MIND MYT

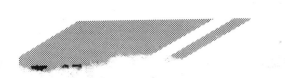

To Franco Ramaccini, a sceptic, a friend

MIND MYTHS

Exploring Popular Assumptions About the Mind and Brain

Edited by

Sergio Della Sala

JOHN WILEY & SONS

Chichester · New York · Weinheim · Brisbane · Singapore · Toronto

 National   01243 779777
 International (+44) 1243 779777
 e-mail (for orders and customer service enquiries):
 cs-books@wiley.co.uk
 Visit our Home Page on http://www.wiley.co.uk
         or http://www.wiley.com

Other Wiley Editorial Offices

John Wiley & Sons, Inc., 605 Third Avenue,
New York, NY 10158-0012, USA

WILEY-VCH Verlag GmbH,
Pappelallee 3, D-69469 Weinheim, Germany

Jacaranda Wiley Ltd, 33 Park Road, Milton,
Queensland 4064, Australia

John Wiley & Sons (Asia) Pte Ltd, 2 Clementi Loop #02-01,
Jin Xing Distripark, Singapore 129809

John Wiley & Sons (Canada) Ltd, 22 Worcester Road,
Rexdale, Ontario M9W 1L1, Canada

Library of Congress Cataloging-in-Publication Data

Mind myths : exploring popular assumptions about the mind and brain /
  edited by Sergio Della Sala.
      p.   cm.
   Includes bibliographical references and index.
   ISBN 0-471-98303-9 (alk. paper)
   1. Mind and body.   2. Brain.   3. Intellect.   I. Della Sala,
  Sergio.
  BF 161.M556 1999
  153—dc21   98-38574
                                                      CIP

British Library Cataloguing in Publication Data

A catalogue record for this book is available from the British Library

ISBN 0-471-98303-9

Typeset in 10/12pt Novarese by Dorwyn Ltd, Rowlands Castle, Hants
Printed and bound in Great Britain by Biddles Ltd, Guildford and King's Lynn
This book is printed on acid-free paper responsibly manufactured from sustainable forestry, in which at least two trees are planted for each one used for paper production.

Contents

Contributors

Neil C. Abbot   Department of Complementary Medicine, University of Exeter, 25 Victoria Park Road, Exeter EX2 4NT, UK

Giovanni Berlucchi   Dipartimento di Scienze, Neurologiche e della Visione, Sezione di Fisiologia Umana, Strada Le Grazie 8, 37134 Verona, Italy

Barry L. Beyerstein   Department of Psychology, Simon Fraser University, Burnaby, B.C. V5A 1S6, Canada

Michael C. Corballis   Department of Psychology, University of Auckland, Private Bag 92019, Auckland, New Zealand

Sergio Della Sala   Department of Psychology, University of Aberdeen, William Guild Building, Old Aberdeen AB24 2UB, UK

Ennio De Renzi   Clinica Neurologica, Università di Modena, Via del Pozzo 71, 41100 Modena, Italy

Steve Donnelly   Department of Physics, University of Salford, The Crescent, Salford M54 UUT, UK

Edzard Ernst   Department of Complementary Medicine, University of Exeter, 25 Victoria Park Road, Exeter EX2 4NT, UK

Susan Frame   Psychology Department, Victoria University of Wellington, Box 600, Wellington, New Zealand

Maryanne Garry   Psychology Department, Victoria University of Wellington, Box 600, Wellington, New Zealand

Ken J. Gilhooly   Department of Psychology, University of Aberdeen, William Guild Building, Aberdeen AB24 2UB, UK

Toby Howard   Advanced Interfaces Group, Department of Computer Science, University of Manchester, Oxford Road, Manchester M13 9PL, UK

Mike Kopelman   UMDS, Division of Psychiatry and Psychology, St Thomas's Hospital, Lambeth Palace Road, London SE1 7EH, UK

Kate Leafhead   UMDS, Division of Psychiatry and Psychology, Guy's Hospital, London Bridge, London SE1 9RT UK

Elizabeth Loftus   Psychology Department, Box 351525, University of Washington, Seattle, WA 98195-1525, USA

Robert H. Logie   Department of Psychology, University of Aberdeen, William Guild Building, Old Aberdeen, AB24 2UB, UK

Michael A. Persinger   Behavioural Neuroscience Programme, Laurentian University, Ramsey Lake Road, Sudbury, Ontario P3E 2C6, Canada

Massimo Polidoro   CICAP (Comitato Italiano per il Controllo delle Affermazioni sul Paranormale), Casella Postale 60, 27058 Voghera (Pavia), Italy

Pat Rabbitt   Age and Cognitive Performance Research Centre, The University of Manchester, Coupland I, Oxford Road, Manchester M13 9PL, UK

James Randi   James Randi Educational Foundation, 201 SE Davie Boulevard, Fort Lauderdale FL 33316-1815, USA

Fernando D. Saraví   Medical School, Universidad Nacional de Cuyo, Mendoza 5500, Argentina

Graham F. Wagstaff   Department of Psychology, Liverpool University, Eleanor Rathbone Building, Liverpool L69 3BX, UK

The drawings are by:

Mr Peter Bates   Department of Psychology, University of Aberdeen, William Guild Building, Old Aberdeen, AB24 2UB, UK

Foreword

While the world would be poorer without myths, it is helpful to be able to separate myth from reality, indeed, it is their implausibility that gives myths such as the Loch Ness Monster or King Arthur's Round Table much of their attraction. Psychology is not lacking in myths, but unfortunately the general public tends to confuse them with reality. *Mind Myths* seeks to address this issue, covering a wide range of popular beliefs about the brain and the mind. It includes the remarkably persistent fallacy that we only ever use 10% of our brains, the assumption that our right brains function as artistic hippies and our left as desiccated accountants, through to the belief that near-death experience gives us a view of life after death. Areas of folk psychology covered range from fallacies about optimal learning strategies and creativity, through to myths about hypnotism and false beliefs about the effects of ageing. The book is edited and introduced by Sergio Della Sala, who has the appropriate but unusual distinction of having had a paper published in *Nature*, on the "miraculous" liquefaction of the blood of St Januarius (San Gennaro), denounced from the pulpit by the Bishop of Naples! In general the book is written in a lively style and will, I hope, be read widely by science journalists, and others who help perpetuate the various myths. It would also make an excellent focus for an undergraduate seminar, providing a stimulating bridge between the psychological laboratory and the rather untilled field of folk psychology. It is, in short, a timely and fascinating book.

Alan Baddeley

Acknowledgements

First of all, I wish to thank all the authors who accepted with enthusiasm my suggestion that they write a chapter for this book. However, and I am sure I share this feeling with anybody who has had the experience of being an editor, I have often mused on the real meaning of ''deadline'', a term that still seems to outrage academics. The word is said to have originated from the Confederate prisoner camp at Andersonville during the American civil war: there was a line on the ground which the prisoners could not pass without being shot dead. I must confess that in my most deepest dreams I envisaged some of the contributors to this volume on the exact verge of that grim line.

I also thank Comfort Jegede, the publishing editor, for her verve and guidance, Melanie Phillips, the editorial assistant, Mandy Collison, the production editor, and Tracy Clayton, the marketing manager, for their continued support, Jo Watson, who patiently amends my Mediterranean grammar, and, as is customary, Miriam, my companion. The readers will be pleased to know that our relationship was not wrecked by my dedication to this book, as has been the case for other less fortunate colleagues, to judge from the prefaces of most scientific books, from which it is clear that scientists, when editing a volume, become bullheaded, vicious misanthropic beasts at home. On the contrary, we had quite a few laughs in devising the captions for the cartoons that Peter Bates had so skilfully drawn. Apropos these vignettes, I should acknowledge all the people whose work has given inspiration.

Finally, I would like to thank Leslie Ord, who wrote the program to collect the data on the questionnaire, and Ruth Drinkwater, Sandra Skilling and Sarah McCrimmon, who helped with the editorial work and made my life easier and my work much more pleasant.

Preface

As with most domains of human knowledge, the various disciplines loosely lumped together as neurosciences, whose aim is to investigate the functioning of our brain and its relationship with our behaviour, are not exempt from personal beliefs, prejudices, faith, hopes, hunches, and ultimately myths. People often respond to scientific reasoning about the mind and the brain by opposing conventional beliefs accepted as truth by the great majority, but supported by little validation in reality; for a discussion see Rothman (1989). Hence the working title of this book, "Neuromythology" (a term borrowed from previous papers, unrelated to our issue, by Landau (1988, 1989, 1990), Rosenberg (1996) and Landau and Nelson (1996), and its final title: Mind Myths. I found a good definition of "myth" in Archeolink, a museum near Aberdeen, the town where I currently live: myths were poetical stories, invented by early humans to explain the mysteries of the universe, of natural events and of life itself. The changing seasons, growth and decay, storms, floods, drought, good and bad fortune, were all attributed to supernatural beings, famous ancestors or ancient heroes. We now have a better understanding of thunderbolts and lightning; they are less mysterious, are less supernatural and terrify us no more. But in the absence of understanding of the mechanisms of the mind and the brain, and the effects of their diseases, we tackle their mysteries by aping every humans invoking divine intervention or taking shelter in simplistic dogmas. This book seeks to contribute to the discussion of the mysteries of the brain and mind, making things as simple as possible, but not simpler. Some people will notice the deliberate ambiguity between the two terms brain and mind which pervades the volume, right from its title (remember Marvin Minsky: "the mind is simply what the brain does", 1987). To avoid misunderstanding, without going into a verbose philosophical dispute, let me state my own materialistic view of the brain–mind (see, for example, Rose (1996) for a brief discussion on the topic). However, I am aware of the Punch motto: What is matter? Never mind; What is mind? No matter (Blakmore, 1994).

There is a gap between what scientists know about brain functions and cognitive mechanisms, and the view that lay people draw from sources of everyday information such as newspaper, the popular press and television. This book is aimed at partly filling this gap. As with other sciences (e.g. physics, chemistry) questions that interest the general public are different (often more general) than most of the endeavours that the neuroscientists undertake in their research. The authors contributing to Mind Myths have addressed, often using a scientific approach, topics of discussions that people are likely to engage in at cocktail parties.

We live in a credulous world. Many of us, like Lewis Carroll's Red Queen, believe "as many as six impossible things before breakfast". I was struck by the notion that about half the population of the USA does not believe in evolution by natural selection and that a significant proportion of the UK population does not think that the earth goes round the sun (Wolpert, 1993, p. ix). Sapolsky (1998, p. 218) maintains that in a recent Gallup poll "25 percent of Americans fessed up to believing in ghosts, while 26 percent admitted to believing in mental telepathy, 47 percent in UFOs, and 49 percent in extrasensory perception"; a similar proportion (49%) believes that it is possible for someone to be physically possessed by the devil.

I wanted to check some of these figures. The opportunity came when we organized an Open Day to celebrate the centenary of our department, the oldest department of psychology in the UK. Among the many other hands-on demonstrations, for fun, we also set up a computer program with a 16-question questionnaire, entitled "Are you a Scientist or a Poet?", which had to be answered as "true" or "false". The questionnaire[1] is reproduced in the box opposite: maybe you would like to spare the time to put yourself to the test (do it before reading on). Of course, the public attending a University Open Day is not exactly representative of the whole population. Nevertheless, we were pleased to see that only 15% of them disagreed that the sun is a star, and only about 24% did not think that the earth takes a year to revolve around it. On the other hand, 31% responded "true" to question number 2, therefore being ready to treat a common cold with heavy drugs, and as many as 43% denied that Galileo was on trial for his scientific achievements, and was only very recently "rehabilitated" (Della Sala, 1997a). Somewhat disappointingly, we realized that 27% of the people who participated maintained that one can bend spoons by the means of mental energy, and an outstanding 69% were convinced that we normally only use 10% of our brain. I do hope that some of them will enjoy this book.

Gullibility is not a sign of poor education. Winer and Cottrell (quoted by Abel, 1997) reported that over one-third of US college students maintain the aristotelian belief that when we look at something, rays, waves or other unspecified energies go out of our eyes, a bit like Leonardo's love-rays. Indeed, about one in five of my own psychology students admitted believing in extrasensory perception and that we emit brain waves with some impact on the material world. They were in good company. The former rector of my own university has been fascinated by fire-walking, which he maintained defied scientific explanation (Hamilton, 1994). He was apparently unmoved by my plea to consider that burning embers do not conduct heat very well, and therefore if one walks reasonably fast, one will not be burned (that's why fire-walkers will refuse to walk on heated metal, or indeed to stand on red-hot coals). He was adopting the well-read believer's logic: I cannot find an explanation, therefore there is no explanation. As is frequently the case, the sentence "science cannot explain . . ." should translate as "I do not know how to explain, but maybe others do." Attributing a supernatural aura to everything we do not understand would mean no end to the supernatural. Hippocrates, the father of medicine, criticized his contemporaries for thinking that epilepsy was "divine" simply because they did not understand it. And the Canon Law (art. 1289,3) remains ambiguous about the distinction between epileptics and the possessed (Della Sala and Berrini, 1979). Is this solely an approach common in the past? Not at all. Addressing the congregation which had flocked into Catania (Italy) on 14 April 1997 to listen to his mighty words, Bishop Echevarría literally maintained that "90% of handicapped people have parents who were not virgin when they married". In this humus of preposterousness and scientific ignorance, irrationality finds its perfect habitat. Shelves of bookshops and newsagents are swarming with newspapers with improbable titles such as "Secret Wisdom", "Unsolved", "The Unopened Files", "Positive Health", "Enlightenment", "Tai Chi and Alternative Health", "New

Questionnaire "Are you a scientist or a poet?"

True or False?

1. The last dinosaur died before the first human appeared

2. Antibiotics kill viruses

3. Electrons are smaller than atoms

4. The Catholic Church admitted only as late as 1992 that Galileo was right after all in maintaining that the earth does revolve around the sun

5. The earth takes a year to revolve around the sun

6. The sun is a star

7. Occam's Razor is a medieval Bavarian technique for carving meat

8. Humans have the same number of vertebrae (neck bones) as giraffes

9. Human beings normally only use 10% of their brain

10. Cutting hair makes it grow faster

11. The brain operates on about the same amount of power that would light a 10-watt bulb

12. The universe is 6000 years old

13. Zadig is a Brazilian soccer player famous in the 1950s

14. The capital of Australia is Sydney

15. Any particularly gifted person can bend spoons using only mental energy

16. The average brain weighs between 1100 and 1300 grams

Scores
12–16: Born to be a scientist
8–11: Hits and misses, but still impressive
4–7: Keep it up, you have some potential
0–3: Science is not all, you might enjoy poetry

Solutions (True = t; False = f): 1t, 2f, 3t, 4t, 5t, 6t, 7f, 8t, 9f, 10f, 11t, 12f, 13f, 14f, 15f, 16t

Age'', ''Nexus'', ''Enigma'', ''Green Egg'', ''Magical Blend'', ''Magonia'', ''The Kabbalist'', ''Avalon'', ''Gnosis'', ''Shaman's Drum'', ''The X-factor'', ''Vision: Explaining the Unexplained'', and even more traditional magazines such as *LIFE* produce their special issue on paranormal phenomena from the believers' stance (Miller, 1997).

If it is true that believers' books abound and they sell like hot cakes (Ridley, 1995), there is also a plethora of books by sceptics, attempting to debunk the usual beliefs: little green men, extrasensory perception, creationism, alien sight and abduction. Likewise, we are inundated by bold neurological explanations of consciousness, astonishing hypotheses revealing that the brain is worth something, best-sellers unlocking the mysteries of the brain, and a surplus of enchanting anecdotes mistaken for science.

John Allen Paulos stated that the motivation for any book is, at least partly, anger (Paulos, 1988, p. 32). Indeed, this book also has its origin in dissatisfaction. I have often had the opportunity to participate in meetings attended by people with different backgrounds, and I could appreciate that a number of misconceptions about brain mechanisms are taken for granted even by well-read, educated people. These topics include the ''use of only 10% of the brain'', the ''resuscitation from coma thanks to the patient's favourite songs'', ''the creativity of the right hemisphere'', ''the trust in magic tricks to prevent ageing'', the ''energy of the brain'', and the ''false memory syndrome''. Attempting to counterbalance this misinformation with a ''scientific view'' on the different topics, I realized that such a source was not available and only taken for granted in technical books. However, the functioning of the brain and the mind fascinates and challenges virtually everybody (Greenfield, 1997). Hence the idea of *Mind Myths*: to provide the necessary information to those readers, not necessarily expert in the neurosciences, who are curious about neurological and cognitive phenomena they hear of, and do not know how to find out whether the evidence on which such claims are based is reliable or not.

I had a list of the questions that friends had asked me, and a list of people I know of who could attempt to tackle these questions: the match between these two lists formed the basis for the project. The general tone of the book was intended to be scientifically oriented but clear to educated lay people. However, I hope that the book may also please experts in the different disciplines of the neurosciences and may be used as an additional textbook for students in their first years of science, neuroscience and psychology. It does not require specific prior knowledge, but the student should be familiar with scientific language. In editing it, both the contributors and myself have tried to avoid a patronizing approach, bearing in mind the risk of thinking as the venerable Professor of Worldly Wisdom, mighty member of the Erewhonian College of Unreason, that ''it is not our business . . . to help students to think for themselves. Surely this is the very last thing which one who wishes them well should encourage them to do. Our duty is to ensure that they shall think as we do, or at any rate, as we hold it expedient to say we do'' (Butler, 1985, p. 189). I hope that we have, at least partly, succeeded.

As is the case with most edited books, this volume has its ups and downs, chapters are not homogeneous in style, and the editor does not necessarily agree with all that has been said by the various authors (and vice versa, I am sure). However, on the whole, I hope it does convey the message that the mysteries of our mind should not be dismissed with dogmatic beliefs, but confronted with respect, and investigated with some method. This book is not about solving mysteries or disclosing secrets, and I have no intention of propagating scientific rage or stressing the supremacy of reason. Indeed, I find rather odd the opinionated tone sometimes used by professional sceptics and invincible reductionists. Alas, it is simplistic to maintain that cases of bizarre behaviour or unusual findings "are all easily explained and understood in terms of contemporary psychology and what is currently known about the functioning of the human nervous system" (Baker, 1992, p. 23). In fact, nothing is that easy, especially when we are dealing with something as intangible as the mind (see Stannard (1996) for a discussion). As Brecht wrote in his *Galileo*, "The chief aim of science is not to open a door to infinite wisdom but to set a limit to infinite error." It is not by contrasting a dogma with another dogma that we will succeed in disseminating the results of our science, but by educating as many members of the general public as possible about its ethics and its methods (Latour, 1998), about what it can and cannot achieve, about what we do know and do not yet know. For instance, a concept that is not so obvious is that there is a difference between science and technology. Technology is based on science; science produces ideas, whereas "technology results in the production of usable objects" (Wolpert, 1993, p. 25). This is why I find it obnoxious that we should be forced to struggle to find an immediate possible application of our work, by grant-giving committees and by colleagues who have capitulated. I think that scientists should make an effort in explaining that, often, what they do has no immediate outcome, and perhaps never will have (Feynman, 1985). Investigating the functioning of the brain and of the mind is sometimes an exercise solely directed at adding to our knowledge, with no obvious pragmatic implication.

Generally, factual information is perceived as comforting, and the sceptical scientific approach as distant and somewhat dull. Science is typically counter-intuitive and probabilistic. Good scientific theories should always generate more interesting questions, in contrast to the dogmas of beliefs, which are unchangeable by new evidence. Science can rarely give definite answers, for it advances by wearing away the tenebrae of natural mysteries, the extensions of which are very far from defined. Scientific knowledge, in any given field and in neuroscience in particular, is formed by a set of theories which serve (temporarily) the purpose of allowing us to account for various observed phenomena. And it is true that in science "novelty emerges only with difficulty, manifested by resistance, against a background provided by expectation" (Kuhn, 1970). Therefore, the eccentric, elaborate, contradictory and sometimes preposterous scientific approach is seen as detached and cold. This notion pairs up with the well-rooted popular opinion that scientists are absent-minded, socially unfitted, generally graceless and flabby. "I don't believe in science. You know, science is an intellectual dead end. It's a lot of little guys with tweed suits, cutting up frogs" says Woody Allen in *Sleeper*. In the case of neuroscientists, this stereotype is only matched by that of the mad professor, often characterized with a negative twist, spread by film-makers. I hope that this book might have a small part in showing that science, the science of the mind, can be fun and creative. Science is not simply a heartless pursuit of objective information. It is a creative human activity (Gould, 1980, p. 201). Scientists often fail to realize that not everyone sees the world as they do, or indeed has the same priorities. They are therefore perceived as arrogant, elitist and uncaring (Coghlan, 1997), and it is true that deep down some of them do believe that the lay person is ignorant and irrational (Anderson, 1997), and so they run the danger of advocating "the superiority of science". Moreover, there is no doubt many of us have large, encumbering egos, a fact well demonstrated by the way in which The Institute for Scientific Information recently publicized its updating of published articles. Their alluring brochure, aimed at convincing researchers to subscribe, recites: "That's right, *your* name and *your* work is included in the ISI". Pathetic? It works. I, for one, have subscribed.

Indeed, there is total absence of irony in the way in which scientists refer cumulatively to their work, as "The Literature". I appeal to the readers' tolerance if they see hints of this hubris also in *Mind Myths*. We have to accept that sometimes we really cannot do without it.

This is a large book, but it is far from comprehensive and could have been much longer. Several relevant issues have been omitted which I hope will receive due attention in the near future. Academics are often reluctant to devote their precious time to the investigation of fringe phenomena (Newman and Baumeister, 1996), though I must agree that it is necessary to recognize that some claims really are outside the realms of scientific investigation. "If not, one might just as well investigate, as science, the production of rabbits out of hats" (Wolpert, 1993, p. 139).

Finally, a plea to bookshop managers: please, do shelve this volume in the "science" rather than self-help section, even if it has the word "mind" in its title. Consider that, as a rule, you do not shelve dissertations on Schroedinger's cat or on the biochemistry of galanthamine in the "pet and garden" section, and nor do you shelve treatises on the riddle of black holes in the DIY section. I appeal to your undoubted acumen. I abhor the idea of seeing this book cheek-to-cheek with volumes devoted to the science of the zodiac: I am a Libran, and, notoriously, Librans do not believe in astrology.

We will begin our journey through the myths of the mind by appraising our knowledge on some of the most common myths about brain functions.

NOTE

1. A few of the questions are taken and adapted from published sources (Sagan, 1996; Seuling, 1991; *The Skeptic*, Editorial, 1997).

Section 1

BRAIN MYTHOLOGY

CHAPTER 1

Whence Cometh the Myth that We Only Use 10% of Our Brains?

BARRY L. BEYERSTEIN

> It ain't the things we don't know what gets us in trouble, it's the things we
> know that just ain't so.
>
> *Artemus Ward*

Had our esteemed editor decided to offer a prize for the most popular piece of neuronon-sense in this collection, I believe that I, for once, would be holding the winning ticket. Although the notion that normal people ordinarily use only a tenth of their brains probably ranks as the premier brain-howler of all time, its implausibility has done little to dampen its popularity over generations and continents. I recall it being intoned by teachers in "pep talks" at school, and it remains one of the most likely questions I can expect when I discuss brain matters with community groups on behalf of my university's speakers' bureau. And if I should forget to disabuse them of it beforehand, the 10% myth is sure to be raised by someone each time I teach my freshman "Brain and Behaviour" course. Most often, those who pose the question react with mild dejection when I tell them "it just ain't so" – perhaps a clue as to why this dubious assertion refuses to die. Anything this impervious to evidence must speak to widely felt longings. That is to say, it would be nice if it were true, for, like so many congenial falsehoods, the 10% myth lays open a variety of attractive possibilities.

The most recent luminary to hit me with the "10% solution" was none other than the spoon-bender extraordinaire, Uri Geller. When Geller and I locked horns on Jim Bohannon's national radio programme out of Washington, DC, Geller patiently explained that the reason he could do psychic feats and I could not was that he had discovered how to break through the 10% barrier. It's all a matter of overcoming the crippling doubts spread by crepe-hangers like me. Coincidentally, he just happened to have authored a new self-help book that would share the secret with the rest of us. The magic crystal is included at no extra charge.

In debates with supporters of paranormal or pseudoscientific beliefs, I frequently encounter the claim that "scientists say" we use only 10% of our brains. Curiously, though, none of them has ever been able to tell me which scientists these were or what their reasons were for saying it. Taking the figure as a given, anyway ("Everyone knows that . . ."), proponents usually proceed to argue that if we don't know what that untapped reservoir of brain stuff is doing, it could be harbouring awesome mental powers that only a few adepts have mastered. Members of this enlightened minority could be tapping their latent cerebral potential to accomplish levitation, psychokinesis, clairvoyance, precognition, telepathy or psychic healing, for instance. Or, say other believers, it could be used to achieve voluntary control of bodily functions, perfect learning and recall, transcendence to higher planes of knowledge, or other fantastica scarcely conceivable to mere mortals condemned to subsist on the drudge-like 10%.

Those who passed first-year logic will recognize this as a classic fallacy, the "argument from ignorance". In this gambit, one debater presses the other to concede that in what we (admittedly) don't yet know lies the proof of whatever the first party believes to be true. Lacking solid evidence of their own, those with their backs to the wall often argue that if sceptics cannot prove that something is not the case, this somehow counts as evidence that it is true. The one-tenth figure is, of course, unlikely, but even if it were accurate, it would in no way entail the existence of paranormal powers of mind, which must stand or fall on their own merits. To date, the demonstrations have been less than convincing (Alcock, 1981; Hyman, 1992).

Having been assailed with the 10% myth by teachers, athletic coaches, habitués of the motivational speakers' circuit, hawkers of self-help literature, and a bevy of occultists, I was eventually driven to search for its origins. I had become curious as to why it persists in the face of strong doubts arising from our growing knowledge about the structure and function of the brain. Some preliminary speculations on the topic (Beyerstein, 1987) generated several thoughtful suggestions from readers. Since, as will be apparent by the end of this chapter, much about this question remains unsettled, I would be pleased to hear from present readers as well.

As someone who spends much of his professional life pondering how the brain works, I am quite prepared to admit the enormity of what we do not yet understand about how this kilo-and-a-half of grey matter manages to produce thoughts, feelings, and actions. None the less, I am at a loss to understand how my informants came to know with such pontifical certainty that we normally use only 10% of it. To the best of my knowledge, this alleged "fact" appears nowhere in the literature of neurophysiology or physiological psychology. On the contrary, it is at variance with most of what we do know about the brain; for an overview of the field, see Kolb and Whishaw (1996), Rosenzweig, Leiman and Breedlove (1996) or Kalat (1995).

The "dormant brain" thesis seems to be another of those shibboleths that has insinuated itself into our cultural storehouse of "truths" through mere repetition. Its place in this pantheon of conventional wisdom is made secure by a phenomenon known as "source amnesia" or "cryptomnesia" (Schacter, Harbluk and McLachlan, 1984; Baker, 1992). It seems that the brain stores factual data somewhat differently from the information about where, how and from whom we learned it. Knowledge of the latter sort can fade completely without diminishing our sense of certainty that the facts themselves are true. In this way, people often become convinced they are repeating reliable scientific findings when, in reality, they were actually picked up from an issue of *The National Enquirer* or an episode of *The X-Files*.

SOME SHORTCOMINGS OF THE 10% MYTH

Doubts from the Study of Brain Damage

Certain things they already know should give pause to those who believe in the 10% myth. For instance, when I am asked if the one-tenth figure is true, I often draw the questioner's attention to the well-known consequences of strokes and penetrating head wounds. There is virtually no area of the brain that can be damaged without loss of some mental, vegetative or behavioural capacity (Rosner, 1974; Damasio and Damasio, 1989). If 90% of the brain normally lies unused, there should be many parts of it that could sustain damage without disturbing any of these abilities. Obviously, that is not the case – brain injury just about anywhere has rather specific and lasting effects (Sacks, 1985). Most people are intuitively aware of this, as shown by their answers to the counter-question I sometimes pose: "How well do you think you would cope if you were suddenly to lose the functioning of 90% of your brain?" We all know of stroke victims who have lost relatively small amounts of brain tissue and are severely debilitated. Although there is usually some recovery of function after brain damage, if nine-tenths of the brain were normally held in reserve, we should see far more restoration than we typically do.

Doubts from the Study of Evolution

By now, all but the most fervid religious fundamentalists accept that the human brain is the product of millions of years of evolution (Oakley and Plotkin, 1979). Given the conservatism of natural selection, it seems highly improbable that scarce resources would be squandered to produce and maintain such an underutilized organ. Metabolically speaking, the brain is costly to run. For instance, at 2% of total body weight, the brain accounts for 20% of the body's resting oxygen consumption and a similar proportion of the nutrient-bearing bloodflow from the heart. Simply fuelling the sodium–potassium pumps that allow neural membranes to process information consumes a wildly disproportionate chunk of your daily caloric intake. How long would you continue to endure huge power bills to heat all 10 rooms of your home if you never strayed beyond the kitchen?

Doubts from Brain Imaging Research

The brain has evolved a certain amount of redundancy in its circuitry as a safety precaution, but little, if any of it, lies perpetually fallow. Modern imaging techniques soundly refute the notion that there are large areas of the brain that are unused most of the time. The electroencephalogram (EEG), computerized axial tomography (CAT) scans, positron emission tomography (PET) scans, functional magnetic resonance imaging (fMRI), magnetoencephalography (MEG), and regional cerebral bloodflow (rCBF) measures are all tools for inferring the functions of anatomical structures in the living human brain (Roland, 1993; Baranaga, 1997). These imaging techniques show that, even during sleep, there are no completely silent areas in the brain. In fact, such sites of neural tranquillity would be signs of serious pathology.

Doubts from the Localization of Function in the Brain

From the foregoing devices, and from observing the consequences of head trauma and the effects of electrically stimulating various sites in the brain, it has become apparent that the cerebrum does not function as a homogeneous unit. Unique psychological processes are handled in different anatomical regions (Figure 1.1). This is known as the doctrine of "localization of function". The history of neurology has witnessed a see-saw battle between the localizationists[1] and those who preferred the opposing concept of "mass action", the idea that the brain functions holistically in virtually every act (Krech, 1962). Whether they realize it or not, most supporters of the 10% notion implicitly adopt some version of the mass action position. Modern research, on the other hand, has come down firmly on the side of the localizationists, although we now know that the way in which the brain breaks complex chores into sub-tasks and parcels them out to distributed processing units differs from most common-sense assumptions about how this might be achieved (Gazzaniga, 1989; Petersen et al., 1990).

Clinical neurologists were among the first to recognize that localization of function exists. For instance, from the 1860s on, Aubertin, Broca, Dax and Wernicke began to convert mass action supporters with their demonstrations that the brain mechanisms for language and speech were both lateralized to one hemisphere and localized within the dominant one. Today, we know that specialization for certain mental operations is so precise that small lesions in an area on the underside of the temporal lobe, for example,

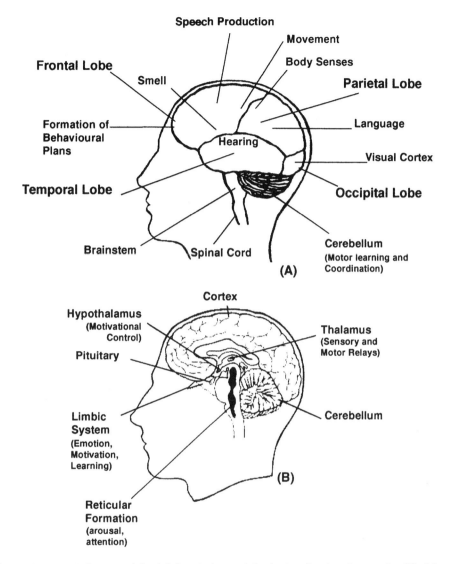

Figure 1.1   (A) Side view of the left hemisphere of the brain, showing (in oversimplified form) its major functional divisions. (B) Midline view of the brain and its functions.

can leave a patient able to perceive most objects as before, but unable to identify human faces (Damasio, Tranel and Damasio, 1990).

Along the same lines, it was demonstrated in the 19th century that moving a weak electrical probe from site to site on the exposed surface of the brain evokes different psychological phenomena as successive points are stimulated (Young, 1970). The pioneering experiments by Fritsch and Hitzig in Germany and Ferrier in England eventually led Barthelow in the USA and Penfield in Canada to apply this technique with conscious neurosurgical patients, who could report their subjective reactions as their brains were being stimulated. Systematically mapping the cortex in this fashion has confirmed beyond doubt that the brain allocates different tasks to different regions of its anatomy (Krech, 1962; Penfield and Perot, 1963). Understanding the nature of this cortical specialization has permitted the development of technologies such as sensory prostheses for the blind, where patterned electrical stimulation is delivered to the visual areas of the cerebral cortex (Dobelle and Mladejovsky, 1974). The upshot of decades of work, stimulating deep structures as well as the cortex of conscious human patients, is that probing from stem to stern has failed to flush out the freeloading nine-tenths of the brain that some stubbornly contend is lacking an immediate assignment.

Doubts from Microstructural Analysis of the Brain

Because the foregoing studies have established that perception, language, movement, emotions, etc. are all handled by different parts of the brain, it is no longer viable for those who believe in the 10% myth to assume that all mental processes are confined, ghetto-like, in some small corner of the whole organ. Thus, in order for supporters of the 10% solution to accommodate the known dispersal of functions throughout the brain, they must contend instead that 90% of the volume of each one of these specialized modules lies dormant. This too seems implausible in light of research where electrodes are inserted directly into these processing units to map their functional microcircuitry.

Microelectrodes, capable of isolating the electrical responses of single neurons, are used to study information processing at the level of individual cells in the living animal (Barlow, 1972). With the aid of a stereotaxic positioning device, the electrode is moved through an area to be mapped, sampling the different functional characteristics of cells in that population as it goes. Moving the tip of the electrode as little as a few micrometres (thousandths of a millimetre) will cause the electrode to lose the cell it was monitoring and to lock onto the responses of the next one in line. While, for obvious reasons, recordings of this type are used routinely only with non-human animals, the procedure has been tried experimentally with human neurosurgical patients under strict ethical guidelines. Results from these human volunteers show a similar organization and response pattern to those seen in other higher mammals (Marg, Adams and Rutkin, 1968). Scientists using this "single-unit recording" technique should have noticed by now if nine-tenths of each functional module were inoperative. Had that been the case, they should have encountered great gaps through which passage of the electrode failed to detect any active neurons. Again, that is not what typically occurs.

Doubts from Metabolic Studies

Similar questions about the 10% mantra are prompted by techniques that map the functional specializations of the brain by tracking differential rates of cellular metabolism. The assumption is that a given psychological task will maximally activate those specialized neural modules that contribute to its completion. It follows that cells that are exercised in this fashion will require more glucose, their principal source of energy, and that they will absorb their additional fuel requirements from the blood supply to the brain. In the 2-deoxyglucose method, a radioactively tagged molecule similar to glucose is injected into the bloodstream (Sokoloff, 1977). Like glucose, it will be absorbed in greater amounts by neurons that are strongly activated, but, unlike the natural sugar, 2-deoxyglucose cannot be metabolized and thus it accumulates wherever cells are working hardest. After the behavioural task has been completed, the brain must be removed and cut into thin slices which are placed on paper coated with emulsions sensitive to the radioactive emissions of the ''tag''. When this radiograph is developed, the areas of maximal radioactivity will reveal which modules were recruited by the preceding task. If 90% of the neurons in each functional module were quiescent, large ''holidays'' should appear in these radiographs. Perusal of maps for a variety of different abilities shows, once again, no evidence of that kind of dormancy within modules. Obviously, this technique is suitable only for use with non-human animals, but the PET scanner, mentioned earlier, allows the same basic strategy to be used with intact human brains. Recording the radioactive particle decay from outside the head, the PET scanner's spatial resolution is necessarily much less fine, but it too offers no support for the 10% myth.

Doubts from the Study of Neural Disuse

The industrialist Henry Ford once said, ''Whatever you have, you must use it or lose it.'' Bedridden patients and astronauts know that muscles atrophy from disuse and so, apparently, do brain circuits. Much research indicates that neural systems that are underutilized early in life either fail to develop or deteriorate permanently (Hirsch and Jacobson, 1975). If early environmental deprivation results in failure of the deprived brain circuitry to develop, remedial stimulation in later life will not completely overcome the resulting behavioural deficits (Beyerstein and Freeman, 1976). Thus, if the brain really had the idle capacity suggested by the 10% myth, it is likely that the neurons supposedly held in reserve would be useless by the time they were called into service. If 90% of our brains was really idle, the result would probably be large areas of cellular degeneration. No such signs are apparent when normal brains undergo histological examination at autopsy.

Straws for Believers to Grasp

Despite the foregoing objections, diehard supporters of this cherished illusion might attempt a rescue by arguing that the 10% figure refers not simply to neural volume, but rather to underutilized storage capacity or failure to reach peak processing speed, maximal neural interconnectivity, or some other index of brain efficiency. Be that as it may, I know of no way to determine the theoretical limits of such processes in order to estimate the average person's proportional achievements. At any rate, research suggests that it is not lack of storage capacity that hinders performance most; the bottleneck is more likely to arise from difficulty in retrieving what we've safely stored in our brains.

HOW MIGHT THE 10% MYTH HAVE ARISEN?

After several years of digging, including much help from friends, colleagues, students, and readers of my earlier efforts, I confess that I have been frustrated in my attempts to unearth the ultimate source of the 10% myth. Perhaps no Boswell was on hand to record the seminal utterance, but some interesting clues have turned up during my search. Although its origins remain obscure, there is little doubt that the primary disseminators (not to mention beneficiaries) of the 10% myth have been the touts and boosters in the ranks of the self-improvement industry, past and present.

Positive Thinking and the 10% Myth

The quintessentially American phenomenon known as the ''New Thought'' movement blossomed following the American civil war among the prosperity-obsessed yet anxiety-ridden middle classes (Meyer, 1965). It offered a mix of religious revivalism and popular psychology that promised health, affluence, personal charisma, mental agility and peace of mind to all who would follow the positive thinking nostrums that its promoters called ''The Mind Cure''. These merchants of success, from Phineas P. Quimby and Mary Baker Eddy to Dale Carnegie, Norman Vincent Peale and the gurus of today's Human Potential Movement, have sought to secularize and bolster an allegedly sagging Protestant ethic with a patchwork of homespun theology (now broadened to include Eastern as well as Western banalities), pop-psychology, and pseudoscience (Beyerstein, 1990).

   Whatever the source of the 10% myth, it is apparent that it was already commonplace by the early part of this century, thanks in large part to the positive thinking revolution. Although the self-help messiahs may not have created the myth, its usefulness to them is undeniable. In a letter to the editor, responding to my earlier speculations on the subject, Decker (1994) reported that the 1929 edition of the *World Almanac* contained an advertisement for The Pelham Institute, purveyors of self-improvement study courses. As can be seen in Figure 1.2, the idea that we use only 10% of our brains is presented in a chatty style that suggests readers were, by then, already expected to recognize it as a comfortable truism. Decker also noted that the same edition of the *World Almanac* contained a similar advertisement for the works of David V. Bush. Bush, whose almost sole claim to fame is that he was fortunate enough to have retained H.P. Lovecraft as his ghostwriter, refers to vast, untapped resources of the mind that he could help clients to develop. Bush, however, apparently declined to specify the exact percentage waiting in the wings.

   If the 10% myth had not existed, the self-improvement crusaders would have had to invent it. As it became impossible to ignore the central role of the brain in everything we do, the need arose for a neural scapegoat to explain why most people are not as productive and happy as the positive thinkers were telling them they ought to be.[2] In inspirational tomes such as those of Orison Swett Marden (Marden, 1909, 1917) and his competitors, the initial references to unused inner potential tended to be unmistakably metaphorical. But as they warmed to the task, these writers would gradually begin to reify the metaphor. By the end of these uplifting works, the word would often be made flesh, with the author now discussing our hidden powers of mind in terms of actual areas of unused brain mass. Such a progression is evident in Marden's (1917) best-seller, *How to Get What You Want*:

> Now why not plan to bring out this enormous residue, this locked up ability which has never come out of you? . . . The finding of the larger possibilities of man, the unused part, the undiscovered part, is the function of the New Philosophy. (Marden, 1917, p. 11)

> The New Philosophy especially appeals to that unknown part of us which is still waiting to be discovered, that part which is still locked up tight in the within of us [sic]. (Marden, 1917, p. 20)

> The great majority die without deveoping their possible efficiency of hand, or tongue, or brain; without developing any of the special gifts locked up in the great within of themselves. (Marden, 1917, p. 191)

   In his earlier work, *Peace, Power, and Plenty* (1909), Marden had already blurred the distinction between the mystical states of mind he believed in and the physical structure

Advertisements—Educational.

The Gambler

He gambles that a "lucky break" will come to him in the course of time

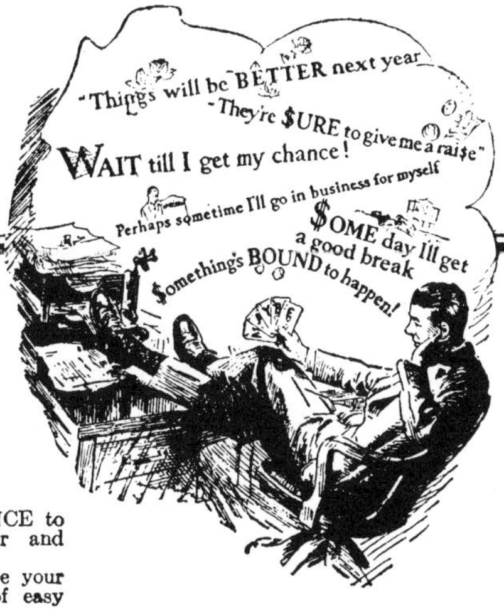

"Things will be BETTER next year"

"They're $URE to give me a raise"

WAIT till I get my chance!

Perhaps sometime I'll go in business for myself

$OME day I'll get a good break

Something's BOUND to happen!

MOST men live in the HOPE that their "lucky break" will come TO-MORROW or NEXT WEEK OR NEXT YEAR. They risk their whole lives on what may COME to them in TIME.

Gambling on what TIME and FATE have in store for you is more costly than any gambling known. You lose MORE than money. You lose your SELF-RESPECT. You lose the self-respect of those about you.

And as each year passes your CHANCE to amount to anything becomes slimmer and slimmer.

You get discouraged. Perhaps you hide your shortcomings behind a whole flock of easy EXCUSES.

But the hard, cold world doesn't care about you. You've got to look out for YOURSELF.

There's ONE SURE WAY—yes, ONLY one—to get what you want out of life. Make your own BRAIN just a little bit more effective and you will MULTIPLY your earning power.

There is NO LIMIT to what the human brain can accomplish. Scientists and psychologists tell us we use only about TEN PER CENT of our brain power. The mind is like a muscle. It grows in power through exercise and use. It weakens and deteriorates with idleness.

What can you DO about it? That is the question you are asking yourself. Here is a suggestion.

Spend 2c for a postage stamp. Send in the coupon below for a free copy of "Scientific Mind Training."

This little book will tell you how Pelmanism has shown over 650,000 people the secret of self-confidence, of a strong will, of a powerful memory, of unflagging concentration; how to acquire directive powers, how to train your imagination (the greatest force in the world), how to make quick, accurate decisions, how to reason logically —in short, how to make your brain an instrument of all-around POWER. It tells you how Pelmanism will help you to banish the negative qualities like forgetfulness, brain fag, inertia, indecision, self-consciousness, lack of ideas, mind wandering, lack of system, procrastination, timidity.

Men like Judge Ben. B. Lindsey, Sir Harry Lauder, Prince Charles of Sweden, Jerome K. Jerome, the famous novelist; Frank P. Walsh, Chairman of the National War Labor Board, and hundreds of others equally famous, praise the simple method of increasing brain power and thought power described in this free book.

You have only TWO CENTS to lose by writing for your copy. You may GAIN thousands of dollars, peace of mind, happiness, independence.

Thousands who read this announcement will DO NOTHING about it. The effort and the will needed to send for this book—which is FREE—may be lacking.

Other thousands will say, "I can lose only TWO CENTS. I may GAIN a great deal by reading "ScientificMind Training,"I will send for it NOW."

The thousands who are open minded will ACT on their impulse to send the coupon. They will be better, stronger minded for having TAKEN SOME ACTION about their lives, even if they do nothing more than to READ a booklet about the inner workings of the mind. For your own sake—and for the sake of your beloved ones, don't continue to GAMBLE. Mail this coupon today—NOW.

THE PELMAN INSTITUTE OF AMERICA
Suite 1141, 71 West 45th St., New York City.

71

Figure 1.2   A reproduction from the 1929 *World Almanac*, showing how the 10% myth was spread by the self-improvement industry.

of the body by introducing his notion of "mental chemistry". According to Marden, this gives the mind miraculous powers over bodily processes, and in a chapter titled "Why grow old?" he explains how positive thinking can halt the ageing process. To add authority to his outlandish vision of mind–brain power, Marden at one point quotes the mystical philosopher, Emanuel Swedenborg (1688–1772). Swedenborg was also an early influence on William James who, as we shall see, played his own part in popularizing the 10% myth:

> Every volition and thought of man is inscribed on his brain. Thus, a man writes his life in his physique, and thus angels discover his autobiography in his structure [when they assess the individual for admissibility into heaven]. (Swedenborg, quoted in Marden, 1909, p. 87)

Always returning to his central themes – the prodigious but latent powers of the mind, and the ability of positive thinking to produce health, wealth and happiness – Marden gathered testimonials from many prominent educators, clergy, and editorialists of his day, not to mention from President William McKinley himself.

Of course, most self-improvement books do contain some useful, common-sense advice amidst the blather, such as tips on how to organize one's time, enhance attention and motivation, and strengthen interpersonal skills. The problem with most works of this genre is the overblown nature of their claims and their frequent appeal to occultism and pseudoscience to back them up. When these exaggerated benefits fail to materialize, dejected readers are often left feeling even more inadequate than before.

The Numerological Connection

Speaking of the occult, I suspect that the lucky choice of the number 10 for the denominator in our fictitious fraction has served to enhance the attractiveness of the one-tenth myth. Among magical thinkers, numerology – the belief in the magical power of numbers – is rarely far from the surface, and 10 is a perennial favourite in this camp. Probably because nature equipped us with 10 fingers and 10 toes, our ancestors developed a primitive reverence for the number 10. The special significance accorded to decades and centenaries and the mounting frenzy over the approaching millennium are manifestations of this enduring fascination with 10 and its multiples. Pundits are fond of representing historical trends by reference to decades: e.g. the "roaring 20s", the "rebellious 60s", and the "greedy 80s", as if mass social trends broke so neatly into arbitrary epochs. The Ten Commandments, the 10-best-dressed list and the top 10 hit parade are but a few manifestations of the special status accorded to this number. It is a safe guess that had someone postulated that we only use one-eighth of our brains, the myth would have had a harder time on the road to immortality. One-seventh, on the other hand, might have enjoyed a better reception among the numerologicaly besotted, but it doesn't pack quite the same punch if one's aim is to drive home the enormity of the unused brain potential supposedly there to be tapped.

'Big-Name' Spreaders of the Myth

The 10% myth continued to rattle around the self-improvement industry until mid-century, when it became a staple of courses like those of the Dale Carnegie organization; these days, it resurfaces regularly in the promotional ballyhoo spread by the hawkers of

Transcendental Meditation, Scientology, and Neurolinguistic Programming. Motivational speakers still love it and I continue to encounter it in the advertisements for a variety of crackpot "brain-tuner" devices so dear to New Age entrepreneurs (see Chapter 4).

Although the 10% myth does not appear in the text of the original 1936 version of Dale Carnegie's How to Win Friends and Influence People, the popular adventurer, journalist and documentary film narrator, Lowell Thomas, gave it a strong boost in the foreword he wrote for the first edition of that book (which, by the 1956 reprinting, had sold nearly five million copies):

> Professor William James of Harvard used to say that the average man develops only ten percent of his latent mental ability. Dale Carnegie, by helping business men and women to develop their latent possibilities, has created one of the most significant movements in adult education. (Thomas, in Carnegie, 1936, p. 12)

Carnegie himself picked up the theme in How to Stop Worrying and Start Living, which was published in 1944:

> The renowned William James was speaking of men who had never found themselves when he declared that the average man develops only ten percent of his latent mental abilities. "Compared to what we ought to be," he wrote, "we are only half awake. We are making use of only a small part of our physical and mental resources. Stating the thing broadly, the human individual thus lives far within his limits. He possesses powers of various sorts which he habitually fails to use". (Carnegie, 1944, p. 123)

Although Carnegie put quotation marks around the passage he attributed to the pioneering American psychologist William James (1842–1910), he failed to cite a source for this quotation. One of the informants mentioned by Dwight Decker in a 1994 posting to the Internet newsgroup, "sci.skeptic", thought he remembered James discussing the 10% estimate in his two-volume text, The Principles of Psychology (James, 1890). However, both Decker and I were unable to find such a statement in this, James' magnum opus.[3] The prize for persistent sleuthing on this score goes to another reader, Richard G. Everit, of Walnut Creek, California. Everit (personal communication) wrote that he had traced the passage quoted by Carnegie to a lecture that James delivered to the American Philosophical Association in December of 1906. This lecture, entitled "The Energies of Men", was delivered at Columbia University and later reprinted in the January 1907 issue of the Philosophical Review. Everit noted that a popularized version of this paper also appeared in the October 1907 edition of the American Magazine – by then, its title had acquired a more inspirational tone: "The Powers of Men". It seems likely that this article, or a quotation from it, may have been Carnegie's source. It is also possible that James himself may have uttered words to this effect in some of his frequent public addresses and that he was quoted (or misquoted) elsewhere. Trained as a medical doctor, James was too good a physiologist to believe that we literally use only 10% of our brains, but he may well have uttered it metaphorically in his voluminous popular writings, for, as Fellman and Fellman (1981) note, James' speculations about the powers of mind and his advice on human perfectability reached a large audience via his frequent contributions to publications such as the widely read Popular Science Monthly.

Hucksters have long known that a reliable way to add instant credibility to almost any assertion is to attribute it to a famous and respected figure. By the mid-20th century, the surest way to appropriate an unassailable mantle of truth for an idea was to attribute it to

Albert Einstein. There are instances, in the political sphere for example, where Einstein's enormous public prestige lent disproportionate weight to speculations he made in areas outside his scientific expertise. In what is possibly a myth about a myth, Albert Einstein is supposed to have alluded to the 10% explanation at some time or other in reply to the constant barrage of questions about the source of his brilliance. Prevalent as this tale is, once again its provenance is suspect. Although I have been told dozens of times that Einstein said it, I have been unable to determine when, where, or even if, he did. Neither, apparently, have those who have made an effort to chronicle Einstein's vast accumulation of writings, interviews, and quotations. In a reply to my research assistant, Anouk Crawford, Jeff Mandl, assistant curator of the Albert Einstein Archives, wrote:

> We are not aware that Albert Einstein ever stated that human beings exploit only 10% of the capacity of their brains. Upon receiving your note, we examined our holdings but found no remarks of his on the subject.

As with William James, it remains possible that Einstein said something along these lines in unrecorded remarks that have spread by word of mouth. But even if he did utter it, Einstein's genius as a physicist would not have elevated his opinions about neurology or psychology beyond those of any other intelligent amateur. And, as with Mark Twain, Abraham Lincoln and Winston Churchill, people with faulty memories or a desire to ''gild the lily'', as it were, may not have been above putting words in Einstein's mouth. Perhaps some hopeful 10% supporter simply decided that if Einstein didn't say it, he ought to have. The public apparently remains convinced that he did.

Another possible boost for our favourite brain myth may have come from popular depictions of Freudian psychoanalysis. Despite their scientific shortcomings, Freud's theories have grabbed the modern imagination. They have been influential not only in psychiatry, but in numerous works of pop-psychology, literature and film. As almost everyone knows, Freud postulated a three-tier model of the mind, composed of the ego, the superego, and the id. Diagrammatically, it was once popular to portray the Freudian view of the mind as shown in Figure 1.3. The conscious ego was depicted as the tip of the iceberg, with the other, much larger and non-conscious, echelons lurking beneath the surface. Freud himself always believed that, someday, actual structures would be found in the brain that would map onto these components of his model. This has not happened, but it was all very convenient, none the less, for generations of pop-psychologists who were even less interested than Freud in gathering empirical data. All the positive thinking fraternity really wanted was another big name to misappropriate in their haste to link the presumably massive unconscious part of the mind to the promises of life-changing bursts of creative energy that they were selling to their ever-hopeful clientele. While the parallels between Freudianism and the positive thinkers' versions of the 10% myth were far from exact, they were close enough to inspire this forgiving audience – and to provide the myth with yet another source of unearned credibility.

WHY DOES THE 10% MYTH REFUSE TO DIE?

If it has been known for ages that the 10% myth makes no sense neurologically, one must wonder about its remarkable longevity. I would suggest that this parable of neural tithing

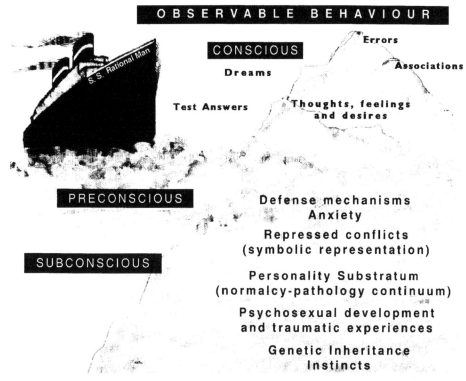

Figure 1.3 A typical textbook depiction of the Freudian model of the mind. By using the iceberg metaphor, these authors helped spread the idea that much of the mind is latent or submerged. Some readers may have mistakenly assumed that this was support for the "10% myth".

in ordinary folks continues to thrive because it is a soothing allegory for the universal human desire to be more talented, influential, and prosperous. As we have seen, a huge industry has evolved, catering to our noble longing for self-betterment. It is comforting to believe that we all possess huge reserves of untested ability, and if this fantasy can be canonized by reference to brain science, so much the better for would-be profiteers.

Stretching the Facts for Fun and Profit

Pseudoscientists are well aware that a good way to promote a dubious product is to associate it in the public mind with whatever is currently most prestigious in the realm of legitimate science. Even before President Bush declared the 1990s the "decade of the brain" (why only 10 years for such a massive task, one might ask?), it had become common in the self-improvement industrial complex to borrow a patina of scientific respectability for questionable assertions by hitching them to the coat-tails of reputable findings in neuroscience (Beyerstein, 1990).

Brain researchers themselves have obligingly provided a number of statements over the years that could be innocently misunderstood, or venally stretched, to suit the purposes of the human potential entrepreneurs and their 10% myth. One example of this may have been public misinterpretation of neuroanatomists' pronouncements that the supporting glial cells in the brain ("white matter") outnumber the neurons ("grey matter") – which do the actual mental work – by a factor of 10 to 1. The role of glial cells is discussed further in Note 7. In this trivial sense, we do, strictly speaking, use less than a tenth of our total brain cells to produce all psychological phenomena, even if the support of that overwhelming mass of glial cells is indispensable to the process.[4] However necessary the glial cells' support functions are for neurons, as far as I know no one has yet begun to market mental exercises or other self-improvement products that promise to transform glial cells into auxiliary "thinking stuff" in order to ensure top grades or a coveted promotion. One hesitates to even mention such an idea, for although this has apparently not yet occurred to the brain hucksters, there is hardly any notion too far-fetched for them to put on the market.

Another possible misinterpretation of neurologists' speculations that could have abetted the 10% myth was raised by Dwight Decker in his 1994 Internet posting, mentioned earlier. Decker suggested that the 10% credo might have been helped along by readers who misconstrued certain statements contained in the entry on the brain in the 1911 edition of the *Encyclopedia Britannica*. Describing the progress to date in assigning functions to cortical areas, the encyclopedia opines that "it is true that the greater part of the cortex remains *terra incognita* unless we are content with mere descriptive features concerning its coarse anatomy". Thus, some readers may well have stumbled from "We don't know what it does," to "It doesn't do anything."

A similar misunderstanding that might have contributed to the 10% myth has been suggested by Professor James Kalat of the Psychology Department at North Carolina State University.[5] Also in an Internet posting, Kalat draws our attention to the following quotation from R.S. Woodworth, another pioneer of American psychology. In one of Woodworth's (1934, p. 194) textbooks, he writes:

> The total number of nerve cells in the cerebral cortex is estimated to be about 14,000,000,000. Many of these are small and apparently underdeveloped, as if they constituted a reserve stock not yet utilized in the individual's cerebral activity.

We now know that these so-called "interneurons" exist throughout life and that, though they are small, they are not necessarily immature. They are also known as Golgi type II neurons and they are involved in forming new interconnections among the larger and more static Golgi type I neurons in the cortex (Hirsch and Jacobson, 1975). Building new circuitry in this way is one of the ways in which new experiences leave their traces in the brain. Kalat may well be right that some of the earlier generation of students who were exposed to Woodworth's influential text might have gone away thinking that this large number of "baby" neurons was simply a back-up pool awaiting special new enhancement techniques, to be supplied by the emerging cadre of brain-trainers, that could propel them to maturity and generate vast new mental powers.

I also believe that the vision of a largely dormant brain acquired some of its unearned scientific gloss from lay persons' misinterpretations of early neurological experiments with lower animals. Pioneering studies by Karl Lashley, for instance, seemed to show that large portions of rat cortex could be removed with apparently little disruption of behaviour (Krech, 1962). These findings led Lashley to become one of the last great proponents of the holistic or "mass action" view of brain function discussed earlier. His notion of equipotentiality suggested that loss of function was proportional to amount of cortex lost, not the site of the loss. The apparent lack of disruption caused by Lashley's lesions was at least consistent with the idea that there is massive redundancy in the brain. Later, more sophisticated behavioural tests did expose functional deficits that weren't obvious with Lashley's testing methods.

In a similar vein, popular confusion regarding certain terms used by early comparative neurologists may have contributed to the misapprehension that we use only 10% of our brains. As depicted in Figure 1.4, research has shown that, with evolutionary advancement, the cerebrum of mammals has enlarged greatly, but that a progressively smaller *proportion* of its mass is concerned with strictly sensory or motor duties. This was demonstrated in the 1930s by studying the cerebral cortex in a variety of species from different levels of the evolutionary tree. Electrical stimulation of cortical cells and experimentally produced cortical lesions seemed to have minimal effects in these increasingly large

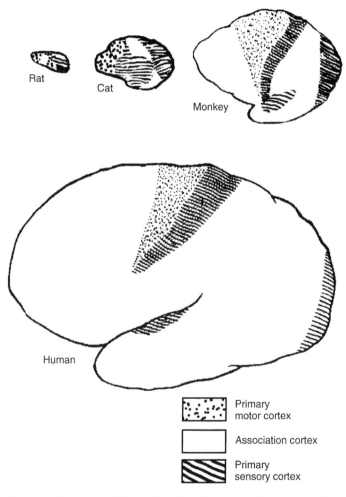

Figure 1.4 Left-hemisphere views of the brains of various mammalian species (drawn only approximately to scale). The diagrams show the absolute increase in size with evolutionary change, as well as the proportional increase in "association cortex". Because some authors choose to call this association cortex "silent cortex", some readers may have mistakenly thought it was literally "silent".

non-sensory and non-motor areas in the brains of the higher species. For that reason, those areas were referred to by some researchers as "silent cortex", although they did not intend this to mean that these regions were literally silent or unused. As we have seen, they are anything but silent – these areas, which today are usually referred to as "association cortex", are responsible for our most uniquely human characteristics, including language, mental imagery, and abstract thought. Areas of maximal activity shift in the brain as we change from one task to another or vary our attention and arousal levels, but there are normally no dormant regions awaiting new assignments.

The term "silent" had a certain allure, however, and its connotations helped some customers of the self-help industry to misconstrue the intent of certain popular works on the brain, published in the 1950s and 1960s, that still leaned toward some aspects of Lashley's concept of mass action. For instance, the influential British neurophysiologist Walter (1963), in *The Living Brain*, a book aimed largely at the intelligent lay person, had the following to say:

> It is true that certain parts of the brain have a regular and recognizable microscopic appearance and respond in a fairly predictable fashion when stimulated electrically, and when diseased or damaged they are associated with certain diagnostic signs or symptoms. But the exceptions to these rules are so numerous and their experimental foundation is so tenuous, that there is now a tendency to support an entirely "holistic" view of brain function, to suppose that all parts are engaged in any sense or any action, and that the location of function is more a probability than a place . . . That we can conceive of it at all is due to the obscure workings of the brain regions which yield least to experimental probing, the association areas, sometimes called "silent" because their oracles are dumb when threatened by the experimental intruder. These regions make up the greater part of the human brain . . . (Walter, 1963, p. 71)

In this way, however inadvertently, widely read books such as Walter's fostered the mistaken notion that "silent cortex" meant that the brain contains large unused areas. It is no disservice to the memory of truly great researchers such as Karl Lashley and Grey Walter to note that subsequent research overtook their notions of a holistic brain by finding many specific functions in what was previously called "silent cortex". Ironically, though, this later research showed that Lashley and Walter were, in a sense, right after all, but in a somewhat different way than they had intended. Large portions of the brain *are* activated by most mental tasks. It is just that this comes about because the brain breaks complex undertakings into many parallel operations which it then directs to widely dispersed and highly specialized processing modules throughout the cerebrum (Gazzaniga, 1989). This can give the appearance of "mass action" but, in fact, the whole brain is operating more like a symphony orchestra, i.e. a collection of individual sections, each blending its own unique part into the performance of the whole composition. Walter's ideas have also been partially vindicated in that modern views of brain modularity suggest that the task-oriented assemblies of these units are more fluid and temporary than was once thought. Although the modules are indeed highly specialized, different but similar ones might be recruited into temporary networks to accomplish the same task on subsequent occasions. This ability to pick and choose "on the fly" also means that damage to one module leaves open the possibility of substituting another, though perhaps less efficient, assemblage to do the job after trauma to the brain.

It is also possible that what might have given rise to William James' speculation that we only use a small part of our brains (if indeed he said this, as opposed to suggesting that we use only a small part of its *creative potential*) were anecdotal accounts of people who had suffered drastic losses of brain tissue due to accidents or disease, but seemed, none the less, to function more or less normally. Most of these cases were poorly documented and specialists trained to spot more subtle cognitive deficits were typically not consulted. Although they were probably exaggerated for dramatic effect, these stories gained considerable notoriety (Corliss, 1993), especially among mystery-mongers who delight in finding anomalies that science allegedly cannot explain. It seems reasonable to think that they might have lent another bit of credence to the 10% myth.

There have been better-documented cases recently, however, that confirm the remarkable ability of immature brains to reorganize and recover from neural damage. Young children have been known to recover a surprisingly high level of functioning after loss of an entire cerebral hemisphere to injury or disease (Kolb and Whishaw, 1996, Chapter 10). This is far less than 90% of their brains, of course, but because, after birth, dying nerve cells are replaced sparsely if at all, these patients must be making do with whatever neurons remain, raising the possibility at least that there may have been some unused parts lying around. In fact, it seems instead that the functions of the destroyed areas actually ''crowd in'' alongside those the intact areas were already handling, rather than colonizing previously unused areas. Immediately following the surgical removal of one hemisphere, these children experience devastating disruptions of behaviour and consciousness but, gradually, most abilities, including language, show substantial recovery. Unfortunately, this ability of the remaining neural tissue to assume additional duties when other parts of the brain are decimated wanes with age, as a visit to any neurological ward will quickly convince you.

Even among those who suffer brain damage as young children and regain near-normal functioning, some deficits do remain, although it sometimes requires fairly sophisticated tests to reveal these frailties. The ability to achieve such a high degree of recovery seems to be largely lost by the time of puberty. Much recent research has been devoted to finding ways to suppress certain processes in mature brains that largely prevent adult neural tissue from re-establishing functional connections after brain damage.

The Gospel According to Lorber

Popularized accounts of dramatic sparing of function in some youngsters with a different kind of brain damage have strengthened the hands of those committed to the proposition that we don't really need all that extra brain substance in the first place. In my experience, an otherwise informative UK television documentary featuring some remarkable teenage neurological patients has done more to rejuvenate a version of the 10% myth than any other recent event.[6] This programme, created by the British producer/director Hilary Lawson and narrated by Michael O'Donnell, is replayed regularly throughout the English-speaking world, because of its striking and counter-intuitive contents. Given the deliberately provocative title, ''Is Your Brain Really Necessary?'', the telecast employs the ever-popular theme of a brave outsider struggling against a mulish establishment to suggest that, once again, the so-called ''experts'' aren't as bright as they think they are. Along the way, the programme encourages the misapprehension that there is a huge reserve of unnecessary brain mass that can be casually dispensed with. The show features the Sheffield University paediatrician, Professor John Lorber, who discovered the patients highlighted in the programme. Lorber, who has a reputation for being deliberately controversial, sets the theme when he opines on camera:

> My hunch is that we all have a substantial reserve of neurons and brain cells . . . that we don't need and don't use . . .

Lorber prefers this interpretation to account for an admittedly extraordinary group of patients referred to his paediatric practice, initially because of fairly minor, unrelated complaints. Most of these young people were in mid- to late adolescence at the time the programme was made. They were of normal or above-normal intelligence and were coping well, educationally and socially but, astonishingly, CAT scans had revealed that their cerebral hemispheres had been compressed into a slab only a centimetre or so thick in places.

This compression of the brain had been caused by an enlargement of the underlying fluid-filled ventricles, as shown in Figure 1.5. It is likely that this compacting of the higher cerebral centres occurred insidiously as the normally circulating cerebrospinal fluid (CSF) in the ventricles and the subarachnoid spaces slowly dammed up behind partially con-stricted outflow ducts. This condition is known as hydrocephalus. Most commonly, it begins in infancy and the pressure build-up progresses quite rapidly, with devastating results. It is presumed that in Lorber's patients the onset was somewhat later, during childhood, and that the excess CSF accumulated more slowly, applying more moderate but constant pressure on the cerebrum, over a more extended period.

Before modern surgical treatments became available to drain the accumulating CSF, the rapidly increasing pressure in the more typical infant-onset cases of hydrocephalus would cause the still plastic cranium to balloon out grotesquely. Such an enlargement was possible because the infant skull has not yet fully calcified. The expected outcome was

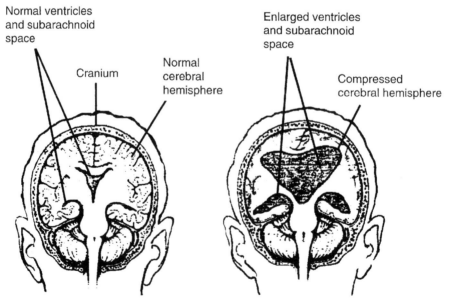

Figure 1.5   The left diagram shows the usual size of the brain's fluid-filled ventricles and sub-arachnoid spaces. The right diagram shows an enlargement of these areas that are normally filled with cerebrospinal fluid (CSF). The enlargement is due to an accumulation of CSF caused by the disease, hydrocephalus. This enlargement of the spaces containing the accumulated CSF has com-pressed the overlying brain tissue drastically.

severe mental and motor retardation, and, most often, death. In Lorber's presumably later-onset cases, the cranium had probably already fused by the time the hydrocephalic accumulation began, trapping the cerebral hemispheres "between a rock and a hard place". The absence of mental retardation in these young adults, despite their tremendous cerebral shrinkage, led Lorber and the producers of the show to ask the disingenuous question that became the title of the episode: "Is Your Brain Really Necessary?" Although the programme contains a few demurrals here and there, and Lorber concedes occasionally that there might be more conventional explanations, it is clear that the producers' sympathies lie with the "excess cerebral baggage" interpretation – i.e. that most of the normal cerebral mass is superfluous. No doubt, this kind of sensationalism helps many viewers to recall the documentary's misleading slant.

The facetiousness of the programme's question/title is apparent if one looks at the vegetable-like existence of children unfortunate enough to be born with a similar impoverishment of the higher cerebral centres due to failure of these areas to develop normally (so-called anencephalic infants). Obviously, the adolescents in Lorber's care must have endured substantial compression of comparable areas of their brains, but they are not living essentially without them, as the documentary manages to imply. Lorber, engaging in characteristic hyperbole, is quoted in one article as saying that one of these boys is "socially completely normal. And yet [he] has virtually no brain" (Lewin, 1980).

What Lorber's remarkable cases demonstrate is not, as the show coyly suggests, the irrelevance of higher brain centres to our mental lives, but rather the ability of this amazing organ to adjust to massive disruptions, providing they occur slowly enough and early enough in life. It has been known for some time that, for certain functional units at least, a series of small brain lesions in the same general area is less devastating than one massive lesion, even if comparable amounts of tissue are ultimately destroyed (Kalat, 1995, p. 543). In multiple infarct disease, for instance, a series of tiny strokes occurs over an extended period. These patients are often able to cope reasonably well until they die of other causes, and pathologists are frequently surprised to see the extent of cellular damage in their brains when they are finally subjected to autopsy. This is presumed to be possible because, in the case of temporally spaced damage, there is time for the remaining neurons to adjust. Neurons in intact regions can sprout new collateral offshoots that can reinnervate some of the cells that were deprived of their input by cell death in the damaged regions. And, in addition, the whole system has time to learn new strategies to cope with the loss of the damaged areas (see the discussion of brain modularity and parallel processing, above).

The CAT scans shown in the Lawson/Lorber television documentary cannot reveal how much of the thinning of the cerebral hemispheres in these patients was due to neuronal loss and how much to compacting of brain cells into less than their normal volume. Nerve cells are normally bathed in a sea of intercellular fluid. Perhaps some of the volume of this fluid, and not only neural volume, has been reduced. In addition, there is also reason to believe that the greater share of cell loss in such cases may be among the supporting glial cells rather than in the neurons that actually mediate mental functions.[7] Glial cells perform essential support functions for neural circuits, but if their numbers are thinned, cortical function could be maintained, providing a sufficient number remain. It is also possible that the cortex in these patients (which is normally quite infolded) has been smoothed out by the growing internal pressure, but has retained its essential organization and connectivity.

PET scans shown in the same television documentary revealed varying effects among Lorber's patients. Generally speaking, having these patients engage in various mental tasks resulted in activation of areas in the compressed slabs of cerebral tissue that were more or less homologous to the distribution found in normal brains. However, there was also some evidence that certain functions may have changed their relative positions in some of these patients.

The fact that these young people can get by with reduced cerebral volume does not imply that they would not have put any additional tissue to good use had it been retained. I also suspect from watching the documentary that, at least in some cases, their degree of normality may have been exaggerated somewhat for dramatic effect. Most descriptions of these cases have appeared in the popular media, who love to emphasize Lorber's bombastic claims that he is about to overturn several centuries' worth of brain research.[8] The paucity of data on these cases published in peer-reviewed sources suggests that some of the claims Lorber is given to making in the mass media may have had more difficulty getting past more sceptical scientific reviewers. For example, Kenneth Till, a British neurosurgeon, has cautioned that the sorts of scans Lorber has used can sometimes produce underestimates of the actual amount of brain tissue left (Lewin, 1980). At any rate, it is not the case, as Lorber says on camera, that these adolescents have ''virtually no brain'' above the brainstem.

Lorber also asserts in the documentary that the functional sparing exhibited in his cases overthrows the established doctrine that, in mammals, no new neurons are produced after birth. He was not the first, however, to suggest that this dogma is only substantially, not absolutely, correct (Altman, 1967). A recent panel convened by the New York Academy of Sciences has confirmed that there is in fact more cell division and replacement of neurons in mature brains than previously thought. But if you think about it, the ''regrowth'' explanation floated by Lorber actually undermines his suggestion that much of the brain is unnecessary. Why would the brain need to regrow damaged parts if they were superfluous to begin with? Lorber also undervalues the fact that the axons and dendrites that connect neurons into functional circuits continue to grow and form new circuits throughout life. Much of the postnatal increase in the volume of normal brains is due to the ramification of these axonal and dendritic interconnections. Thus growth of new functional interconnections could account for some sparing of abilities without requiring new cell division to form replacement neurons as Lorber suggests. These conventional alternatives seem more likely because the compression probably occurred slowly, giving time for these collateral connections to become established.

Although Lorber will be disappointed that, contrary to his predictions, the leading textbooks in neurology will probably not have to be scrapped, his cases are an eloquent testimonial to the resilience of the young brain and its ability to reorganize and carry on after major insults. It is unfortunate that the producers did not make this their take-home message, instead of the misleading impression they chose to leave. Had they done so, their programme would have served a useful educational purpose. The audience should also have been warned that mature brains subjected to more rapid increases in intracranial pressure, due to growing tumours for example, certainly experience much more drastic impairments. None the less, Lorber's brain images do supply a useful corrective in that they serve to remind neurologists and neuropsychologists that deeper structures in the brain (which are relatively unharmed in such cases) may contribute more to our mental abilities than our fascination with the intricacies of the cerebral cortex sometimes leads us to think. Leading theorists such as Ronald Melzack (Melzack, 1989) are beginning to reawaken interest in the possible contributions of these midbrain and brainstem areas to higher mental processes.

CONCLUSION

After much searching, I have come to the conclusion that the 10% myth arose most likely from various attempts to reify popular metaphors about latent powers of the mind. This has been helped along by a combination of honest and self-serving misconstruals of the rightfully modest admissions by neuroscientists concerning the limits of our current understanding of the brain. Despite the enormous amount that has been learned, it is only honest to confess how much remains to be discovered. Such modesty would have been even more appropriate at the dawn of the 20th century when the myth appears to have taken off. It seems likely that some early investigator's (probably optimistic) estimate that researchers only knew what 10% of the brain does may have been misinterpreted as an assertion that we normally only need or use 10% of it.

In the final analysis, I think that the persistence of this curious assertion is yet another testimonial to the comforting nature of most occult and New Age beliefs. It would be nice if they were true – death would have no sting, merely thinking about desirable outcomes would bring them to pass, and there need be no shortfalls in life, materially or mentally. The 10% myth conveys the welcome message that we could all be Einsteins, Rockefellers or Uri Gellers if we could just engage that ballast between our ears.

The ubiquity of the 10% myth is reminiscent of the so-called ''urban legends'' studied by the American folklorist, Jan Harold Brunvand (Brunvand, 1982, 1986). Brunvand has dubbed these mini morality plays ''FOAF-lore'' (for ''Friend-Of-A-Friend''), because attempts to verify them invariably lead to an infinite regress. The allegedly true story always seems to have happened to a ''friend of a friend'', who, upon being approached, says it happened to a ''friend of a friend'', and so on. Brunvand (1986, p. 165) notes several reasons for the popularity and longevity of urban legends, e.g. they generally have a gripping story line, have a small element of embedded truth, and frequently provide the opportunity to be politically incorrect without incurring social wrath (''Don't blame me, I'm just telling it like it happened,'' the teller declares). Above all, they offer a vehicle for advancing a warning, incitement or moral lesson that is either stated or implied. Despite the implausibility of many of the story lines in these legends, their underlying messages play on widely held hopes, prejudices and anxieties, and they have an exhortative quality that makes people want to suspend their scepticism. Consequently, people in all walks of life tend to believe and spread these tales, and the media continue to recycle them with minor variations and almost clockwork regularity. As we have seen, variants of the 10% myth exhibit many of these same qualities. I've been told many times about ''this guy who went in for an x-ray, and, ya know, they found that his head was full of nothing but water, but he was smart as a whip, anyhow . . .''

The concept of a trusty ''cerebral spare tyre'' continues to nourish the clientele of ''pop-psychologists'' and their many recycling self-improvement schemes. As a metaphor for the fact that few of us fully exploit our talents, who could deny it? As a spur to hope and a source of solace, it's probably done more good than harm, but comfort afforded is not truth implied. As a refuge for occultists and flim-flam artists seeking the neural basis of the miraculous, the probability of its being true is considerably less than 10%.

NOTES

1. Gall and Spurtzheim, in the 19th century, carried the defensible notion of functional specificity too far. Their doctrine of phrenology asserted that the cerebrum was divided into tiny islands, each responsible for a particular psychological trait or ability. Although the phrenologists were wrong about how the brain maps these entities onto its anatomy (and several other things as well), they were correct in the assumption that localization exists. Unfortunately, their excesses (which were not as absurd then as they seem today, given what was known at the time) served to sully the idea of functional specificity for a generation or more (Clarke and Jacyna, 1987). This left advocates of holistic functioning firmly in command until the weight of clinical evidence and modern research data showed that, in principle if not in detail, the phrenologists' concept of localization had been right all along.
2. It is ironic that the self-improvers were, by buying into the 10% myth, promoting the materialist view that mind equals brain function (which, even today, is not the majority opinion in the population at large), while at the same time they remained true to their revivalist roots by heavily lading their writings with dualistic references to the God-given, spiritual nature of mind.
3. Independent checks by my research assistant, Sheri Kashman, and my brother, Dale Beyerstein, chair of the Philosophy Department at Vancouver's Langara College, also failed to find any reference to the 10% myth in James' *Principles*.
4. Multiple sclerosis sufferers will attest to the major perceptual and motor disruptions that follow destruction of massive amounts of glial cells by that disease.
5. I am indebted to Ron Apland, of the Psychology Department at Malaspina College in Nanaimo, British Columbia, for bringing Kalat's suggestion to my attention. I also acknowledge with thanks some helpful suggestions from Professor Robert Keefer of St Mary's College, Gettysburg, Pennsylvania.
6. Lawson's documentary has also been cited by fundamentalist Christians of my acquaintance as evidence against assertions I have championed elsewhere (Beyerstein, 1988a) that mind is identical with brain function. They detest this materialist view of mind because it argues against the dualistic alternative they prefer, i.e. that mind is equivalent to the immaterial and immortal soul. If, as Lawson's documentary stops just short of asserting, the brain really isn't necessary for higher thought processes, this makes dualistic, spiritual beliefs (including that of an afterlife) easier to hold.
7. Glial cells are fatty tissues ("white matter") that provide metabolic and physical support for neurons. They also comprise the myelin sheaths around the axons of some neurons that provide insulation and speed up neural conduction. Glial cells are estimated to be much more numerous than neurons, so some loss, due to intracranial pressure produced by hydrocephalus early in life, might be sustainable without major functional disruptions.
8. Although Lorber usually refrains from putting numbers on his estimates, the popular media have not been so circumspect. Frequently, the magic 10% rears its head in reporters' accounts. As an unsigned column in the May 1981 issue of *Monthly Science Digest* put it, "Dr John Lorber . . . believes that people with as little as one-*tenth* normal brain size are capable of superior intellectual achievement" (italics in original). Almost imperceptibly, the magazine made the huge jump from one-tenth normal cortical thickness to one-tenth of a brain.

CHAPTER 2

Are We in Our Right Minds?

MICHAEL C. CORBALLIS

INTRODUCTION

Everybody now knows about the left brain and the right brain. The left brain is verbal, rational, linear, computational, and scientific. The right brain is spatial, intuitive, emotional, creative, and artistic. The left brain epitomizes industrial, military Western culture, while the right brain has the glamour and mystery of the East. The left brain is boring, while the right brain is fun.

These notions came to light in the latter years of the 1960s, largely as a result of research carried out on people who had undergone the so-called "split-brain" operation for the relief of intractable epilepsy. The basic idea behind the operation was that an epileptic disturbance originating in one hemisphere of the brain could be prevented from reaching the other, and so causing a major seizure, if the connections between the hemispheres were cut. This rather drastic treatment was largely successful in at least reducing the frequency and severity of seizures. What was really interesting about the patients, though, was that the two sides of the brain were effectively separated from one another, at least with respect to higher mental functions, so it became possible to assess each side without interference from the other.

The leader of this research was Roger W. Sperry, who received the Nobel Prize for his work in 1981. Sperry and his colleagues were quickly able to show that only the left brain could actually name objects or words presented to it, while the right remained speechless (Gazzaniga, Bogen and Sperry, 1967; Sperry, 1982). The right brain of at least some patients was shown to be able to *understand* language, though, and could direct the left hand to point to the names of objects presented to it, or to point to objects whose names were presented to it. The right brain's ability to comprehend was clearly below that of the left, but still came as something of a surprise, since a century of research on the effects of damage to the left brain had suggested that the right brain had little ability to either comprehend or produce language (Sperry, 1982). It is still a matter of controversy as to whether studies of the split brain have painted an accurate picture of right-brain verbal capacities in normal people.

But what was more interesting was the idea that the right brain might have special abilities of its own, abilities perhaps not shared by the left. Until the 1960s, the right brain, or hemisphere, had generally been considered subordinate to the left, and was known as the "minor" or "non-dominant" hemisphere. Then, experiments on the separated right hemisphere began to reveal a few activities in which it scored better than the left. These were largely spatial, as in matching parts of shapes to wholes, or in imagining shapes in different orientations, or in directing spatial attention. The right hemisphere also proved somewhat better at identifying melodies, although the left hemisphere appears to be the more specialized for rhythm. There is some evidence that the right hemisphere is the more specialized for emotion, although there is an alternative view that the right hemisphere is specialized for negative emotions and the left for positive ones. Although the compendium of suggested right-hemispheric functions is quite broad, the advantages are usually slight, and the functions themselves are often simple perceptual ones (review: Corballis, 1983). Research has shown nothing in the right hemisphere comparable to the remarkable dominance of the left hemisphere for speech. Michael Gazzaniga, one of Sperry's original collaborators and a long-time researcher on the split brain, was even moved to remark that "It could well be argued that the cognitive skills of a normal disconnected right hemisphere without language are vastly inferior to the cognitive skills of a chimpanzee" (Gazzaniga, 1987, p. 535).

Korb '98

Figure 2.1   Dr G. exercises his right hemisphere.

In fairness, it should be said that it is not easy to test the right hemisphere because of its limited verbal comprehension, and it may possess abilities untapped by research. Moreover, Gazzaniga's extreme view provoked rebuttals from Zaidel (1983) and Bogen (1993, 1997), among others. But he was not repentant, and 4 years later still insisted that "the vast majority of the cases from all [split-brain] surgical cases reveal little cognitive capacity in their right hemispheres" (Gazzaniga, 1987, p. 120). What this controversy shows is that the supposed creative, intuitive skills of the right hemisphere are far from proven, and are based more on speculation and the power of myth than on any incontrovertible scientific evidence. My own view is that the apparent superiority of the right hemisphere in some spatial or non-verbal skills is a secondary consequence of the left hemisphere's involvement with language (Corballis, 1983). It is not that the right hemisphere is specialized, but rather that the left hemisphere has forfeited some of its competence in non-language functions. I will return to this later.

THE MYTH-MAKERS

The paucity of evidence did not stop the myth-makers, who greeted the right brain as though it were some long-lost but exotic uncle. First off the mark was Joseph E. Bogen, one of the surgeons who carried out the split-brain operation in the 1960s. In a free-floating but scholarly review, he suggested that the right hemisphere might be considered to harbour an "appositional mind", complementary to the "propositional mind" of the left hemisphere (Bogen, 1969). Besides drawing on neurological evidence and evidence from the split brain, Bogen referred to long-standing notions about the dual nature of the mind, including the Chinese concepts of Yang and Yin, the Hindu distinction between intellect (*buddhi*) and mind (*manas*), Hobbes' notions of unordered versus directed thinking, and the everyday distinction between reason and intuition. Bogen and his colleagues also undertook a study comparing different ethnic and racial groups on a battery of tests purported to be sensitive to the different specialized capacities of the two hemispheres. Among the groups they tested, Hopi Indians were the most "right-brained" in their profile of abilities, followed by urban Afro-American women, urban Afro-American men, rural whites, and urban whites (Bogen et al., 1972). The idea that primitive peoples might be more right-hemispheric than those from industrialized societies is a common one, smacking somewhat of 18th-century Romanticism and the concept of the "Noble Savage", and is probably not without a touch of condescension. The "pernicious myth of the right-brained Indian" is neatly dismantled by Chrisjohn and Peters (1986).

The dual brain was enthusiastically pursued by Robert E. Ornstein in his best-selling book *The Psychology of Consciousness* (Ornstein, 1972). Part of Ornstein's message was that society in general, and educationalists in particular, had placed far too much emphasis on left-brain thinking, and that there was a need to liberate the creative powers of the right brain. So quickly did this idea grow that by 1977 the editor of *Psychology Today* called it "the fad of the year" (Goleman, 1977, p. 89). Betty Edward's 1979 book *Drawing on the Right Side of the Brain* (Edwards, 1979) which purported to teach people how to draw by exploiting the creative and spatial powers of the right hemisphere, has been possibly even more successful than Ornstein's book. Picking up on Bogen's theme, anthropologists argued that differences between the two hemispheres might explain cultural differences (e.g. Paredes and Hepburn, 1976). Even science itself was not immune. In his 1977 book *The Dragons of Eden* Carl Sagan, the noted cosmologist and popularizer of science, portrays the right hemisphere as the creative but paranoid instigator of scientific ideas, often seeing patterns and conspiracies where they do not exist (Sagan, 1977). The role of the rational left hemisphere is to submit these ideas to critical scrutiny.

The two sides of the brain turned out to be good for business, and in 1976 a professor in the Faculty of Management at McGill University was moved to write in the *Harvard Business Review* as follows:

> The important policy processes of managing an organization rely to a considerable extent on the faculties identified with the brain's right hemisphere. Effective managers seem to revel in ambiguity; in complex, mysterious system with little order. (Mintzberg, 1976, p. 53)

Korb '98

Figure 2.2 Dr B.'s left hemisphere wonders what the hell his right hemisphere can be up to.

Nearly 20 years later, the same theme persists, as in books such as Harry Alder's *Right Brain Manager: How to Harness the Powers of Your Mind to Achieve Personal and Business Success* (Alder, 1993).

In his 1977 *Psychology Today* article, Goleman suggested that the fad would soon peak, but he was wrong. A decade later, Harris (1988) noted that it was still going strong, and it shows no signs of abating even in the late 1990s. The authors of *Superlearning* 2000, published in 1994, have the audacity to write as follows:

> Yes, it's the left brain/right brain, and you've heard it before. *Superlearning* helped popularize the idea in the early 1980s (Ostrander and Schroeder, 1994, p. 176)

In the early 1980s it had been swilling around in the popular press for at least a decade.

Needless to say, there was – and still is – money to be made. Right-brain education programmes such as "The Neuropsychology of Achievement", described in Trubo (1982), and the "Applied Creative Thinking Workshop" (Hermann, 1981), were aimed particularly at business managers, personnel directors, and so forth. As of 1986, a scheme known as "whole-brain learning" was available on tape for $195, and provided "mind–brain expansion" through "megasubliminal messages", three hearable by the left brain and four hearable by the right brain. Those interested in the scheme were invited to pay $1400 to attend seminars so that they might become "certified in accelerated teaching and learning" (Harris, 1988). Programmes like *Superlearning* and *Neuro-Linguistic Programming*[1] (Bandler and Grinder, 1979), which pay extensive homage to the supposedly complementary functions of the two sides of the brain, continue to draw fee-paying converts and are big business worldwide.

Figure 2.3 A chartered accountant receives an unexpected phone call.

The duality of the brain was enthusiastically received in educational circles. In 1977, an art teacher, anticipating Betty Edwards, was quoted in the *Los Angeles Times* as saying that the essence of her method was to teach people to "gain access to the right hemisphere and be able to put it to use for education in general" ("The Art of Putting the Brain to Work," 1977, Part IV, p. 20). Another author chimed in by deploring the overemphasis on left-hemispheric values in US schools, and "the tragic lack of effort to develop our children's right brain strengths. That potential – a source of equally essential creative, artistic, and intellectual capacity – is at present largely unawakened in our schools" (Garrett, 1976, p. 244). Suggested ways to enhance right-brain participation in the classroom included being more tolerant of children's wrong answers and of their excursions into dreams and fantasy (Brandwein, 1977), and greater use of television and of such meditation devices as transcendental meditation, yoga, Sufi, biofeedback, biorhythms, and hypnosis (Grady and Luecke, 1978). And so it goes on. Zdenek (1985) interviewed a number of creative writers and artists, and informed a rather bemused Charles Schulz, the cartoonist, of the ways in which he had been putting his right brain to use. But at least she managed to cheer him up: "Well, I'm glad you came all the way up here," he said at the end of the interview, "You helped the sadness go away" (Zdenek, 1985, p. 74).

The right hemisphere has even managed to invade the world of English literature, a remarkable achievement when one considers that it has little, if any, language capacity. In 1983 a professor of English published a book entitled *Writing the Natural Way: Using Right-Brain Techniques to Release your Expressive Powers* (Rico, 1983). In New Zealand, the syllabus for the teaching of English in schools divides languages into three categories: written language, spoken language, and something called *visual* language. This last category seems to include film, television and theatre, as well as posters, computer-generated text and fax machines. It is, in part, a kind of concession to political correctness, so that children who have little ability in spoken or written language may nevertheless hope to find expression for other talents, but it is no doubt intended also to cater for right-brain activity. One trenchant commentator, himself a distinguished poet, novelist and critic, foresees dire consequences for the literacy of New Zealand children (Stead, 1997).

For the ultimate in dual-brain rhetoric applied to literature, though, we can do no better than turn to the late Poet Laureate, Ted Hughes. He has this to say:

> An explanation for some aspects of the poetic effect of Shakespeare's device is suggested by what is now known of the co-operative inter-activity of the left and right hemispheres of the brain. We are told that, in general, the left side processes verbal language, abstract concepts, linear argument, while the right side is virtually wordless, and processes sensuous imagery, intuitive ideas, spacial [sic] patterns of wholeness and simultaneity . . . By nature the two sides presumably live in a kind of happy marriages. A noisily chattering society is supercharged with right-side participation: music, song, dance, colour, imagery – and a vernacular tending naturally to imagery and musicality . . . But, as history demonstrates, the onset of rationality institutes proceedings for a kind of divorce. (Hughes, 1992, p. 157)

Hughes goes on to convince us that William Shakespeare had two sides to his brain. There must be something to the idea, since nearly a century ago Rudyard Kipling wrote the following poem, which appeared in 1901 in *Kim*:

> Something I owe to the soil that grew –
>   More to the life that fed –
> But most to Allah who gave me two
>   Separate sides to my head.
>
> I would go without shirt or shoes,
>   Friends, tobacco or bread
> Sooner than for an instant lose
>   Either side of my head.

HISTORY REPEATS ITSELF

If this seems to be remarkable prescience on Kipling's part, it should be explained that there was an obsession with the left and right brains in the latter part of the 19th century that eerily foreshadows the present one. In the 1860s, the French physician Paul Broca reported observations from brain-injured patients indicating that the loss of speech (which he called *aphemia*) was associated with damage exclusively to part of the left hemisphere of the brain (Broca, 1865).[2] Shortly afterwards, the German neurologist Wernicke (1874) associated the loss of language comprehension with another part of the left hemisphere. These two parts of the left hemisphere, Broca's area in the frontal lobe and Wernicke's area around the junction of the parietal, occipital and temporal lobes, are still regarded as the major language-mediating areas of the brain.

Even though the left hemisphere was thereafter widely considered the "major" or "dominant" hemisphere, there were some who found odd jobs for the right hemisphere to do. The British neurologist Jackson (1864) speculated that if "expression" resided in the left hemisphere, then maybe "perception" resided in the other, an idea that was echoed independently by the French neurologist De Fleury (1872) and the Austrian physiologist Exner (1881). Speculation took a different turn when the French neuroanatomist Luys (1881) noted personality differences between those with left- and right-hemispheric damage, and suggested that the "emotion centre" was in the right hemisphere, complementing the "intellectual" centres in the left. It had also been noted that patients with hysterical disorders tended to show left-sided symptoms. Although this was first observed by Briquet in 1859, even before Broca's discoveries were made known, it was widely attributed to Jean-Martin Charcot, well known for his work on hypnosis and hysteria, and was even dubbed "Charcot's rule".

And then the game was on. Brown-Sequard (1877) argued that the left hemisphere represented "the life of relations" and the right hemisphere the "organic life", and that right-hemispheric damage was likely to lead to "troubles of nutrition", such as bedsores, oedema, pulmonary congestion, and involuntary evacuation of faeces and urine. He went so far as to believe that each side of the brain was a complete brain, each with separate bilateral control of the whole body, and continued to expand on this theme until well into his old age (Harrington, 1985). Luys (1879) maintained that the left hemisphere was the repository of civilization, with the right hemispheres representing the primitive, prehuman side of our nature. Madness was the result of an imbalance, with the right hemisphere assuming dominance. Another influential theorist, Delaunay (cited in Harrington, 1985), associated the left and right sides of the brain with male and female characteristics, and in

1898 another French physician declared: ''The terms 'male hemisphere' and 'female hemisphere' should render rather well the differences in the nature of the two brains, of which one, more intellectual, is more stable, and of which the other, more excitable, is also more rapidly exhausted'' (Klippel, 1898, pp. 56–57).

The dual brain was also used to account for cases of dual personality, with the left hemisphere representing the educated, civilized Dr Jekyll and the right hemisphere the crude, passionate Mr Hyde. One extraordinary case, known as Louis V, apparently suffered hemiparalysis and hemianaesthesia that could be transferred from one side of the body to the other. This transfer was accompanied by changes of personality: ''Louis V, directed by the right hemisphere is a different individual than the Louis V who corresponds to the left hemisphere. The right-sided paralysis [implying right-hemispheric control] only allows the violent and brutal aspects of his character to appear; the left-sided paralysis [implying left-hemispheric control] transforms him into a peaceful boy'' (Bourru and Burot, 1888, p. 127).

These claims soon led to therapies directed to one or other side of the brain. A technique known as ''metallotherapy'' was developed in which metal discs, and later magnets, were applied to the sides of the body in order to transfer symptoms from one side to the other, and it was soon claimed that these techniques were also able to effect changes in personality and intellect. This was known as ''psychic transfer'' (Binet and Feret, 1885). Hypnotic techniques were also developed, especially in France, to hypnotize each side of the brain separately. In one extraordinary case, a hypnotized person was said to simultaneously express horror on one side of the face and calm contentment on the other through having one hemisphere induced to hallucinate an attack by dogs and the other a pleasant country fete (Dumontpallier and Magnan, 1883). There were visions of a brave new world in which magnets and hemihypnotic techniques might produce a doubling of mental faculties. John Jackson, one of the founders of the British Ambidextral Culture Society in 1903, wrote of a new age in which ''each hand shall be absolutely independent of the other in the production of ANY KIND OF WORK whatever; . . . if required, one hand shall be writing an original letter, and the other shall be playing the piano, with no diminution of concentration whatever'' (Jackson, 1905, p. 225).

Needless to say, there were spoilsports. From about 1885, Bernheim began a campaign to discredit metallotherapy, suggesting that the claimed effects were due entirely to ''suggestion''. Hemihypnosis soon lost credibility because its proponents had naively assumed that one could gain access to one half of the brain by having the patient cover one eye and directing their attention to the other. In the 1880s, there was some confusion as to how information from the eye reached the brain, but it was widely thought that the fibres from each eye projected wholly to the opposite hemisphere. It was later established that there is partial decussation of the optic tract, so that each eye actually projects to both side of the brain. It is each *side of the retina*, not each eye, that projects to one side of the brain. By the time this fact was made clear, however, the whole fanciful facade of hemihypnosis, metallotherapy and assorted other dual-brain techniques had collapsed. The historian Harrington (1987) states that she could find almost nothing written on the dual brain from 1920 until 1960, when the cycle was destined to repeat itself.

It is entirely to Harrington's credit that this earlier episode is recalled at all. The great majority of researchers on laterality from the 1960s on were oblivious to the fact that they were repeating history, until Harrington (1985, 1987) revealed all.[3] And if history is truly to repeat itself, the present-day phase is likely to soon burn itself out, notwithstanding its resilience over the past 30 years.[4] It is to be hoped that when the next cycle emerges in the 2060s, there is another astute historian who can remind our great-grandchildren of the excesses of the previous two centuries.

What can we learn from history? We have seen that the laterality myths of the late 19th century were in many ways similar to those of today, but there was at least one important difference. In the earlier version, the right hemisphere was clearly inferior to the left; it represented the primitive, uncivilized, brutish, and, dare I say, female side of the human condition. In these respects, of course, it echoes the prejudices of the time, and in particular the prejudices of a dominant, "civilized", male-oriented Europe – "dead white males", to borrow a feminist expression. Small wonder, then, that the right hemisphere, despite the array of functions attributed to it, was referred to as the minor or non-dominant hemisphere – non-dominant, that is, unless some disease caused it to assume dominance and induce madness in the hapless victim. Notwithstanding Gazzaniga's (1987) unflattering depiction of the right hemisphere as a sort of retarded chimpanzee, the modern myth-makers are much more respectful of the right hemisphere, even elevating it to a creative genius struggling for release. This again owes more to the prejudices of the time than to the neurological facts. The 1960s and 1970s were a time of protest, against the Vietnam War, and against the military–industrial establishment. The right hemisphere became a symbol for the creative, exploited people of the East against the brutal Western juggernaut. In the protest slogan "Make love, not war", the right hemisphere was love, and the left hemisphere war.

In homage to the feminist movement, too, the creative, intuitive, feminine side of our nature is associated with the right hemisphere, to be released from the slavery imposed by the bullying, masculine left hemisphere. In neuropsychological terms, however, the evidence on sex differences is muddled, to say the least. Women are widely regarded as more intuitive and better able to express emotion than men, suggesting greater right-hemispheric involvement, although the actual evidence for hemispheric differences in these attributes is far from clear. But women are also widely regarded as more verbal than men, and men more spatial than women, yet verbal ability is associated with the left hemisphere and spatial ability with the right. Indeed, in the 1980s, the neurologist Norman Geschwind saw fit to reverse the polarity by arguing that, far from being dominant, the left hemisphere in males was likely to be deficient. He suggested that the male sex hormone testosterone inhibits the early growth of the left hemisphere, which might explain why men are more likely than women to be left-handed and to suffer from language disorders, such as reading disability and stuttering. The influence of testosterone was also said to increase the likelihood of autoimmune disorders, especially in hapless males and left-handers (Geschwind and Behan, 1982; Geschwind and Galaburda, 1987). In a way, though, Geschwind's theory couples the 19th-century idea of a brutish, primitive, right hemisphere with the more contemporary feminist depiction of men as violent; according to another feminist slogan of the 1980s, "All men are rapists". Again, we see that the popularity of a theory may owe more to the culture of the age than to the neurological evidence. Geschwind's theory has not held up well in the face of empirical research (e.g. Bishop, 1987; Bryden, McManus and Bulman-Fleming, 1994), and seems already destined for the dustbin of history.

History shows us, then, that the hemispheres serve at least in part as pegs upon which to hang some of our cultural preconceptions. But this is a trend that goes back much further than the 19th century, except that in the beginning it was not the hemisphere – it was the hands.

READING THE HANDS

Throughout history, people of diverse cultures have associated different values with the two hands, or more generally with the two sides of the body. In general, these values are the reverse of those associated with the two cerebral hemispheres, presumably because of the crossed connections between the two sides of the body and the two sides of the brain. Positive values tend to be associated with the right hand and negative values with the left, although in some cases the attributes mapped onto the two sides of the body are complementary without being value-laden.

In the Pythagorean table of opposites, recorded by Aristotle, the right was associated with the limited, the one, the odd numbers, the light, the straight, the good, and the male, while the left was associated with the unlimited, the many, the even numbers, the dark, the curved, the evil, and the female. Many similar examples can be drawn up from quite unrelated cultures (Needham, 1973). For example, to the New Zealand Maoris, the right was the sacred side, the side of the gods, the side of strength and life, while the left was the side of profanity, demons, weakness, and death (Hertz, 1909). And we should not, of course, forget the Bible:

> And He will set the sheep upon His right hand and the goats upon His left. Then shall the King say to those upon His right, ''Come, ye blessed of my father, and inherit the Kingdom prepared for you from the beginning of the world.'' . . . Then shall He also say to those on the left, ''Depart from me, ye accursed, into everlasting fire prepared for the Devil and his Angels''. (Matthew 25:33–34; 41)

According to Barsley (1970), there are over 100 favourable references to the right hand in the Bible, and about 25 unfavourable references to the left hand.

The universality of left–right symbolism, with the right nearly always associated with positive attributes and the left with negative ones, no doubt reflects the fact that the majority of people in all human societies are right-handed. It has sometimes been argued that some nation or race of people were predominantly left-handed. In a popular article written in 1956, Trevor Holloway asserted that ''The Antanalas of Madagascar are unique among the races of the world for almost every member of this tribe of 100,000 is left-handed'' (Holloway, 1956, p. 27). I have been able to find no basis for this extraordinary claim. It has also been suggested that the ancient Hebrews must have been left-handed because Hebrew is written from right to left (e.g. Blau, 1946), but up until about 1500 AD there were about as many right-to-left scripts as left-to-right ones, and the gradual predominance of left-to-right writing is almost certainly due to historical events unrelated to handedness (Hewes, 1949). It was also thought for a time that the ancient Egyptians were mostly left-handed because they usually depicted humans and animals in right profile, whereas it is more natural for right-handers to draw left profiles. But this was probably simply a reflection of the widespread cultural belief that the right side is sacred and the left side profane, so that the left side of the face or body should be hidden from view. Dennis (1958a) pointed out that if one considers how the use of the hands themselves is depicted, the evidence for right-handedness in ancient Egypt is comparable to that in modern societies. As long ago as the 1860s, Andrew Buchanan wrote boldly but almost certainly correctly as follows:

> The use of the right hand in preference to the left must be regarded as a general characteristics of the family of man. There is no nation, race, or tribe of men on earth at the present day, among whom the preference does not obtain; while in former times, it is shown to have

existed, both by historical documents and by the still more authentic testimony of certain words, phrases, and modes of speaking, which are, I believe, to be found in every spoken language. (Buchanan, 1862, quoted by Wilson, 1872, p. 198)

Another near-universal aspect of left–right symbolism is the association of males with the right and females with the left. To the Maoris, the expression *tama tane* refers to the right, but literally means "male side", while *tama wahine*, literally "female side", refers to the left (Hertz, 1909). Hertz also quotes a Maori proverb: "All evils, misery, and death come from the female element" (Hertz, 1960, p. 97). Empedocles, the Sicilian, argued in the 5th century BC that males were hotter than females and the right hotter than the left, so that sex was determined by relative placement in the womb. Perhaps he was right: Mittwoch (1977) reported that in hermaphrodites testes are more likely to be found on the right and ovaries on the left, and she went on to suggest that the same opposing tendencies are present in normal males and females, but are overridden by the influence of the sex chromosomes. The association of the female with the left has not always implied disrespect or inferiority. In the matriarchal Isis cult of ancient Egypt, honour was given to Isis over Osiris, and to mother over son, to night over day, and the Isis procession was led by a priest carrying an image of the left hand.

THE SYMBOLIC POTENCY OF LEFT AND RIGHT

We may now wonder what it is about left and right that inspires such symbolic potency. Perhaps it is in part the sense of paradox that the two hands seem to present: "What resemblance more perfect than that between the hands," exclaimed Hertz (1960), "and yet what a striking difference there is!" (p. 89). Part of the paradox is simply that the hands are mirror images, and the mirror-image relation itself has a paradoxical property: shapes that are mirror images, like a left and a right shoe, may be said to be identical in the sense that every point on the surface of one can be mapped uniquely onto a point on the other, yet a shape cannot occupy exactly the same space as was previously occupied by its mirror image – except in trivial cases of shapes that are themselves symmetrical. Lewis Carroll, who was obsessed by mirrors, reminds us of this in *The White Knight's Song*:

> And now, if e'er by chance I put
> > My fingers into glue,
> Or madly squeeze a right-hand foot
> > Into a left-hand shoe . . .

The left-hand foot, to use Carroll's quaint terminology, fits easily into the left-hand shoe, but the seemingly identical right-hand foot does not.

But what Hertz probably had in mind was not the mirror-image relation *per se*, but rather the fact that the difference in the functional capacities of the hands seems to belie their identical structure. You cannot easily tell people's handedness by inspecting the physical structure of their two hands, but it is at once apparent if you ask them to write or throw with each hand in turn. Parity, as physicists are wont to say, is not conserved.

I have suggested that this apparent mismatch between function and structure may have encouraged a sort of Cartesian wish-fulfilment (Corballis, 1980). Descartes (1985) argued that humans were distinguished from all other animals by virtue of a non-material influence that could influence the material brain through the pineal gland. The superiority of one hand over its seemingly identical twin might therefore be taken as a manifestation of this non-material power that sets us humans apart, and endows us with consciousness and free will. It has also been generally assumed that the predominance of right-handedness is unique to humans, which is a further indication that there is something special about it – and us. We now know, however, that we are not entirely alone in our handedness. For example, parrots are just as strongly biased toward the use of the left foot in picking up small objects (Friedman and Davis, 1938), and under certain conditions chimpanzees also seem to be right-handed (Hopkins, 1996), although this asymmetry applies to only about 67% of chimpanzees, as against about 90% of humans. On these criteria, then, we might have to allow some glimmer of consciousness of our near relative, the chimpanzee, but accord full human rights (or lefts) to the parrot.

The same apparent mismatch between function and structure applies to the human brain. Like most of the body, the brain is very largely structurally symmetrical, with the left side the mirror image of the right. Yet the discoveries of the 19th century and the later split-brain work revealed functional asymmetries that seem to belie that symmetry. One can perhaps detect a whiff of Cartesian wish-fulfilment in the views of Sir John Eccles, who has argued that only the left hemisphere of humans is capable of consciousness (Eccles, 1965), and in particular self-consciousness (Popper and Eccles, 1977), while the right hemisphere is a mere "computer" comparable to the brains of other animals. Zangwill (1976) dismissed these ideas as "little more than a desperate rearguard action to save the existence and indivisibility of the soul" (p. 304), and Eccles (1981) later conceded "limited self-consciousness to the minor [sic] hemisphere" (p. 105).

Of course, one function that we can attribute to the left hemisphere is language itself, but even this is not without a touch of Cartesian wish-fulfilment. Descartes (1985) considered language one of the objective signs of the non-material influence that uniquely endows humans with freedom from mechanical control, an idea picked up by Noam Chomsky, a neo-Cartesian and the foremost linguist of our time:

> . . . a chimpanzee is very smart and has all kinds of sensorimotor constructions (causality, representational functions, and so forth), but one thing is missing: that little part of the left hemisphere that is responsible for the very specific functions of human language. (quoted in Piattelli-Palmarini, 1980, p. 182)

There is increasing evidence for systematic functional asymmetries in the brains of non-human animals (review: Bradshaw and Rogers, 1993), including some evidence for a left-hemispheric specialization for vocal communication in monkeys (Peterson et al., 1978), and there are some hardy souls who even challenge the view that language is specific to humans (e.g. Savage-Rumbaugh and Lewin, 1994). This is not to deny, of course, that the left hemisphere is dominant for language in most people. The point is simply that Cartesian wish-fulfilment may lead to exaggerated claims, especially of human uniqueness.

The discrepancy between functional asymmetry and structural symmetry is not absolute, since the two sides of the brain are in fact not perfect anatomical mirror images of each other. There are some fairly systematic asymmetries that are at least weakly correlated with left-cerebral dominance for language. For example, Geschwind and Levitsky (1968) reported that the temporal planum, which is part of Wernicke's area, is larger on the left than on the right in the majority of cases, and this asymmetry is even evident in newborns (Witelson and Pallie, 1973). These and other anatomical asymmetries of the brain (LeMay, 1976) are present in only about two-thirds of human brains, whereas the proportion of people with left-hemispheric dominance for language is probably over 90% (Corballis, 1983). In any event, the anatomical asymmetries of the brain pale beside the overwhelming structural symmetry, and do not come close to explaining the complementary functions so often attributed to the two sides.

ON SYMMETRY

In the frenzied effort to discover asymmetries of the brain, we are apt to forget that there is a very striking characteristic that we share with all other animals – bilateral symmetry. This is itself an evolutionary adaptation. To freely moving animals, the world is essentially indifferent with respect to left and right. Limbs are symmetrically placed so that movement, whether we walk, run, fly or swim, can proceed in a straight line. Our eyes and ears are symmetrically placed because the events that matter to us are as likely to occur on one side as the other. Predators or prey may lurk on either side, and an animal with sense organs on only one side would be easy meat for an attacker on the other side. Since the brain is largely concerned with inputs and outputs, the symmetry of the limbs and sense organs dictated a symmetrical plan for much of the brain. The psychological consequences of bilateral symmetry are discussed at length elsewhere (Corballis and Beale, 1976).

Even in the face of the evidence for the asymmetrical representation of language in the brain, the French physician Pierre Marie was so impressed with the brain's symmetry that he thought that each hemisphere must at least have the potential for language (Marie, 1922). There is, in fact, good evidence that if the left hemisphere is incapacitated or removed early in life, the right hemisphere can take over, with little or no loss of efficiency (Basser, 1962). At one time, it was claimed that people who have undergone the removal of the left hemisphere in early childhood later show deficits in syntax, supposedly the essence of language and the preserve of the left hemisphere (Dennis and Kohn, 1975; Dennis and Whitaker, 1976), but this has been disputed on methodological grounds (Bishop, 1988). Moreover, there is clear evidence that syntax is preserved in at least some cases of people whose right hemispheres have taken over language following incapacitation of the left hemisphere in childhood (Ogden, 1988; Vargha-Khadem et al., 1997).

These facts do not suggest that nature has endowed us with a left hemisphere uniquely equipped to perform the special functions of language, and a right hemisphere wired for quite different and, I must repeat, complementary functions. Cerebral asymmetry is altogether more fluid than this static picture allows. It seems more likely that we are endowed with two hemispheres that are ready for anything, and that some switch operates early in development to tip the balance towards the left-hemispheric representation of language. That switch may well depend on genetically controlled growth gradients (Corballis and Morgan, 1978). In particular, there is evidence that, between the ages of 2 and 4, the left hemisphere undergoes a growth spurt that may be instrumental in ensuring the syntax is firmly lodged in that hemisphere (Thatcher, Walker and Guidice, 1987). But if something goes wrong with the switching mechanism, or if the left hemisphere is incapacitated, the faithful right hemisphere is following along behind, ready to oblige.

Another point to note is that, when the right hemisphere does take over language in these cases, it does so at the expense of the spatial functions usually associated with that hemisphere (e.g. Ogden, 1989; Vargha-Khadem et al., 1997). What this seems to suggest is not that the right hemisphere is intrinsically specialized for spatial function, or for intuition or creativity or any of the other transcendent properties attributed to it, but rather that whichever hemisphere gets burdened with language loses some of its capacity for everything else (Corballis, 1983, 1991; Corballis and Morgan, 1978; Le Doux, Wilson and Gazzaniga, 1977; Ogden, 1989).

THE VEXED PROBLEM OF LEFT-HANDERS

This brings us to that much maligned minority, the left-handed. Through most of history, and in most cultures, the negative associations with the left have meant that left-handedness has been generally discouraged, and there is still many a left-hander who was forced to switch to the right hand for writing and eating. The American psychiatrist Blau (1946) dismissed left-handedness as "infantile negativism". Even the sexual identity of left-handers was called into question by Fliess (1923), a colleague and close friend of Sigmund Freud:

> Where left-handedness is present, the character pertaining to the opposite sex seems more pronounced. This sentence is not only invariably correct, but its converse is also true; where a woman resembles a man, or a man resembles a woman, we find the emphasis is on the left side of the body. Once we know this, we have the diviner's rod for the discovery of left-handedness. This diagnosis is always correct. (Fliess, quoted in translation by Fritsch, 1968, p. 133)

Sir Cyril Burt, the British educational psychologist, anticipated Blau in describing left-handers as wilful or "just cussed", and echoed Fliess by noting that "Even left-handed girls . . . often possess a strong, self-willed and almost masculine disposition." He went on to complete the demolition of left-handers as follows:

> They squint, they stammer, they shuffle and shamble, they flounder about like seals out of water. Awkward in the house, and clumsy in their games, they are fumblers and bunglers at whatever they do (Burt, 1937, p. 287)

Among the fumblers and bunglers are Alexander the Great, Julius Caesar, Charlie Chaplin, Charlemagne, Cicero, Gerald Ford, Rod Laver, Harpo Marx, Michelangelo, Leonardo da Vinci, Paul McCartney, John McEnroe, Martina Navratilova, Ronald Reagan, Babe Ruth, Ringo Starr, Emperor Tiberius, Harry Truman and Bill Clinton.

Much of the prejudice against left-handers has dissipated, especially in Western countries. But left-handers are a little awkward in the house of dual-brain theory. Following his discovery of left-hemispheric dominance for language, Broca (1865) conjectured that in left-handers this would be reversed, and the right hemisphere would be dominant for language. This became known as Broca's rule. One might then have simply supposed that the left hemisphere would contain the functions attributed to the right hemisphere in right-handers. But Broca's rule turned out to be wrong, and studies have shown that the majority of left-handers, perhaps as many as 70% of them, are left-dominant for language. To be sure, a higher proportion of left-handers than right-handers are right-dominant for language, but there is also a substantial minority who appear to have bilateral representation of language (Milner, 1975). The best explanation for these findings is that most left-handers belong to a minority who do not exhibit the strong lateralizing influence that controls handedness and cerebral asymmetry in most right-handers. In this minority, which includes some right-handers as well, handedness, cerebral dominance for language and other asymmetries are determined at random. It has been suggested that whether or not the lateralizing influence is expressed may depend on a single genetic locus (Annett, 1985, 1995; McManus, 1985).

This poses a problem already for dual-brain theory, since it implies that left-handers do not have brains in which different functions are neatly divided between hemispheres. A glance at the list of left-handers suggests that they are not deficient in creativity or in artistic ability. Indeed, there are some reasons to believe that left-handers may be slightly superior to right-handers in mathematical and artistic skills, and perhaps slightly inferior in musical and verbal talents (e.g. Smith, Meyers and Kline, 1989). There is a long but contentious history of claims that left-handers may be slightly more at risk for reading disability and stuttering (review: Corballis, 1983), but a more bilaterally symmetrical brain may provide a slight advantage in spatial skills (Annett, 1985).

Any advantage of possessing an asymmetrical brain probably has to do with the programming of complex motor skills, such as speech, rather than with the division of mental capacities into packages of opposites. If something as complex as speech involved neural circuits in both hemispheres, it might be prone to interhemispheric delays and interferences that could potentially create dysfluencies (e.g. Corballis, 1991; Passingham, 1982). But there is also evidence that the dominance of one or other hemisphere is achieved by a pruning of the non-dominant hemisphere. Annett (1985, 1995) has proposed that this is under genetic control. The gene has two alleles (alternative forms), one that prunes, and one that does not. In homozygotes with a double dose of the pruning allele, the right hemisphere may be so diminished as to create spatial difficulties to offset any verbal advantage.[5] Conversely, those who lack the pruning allele have full right-hemisphere function, are about equally divided into left- and right-handers, but possibly risk language disorder. The ideal is to be heterozygotic, with one copy of each allele, which minimizes the risk of both spatial and language disorders. It may be this so-called heterozygotic advantage that has maintained both alleles in the population, and held the proportion of left-handers approximately constant for at least the last 5000 years (Coren and Porac, 1977).

This is just a theory, as the postulated gene has not been located, let alone sequenced, but it makes reasonable sense of quite a lot of evidence. It does not make much sense in terms of the dual-brain theory. What evolution has staged is not a trade-off of left- against right-hemisphere functions, but rather a trade-off of asymmetry against symmetry. A symmetrical brain may confer advantages of spatial orientation and locomotion in a world without left–right bias, while an asymmetrical brain may make it easier to program complicated sequences of action, as in speech. The majority of us probably belong to the heterozygotic compromise.

CONCLUSIONS

We do have asymmetrical brains, and this is a fact of considerable interest and importance. But our brains are also highly symmetrical, the result of hundreds of millions of years of evolution in a world in which the difference between left and right is of virtually no consequence. It is only in the world constructed by humans that the left–right polarity matters, as in reading and writing, shaking hands, driving, etc., but this is in turn a consequence of our own asymmetry. The most likely explanation for our asymmetrical brains is that certain complex computations are inefficient if constrained by symmetrical circuits, and are better accomplished within a hemisphere than by circuits straddling the hemispheres. The advantages of asymmetrical representation would apply particularly to computations that are not constrained by the forces that led to symmetry in the first place, namely, linear movement and ability to detect and react to spatial events in the environment. Spoken language meets these criteria, since it is internally generated and is manifest in time, not space.

Even so, the representation of language in the brain is established against a background of structural symmetry, and we have seen that each hemisphere has at least the potential to accommodate it. The asymmetrical representation of language does confer some disadvantages, such as a slight bias towards processing words in the right ear or the right visual hemifield, and a corresponding bias of spatial attention and spatial processing towards the left side of space. The fact that these biases are slight suggests that symmetry is still of overriding adaptive significance. If the left hemisphere were to be totally occupied with language, then we might indeed be easy prey to monsters who lurk on the right. Shortly after the developments of the 1960s that led to the modern left brain–right brain cult, Brenda Milner, one of the pioneers of modern neuropsychology and a careful researcher of cerebral asymmetry, warned against overemphasizing the asymmetries of the brain at the expense of the considerable functional overlap between them (Milner, 1971), but her warning has been little heeded.

Given the nature of evolution, it is likely that cerebral asymmetry has achieved by tinkering with what was already there, rather than by a rewiring of cerebral circuits. The kick needed to give the left hemisphere first option for language may have been as simple as a growth spurt favouring that hemisphere at a critical period in the development of syntax, or it may have been a pruning mechanism that slightly retarded growth in the right hemisphere – or both. It is extremely unlikely that the incremental processes of natural selection somehow managed a rewiring of both cerebral hemispheres so that one became specialized for the complex temporal sequencing required for language, while the other was adapted to complementary spatial, intuitive and emotional functions. This is not to say there are no asymmetries in the way in which these different functions are represented in the brain; the problem lies in the simplistic notions that the two hemispheres somehow embody opposite ways of thinking, and that the right hemisphere's talents have been subjugated. To understand how the mind works, we need to consider both cortical and subcortical regions, as well as the so-called limbic system that lies between them, and it will not do to simply throw our different mental capacities into bins called left-hemispheric and right-hemispheric.

Does the dual-brain myth do any harm? It is perfectly acceptable to contrast intuition with reason, or holistic thinking with analytical thinking, or emotion with logic, and it might be argued there is no harm in linking these polarities with the two cerebral hemispheres. The main difficulty is that reference to the brain can be seen as a legitimizing force that gives scientific credence to dubious practices. The idea that there may be hidden talents lying dormant in a subjugated right hemisphere is a powerful and reassuring one; almost as reassuring, perhaps, as the idea of life after death, and ripe for exploitation in much the same way. Unscrupulous therapists, healers and educators, and some who are simply naive, offer ways to release that hidden potential, and so discover "the stranger within"

(Joseph, 1992), whether through music or meditation or electrodes – or breathing through the left nostril for a while.[6] There is always a market for those who would exploit our fears and disappointments.

My *Chambers Concise Dictionary* (1989 paperback edition) defines a myth as "an ancient traditional story of gods or heroes, esp. one offering an explanation of some fact or phenomenon". Except for the word "ancient", this is not a bad definition of science, where our modern gods are genes and muons and black holes. We do, of course, go beyond the evidence in constructing theories, and the view of cerebral asymmetry I have presented in this chapter no doubt contains its share of myth. The problems arise when we allow the myth to escape from scientific scrutiny and become dogma, and when that dogma creates financial opportunities for charlatans and false prophets. That is what I think has happened with the left brain and right brain.

NOTES

1. This is a thoroughly fake title, designed to give the impression of scientific respectability. Neurolinguistic programming has little to do with neurology, linguistics, or even a respectable subdiscipline called neurolinguistics.
2. Actually, the evidence for an association of speech with the left side of the brain is evident in case studies going back to the 17th century, but was not noticed (Benton, 1984). The first to make the association was not Broca, but an earlier French physician called Marc Dax, who reported it at a medical society meeting in Montpelier in 1836. Dax did not publish his work, and his observations were ignored until his son Gustav, provoked by Broca's claims, arranged to have his father's paper published (Dax, 1865).
3. I am myself indebted to Harrington for the examples presented here. Her 1985 article and 1987 book give much more information, and make fascinating reading.
4. I mention this with some foreboding, having recently helped launch and co-edit a journal entitled *Laterality*.
5. This might lend some credence to Gazzaniga's (1983) idea that the right hemisphere's cognitive skills are "vastly inferior" to those of a chimpanzee. Well, a pruned chimp, at least.
6. Another secret I can reveal is that lying on the left side enhances left-brain function, while lying on the right side tunes up the right hemisphere. Lying through the teeth is best left to the therapist. These revelations are from *Superlearning* 2000 (Ostrander and Schroeder, 1994).

CHAPTER 3

Energy and the Brain: Facts and Fantasies

FERNANDO D. SARAVÍ

Although the scientific study of central nervous system (CNS) function has been established for several hundred years (for a survey see Brazier (1959)) and is currently advancing at an increasing pace, ancient and in most cases outdated conceptions about how the brain works and what it is able to do still remain with us. Interestingly, as we will show below, attempts have been made to link conceptions arising from old philosophical or religious worldviews with modern scientific findings, usually through reformulations of their tenets in scientific language. In so doing, proponents have often revamped the old ideas, borrowing from physical notions, of which "energy" stands apart as a favourite.

In this chapter, I first examine and discuss several examples of use and misuse of scientific jargon related to energy and its transformations to support non-scientific conceptions. Afterwards, I present an outline of current scientific understanding of bioenergetics as related to CNS function, and finally discuss some common misconceptions on the subject. It should be clear from the start that, even when some of the "energies" to be dealt with have religious or esoteric roots, the following discussion will be limited to the available scientific evidence.

ENERGY AND "ENERGIES"

The word "energy" is derived from the Greek *energeia*, which has "activity" as its basic meaning, and this in turn stems from *ergon*, which means deed, action or work. In everyday language, the term has – like its Greek parents – a range of meanings, including:

> "1 a: dynamic quality |narrative ~| b: the capacity of acting or being active |intellectual ~| 2: vigorous exertion or power: EFFORT |investing time and ~| 3: the capacity for doing work 4: usable power (as heat or electricity); *also*: the resources for producing such power". (*Merriam-Webster's Collegiate Dictionary*, 1993)

In the physical sciences, energy is a fundamental magnitude, which is often tautologically defined (Harten, 1977, p. 32) as the capacity to do work. In fact, in their physical sense, energy and work are used as interchangeable terms. Depending on the kind of work involved, energy may be classified as mechanical, electrical, chemical, etc. Energy and its transformations are what physics is about; the law of conservation of energy may be considered the main tenet of physics. We shall return to this point later, but attention should first be paid to some broader conceptions relevant to the present discussion.

Most, if not all, proponents of New Age thinking (e.g. mind control, holistic medicine, paranormal claims) believe in some kind of loosely defined, pervading "universal energy" which is at the root of all physical phenomena, including life itself. As such, this "energy" is the link that is supposed to explain healing powers, mind-over-matter and other paranormal feats.

For example, in traditional Chinese medicine this universal energy is known as Ki (also transliterated Ch'i or Qi) and is conceived as flowing through the body, near to its surface, in a system of conduits called chings or meridians. The ancient practice of acupuncture is aimed to correct "energetic" (Ki) imbalances through the insertion of needles at specific points along the meridians (Sussmann, 1978); see the critique by Huston (1995). Although it has been claimed that the existence of the Chinese meridian system could be demonstrated through radioisotopic techniques (De Vernejoul, Darras and Beguin, 1984) it seems clear that, instead of showing acupuncture meridians, tracer uptake and flow allow visualization of venous and lymphatic drainage (Simon et al., 1988; Broch, 1991; Guiraud and Lile, 1993).

The equivalent concept in Indian (Vedic) traditional medicine is *Prana*, the "cosmic life force". It flows mainly from the air (*prana* means "breath" in Sanskrit) and this is the reason why breathing exercises or *pranayama* are central to Yogic practices. The *prana* is conceived as having an inherent, selective affinity for the mind (Yesudian and Haich, 1986, p. 53). Lest *prana* may be thought of as a prescientific term for oxygen, we are informed that it is more abundant at high altitude, while, of course, the opposite is true for oxygen pressure. Within the body, *prana* finds its way to seven *chakras* or energetic vortices located in the midline, which in the traditional system have no precise anatomical counterparts, even though they have been related to endocrine glands by modern proponents. "Energetic" balance through exchange of life energy among the *chakras* is required for health.

Samuel F. C. Hahnemann (1755–1843), founder of homeopathy, taught that an intelligent and self-determined vital force "rules with boundless power and keeps all the parts of the organism in admirable and harmonious operation" (Hahnemann, 1991, p. 91). Disturbances of this vital force are to be blamed for all diseases. Similar conceptions may be found in most unscientific health systems, including, among others, chiropractice, Bach's flower remedies and psychic surgery (Reisser, Reisser and Weldon, 1987; Saraví, 1993a; Zwicky et al., 1993).

As mentioned above, the notion of a universal energy that abides in humans as an "energetic body" has been invoked as an explanation for putative paranormal phenomena such as deliberately caused bodily damage phenomena (Hussein et al., 1994), popular "mind control" techniques (Murphy, 1985; Silva and Miele, 1985), clairvoyance, telepathy and psychokinesis (Coxhead, 1980).

The notion of an energetic body besides the physical one was clothed with "scientific" respectability by Ostrander and Schroeder (1970, pp. 196–217) among others. They reported that in the USSR a method had been developed to demonstrate the human aura. In the late 1930s, an electrician named Semyon Davidovich Kirlian found that an object submitted to a high-frequency alternating electrical field shows a luminescent halo. If the object is in contact with a photographic plate, a permanent picture of the light pattern surrounding the object while the current is flowing may be obtained. Speculation about the meaning of this phenomenon ran wild, and possible scientific applications were suggested; the Kirlian halos were linked to acupuncture meridians (Sussmann, 1978, pp. 246–250) and to normal and altered physiological and psychological states (Tagle, 1995). However, Kirlian had merely rediscovered a physical phenomenon first described by Georg Lichtenberg in 1777, and photographed since 1851 (Broch, 1987, p. 69). Unfortunately for quacks and psychics, the glowing halos that the Kirlian photographs show are due to air ionization caused by the high-voltage electrical fields supplied. In other words, instead of allowing visualization of an energy body, the device simply records the effect of the energy supplied by the external field (Broch, 1987, pp. 74–75; Saraví, 1991). The intensity, colour and specific pattern of the halo are affected by prosaic physical variables such as time of exposure, humidity of the sample, applied pressure, and type of photographic paper (Watkins and Bickel, 1986, 1989).

PLAYING WITH WORDS

What do all these mysterious "energies" related to paranormal phenomena have in common? A tentative list follows.

They Have No Known Physical Correlates

In all physical phenomena involving energy transfer, one or more of the following forces are at work: electromagnetic, gravitational, weak or strong nuclear forces. The latter two operate at subatomic distances, and therefore are of relevance to nuclear physics. On the other hand, gravitational forces between relatively small objects – or very distant large ones – can safely be neglected when compared with the earth's gravitational field (Culver and Ianna, 1984, pp. 103–121). This leaves only some kind of electromagnetic force as a viable candidate, and this has not been demonstrated; on the contrary, not only are proofs lacking, but there is some evidence against the existence of such a force, now that Kirlian photographs can be seen as spurious. However, proponents of extraordinary energies keep on trying to imagine some explanations for phenomena whose very existence is doubtful in the first place. As has been observed by Gardner in his chapter on parapsychology and quantum mechanics (QM):

> It is a sad history. When Maxwell's theory of electromagnetic fields was new, it was fashionable to theorize about how magnetic forces could account for psi. When relativity theory was new, it was fashionable to explain psi by forces in hyperspace that move in and out of our world. Today the big mysteries of physics are on the microlevel. It is not surprising that true believers, eager to underpin psi with science, would turn to QM. (Gardner, 1985, pp. 594–595)

They Cannot be Quantified

Since the energies invoked as explanations of the paranormal cannot be identified, there is no way to quantify them. Of course, this is in sharp contrast with real-world physical phenomena, in which the forces are known and energy exchanges may be readily measured.

They Are Often Depicted as Having Positive or Negative Signs

Even when their nature is unknown, and therefore unmeasurable, the "energies" are often conceived as "positive" or "negative". Sometimes "positive" energy is seen as good and "negative" energy as bad; in other cases, especially where there is influence from Taoism, these energies are seen as opposite entities that must be balanced against each other.

From a physical viewpoint, giving plus or minus signs to energy is sheer nonsense. When physicists speak of "negative" energy, they refer to an energetic deficit. For example, a body located in the earth's surface, or an electron bound to the positive atomic nucleus, have negative potential energy because work must be performed (energy must be supplied) in order to release them from the gravitational or electric fields, respectively. Thus "negative" does not refer to a different kind of energy, but to its non-existence.

They Are Conceived as Having Intelligence

The bottom line is that the universal energy that supposedly abides in humans is endowed with some kind of innate, dormant intelligence that is there, waiting to be unleashed. In a fanciful paper devoted to so-called deliberately caused bodily damage, in which instant healing is supposed to occur, Hussein et al. (1994) state that the body knows exactly which tissues are damaged, and also how to instantly heal those injuries. They go on to note that:

The intelligence and knowledge revealed in these two points are beautifully described in Grad's (1991) words who wrote about what he terms as healing energy saying that: "It knows what to do". That is, it carries within itself both intelligence and information. This is very apparent in the healing process, during which time the healer simply transmits the energy, or stimulates it within the body of the patient. From then on, the energy then appears to know what to do on its own, without the healer being involved. (Hussein et al., 1994, p. 27)

In a chapter that opens with a quote about "energy" from William Blake's *The Marriage of Heaven and Hell*, Michael Hutchinson asserts:

What they [the scientists] have discovered is that the brain is far different and far more powerful than most of us imagine. That, given the proper type of stimulation, the human brain can perform seemingly miraculous feats with ease. That the ordinary human brain, in other words, has extraordinary or exceptional powers; that these powers are not extraordinary at all [sic], but, for most of us, simply dormant, undeveloped; and that these powers can be activated or switched on by the right type of stimulation. And, most importantly that we can learn to activate these powers, in the same way, and almost as easily, as we can learn to ride a bicycle or play the piano. (Hutchinson, 1994, p. 21)

Besides being personally very disappointing for me, since I perform very poorly as a bicycle rider and could never learn to play the piano, the recipes proposed a series of "mind-expanding" techniques and hi-tech paraphernalia, together with nutritional advice, involving plenty of food supplements – this may be amusing, but it is very doubtful whether the brains of the purchasers would be as enriched as much as the bank accounts of the suppliers.

In conclusion, New Agers' and psychobabblers' "energy" has only a remote relationship with its physical, scientific counterpart. For them, it is just a word conveniently invoked to explain phenomena whose very existence is far from certain. Figure 3.1 is a sketch of an "energized" man taking advantage of several "energies". However, as we will see below, his brain surely would rather prefer a more prosaic diet.

BRAIN ENERGY UTILIZATION

At this point, and before we proceed to consider some other fanciful proposals about mysterious "energies" affecting brain function, it is necessary to clarify what is scientifically established about brain energy metabolism. In this section, we will be primarily concerned with the sources of energy that the brain can utilize and the ongoing metabolic processes demanding energy.

The CNS receives its nutrients from the blood supply. A 1500-g brain from a 75-kg man, for example, has an average cerebral blood flow close to 700 ml/min and an average cerebral oxygen consumption of 45 ml/min or 2 mmol/min (Madsen et al., 1993).

When it comes to picking up nutrients from the blood, brain tissue is quite selective. While prolonged fasting results in an increased capacity for ketone body consumption, under normal conditions nearly all the energy is obtained from glucose (Nehlig, 1993; Amiel, 1995). In adults, the brain is responsible for about 55% of total body glucose consumption under resting conditions (Amiel, 1995).

Although glucose is the major metabolic fuel at all ages, glucose consumption, expressed per unit of brain weight, is relatively low in the newborn, reaches adult levels in

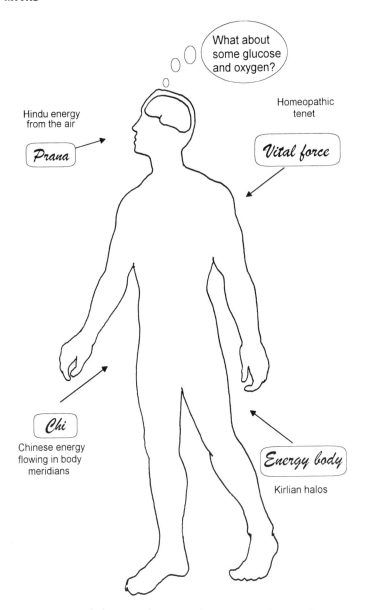

Figure 3.1   A man "energized" by several purported sources. His brain cells are wondering whatever happened to their usual diet.

the 2-year-old infant, is higher than in adults from ages 3–8, and then gradually declines to adult levels in the following years. The higher consumption from ages 3–8 is thought to reflect extra needs related to brain development (Nehlig, 1993; Clark et al., 1994; Nehlig, 1997). In both rodents and humans, there is evidence that increases in blood glucose improve performance in learning and memory processes; see the review by Gold (1995).

Most of the glucose incorporated undergoes oxidation to water and carbon dioxide. The overall reaction is:

$$C_6H_{12}O_6 + 6O_2 \rightarrow 6CO_2 + 6H_2O + energy$$

The energy released comes from the reduction in chemical potential energy of the products (carbon dioxide and water) compared with the parent compound (glucose).

The oxidation of glucose allows the cell to generate adenosine triphosphate (ATP), which is the main cellular energy currency. Glucose metabolism to carbon dioxide and water is actually the result of two consecutive processes, namely glycolysis and oxidative phosphorylation, that occur in different cellular compartments. Glucose is then degraded to pyruvate; if oxygen is available, pyruvate is transferred into the mitochondria (the cell's "power engines"), where it undergoes a complex series of reactions with a high yield of ATP.

A continuous oxygen supply is critical for brain function, since ATP reserves are small compared with its hydrolysis rate. Assuming a constant ATP consumption rate, if ATP production were shut off, the reserves would be barely enough for just 1 min. Glucose supply is also critical; brain glucose reserves – as glycogen – could enable normal ATP production for 3 min (Bickler, 1992). Every hour, the brain consumes about 3.6 g (20 mmol) of glucose and 2700 ml (120 mmol) of oxygen. About 0.76 mol of ATP is generated, which upon hydrolysis liberates 46.7 kJ.

The human brain accounts for about 2% of total body weight, yet under basal conditions (at rest) it demands about 20% of total body energy consumption (Owen, 1988). This means that cerebral energy requirements per gram of tissue are 10-fold higher than the whole-body average. Although there are activity-related fluctuations in local energy consumption (see below), average global brain energy consumption is rather constant under most conditions. Important exceptions are seen under deep sleep or general anaesthesia and during an epileptic crisis (Erecinska and Silver, 1989). In the former conditions, energy requirements may be halved, while they may be increased two- to fourfold as a consequence of the intense, synchronized and – fortunately – short-lasting increase in electrical activity that characterizes a grand mal seizure.

WHAT DOES THE BRAIN NEED ENERGY FOR?

As in other organs, brain energy requirements may be considered to be the sum of basal metabolism (i.e. the minimal energy quantity supporting cellular function in the absence of nervous activity) and an activation metabolism, or extra energy needed in the presence of nerve impulse propagation and synaptic transmission (Astrup, 1982). Although precise estimation of the relative contributions of basal and activation metabolism to brain energy consumption is difficult, it seems that about 75% of total energy consumption corresponds to the latter. It should be noted that this percentage may vary dramatically between different functional states.

Communication among nerve cells, or neurons, takes place by two main processes. One is impulse transmission, and the other synaptic transmission. Compared with the extracellular fluid bathing them, neurons have a high intracellular potassium ion (K^+) concentration and a low intracellular sodium ion (Na^+) concentration. Under resting conditions, there is a transmembrane electrical potential difference; intracellular fluid is about 60–80 mV more negative than extracellular fluid. Electrochemical gradients favour Na^+ entry into the cell and K^+ loss from it. Since the neuron plasmatic membrane or neurolemma is leaky, Na^+ has to be extruded from, and K^+ introduced to, the cytoplasm against their electrochemical gradients. This is accomplished by the Na^+/K^+-ATPase, an enzyme located in the neurolemma and energized by ATP hydrolysis (Figure 3.2A). In the absence of nervous electrical activity, this maintenance process accounts for about half of the basal metabolism (the remainder may be attributed to other active ion transport processes involving Ca^{2+} and Cl^-, to synthesis of cellular components and to axonal transport of materials).

When a neuron is excited, there is an abrupt increase in Na^+ permeability that allows increased entry of this ion, down its own electrochemical gradient, into the cell. The transmembrane potential is first reduced towards zero and then inverted (inside positive). The change in membrane polarity is short-lasting, first because the kinetics of the membrane channels responsible for the increased Na^+ entry make it self-limited, and second because there is a delayed increase in K^+ permeability that allows this ion to leave the cell and accelerates the recovery of the resting transmembrane potential. Areas of the membrane that have been thus activated act as current sources for neighbour regions still at rest, and the process is repeated (Figure 3.2B). Thus, electrical activity spreads as a wave called an action potential, at a velocity that depends on the electrical properties of the nerve fibre, or axon, and whether or not it is covered by an insulating myelin sheath.

When an action potential reaches the most distal parts of the axon, where presynaptic terminals are present, the resulting depolarization causes calcium ion (Ca^{2+}) entry through specific channels down its own electrochemical gradient. In turn, Ca^{2+} triggers the liberation of specific chemical messengers or neurotransmitters, which are synthesized by the neuron and stored in nerve terminals. The neurotransmitter diffuses through a narrow synaptic cleft and reaches specific receptors on the neurolemma of a postsynaptic neuron. Depending on the nature of the neurotransmitter and of the receptor, either excitatory or inhibitory actions may result. The first occurs when the neurotransmitter–receptor interaction leads to a depolarization of the postsynaptic neuron, which increases the probability of firing an action potential. Inhibitory synaptic action is usually the result of membrane hyperpolarization (shift towards more negative values than the normal resting potential).

Since transmission of nerve impulses harnesses already existing electrochemical gradients, and synaptic transmission relies on already synthesized neurotransmitters, these processes do not require ATP consumption by themselves. However, when the party is over, someone has to wash the dishes; energy is certainly required for recovery processes.

Recovery processes are especially critical in the CNS, where cells are tightly packed, with narrow intercellular clefts and a restricted extracellular space that is just 15–20% of total volume (Rosenberg and Wolfson, 1991, p. 202). In these conditions, repetitive activation of neurons will result in fast extracellular accumulation of K^+ which, if high enough, may abolish further action potential generation (Figure 3.2C).

ENERGY-CONSUMING CELLS

Neurons are not alone in their fight against overwhelming ionic or neurochemical changes. It has been shown that astroglial cells, which are heterogeneous supporting or glial cells that constitute about 50% of brain cells by volume (Pope, 1978) and outnumber neurons by an order of magnitude, have a prominent role in recovery processes triggered by synaptic transmission. Astroglial cells, or astrocytes, are well suited for the task (Figure 3.3). They have prolongations (end feet) that surround blood vessels, and specialized glucose transporters are present in the astroglial membrane; they are thus are a main site of glucose uptake from the blood. Additionally, astrocytes and prolongations that ensheath synaptic connections between neurons, and possess neurotransmitter

A

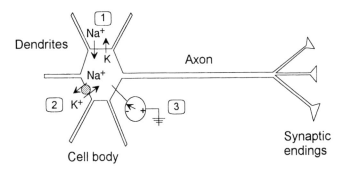

Dendrites

Axon

Cell body

Synaptic
endings

B

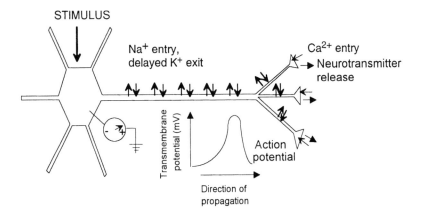

STIMULUS

Na$^+$ entry,
delayed K$^+$ exit

Ca^{2+} entry
Neurotransmitter
release

Transmembrane
potential (mV)

Action
potential

Direction of
propagation

C

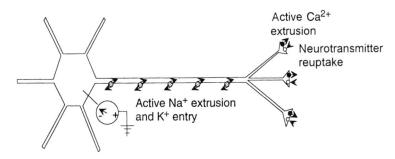

Active Ca^{2+}
extrusion

Neurotransmitter
reuptake

Active Na$^+$ extrusion
and K$^+$ entry

Figure 3.2   Schematic view of a neuron at rest (A), during impulse propagation (B) and during recovery (C). In A, Na$^+$ and K$^+$ leaks (1) and active transport (2) are depicted only for the cell body or soma, even when these processes occur all over the membrane; (3) indicates resting transmembrane potential. In (B) the propagated activity is shown in the axon, even when the cell body is also depolarized. Similarly, in (C) the recovery processes are only depicted for the axon.

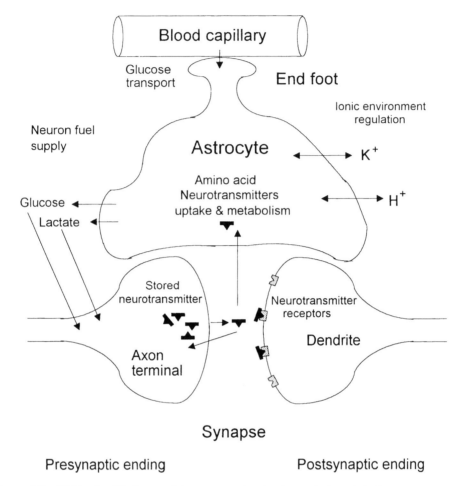

Figure 3.3   Highly simplified view of the astrocyte's roles in regulation of the brain microenvironment. See the text for explanation.

receptors on their surface. They also have several specialized membrane neurotransmitter and ion transport systems.

There is evidence that the increased metabolism triggered by neural activation is not prominent where the neuronal cells bodies are located, but occurs mainly in the neuropil, i.e. regions of high synaptic density (Collins, 1991; Magistretti and Pellerin, 1996; Sokoloff et al., 1996). Part of the raised metabolic activity takes place in neurons, but a large proportion is due to increased astrocyte glucose consumption.

Astrocytes are also very efficient in buffering otherwise potentially harmful increases in excitatory amino acid extracellular concentrations (Tardy, 1991; Schousboe, Westergaard and Hertz, 1993; Hansson and Rönnbäck, 1995). Most glutamate uptake occurs as cotransport with Na^+. This results in increases in astroglial intracellular Na^+ concentrations, which in turn activate the Na^+/K^+-ATPase (Sokoloff et al., 1996; Stanimirovic, Ball and Durkin, 1997). In astrocytes, this enzyme is mainly fuelled by ATP generated through glycolysis, with lactate as the main end product, even in the presence of oxygen (Pellerin and Magistretti, 1996). Lactate is released to the extracellular fluid, where it is taken up by neurons and used – after its previous conversion to pyruvate – as a mitochondrial fuel, with ATP, carbon dioxide and water as end products (Magistretti and Pellerin, 1996). Neurons cannot use blood lactate, because the transfer of lactate is limited by the blood–brain barrier; however, lactate generated within the brain is readily used by nerve cells (Figure 3.3). Indeed, under some conditions, lactate is preferred to glucose as a neuronal energy source (Schurr et al., 1997).

NEW TECHNIQUES ALLOW BRAIN ENERGY METABOLISM TO BE STUDIED IN INTACT SUBJECTS

Technical improvements in the past two decades have enabled researchers to non-invasively study in vivo brain energy metabolism. Magnetic resonance (MR) spectroscopy techniques can identify and quantify high-energy phosphorus compounds, such as ATP and phosphocreatine (Henriksen, 1994; Van der Thillart and van Waarde, 1996), and are providing useful information about both normal brain function and pathological states (e.g. Younkin, 1993). Near-infrared spectroscopy measures oxygen delivery and the redox state of the mitochondrial oxygen-binding enzyme, cytochrome oxidase (Benaron and Stevenson, 1994; Cooper et al., 1994). Both techniques may be combined to improve our understanding of brain energy metabolism (Chance, 1994; Wyatt, 1994).

Positron emission tomography (PET) studies allow quantification of local cerebral blood flow and glucose consumption (Phelps, Mazziotta and Huang, 1982; Friston et al., 1991; Mazziotta et al., 1991; Horwitz et al., 1995). Local cerebral blood flow is tightly coupled to local oxygen and glucose consumption, even when the coupling ratio may vary under special circumstances (Kuschinsky, 1987; Bryan, 1990). A large number of studies have been performed on higher nervous functions (reviews: Démonet, Wise and Frackowiak, 1993; Petersen and Fiez, 1993; Watson, 1996; Cabeza and Nyberg, 1997) and in a number of diseases, such as dementias, schizophrenia, and sleep disorders (Buchsbaum, 1995; Nordberg, 1996; Maquet, 1997).

Recently, functional MR imaging has been employed to detect changes in local cerebral blood flow and oxygen status with high spatial and temporal resolution (Hinke et al., 1993; Kim et al., 1993; Ogawa et al., 1993; Shaywitz et al., 1995; McCarthy et al., 1996). The combination of PET and functional MR imaging is providing new information on brain energy metabolism as related to normal and abnormal function (Apkarian, 1995; Fried et al., 1995; Friston et al., 1996; Liddle, 1996; Bakker and Pauwels, 1997).

An interesting finding is that metabolic requirements for complex tasks may be reduced by training. Haier et al. (1992a) found that as the performance of normal volunteers in a computer game improved with practice, local glucose consumption in several areas was reduced compared with that found initially. Moreover, the same group showed that brain glucose metabolic rate was inversely correlated with psychometric measures of intelligence (Haier et al., 1988) and that those subjects showing the largest decreases in glucose consumption upon training with the above-mentioned computer game were those who scored higher in intelligence tests (Haier et al., 1992b). Thus, it seems that more intelligent subjects are also more efficient from a metabolic viewpoint.

Now, we may summarize known facts about brain energy utilization:

1. The only source of energy available for central nervous system function is chemical energy, namely oxidation of glucose to generate ATP.
2. Several "housekeeping" processes, like protein and phospholipid synthesis and maintaining resting membrane potential, require energy, but a large and variable portion of total energy consumption is needed for supporting recovery processes, including fuelling active transport of ions and neurotransmitter uptake.
3. Active ion transport is responsible for a large part (50–70%). of brain energy consumption.
4. Since energy reserves are small, normal brain function needs a continuous income of chemical energy supplied through the circulation.
5. If this source is shut down, overwhelming ionic and neurochemical changes lead within seconds to a standstill in neural function, and later to neuronal death unless supply is resumed.
6. Apart from blood-borne nutrients, there is no alternative source of energy known that may sustain brain function.

MISCONCEPTIONS ABOUT ENERGY AND ITS TRANSFORMATIONS

A theme that pervades a large part of the popular literature on brain "powers" is the idea that matter and energy are freely exchangeable under physiological conditions (e.g. Silva and Miele, 1985, p. 116; Pistarini, 1991). In order to support their claims "psimongers" often refer to Albert Einstein's famous equation relating mass (m) and energy (E), $E = mc^2$, in which c is the speed of light in a vacuum (approximately 3×10^8 m/s). They envisage the transformation of matter into energy as an ongoing process occurring normally in the body. This reveals a profound misunderstanding of energetic transformations in living systems. For example, combustion process involve no transformation of matter into energy, but the much more modest changes in free energy arising from reductions in the potential energy of the chemical bonds (Oyle, quoted by Reisser, Reisser and Weldon, 1987, p. 36).

The difference is enormous. One mole of glucose (180 g) yields about 3.1 kJ upon combustion to carbon dioxide and water. If the same amount of glucose were completely transformed into energy, it would release 1.62×10^{13} kJ. In more familiar terms, this amount of energy is enough to provide electric power to a medium-sized city for at least one full year. On the other hand, if the brain were powered by this kind of transformation, about 0.3 micrograms of glucose would be enough for a lifetime.

Another kind of common misconception concerns the reversibility of energy transformations. Since, as a rule, bioenergetic reactions take place under conditions far from equilibrium, they are essentially irreversible. Heterotrophic organisms cannot, for example, synthesize glucose starting from carbon dioxide and water (autotrophs can do it through photosynthesis because they are able to harness electromagnetic energy from the sun). However, basic bioenergetics is not a pet subject for most energy gurus. One popular author writes:

We have already discussed how stimuli such as light and sound can act as nutrients to the brain. We have already seen how light and sound can have profound energizing, healing effects by stimulating the brain's electrical activity . . . But there is a more direct way to send electrical impulses into the brain: Use the same rhythmic pulsations of electricity that power the brain cells themselves. If light and sound are nutrients that enrich the brain with their electrical impulses, then surely the electrical impulses themselves, if delivered in the proper form and at the proper intensity, must be like the purest nutrient. (Hutchinson, 1994, pp. 95–96)

Attempts at electrical brain stimulation have a long history, starting with the dawn of the Christian era (Schechter, 1971; Stillings, 1983; Devinsky, 1993). In the present context, however, we must restrict ourselves to the following two questions: first, how is it possible to electrically stimulate the intact brain, and second, may electrical stimulation act as a brain nutrient?

Electromagnetic energy effects on living systems have been the focus of a wealth of research; see, for example, Adey (1981), Faber and Korn (1989), Goodman, Greenebaum and Marron (1995), Olivotto et al. (1996) and Blank and Goodman (1997). It has been shown that they may exert a trophic effect on nerve cell development; for an overview, see Borgens (1986). However, electricity can hardly qualify as a brain nutrient.

Purported brain electrical stimulation was a common theme in old quackery (Macklis, 1993). For example, at the turn of the century an advertisement for an electromagnetic brush hailed it as "Substitute for Medicine", "Joy to Invalids", and "The Friend of Humanity", and proclaimed that through its daily use there would be no "sleepless nights, no softening of the brain, no paralysis, no sudden death" (Barker, 1994). Although an editorial in a scientific journal some years ago proclaimed that the field of biomedical uses of electromagnetic devices was "no longer filled with quacks and black magic" (Szeto, 1983), unproven methods of "electrostimulation" for improving brain function have proliferated recently. Typically, they are not rigorously validated. For example, a popular Argentine magazine featured in its science section an article with the title "Journey to the Center of the Brain", about a method of weak electrical stimulation of the brain in which we are told how an "Argentine physician invented a system that, through the emission of electrical currents to the brain (that the individual does not perceive, though the organ does [sic]), allows recovery of patients with behavioral, learning and motor problems" (Palomar, 1991). No details about electrical stimulation parameters or electrophysiological measurements are given. Hutchinson (1994, pp. 95–101) also describes several "craniostimulation devices" that are supposed to improve alertness and concentration, to optimize brain function, to have antidepressant effects and, most important, to cause personality transformation (presumably for good!). Thus, the Victorian electromagnetic brush is back again, if it ever really left us in the first place.

In real life, brain electrostimulation through electrodes placed on the scalp has proved to be a far trickier business. As an expert wrote: "Electrical stimulation has 3 main limitations: it can be painful, it is difficult to stimulate deep nerves owing to limited depth of penetration, and structures with an overlying layer of bone, such as the brain, are virtually inaccessible" (Barker, 1994, p. 96). Although these problems are not insurmountable, they are so troubling that alternatives, mainly through magnetic stimulation, have been sought (Rothwell et al., 1991; Barker, 1994; Devinsky, 1993). However, proponents of brain electrostimulation devices for self-treatment have circumvented these technical problems with the same approach employed by homeopathy, namely reducing the ''doses'' until they can cause no harm, although then – again, as with homeopathy – the chances are that they can cause no good either.

As for the second question, whether electricity can qualify as a brain nutrient, it is, of course, not mentioned as such by textbooks on nutrition. Nor does it appear in the recommended daily nutritional allowances. This is hardly an involuntary omission.

Even if – and it is a great if – commercial stimulators were really able to somehow reach brain cells, electricity cannot serve as a nutrient, since there are no known mechanisms by which electrical currents could be transformed by neurons or glia into a useful form of chemical energy like ATP. Indeed, if neurons were stimulated to fire action potentials by electricity, the resulting membrane ionic fluxes and neurotransmitter release would lead to increased metabolic energy consumption from the usual diet of blood-borne glucose and oxygen for recovery processes, as explained above.

ENERGY AND PARANORMAL CLAIMS

The process of information transfer requires some kind of energy exchange and, as such, may be included in our present survey. As noted by Zusne (1985), information transfer within the individual, from one subject to another, or from the subject to the environment or vice versa, may be conceived from either a scientific or a non-scientific point of view. The first relies on known experimental data, while the non-scientific (magical) conceptualization obviously does not need to explain how information transfer is actually accomplished; no precise mechanisms have to be invoked, and no cause–effect relationship need be demonstrated or supported by experimental or clinical data. In short, the process is just assumed to somehow happen.

Postulated paranormal phenomena, such as telepathy as a special kind of perception and psychokinesis as a direct mind–brain influence on matter, remain anchored in magical thinking when it comes to explaining how they could actually happen. Of course, there is little, if any, experimental evidence that these phenomena actually exist (Marks, 1986; Saraví, 1993b). However, our concern here is whether plausible mechanisms for them may be envisaged from our knowledge of CNS function.

In the first half of the 19th century, Johannes Müller (1801–1858) postulated his law of ''specific sensory energies''. Stated in modern terms, each sensory nerve carries information normally arising from stimulation of specific sensory receptors, which are usually highly sensitive to one kind of stimulus and much less sensitive to stimuli of other kinds (Zimmerman, 1978; Martin, 1991). The classical example is the eye. The cones and rods of the retina are highly sensitive to electromagnetic radiation in the wavelength range 400–700 nm; in fact, it has been shown that rods can be excited by a single photon (Baylor, Lamb and Yau, 1979). Mechanical energy applied, for example as a blow in the eye, may also excite photoreceptors, but much more energy is required.

Each sensory modality has complex, but none the less recognizable, pathways and connections, and this ''wiring'' largely determines the nature of the sensorial experience evoked by stimulation of the corresponding receptors. Thus, sensory receptors specialized in detecting chemical, electromagnetic or mechanical stimuli evoke the corresponding sensation. However, if the receptors are bypassed, e.g. through electrical stimulation of the afferent nerves, excitation of a sensory pathway will still evoke the same kind of sensation associated with natural stimulation of the appropriate receptors.

For all major sensory modalities, there is a solid and growing body of knowledge regarding receptor structure and function, afferent pathways, central connections, subcortical and cortical processing and association areas linked to integration of different sensory modalities (for a fine introduction, see Kandel, Schwartz and Jessell (1991), Part V). On the other hand, for putative paranormal phenomena such as telepathy, no information whatsoever exists regarding receptors, pathways, relay nuclei or cortical processing areas. There are no known pathways or centres that may evoke a telepathic sensorial experience upon stimulation. Only through an appeal to magical thinking may telepathy be thought of as a plausible biological phenomenon.

The same applies to "mind-over-matter" phenomena. In 1924, Sir Charles Sherrington wrote: "To move things is all that mankind can do; . . . for such the sole executant is muscle, whether in whispering a syllable or in felling a forest" (quoted by Ghez, 1991, p. 548). In other words, as far as is currently known, normally only through muscular action, either subtle or gross, can the brain exert a voluntary influence on the environment.

The living brain does indeed emit energy. As a result of its ongoing metabolic processes, most of this energy appears as heat. It was stated above that aerobic metabolism allows the synthesis of 38 moles of ATP per mole of glucose consumed. Now it should be added that the overall efficiency of biochemical mechanisms coupling glucose combustion to ATP generation is close to 40%. The balance, which is the larger part of the total energy released, is dissipated as heat (Quintero Osso, 1992). Other processes also generate heat, e.g. ionic currents through Joule heating i.e. the production of heating caused by the flow of ions and electrons. However, as a most degraded form of energy, heat is not a likely information carrier, except when used, through highly sensitive devices, to obtain two-dimensional maps of cerebral activation (Shevelev et al., 1993).

From known rates of oxygen consumption, an estimation of brain power may be made. When burning glucose, each millilitre of oxygen yields about 20.2 J. Average whole-brain oxygen consumption is close to 45 ml/min, or 0.75 ml/s. This corresponds to 0.75 ml/s $\times$ 20.2 J/ml = 15 W. This is just about 25% of the power released by a common electric light bulb. Besides that, this energy, released as heat, is not available for performing work.

Of course, ongoing brain electrical activity should also be considered. When it is registered through electrodes applied on the scalp, the resulting record is called an electro-encephalogram (EEG). The recorded waves are thought to correspond mainly to subthreshold excitation of the main cortical neurons, or pyramidal cells (Harmony, 1990). Since moving electrical charges generate a magnetic field, the electrical activity may also be detected as changes in magnetic phenomena (Reite and Zimmerman, 1978).

However, the magnitude of the potential differences registered through an intact skull is attenuated by the distance to the source and is thus very small, typically a few tenths of microvolts (Brazier, 1977, p. 218). The result is that even the routine recording of an EEG using standard equipment is fraught with several sources of interference (Schröter, 1985). Even when the skull and scalp are "transparent" to magnetic fields, magnetic phenomena, mostly from synaptic events occurring in the brain cortical fissures, require a magnetically shielded room and a special superconducting quantum interference device or SQUID (Hari and Lounasmaa, 1989; Renault and Garnero, 1996; Hari and Salmelin, 1997).

Thus, it is hardly conceivable that the brain exerts any purposeful direct influence on the surrounding environment. It is true that recent advances in bioengineering may enable handicapped people to control computers through their brain waves (Lusted and Knapp,

1996). However, even this currently very modest feat demands sophisticated interphases especially tailored to harness the feeble electroencephalographic signals.

CONCLUSION

Brain energy utilization has been the focus of a great deal of research in the last few decades, and has enhanced our knowledge of normal and deranged CNS function. However, neither clinical nor experimental data, from the living subject to the molecular level, lend any support either for mystical conceptions of mysterious "energies" related to brain function or paranormal phenomena. Of course, true believers will not be discouraged by these facts, but they can indeed make a difference for those who think that keeping an open mind does not mean to be blind and deaf to scientific evidence.

CHAPTER 4

Pseudoscience and the Brain: Tuners and Tonics for Aspiring Superhumans

BARRY L. BEYERSTEIN

There's a sucker born every minute.
Phineas T. Barnum

There's a seeker born every minute.
Barry Beyerstein

The prestige of science in the modern world is such that a few areas outside religion and the arts are content to be seen as overtly unscientific. Given the deference that science is routinely accorded in most walks of life, it was inevitable that it would attract many impersonators. These imitators display the trappings of legitimate sciences but lack their rigorous methods, reliable findings, and valid insights (not to mention their many dependable technological offshoots). Critics such as Bunge (1984) have dubbed these thinly disguised pretenders "pseudosciences" and described their *modus operandi*, which is to seek out whatever is currently most fashionable in authentic research and then sell themselves to a largely scientifically illiterate public as an extension of the genuine article (Pratkanis, 1995). From their outset, the neurosciences have captured the public's imagination with their enviable achievements, thereby making themselves attractive targets for counterfeiters. Because valid applications of new discoveries in brain research could enhance a purchaser's cognitive abilities, mood, job performance and net worth, it was predictable that hucksters would begin to trade in products that claim to refurbish the brain as a route to personal betterment. Unfortunately, this merchandise rarely lives up to its advance publicity (Beyerstein, 1990).

Pseudoscientists' motives are sometimes purely meretricious but more often they stem from a sincere but deluded fixation on some eccentric theory that the holder is absolutely sure will revolutionize science and society. More often than not, these victims of self-deception are woefully unfamiliar with the authentic research that should guide their work. Cursory examination of their pronouncements invariably exposes well-worn mystical and occult underpinnings and the discarded science of bygone eras dressed up in modern-sounding jargon. Oddly enough, practitioners of these false sciences tend to be simultaneously envious and contemptuous of the genuine researchers who scorn their half-baked notions and unworkable contraptions. Pseudoscientists slavishly copy the outward appearances of their orthodox role models and glory in any shred of support they can misappropriate from bona fide research, but at the same time they extol their own marginality and lack of credentials as proof of the independence of thought and freshness of insight that should, as they see it, loosen the purse-strings of potential supporters.

Pseudosciences, almost by definition, are unfalsifiable – that is, there is no failed prediction or conceptual gaff that their defenders cannot explain away with *ad hoc* reasoning, or contort in some other fashion to protect their fanciful beliefs (Gardner, 1957, 1981; Radner and Radner, 1982; Sagan, 1996). Pseudoscientists are recognizable by their isolation from mainstream science, the grandiose and irreproducible nature of their claims, and their near-paranoid insistence that they are being persecuted by a closed-minded, self-serving "Establishment". As far as these self-styled pioneers can see, the only reason they have not achieved the recognition they deserve is that they are locked in an uneven power struggle with a bigoted elite that dismisses outsiders out of hand. Those who see themselves as unfairly shunned by this brainwashed in-group accuse it of both lacking the vision to understand their revolutionary discoveries and at the same time plotting to suppress or steal their breakthroughs because they threaten the comfortable *status quo*.

Most members of this band of scientific poseurs are untutored tinkerers who fail to appreciate the depths of their own ignorance, but occasionally competent, even famous, scientists will latch onto unsupportable notions and champion them to the detriment of their reputations and the chagrin of their colleagues. Linus Pauling's excessive claims for vitamin C (Barrett, 1995) and Jacques Benvineste's espousal of homeopathy (Gardner, 1989; Randi, 1989) are two recent examples of top scientists whose later "breakthroughs" the scientific community has found hard to accept (Park, 1997). Reed (1988, Ch. 4) described this curious form of tunnel vision that occasionally afflicts otherwise smart and well-informed individuals in his discussion of what he called "delusion in the service of an over-valued idea".

Pseudoscientists have learned that an effective way to amass cash and converts is to begin with an uncontroversial claim from a respected branch of science and to proceed by imperceptible steps to stretch it to absurd but lucrative proportions. Dale Beyerstein (Beyerstein, 1992a) has dubbed this ploy "nonsense piggy-backing on reliable know-ledge". In describing this favoured strategy of pseudoscientists, he drew his examples from graphology, also known as "handwriting analysis" (Beyerstein and Beyerstein, 1992). Although graphology amounts to nothing more than the ancient rituals of divination by magical correspondences (Beyerstein, 1992b), it sells itself as an extension of modern brain research and differential psychology (Beyerstein, 1992c). In asserting that they have a valid method for measuring character and ability, graphologists begin with a few reasonable-sounding assumptions. They then add some true but irrelevant facts from legitimate research and proceed to spin the entire mixture into a web of pseudoscientific claptrap that would be merely amusing if it were not for its ability to damage reputations, relationships, and livelihoods (Beyerstein, 1996a).

Handwriting analysis exemplifies the central theme of this chapter, namely, that brain research has long been the darling of those peddling pseudoscience in the pop-psychology marketplace. Looking for something to add sizzle to their sales pitches, New Age hucksters are repackaging shopworn folk psychology with cheap mysticism and giving it a gloss of scientific respectability by claiming unearned affiliation with neuroscience. In Chapter 1, I describe the emergence of this trend, which began with the self-improvement messiahs of the 19th century who saw the profit potential in tying threadbare positive thinking platitudes to the rapidly developing science of brain research. Their descendants, and those of their ever-hopeful clientele, continue to populate the fringes of that segment of the New Age marketing empire known as "the human potential movement".

The undiminished profitability of misappropriating neuroscience in this fashion can be seen in the fact that the current catch-phrase for marketing graphology is: "Handwriting is brainwriting." Hoping to divert attention from the amply demonstrated futility of their trade (e.g. Dean, 1992), graphologists begin by inviting potential clients to accept two uncon-troversial assertions: the first is that writing is controlled by the brain, and the second is that personality and aptitudes are similarly tied to brain functions. Having lured the gullible this far, graphologists then spring the glaring non-sequitur that, because of the shared depend-ence of writing and personality on the brain, writing must therefore reveal one's psychologi-cal make-up. In response to this logical sleight-of-hand, I have pointed out that the brain also controls vomiting, so by the same token, styles of regurgitation should be equally good indicators of aptitudes, personality, and moral stature (Beyerstein, 1992c).[1]

In the remainder of this chapter, I present a critical look at an array of products that claim to enhance mental performance, allegedly by directly "re-tuning" the circuitry of the brain. Space does not permit me to extend this critique to include the growing number of self-help seminars, books and courses that make extravagant, though unsupported, claims to enhance brain power by purely behavioural means. Fortunately, these products have been reviewed elsewhere, most thoroughly by a National Research Council (NRC) panel that was charged by the US Government to advise its various agencies regarding the reliability of the claims made by the burgeoning performance-enhancement industry (Druckman and Swets, 1988; Druckman and Bjork, 1991). Also recommended along the same line are evaluations by Rosen (1987) and Gambrill (1992) of popular self-help products that make similar claims. The NRC panel and other objective evaluators of these self-improvement packages concur in their main conclusion. They agree that those who hawk these products to an eager public have failed to demonstrate that their wares contain any secret shortcuts to mastery that can substitute for practice, attention to detail, and plain hard work (Beyerstein, 1990).

PHILOSOPHICAL CONTRADICTIONS IN THE "BRAIN-BOOSTER" ALLIANCE

It has always struck me as odd that the dubious tools for brain enhancement discussed in this chapter should appeal so strongly to that segment of the population whose core belief is that a brain is not even necessary for a mental life. I am referring, of course, to the mind-expansionist entrepreneurs of the New Age movement and their clientele. This cadre of mind–body dualists[2] revels in tales of "channelling" the minds of disembodied spirits, espouses reincarnation, and accepts "out-of-body" experiences as proof that consciousness exists independently of brains (Basil, 1988; Schultz, 1989). It is a pillar of New Age dogma that minds are spiritual entities, unfettered by messy and constraining truck with a naturalistic universe that is all too mechanistic and uncaring to suit their tastes (Beyerstein, 1988b). New Agers are, after all, this generation's standard-bearers for an unbroken like of believers in "mind over matter" (Melton, 1988; Webb, 1971).

Given this commitment of the New Age community to mind–body dualism, it is curious that it still supplies the lion's share of the customers for every marvellous new device that clever merchandisers dangle before it for amplifying mental or psychic powers (Hammer, 1989; Beyerstein, 1990). At first sight, any admission by vendors or purchasers of such machinery that one can get at the mind via the brain would seem to be a concession that the brain is the seat of consciousness after all – why else pay good money to massage the cerebral hardware in hopes of improving mental efficiency? Consistency and logic are not considered great virtues in New Age circles, however, and the fact that any such capitulation to mind–brain identity calls into question much of the rest of their spiritualistic worldview seems not to bother these proponents of "post-modern" lateral thinking.

In opposition to the New Agers' mind–body dualism, the vast majority of neuroscientists are material monists who believe that mental processes are identical with states of the brain (Bunge, 1980; Churchland, 1984; Uttal, 1978). According to them, brain states (and hence mental experiences) are subject to the same natural laws that govern everything else in the universe. New Age devotees remain ardent dualists because they need to place mental phenomena outside the causal structure of the physical universe in order to advance the rest of their agenda (Beyerstein, 1987). Topping this wish list is their desire to reinstate a form of animism into the natural order – that is, they nostalgically long for a cosmos where events occur at the whim of unseen spiritual forces and are subject to moral rather than impersonal natural laws, It is therefore startling when holders of such views still think it appropriate to look to the tools of materialistic neuroscience to bolster their concept of mind (which is, in all other respects, adamantly anti-materialistic). It is ironic that those most dedicated to putting mental phenomena outside the physical realm should end up being the most avid consumers of appliances that purport to improve the mind by manipulating a physical organ, the brain.

Let us now examine some of the mind-improving products that their promoters claim to have derived from legitimate brain research – the various "brain-boosters" that so infatuate the enlightenment lobby of the New Age. These products break roughly into three categories: (1) devices that passively record brain waves in the hope that informing people about their status will teach trainees to produce the allegedly beneficial ones at will; (b) devices that attempt to alter brain activity directly by delivering trains of pulsating stimuli; and (3) so-called "smart cocktails", nutritional supplements that are supposed to improve mental functioning by increasing the availability of the raw materials used by the brain's chemical pathways. These products all enjoy thriving sales, notwithstanding the fact that their promoters would have difficulty convincing the publishers of consumer reports that they are a sensible buy.

BRAIN TUNERS

Despite having lived their whole lives in electrified surroundings, many citizens of the industrialized world still approach electricity as if it were some kind of magical force – and all the more so once they learn that the electromagnetic energy that powers their favourite appliances also permeates everything from the far reaches of the universe to the confines of their own heads. Among the scientifically challenged, the frequencies, attractions, waves and fields discussed by electrical engineers are indistinguishable from the "vibrations", "planes" and "sympathies" so dear to occultists and magical thinkers. Their reverent misreading of electromagnetism and neurophysiology allows New Agers to preserve their belief in the mystical powers of mind while appearing to merge them with the dictates of 20th-century science.

Despite the advances of modern neuroscience, surveys say that the majority of the population still regards consciousness in the spiritualistic terms of the prescientific era (see, for example, the results of a large survey published by *Self* magazine in its December 1997 issue). Given the anachronistic beliefs that folk psychology still attaches to anything related to the mind, popular discussions of consciousness generally take dualism for granted, i.e. that mental processes operate in an ethereal, non-physical realm. Those who claim that they can bridge this gap between spirituality and science with electrical gadgetry promise not only the perennially soothing existential assurances but also bankable benefits in the here-and-now. What could be more saleable, after all, than a package that offers spiritual enlightenment with added bonuses such as improved memory, motivation, concentration, and reasoning power – and why not throw in stress reduction, instant relaxation, perfect health and transcendent bliss for good measure? All of this, the full-colour brochures exclaim, awaits those who will purchase this or that device that can harness this all-powerful fount of mental/spiritual "energy" for fun and profit. Enter the brain tuners.

New Age entrepreneurs, undaunted by the inconsistency of claiming to affect a physical commodity (electricity) to influence things they believe to be non-physical ("transpersonal" consciousness and "universal mind-power"), easily push aside such quibbles in their rush to capitalize on the public's joint veneration of electricity and the transcendent powers of mind. The result has been a spate of hardware vigorously marketed as a fast track to "higher" states of consciousness (from which New Age dualists assume all good things flow).

Attempts to support mysticism with contorted versions of quantum mechanics are perpetual best-sellers. Perhaps less well known is the equally interesting history of appealing to neuroscience by the transcendentally inclined. The German psychiatrist, Hans Berger (1873–1941), was initially moved to adapt for human use the apparatus employed by earlier researchers to record the electrical activity of animals' brains because he thought it might reveal a mechanism that could account for psychic phenomena (Beyerstein, 1985). Berger saw the equipment he developed and named the *elektrencephalogram*[3] (Berger, 1929) as a means of reconciling his spiritual beliefs with science. To the dismay of his colleagues, he even devoted part of his inaugural address when he became Rector of the University of Jena to the use of the EEG in the study of clairvoyance and telepathy. In the last publication of his life, Berger outlined his theory of how thoughts could be propagated telepathically by radiating brain waves. Unfortunately, these fluctuating brain currents (at one time known as the "Berger rhythm") obey the inverse square law and drop to infinitesimal levels only millimetres from the scalp.

Electroencephalography outgrew these youthful indiscretions to become a highly productive tool in both research and clinical settings. The EEG was subsequently pulled back to the fringes of science, however, when members of the "counterculture" that swept the industrialized world during the 1960s (Frankel, 1973) developed an interest in brain waves along with their espousal of Eastern mystical philosophy, psychedelic drugs, and altered states of consciousness (Kamiya, 1969; Tart, 1969). Once again, the EEG and other electrophysiological recording devices became preferred vehicles for the rapprochement between science and spirituality that Hans Berger had so avidly sought. These notions gained popularity as reports began to circulate among the forerunners of today's New Age movement that almost superhuman control of physiological functions had been achieved by those who had mastered certain yoga techniques.

Although these overly enthusiastic reports that spiritual adepts had achieved precise control over their autonomic functions proved to have been greatly exaggerated (Holmes, 1984, 1987; Druckman and Bjork, 1991), it did seem that highly practised masters of certain meditative disciplines did show some interesting changes in the alpha rhythm[4] in their EEGs while meditating (Bagchi and Wenger, 1957; Kasamatsu and Hirai, 1966; Fenwick, 1987). A number of studies of adept mediators reported that, at the beginning of a meditation session, their alpha rhythm tended to increase in amplitude and then gradually slow in frequency by about 1–3 Hz (or cycles per second). While this occurred, the alpha rhythm, which is usually more prominent in recording leads attached to the back of the head, started to become more noticeable in the frontal leads as well. It also seemed that whatever years of practice had taught these mediators about focusing their attention did allow them, while meditating, to ignore distracting stimuli that would tend to capture the attention of untrained people, and thereby block their alpha rhythms.

Here again, the mind-expansion fraternity was quick to make the logical error of assuming that correlation implies causation. They eagerly embraced the non-sequitur that the abundance of alpha waves when practised meditators are meditating meant that the alpha rhythm denotes a special state of consciousness which they assumed to be functionally equivalent to whatever it was that these meditators were experiencing at the time. Devotees hastily elevated this allegedly unique state to the lofty status of "alpha consciousness". They began to assert that alpha training could be a shortcut to the lauded psychological and physical benefits of meditation (Beyerstein, 1985). Advertising at the time suggested that these payoffs could be achieved more quickly and cheaply through the electronic marvel of alpha biofeedback[5] – thereby eliminating the need for the tedious drills and time-consuming philosophical instruction required of traditional seekers on the path to enlightenment.

In fact, EEG changes such as these are non-specific and cannot be used to certify the presence of any particular mental contents. The EEG changes reported by the early EEG–meditation researchers are indicative of generally lowered cortical arousal. Physiologically, they are not unique to meditation and, in fact, they are just as consistent with the drowsiness that borders on sleep as they are with any spiritually uplifting state of consciousness. By the same token, although the EEG during meditation is not distinguishable from that of the groggy borderlands of light sleep, neither does this force us to conclude that the mental experience to which meditators aspire could not be distinct, enjoyable, or even beneficial in some way (Neher, 1990). At the very least, practised mediators maintain that they feel different when they are meditating, as opposed to drifting into sleep.

The alpha-enhancement industry, of course, was never distracted by such academic quibbles. Overnight, companies sprang up, selling portable alpha biofeedback devices that were supposed to inform wearers when their brains were producing alpha waves, so that they could learn, by means of operant conditioning,[6] to maximize alpha production and thereby gain the highly praised benefits of alpha consciousness. Aside from doubting whether the cheap circuitry in these crude feedback rigs could reliably pull EEG signals out of the electromagnetic noise that permeates the typical urban environment, most seasoned electrophysiologists doubted whether alpha enhancement would be worth achieving anyway, even if the machinery could be made to work satisfactorily (Beyerstein, 1985).

Two cautionary thoughts occurred to sceptics who had watched similar mind-expansionist claims come and go in the past. First, knowledge of the relevant research in electrophysiology led them to question whether any unique sort of mental contents could be guaranteed when, and only when, alpha waves predominate in the EEG. Second, the old hands considered it unlikely that psychological and physical benefits would accrue to anyone simply for cultivating their alpha waves. With regard to the first of these demurrals, Fenwick (1987, p. 105) pointed out:

> . . . EEG rhythms are very "blunt" indicators of underlying brain activity. They are the result of synchronization of huge pools of cells, and thus their appearance reflects diffuse regulatory processes which are non-specific. Any EEG picture will have multiple causation, and many different states [of consciousness] can lead to similar EEG pictures . . . Thus, extrapolating from EEG rhythms to [specific] mental states is likely to be both hazardous and haphazard.

In addition to pointing out that the new breed of alpha enthusiasts had failed to include the appropriate control groups during their demonstrations of "alpha consciousness", the sceptics reminded the alpha entrepreneurs of several well-known facts from the EEG literature that should have caused them to question their mission from the outset (Beyerstein, 1985). For instance, non-human species, who presumably neither practise meditation nor aspire to higher planes of consciousness, produce alpha waves. Richard Caton had demonstrated this in cats as early as 1875. Similarly, any competent electroencephalographer knows that most people produce alpha waves when they simply close their eyes and refrain from strenuous mental effort.[7] Most meditation buffs would be loath to concede that meditating is nothing more than closing one's eyes while sitting in a quiet place.

Moreover, it had been known for some time that a certain percentage of the normal population produces few or no alpha waves under any circumstances (Golla, Hutton and Walter, 1943) and no one has been able to show that, as a group, they are conspicuously devoid of any of the desirable qualities attributed to high alpha producers by the alpha-conditioning industry. Even those in the human potential movement who eschewed the more grandiose claims for alpha consciousness (such as the widely held belief that alpha waves are a gateway to ecstatic transcendent states or psychic powers) and simply asserted that alpha waves were an index of carefree relaxation soon ran into trouble when they were informed that children with attention deficit/hyperactivity disorder tend to be excellent producers of alpha waves, despite their lack of feedback training and their less than tranquil state of mind (Grünewald-Zuberbier, Grünewald and Rasche, 1975; Beyerstein, 1985). Fenwick (1987) dropped more rain on the parade when he pointed out that alpha waves are often seen in the deepest coma, just prior to death.

Further trouble for the concept of "alpha consciousness" arose when more sceptical electroencephalographers repeated the earlier experiments, this time employing controls for suggestion and compliance effects. In the end, it became clear that the idea that conditioning alpha waves would propel one into transcendent bliss, or even the pleasures of a warm bath, is, like so much in the New Age pantheon, wishful thinking. What studies with proper control groups demonstrated, however, was that the *belief* that alpha biofeedback is euphorogenic can be a powerful placebo (Plotkin and Rice, 1981). In our own laboratory and elsewhere, it was found that people who were predisposed to believe that alpha waves were a sign of meditative joy would report pleasurable experiences, regardless of what actually occurred on their EEGs. We found that volunteers who had bought into the alpha industry's hype – i.e. that alpha waves could be a shortcut to meditative rapture – reliably reported suitably joyous effects although, unbeknownst to them, we had switched the feedback trigger so that it was teaching them to suppress rather than augment their alpha wave output (Beyerstein, 1985). Their praise for the feedback training we had given them was every bit as effusive as that of the group given the standard, alpha-enhancing feedback.

Another blow to the alpha-conditioning craze came when researchers showed that the apparent increase in alpha wave output over the course of a feedback session was probably not learned enhancement after all. Doubts were raised as to whether increased alpha wave density over the time spent on a biofeedback device represents a true, operantly conditioned augmentation of this brain rhythm – as opposed to merely a reflection of the fact that certain attentional factors (which tend to depress the alpha baseline in the early part of the conditioning process) dissipate over time. Critics such as Plotkin (1979) argued that the typical rise in alpha wave production that occurs over the course of an eyes-open feedback session simply reflects the waning attention paid to the external stimulation (such attention tends to block alpha waves when people first attempt the feedback exercises). Recall that most people produce alpha waves if they simply close their eyes and refrain from strenuous mental effort. Opening their eyes blocks the alpha rhythm because they cannot, initially at least, avoid attending to the visual stimulation that is impinging on their retinas. In the "heady" days of alpha's ascendency, people were typically given alpha biofeedback in quiet, dim and generally monotonous settings. Not surprisingly, the interest they paid to these boring surroundings tended to wane as the feedback session progressed. As they paid less and less attention to the things around them, there was a corresponding lessening of the tendency for the alpha rhythm to be blocked, making it appear that these individuals had learned to augment their output. Better-controlled studies have strongly suggested that apparent increases over the eyes-closed alpha baseline were artefacts due to the fact that these baselines had been artificially depressed by apprehensiveness, novelty of the situation, and inability to ignore local stimuli during the early stages when the baseline levels were recorded. As Plotkin and Rice (1981) summarized this research, "there is absolutely no published evidence that the increases in alpha activity that are frequently seen during alpha training have ever constituted an unequivocal case of actual alpha enhancement above optimal prefeedback baseline levels".

The *coup de grâce* for the alpha conditioners was administered when researchers showed that people could learn to produce abundant amounts of alpha waves with their eyes open, under what were decidedly non-blissful conditions. In one study, volunteers were threatened with electric shocks if they failed to increase their alpha wave output (Orne and Paskewitz, 1974). Understandably, these conditions produced an anxious and hostile state of mind, not to mention considerable autonomic arousal. None the less, these trainees learned to control their eye movements and visual attention in ways that permitted them to pump out alpha waves and avoid the threatened shocks, despite being in a mental state that could hardly be said to be approaching nirvana.

With regard to the alleged long-term benefits of cultivating "alpha consciousness" for stress reduction, improved concentration, etc., more careful research has shown that enhancing one's output of alpha waves, by itself, brings no guarantee of benefits of any sort (Plotkin, 1979; Plotkin and Rice, 1981; Beyerstein, 1985, 1990; Druckman and Bjork, 1991).

For a brief while, it looked as though the sagging fortunes of alpha biofeedback might be salvaged by interest in another frequency band in the EEG, the theta rhythm (4–7 Hz). Once again, similar objections were raised and the touted benefits of theta enhancement came to a similarly ignominious end (Beyerstein, 1990; Bruckman and Bjork, 1991). These revelations have not caused retailers to refrain from selling the devices, however.

While the exact meaning of alpha waves in the EEG remains a topic of debate among the best minds in neurophysiology, most agree that the best predictor of their presence is a lowered state of arousal, coupled with reduced engagement in active visual processing (Perlini and Spanos, 1991). As Mulholland and Peper (1971) put it, it is the processes of "looking" rather than those involved in "seeing" that are most detrimental to production of alpha waves. To the extent that certain meditative strategies affect these attentional/visual processes, it would not be surprising to find some correlations between alpha waves in the EEG and self-reports of meditation. Unfortunately, it escaped the alpha entrepreneurs that such a correlation would no more imply that alpha wave production can *produce* a meditative state than opening one's umbrella can make it rain. All of this, of course, begs the question of whether meditation itself is more beneficial than an equivalent period of time spent in any other state of lowered psychological and physiological arousal. It is to that question that we now turn.

IS MEDITATION GOOD FOR YOU?

Amidst the controversy over the putative value of so-called "alpha consciousness", the adversaries tended to overlook the more basic question of whether the mental state that alpha consciousness was supposed to emulate is, itself, worth cultivating. All sides had tended to concede that there was something uniquely worthwhile about the conscious experience associated with the meditative process, over and above any payoffs that accrue to someone who merely relaxes and maintains a lowered state of arousal for a comparable period. Why else, supporters ask, would the practice of meditation have emerged in so many different cultures and achieved such remarkable longevity?

Claims that the mental rituals practised in one or another kind of meditation are beneficial in and of themselves have centred around two basic themes, one mystical and the other more practical. On the mystical side, disciples have always maintained that enlightenment is not something achievable through strenuous study, i.e. from attempts to perceive, analyse and comprehend logically. Rather, it is something that happens "in a flash" to the suitably prepared mind – specifically, a mind that is both morally worthy and cleansed of the minutiae of everyday thought that tend to impair one's ability to apprehend the true meaning of existence (Russell, 1959). Mystical philosophers assert that the purpose of meditation is to foster this receptive, content-free mode of consciousness as a route to the more profound reality that lies beneath the mundane one we normally inhabit. This assumes, of course, that there is some immaterial fount of absolute knowledge, external to the individual, that can infuse the worthy recipient with complete, instantaneous and indisputable understanding of "all that is" (a decidedly dualistic position – see the dualism–monism debate, discussed earlier). These are, of course, metaphysical assumptions that do not lend themselves to empirical adjudication. It seems undeniable, however, that the subjective feelings associated with meditation have offered comfort, hope and enjoyment to people since time immemorial. Modern psychology and neuroscience have offered non-occult explanations for why these conscious states feel like they do (Neher, 1990; Beyerstein, 1996a), but tomes lauding the mystical interpretation have shown no sign of being pushed off the best-seller lists. Whether there are any more tangible payoffs to be gained in return for engaging in the specific mental exercises advocated by the teachers of meditation remains contentious. Among their many spiritually inclined devotees, to even raise such a question is to miss the point of meditating altogether.

Claims of more concrete payoffs are touted primarily by promoters of the secularized versions of meditation aimed at stressed-out, upwardly mobile Europeans and North Americans.[8] Woodrum, a sociologist of religion, has analysed this attempt by TM to downplay its religious agenda in order to broaden its appeal. Woodrum (1978) writes:

> During [its] Spiritual Mystical period (1959–65), the [TM] movement attracted a few salvation oriented persons with a variant of Hinduism. The Counter Culture period (1965–69) brought rapid growth as the diversified organization recruited youths anticipating world transformation and this-worldly bliss. In the Secularized, Popular Religious period (1970–present), TM is marketed as a scientifically validated technique for worldly benefits. Most contemporary transcendental mediators have practical, utilitarian motivations and little commitment, but a hidden religiously oriented inner sect exists whose members' dedication is integral to the movement.

The secular-sounding branch of TM maintains that meditation is superior to simple relaxation as a means of rejuvenating one's vitality and promoting health and mental efficiency (Forem, 1973). Benson (1975), a Harvard physician and early supporter of TM's medical claims, aided the sect's attempt at secularization when he argued that what he referred to as the "relaxation response", supposedly linked in some special way to meditation, produces larger and more beneficial bodily changes than simple rest. With his student, Wallace (who later went to work for the TM organization), Benson asserted that meditation produces a unique "hypometabolic state" of the brain, autonomic nervous system, and other organs, that is distinguishable from the physiological changes produced by, say, hypnotically induced relaxation (Wallace and Benson, 1972).

It is often the case when fundamentally opposing worldviews intertwine with scientific debates that overenthusiastic researchers become more interested in supporting their personal beliefs than arriving at the truth. Many misapprehensions about the physical and psychological benefits of meditation arose because ideologically committed researchers failed to match meditators with comparable control subjects, i.e. ones matched on other possibly relevant characteristics who lowered their mental and physical activity levels for an equivalent interval without engaging in whatever manipulations of consciousness were being advocated by the proselytizers. When appropriate experimental controls were finally put in place, the results were not encouraging for the meditation industry.

Objective researchers have disputed many of the claims of benefits based on in-house research conducted by members of the TM organization. For instance, at the biochemical level, when TM practitioners were compared with properly matched control subjects, it was found that "meditation does not induce a unique metabolic state but is seen bio-chemically as a resting state", essentially like any other condition of lowered arousal (Michaels, Huber and McCann, 1976).

Whenever researchers with no stake in selling meditation have looked into the claims of its various promoters, a consensus has emerged that there may well be benefits to be derived from stepping outside the urban rush to spend a half-hour or so per day in quiet repose. However, just as there is no reason to believe that alpha conditioning is a necessary or cost-effective technique for achieving this desirable state of relaxation, there seems to be little viable evidence that the payoffs for relaxing are any greater if one adds the meditative (i.e. subjective) part of the exercise – as opposed to simply spending an equivalent amount of time in any other state of mental and physical calm (Holmes, 1984, 1987; Blackmore, 1991; West, 1987). Reviewing the literature on the alleged psycho-therapeutic benefits of meditation, Delmonte and Kenny (1985) agreed that meditation can help induce relaxation and alleviate mild anxiety, but they concluded that "there is no compelling evidence that meditation is associated with unique state effects compared with other relaxation procedures".

A major problem for those who promote meditation as a panacea is that of self-selection of its practitioners. People who are attracted to and stay with a meditative regimen are probably fundamentally different in several important ways – such as personality, belief structure, baseline arousal levels, interests and aspirations – from those who don't. This makes it very difficult, even for competent researchers, to match meditators with suitable control subjects who don't meditate, in order to tease apart what is due to meditation *per se* and what is due to these confounding "subject variables". Thus it is hard for the meditation-sellers to say that any marketable differences they see in their meditating customers are due to the mental disciplines of the meditative regimen itself (West, 1987). If there is no such "extra added ingredient", why pay the often high price for meditation instruction if it can be matched for free by anyone with a library card or a wise old uncle?

High-pressure marketing organizations such as TM have profited handsomely from the anxieties of those seeking relief from the psychological and physical ills attributed to the stresses of today's fast-paced lifestyles. A salvo of research papers from TM devotees, largely from the TM-owned Maharishi International University, has claimed special efficacy for the particular mental exercises prescribed by the TM organization. In addition to the usual promises of relaxation, improved health, and heightened mental prowess, the supposedly scientific TM organization also asserts that trainees can learn to levitate and walk through walls, reverse the ageing process, and "develop the strength of an elephant" (Skolnick, 1991). The organization further asserts that if 1% of any local population takes up TM, the crime rate in that vicinity will drop. As far as TM's therapeutic pretensions are concerned, outside evaluators with no personal stake in the outcome concur that TM, or any other form of meditation, is no more efficacious than simple rest, which is considerably cheaper (Randi, 1982; West, 1987; Blackmore, 1991; Druckman and Bjork, 1991).

Other observers of the TM movement have sounded a more ominous note. Persinger, Carrey and Suess (1980, p. 7) agreed with the foregoing critics, concluding that "claims of TM effects are neither unique nor special but are the consequences of procedures associated with suggestion, placebo reactions, simple relaxation, neurotic belief and the mislabeling of vague emotional experiences". These authors then went on to discuss the possible harm that can ensue when dependent or unstable individuals become obsessively involved with meditation to the detriment of their psychological health. The book also documents the kinds of psychological and financial manipulation to which these vulnerable seekers are sometimes subjected. In recent years, the TM movement has branched out to open Maharishi theme parks and engage in sales of traditional Ayurvedic medicines. Concerning the latter products, the science writer Skolnick (1991, 1992) exposed how followers of the Maharishi had misrepresented their affiliation with the TM organization in successful attempts to get supposedly objective evaluations of these traditional remedies published by the *Journal of the American Medical Association* and other prestigious publications. Redressing this gaff, the editors of JAMA published a strongly worded follow-up article that described Ayurvedic remedies as scientifically unproven and part of a deceptive scheme on the part of the Maharishi's supporters to boost declining enrollments in TM courses.

After helping TM try to distance itself from its occult roots, Benson (1996) has returned to the overtly spiritual path in recent years. He now asserts that we are "genetically wired for God" and that prayers for recovery from illness will be answered. Like the earlier claims for TM, the evidence that Benson cites for his expanded claims for spiritual contributions to health have been strongly criticized. Tessman and Tessman, for instance, have found Benson's conclusions to be exaggerated and largely unsupported by objective research:

> It is undeniable that the mind affects the body in many ways. Therein lies a fertile field for rigorous science; also a fertile field for exaggerated claims, uncontrolled studies, flawed statistics, mind-boggling illusions, and anecdotal reports. (Tessman and Tessman, 1997a)

Further disputing Benson's claims, Tessman and Tessman (1997b) found his assertions of therapeutic usefulness of the "relaxation response" in treating sleep disturbances, infertility and chronic pain to be based on misrepresentations of the actual data contained in the scientific publications cited by Benson.

To recap this section, then, there is a serious lack of evidence that the use of biofeedback to condition brain waves is able to produce a unique and beneficial state of consciousness. Nor is there good reason to believe that the subjective experiences of supposedly related meditative states are more beneficial, physically or psychologically, than any other restful state of lowered physiological arousal. We turn now to the claims of the next generation of "brain tuners", those who tout the benefits of driving certain brain frequencies with external stimulation.

BRAIN DRIVERS REPLACE THE BRAIN TUNERS

As it became clear that passively training brain waves could not be counted on to deliver the promised dividends, the self-improvement industry shifted to selling more active ways of driving brain rhythms. It has been known since ancient times that bombarding the senses with repetitive, pulsating stimulation can produce alterations in consciousness – this has been achieved at various times by rapid alternation of shadow and light, rhythmic drumming, or engaging in repetitive chanting, dancing, swaying or breathing (Beyerstein, 1988, 1996a). The ritualistic employment of pounding, rhythmic stimulation to affect consciousness has been discovered independently in many different historical eras and parts of the world (Sargant, 1957, 1973; Neher, 1990). Widely differing religious and political movements have found these manipulations useful in their bids to attract and hold converts. From the whirling dances of the Sufis to the "sawdust trail" travelled by the American tent-revivalist preachers, and from Dr Goebbels' torchlight rallies to the repetitive, mind-numbing chants of the Moonies, the overt messages (and social agendas) have varied immensely, but the techniques have always rhymed. Succeeding generations of charismatic leaders have rediscovered that their exhortations carry more weight when delivered in ceremonial settings that induce physical exhaustion while building emotional tension, often aided by sleep deprivation and fasting. Most often, the crowning touch has been the addition of repetitive sensory bombardment to this potent mind-altering mix, in order to hammer these messages home. There is no doubt that these methods do affect proselytes' state of consciousness and, implicitly or explicitly, the subtext always reads, "See how our rituals produce these feelings of awe and wonderment in you? If we possess this power, it must mean that the 'truths' we are imparting to you are specially favoured by higher forces too. Therefore, you must listen and obey."

Once again, modern technology has helped to perfect techniques discovered by the ancients – and now it can all be done in the comfort of your own home. Electronic wizardry has made it a trivial task to deliver this kind of driving sensory stimulation to the eyes and ears of enlightenment seekers, who remain as eager as at any time in the past to experience what they take to be transcendent states of being (rather than a transient perturbation of their brain activity). The apparatus typically consists of goggles and ear-phones fed by circuitry that delivers flickering lights and pulsing tones at various frequencies to the trainees' eyes and ears (Hammer, 1989; Beyerstein, 1990). In the words of the advertising of the FringeWare organization of Austin, Texas:

> Brain tuners (or mind machines) use rhythmic light and sound to alter brainwave activity. Through a process called entrainment, they "tune" the brain to brainwave frequencies associated with the states of consciousness associated with meditative and trance states.

Though imitators are legion, the initial heavy hitters in this market are the Monroe Institute with its "Hemi-Sync" device and the Zygon Corporation's "brain booster".

They were soon joined by the even more fanciful and grossly overpriced contraptions of the John-David Learning Institute (which adds subliminal messages[9] to the existing melange of pseudoscience in order to produce, so they say, "effortless learning", "ultra intelligence", "the psychoneurology of self-healing", and an enhanced immune system thrown in for good measure). A competitor's come-on trumps this hyperbole by offering the bountiful rewards available to people who use their brain-tuning device to synchronize their bodily energies with those of Mother Earth (whatever those might be). The back pages of *Popular Mechanics* and the *Farmer's Almanac* were once the preferred venue for advertisements seeking to attract paying customers for far-fetched brain-enhancement schemes. By the time my earlier critique of these devices was published (Beyerstein, 1990), popular science magazines such as *Psychology Today*, *Omni* and *Discover* had become the preferred media for delivering these sales pitches.[10] These days, the Internet, various New Age tabloids, television "infomercials" and the growing number of holistic health and psychic fairs have largely replaced these earlier venues as the most lucrative places to troll for customers. The devices being pushed in these places do affect the user's subjective stream of experience for a short time, but then so does a merry-go-round or sustained rapid breathing. But, again we must ask what, if any, good these high-priced "mind-expansion" contrivances do for the customer that he or she couldn't get elsewhere for free.

Shortly after the EEG was invented, it was discovered that presenting pulsating trains of stimuli in the appropriate frequency ranges will cause spontaneous brain rhythms to lock onto these external fluctuations and to resonate in synchrony; for reviews of this phenomenon, known as "photic" or "auditory driving", see Beyerstein (1990). When this entrainment of EEG rhythms occurs, the person typically experiences a mild alteration of consciousness, particularly if the resonating frequencies happen to be around the alpha range (Neher, 1961, 1962). The experience is variously described, but usually in terms that suggest mild disorientation (which can be fun or frightening, depending on the social and psychological context). For instance, participants' narratives tend to place their experience somewhere in the vicinity of vertigo, a mild drug high, or the lightheaded feeling one gets after hyperventilating. Some people report unusual visceral sensations or vague feelings of foreboding as well. More recently, in research settings, placing the head in pulsating magnetic fields has also been shown to drive brain rhythms and to produce certain experiences akin to those that have long been ascribed to the intrusion of paranormal or occult forces (Johnson and Persinger, 1994; Blackmore, 1994).

Studies in the literature have reported both positive and negative reactions to the subjective effects of this kind of driving of one's brain waves (Fedotchev et al., 1996).[11] Whether the resulting mental changes will be perceived as agreeable or disturbing is largely determined, as in all such occasions, by the personality and expectations of the experiencer and the social demand characteristics present at the time the manipulation is tried. As is the case with all mental changes engendered by externally caused alterations in brain physiology, the accompanying subjective effects will be interpreted and embellished by the experiencer in accordance with the meaning he or she ascribes to the event and the hopes, fears and expectations brought to the situation (Beyerstein, 1996a). The experience will be welcomed or abhorred, accordingly. Just as quite different drug experiences can result from the same dose of the same chemical agent (Zinberg, 1984), meditators and users of these brain drivers are subject to the effects of "set and setting",[12] which will strongly colour the nature and interpretation of the "raw" experience.

Robert Monroe, a former business executive with no significant training in psychology or electrophysiology, has latched onto two assertions that supposedly make his devices more spiritually uplifting than those of his competitors (who are content merely to engage in garden variety photic and auditory driving of the EEG). The allegedly special benefits produced by Monroe's Hemi-Sync auditory tapes supposedly arise from their ability to produce binaural beats and hemispheric synchronization. Monroe's tapes feed slightly different sound frequencies into the two ears, a procedure that produces a phantom auditory experience known as ''binaural beats''. These subjective phenomena have interested psychologists and neurophysiologists for decades (Oster, 1973), but no reputable scientist has ever suggested that they were practically useful, let alone helpful in the way that Monroe asserts (Beyerstein, 1990). Monroe, none the less, claims that producing binaural beats is the way to achieve something of even greater value, synchronization of the two cerebral hemispheres. Monroe seized upon the idea that this might be of value after hearing of earlier work with meditators that employed ''coherence analysis'' of the EEG; for a review of this mathematical technique for analysing EEG signals, see Fenwick (1987). Briefly, coherence merely means that EEG frequencies in a set of recording leads attached to different parts of the scalp are fluctuating at approximately the same frequency. Since earlier EEG work with practised meditators had noted some tendency for this kind of synchrony to increase, Monroe, with the usual faulty logic employed by the brain-booster fraternity, assumed that (1) coherence must be unique to meditation and kindred states of spirituality and bliss, (2) getting into this condition must be somehow beneficial, and (3) inducing coherence with driving stimuli would be sufficient to bring about the putative state mentioned in (1) and the payoffs mentioned in (2).

Monroe, in his glossy promotional campaigns, however, has never been able to provide any credible evidence that synchronizing the two hemispheres would be of any benefit in either the short or the long term. In fact, as Fenwick (1987) and Beyerstein (1990) have pointed out, increases in coherence are also seen in patients and schizophrenia, during epileptic seizures and so-called delta comas, and even in brains on the verge of death. Fenwick (1987) has also warned that amateurs who don't really understand the intricacies of EEG recording methods can easily produce an illusion of coherence between EEG channels which is nothing more than an artefact of the faulty recording technique.

Monroe's unsupported assumption, like those of the alpha-training entrepreneurs discussed earlier, was that there is a unique mental state induced by hemispheric synchronization and because they have endowed it with mystical significance, it must therefore be beneficial. When one looks for solid information to back up Monroe's nebulous assumptions, one finds that the ''evidence'' is derived from the usual sloppy metaphors that underlie New Age magical thinking. Because ''balance'', ''harmony'', ''holism'' and ''synchrony'' have nice connotations, it is axiomatic that brain measurements that exhibit these properties will have salutary effects as well. In effect, the promoters are saying that their products must be good for you because the terms used to describe them engender warm and fuzzy feelings. ''You create your own reality,'' New Agers say.

Showing the isolation from legitimate science so common to the classic pseudoscientists described at the beginning of this chapter, the amateur brain dabblers of the Monroe Institute seem oblivious to the fact that, for optimal performance, one does not want all parts of the brain beating in unison. Even if their devices achieved this supposedly advantageous synchrony, they offer no explanation for why any effects would persist between training sessions and why they would enhance overall performance, even if they did. Monroe's rhythm section seems oblivious to the fact that there is considerable specialization of function between the two cerebral hemispheres (Springer and Deutch, 1998) and that optimal performance usually requires *differential* activation rather than synchrony of the two halves of the brain. Moreover, Monroe and his followers have not explained why one would want increased hemispheric synchrony in the EEG when the most synchronous periods we normally find are during sleep and coma – hardly times of peak performance. Likewise, true to the pseudoscientific mould, Monroe and company show no evidence that they are aware of the legitimate research on the effects of synchronization of cortical activity (e.g. Singer, 1993). Synchronization of rhythms between small, highly specialized areas, within the same hemisphere as well as between sites in opposite hemispheres, seems to be the way that specialized units in the brain are linked together temporarily to accomplish complex tasks. Synchronizing a whole hemisphere with the other one would thus seem counterproductive to optimal performance.

The self-taught merchants of the brain-booster industry offer no theory, rationale or believable data of their own to back up their fanciful claims. As usual, the come-ons for the brain-synching boxes are long on testimonials from satisfied users and short on properly conducted outcome research. Testimonials, of course, are useless as hard evidence for any procedure, for reasons I have discussed in detail elsewhere (Beyerstein, 1997). No one disputes that the flickering, booming cacophony produced by these brain blasters can, if sufficiently intense, drive the EEG at the same frequencies, or that this entrainment can affect consciousness. Proof that this has any benefits beyond that of the ubiquitous placebo effect is lacking, however. A "Synopsis of Scientific Articles" contained on the web site maintained by another "brain tuner" outfit, Synectic Systems Inc. (http://www.ecst.csuchico.edu), contains the usual collection of testimonials, poorly controlled one-off case reports, naive neurologizing, and a few studies from peer-reviewed journals that are irrelevant to the promoters' claims. I could not find the words "control group", "placebo effect", "suggestibility" or "demand characteristics" mentioned anywhere in the list of studies summarized on this Web site. It was, however, replete with New Age jargon, grammatical errors, and humorous misinterpretations of reliable scientific data.

The quality of insight that underlies the brain-synching enterprise is nicely exemplified by a visit to the home page of Ed Erst, a devotee and refiner of Monroe's rhythm method (http://www3.eu.spiritweb.org/Spirit/hemisync.html). Erst claims that more precise tuning of the stimulus input frequencies can produce even more specialized and dazzling effects than the "standard" method. For instance, Erst says, within the alpha range (6–13 Hz), driving the brain at 7.0 Hz will permit you to master "mental and astral projections [and mental] bending [of] objects". It is also optimal for performing "psychic surgery", says Erst. Moving all the way from 7.0 to 7.5 Hz will engage "inter-awareness of self and purpose; guided meditation; creative thought for art, invention, music, etc.; contact with spirit guides for direction". According to Erst, 7.83 Hz is optimal for those seeking "earth resonance", whatever that might entail, and 8.0 Hz is the doorway for regression to past lives. At 10.5 Hz, one can expect "healing of the body; mind/body connection; firewalking". Cranking up the dial to the "High Beta" range (30–500 Hz), Erst says, will provide more marvels for the taking: 35 Hz balances one's chakras, whereas 63 Hz is the resonant frequency for astral projection; 83 Hz permits "third eye opening for some people". Why anyone would dally around at 105 Hz, content with nothing better than an "overall view of the complete situation", when increasing the frequency a further 3 Hz will provide "total knowing", is something Erst fails to explain. Impatient folk like myself would probably rush right to the top of the scale (120–500 Hz), where full psychic abilities lie, along with very useful talents such as "moving of objects, changing matter; [and] transmutation".

Another player in the competitive mind machine field, Breakthrough Products, offers nothing new in terms of claims (just the usual offers of super intelligence, a turbocharged immune system, instant smoking cessation, cures for depression, heightened sexual energy and performance, elimination of phobias, accelerated learning, etc.). It does break new ground, however, in appealing to conspiracy buffs in need of mind expansion. According to Breakthrough, the FBI and CIA have had exclusive access to these marvellous technologies for years because a government cover-up has kept ordinary citizens from acquiring them.

An evening's net-surfing will provide much more of the same. One of my personal favourites is FringeWare Inc. of Austin, Texas, who are considerate enough to offer a product line suitable to a range of budgets. Their $500 Synergizer is "a high-end programmable PC-driven mind machine, comprises [sic] a card that plugs into a PC and state-of-the-art goggles and headphone." For the less well-heeled, there is the "Daydreamer", for only $16.95 (post paid). The latter is

> a low-tech machine similar to a tall scuba mask with two circular holes over the eyes. When you blow into a hole at mouth level, a rotor spins, alternatively blocking each eyehole. If you do this with eyes closed while facing a bright light, the flashing effect can alter your consciousness.

Was nirvana ever so achievable at such bargain basement prices?

Not surprisingly, devices such as these have appealed strongly to the corporate clientele of the motivational seminar circuit, the group that, incidently, prides itself as being among the most hard-headed, performance-obsessed segment of society. The pressing need to eek out any sliver of advantage in today's competitive business environment has created a never-ending stream of willing suckers for purveyors of the latest far-fetched self-improvement fad (Beyerstein, 1990). Stuart Coupland is a former graduate student in our laboratory who now heads his own electrophysiology laboratory in the Faculty of Medicine at the University of Ottawa. He was recently moved to put Monroe's Hemi-Sync tapes to a simple test when a friend of his was induced to buy some at a New Age management seminar. In a personal communication to the author, Coupland describes the evaluation study he ran in his laboratory:

> I have a colleague who . . . took a course from a psychologist on creativity in business management. [The trainer] was espousing the use of Hemi-Sync tapes and the Synchro-Energizer, a device to increase theta driving and interhemispheric coherence. I took several individuals who claimed that the Hemi-Sync tapes and the Synchro-Energizer all produced significant psychological benefits [for them] and we did quantified EEG measures . . . and . . . topographic brain mapping of baseline versus [Hemi-Sync/Synchro-Energizer] stimulation conditions. As you can guess, there was no significant difference between the [baseline and the other] two conditions. Interhemispheric coherence was not increased with either technique. In addition, we noted that there was actually increased power asymmetry in the theta and alpha frequency ranges [when the supposedly synchronizing stimulation was in effect].

From what then, might these satisfied customers have derived their subjective benefits? The obvious answer is the placebo effect.

To end this section, I could hardly do better than to quote Dana Nibby, a philosophy student who used to maintain a Web site that genuinely tried to find any redeeming features in the various mind-enhancement machines (http://www.apocalypse.org/pub/u/x/mind.html). Under his electronic ''handle'', Xochi Xen, Nibby writes:

> WARNING! I no longer maintain this site, as my interest in mind machines has dwindled to about zero. There seems to be no good evidence to support the wilder claims about mind machines (that they could make one smarter, etc.). Sure, mind machines can relax you but so can a number of other (cheaper) things . . . If you have any respect for science, however, mind machines will surely fall short of your expectations . . . If you want to make someone smarter, expose [them] to literature, art, etc. . . . . The best thing one can do to make oneself smarter is via reading [and] learning new skills. Take the money you'd be spending on a mind machine to a used book store – that's my advice.

SMART DRUGS AND BRAIN TONICS

Earlier in this chapter, I quoted my brother, Dale to the effect that nonsense often piggy-backs on reliable knowledge. Yet another example can be found in the commercial exploitation of so-called ''smart drugs'' or ''mind cocktails''. Once again, the basic science – upon whose coat-tails these dubious marketing schemes attempt to ride – is sound. These discoveries have fascinating theoretical implications for several areas of neuroscience and have already found limited applications in geriatric medicine. Whether or not they constitute a reliable path to mental superiority for apprehensive Yuppies seeking a competitive advantage in the dog-eat-dog workplace of the 1990s is much less certain. For one thing, much of the work cited by smart-drug peddlers has been done with laboratory animals, and while rats may show moderately improved performance in running through mazes after a dose of one or another of these drugs, how this would ''scale up'' to provide an advantage in securing a coveted promotion at work, or good results in an important examination, is not entirely apparent. In other words, while there may be a measurable change, in practical terms this may well be the classic ''true but trivial'' effect. As the poet Gertrude Stein reminded us, ''a difference isn't a difference unless it makes a difference''.

The organ of consciousness is a chemical machine. It is well established that the efficiency of brain operations is affected by the availability of the basic nutrients that are combined to create the brain's structural and functional chemistry.[13] Reputable scientists such as Wurtman (1988) have documented possible effects of diet on mood and arousal. The question is whether the mass-marketed brain tonics that are supposedly based on this research actually produce any noticeable cognitive advantages for patrons who frequent the growing number of ''smart bars'' springing up in trendy shopping districts across North America, Europe, and Japan. Catering to the same clientele as the other ''brain boosters'' discussed earlier, these bars sell concoctions with catchy names such as ''Blast'', ''Memory Boost'' and ''Rise and Shine''. These drinks are said to contain a variety of ingredients that will allegedly enhance intelligence by improving brain efficiency. They typically contain a mixture of amino acids, fructose, vitamins and caffeine. Many of the major transmitter substances in the nervous system are derived from amino acids such as tyrosine or tryptamine that must come from the diet. So the idea of a dietary brain-booster is not inherently absurd – it just remains to be satisfactorily supported with scientific data. Although the connections between these New Age elixirs and relevant scientific research are tenuous, hundreds of thousands of North Americans spend considerable sums of money each year on these unproven potions (Erlich, 1992). As usual, testimonials from satisfied users are the main evidence supplied when sellers are quizzed. The weakness of such evidence has been discussed above – in short, it includes no controls for expectancy or placebo effects that can easily make useless concoctions seem quite beneficial in uncontrolled trials (Beyerstein, 1997).

The term "smart drugs" is a colloquialism for a diverse group of agents known to psychopharmacologists as "nootropics" (from "noos" [mind] plus "tropein" [towards]). Though individual nootropics differ chemically, and in their mode and sites of action in the brain, each is thought by at least a few reputable investigators to be able to enhance some aspect of mental performance, at least in people whose abilities have been hampered by neurological diseases. Legitimate researchers in this area have sought chemical agents that selectively affect the integrative functions of the central nervous system by altering the chemistry of the mechanisms that mediate arousal, attention, cognition, and memory (Nicholson, 1990; Mondadori, 1994). The drugs studied most intensively in this regard include piracetam (a derivative of the neurotransmitter GABA), hormones such as vasopressin, dilators of cerebral blood vessels such as the LSD relative hydergene, and the antihistamine chlorphenoxamine.

Because the drugs mentioned above have potentially dangerous side-effects, they are regulated by the appropriate government agencies in Europe, Canada and the USA and do not generally appear in the "smart cocktails" being sold in shopping malls across these countries. Some smart-drug afficionados in these jurisdictions have attempted to bypass these regulations in some cases, by establishing a black market in these drugs via the mails, obtaining their supplies from offshore sources.

A number of substances that enhance the effects of the neurotransmitter acetylcholine have also been widely studied because of the well-known role this transmitter plays in the brain's memory mechanisms. Other putative performance enhancers, best described as dietary supplements, are rich in the precursors that the brain uses to assemble certain neurotransmitters that are involved in higher cognitive functions.[14]

Originally aimed at alleviating the dementias produced by conditions such as Alzheimer's disease, Korsakoff's syndrome, or strokes, the aforementioned drugs are assumed to boost failing cortical function by enhancing cerebral bloodflow or other means of resisting cerebral oxygen deprivation, by affecting the brain's energy metabolism, or by strengthening the chemical transmission of information across the synapses of the brain. In laboratory animals, these agents have been shown to enhance performance on a number of different learning and memory tasks and, to a much more modest extent, they have been found to help human patients suffering from memory problems (Mondadori, 1994).

The generalizability of this research, conducted as most of it was on non-human species and human patients suffering from dementia, to ordinary people seeking to improve their memory and reasoning power in everyday life remains questionable. There are beginning to be some reports that certain indices of brain activity in normal people are affected by doses of nootropics such as piracetam (Wackermann et al., 1993), but this remains far from establishing their usefulness for the general, non-diseased population. While their findings are of academic interest, Wackermann and his colleagues were quick to point out that the relevance of their data to the performance-enhancement industry is doubtful. This is especially so because, in this instance, the recorded EEG responses to the drug were of the sort that, in other contexts, would be suggestive of decreased vigilance and hence lowered performance.

A thoughtful review of this very technical field, accessible to the intelligent lay person, was recently published by the British neuroscientist, Steven Rose. Summarizing his review of the literature on the smart drugs being sold to the public, Rose (1993) concludes:

> it was not a cheering experience. In magazines, books and newsletters, smart drug enthusiasts cite an impressive string of scientific papers to support their claims. Using these and other papers reporting experiments on prototype smart drugs, I examined well over 100 studies, some on animals, some on people with dementia, some on healthy people. Most of these are either misleadingly quoted by advocates of smart drugs or describe experiments that are poorly controlled or extravagantly overinterpreted by the researchers.

Rose also noted the worrisome trend, also a sign of approaching pseudoscience, that the more dramatic the claim, the more likely it was to have been published in an unrefereed journal or non-reviewed volume of conference proceedings (often from conferences organized by ''true believers'').

Despite the complex and often disputatious picture of nootropics that exists in the scientific literature, Dean and Morganthaler (1990) none the less promise purchasers of their book, *Smart Drugs and Nutrients*, that they will be able to ''increase [their] mental energy, concentration, and alertness'' with the dietary supplements they recommend. Most of the drugs, as opposed to nutritional supplements, that these authors discuss are rightly unavailable without a prescription. However, the authors, irresponsibly in my opinion, suggest some ways in which people might circumvent the busybodies who want to deny them their right to acquire a few more IQ points. The book's jacket reveals who its target audience is by proclaiming that people will be able to ''perform better in school, on tests, or on the job'', ''improve [their] problem-solving abilities'', and ''maximize [their] ability to memorize material''. This volume adequately summarizes much of the animal research and the clinical trials (with various compounds on people suffering from dementia), but it fails to make a convincing connection between this research and the promised mental improvements in ordinary people. Amid the peer-reviewed research cited, there is a disturbing tendency for these crucial links (the ones that would be needed to show the relevance of the peer-reviewed clinical trials to the everyday purchaser's needs) to be backed up primarily by speculations contained in such fringe science publications as *Durk Pearson and Sandy Shaw's Life Extension Newsletter*. Dean and Morgenthaler's book is dotted with laudatory references to various pop-psychology writers, making one wonder how critically these authors assess their evidence in general. Throughout the book, and to an even greater extent in several of the World Wide Web sites devoted to the pushing Dean and Morganthaler's views, there are the kind of exaggerated claims and the tell-tale tendency to engage in conspiratorial thinking that typified the pseudoscientists discussed earlier in this chapter. The sorts of insinuations one hears from smart-drug enthusiasts, particularly in the health food industry, are, for instance, that the medical establishment, the scientific community and the US Food and Drug Administration are somehow hostile towards, even plotting against, this sort of research – as opposed to merely withholding their approval until the evidence of safety and efficacy is more conclusive.

At this stage, it is fair to say that there are many promising leads in the area of nootropics from reputable laboratories, ones that will be well worth pursuing in future research. However, selling so-called ''smart cocktails'' to the public definitely seems premature at this time. From my own review of studies in the area, I must concur with Rose (1993), who concluded, "what is abundantly clear, however, is that the primary scientific literature does not justify the claim that smart drugs can be of any therapeutic or 'memory-boosting' value to healthy humans".

CONCLUSION

The desire for self-improvement and deeper understanding are two of our most noble human aspirations. Unfortunately, these commendable attributes sometimes go hand in hand with some other prevalent human traits – among them, our penchant for wishful thinking, self-delusion, and grasping for quick fixes. Jumping to congenial, comforting conclusions is something we all do with astonishing ease. The time, toil and tedium required to acquire genuine insight and mastery in any worthwhile field of endeavour – and the payoffs that accrue to those who manage to claw their way to these plateaux – guarantee that anyone promising a shortcut will soon attract a large following, whether deserved or not. I think this has been evident in the areas I have surveyed in this chapter. The goals seem so unsordid that it strikes many as somehow mean-spirited to say, "That's nice, but do you have any evidence that it really works?" In my dealings with those who sell the products I have criticized in this chapter, I have found very few intentional con-artists. Most of the merchandisers I have encountered are sincerely convinced that they are offering good value for the money they solicit. Many even see themselves as great (if woefully misunderstood) benefactors of humanity. As a group, however, they have struck me as quite unaware of how naive their assumptions are and lacking in knowledge of how to test the efficacy of what they sell. Their clients, on the other hand, tend to be equally unaware of how easy it is to convince ourselves that useless products are helping us to achieve ends we can all agree would be quite desirable, if obtainable.

In my meanderings through the world of New Age self-improvement products, I like to apply what I call "the garage sale test". Things that promise spectacular results, and really work, are rarely pawned off for pennies on the dollar soon after purchase. My own collection of these books, course manuals and gadgets has been largely derived, at considerable savings, from Saturday morning jaunts through the maze of hand-painted lawn signs in our neighbourhood. It has been assembled from the garage sales, flea market stalls and rummage sale booths of sadder but wiser purchasers who have come to realize, temporarily at least, that "there ain't no free lunch". Because hope springs eternal, this realization tends to be short-lived and I suspect that I can count on more interesting bargains in the future.

There is, as we have seen, nothing new in the New Age. Its core beliefs are, as outlined above, traceable at least as far back as the mystery cults of the pre-Socratic Greeks (Frankel, 1973). New Agers' criteria for truth are emotional rather than empirical – if it feels good, it must be true. This has been largely responsible for the booming sales climate for the kinds of products described in this chapter. The New Age movement differs from its predecessors only in the modern-sounding jargon it chooses for restating many of these ancient dogmas. The movement is primarily a marketing umbrella that combines numerous threads of ancient magical belief with the modern fascination with the latest in technology. The mind-expansion fraternity plays effectively on our desire to "get ahead" at school or at work by means other than the traditional ones of concerted effort and "learning the ropes". While appealing to our desire for shortcuts, it also taps into our anxieties about the need for help in the increasingly competitive modern workplace. On the other hand, it feeds our nostalgia for a halcyon past that probably never was, and it speaks to the unease many feel about their perceived lack of spiritual meaning in the modern world. Helping to fill this void, the New Age movement has provided a haven for pseudoscientists claiming to have harnessed modern technology to reunite what they see as the falsely separated spiritual and material worlds. The seekers to whom they pitch their wares tend to forget all too easily the wise admonition of the US Justice Oliver Wendell Holmes that "men should be most on their guard when motives are of the highest order".

Notes

1. For a detailed explanation of why graphology seems to work in everyday, informal demonstrations when it invariably fails in properly controlled trials, see Dean et al. (1992) or Beyerstein (1996b).
2. Dualism is the philosophical position that says the universe is composed of two fundamentally different components, one physical and the other spiritual or mental. According to dualists, brains are composed of physical matter and obey the laws of physics and chemistry, whereas minds are ethereal, intangible, and under no obligation to conform to the laws that govern physical matter. For dualists, "mind" is essentially equivalent to the religious concept of the soul. On the other hand, material monists, such as myself, see mental events as identical to, and inseparable from, functional states of the brain.
3. In English it is called the electroencephalogram, or EEG for short. It is a sensitive voltage-measuring device that can record the summed rhythmic electrical discharges of large aggregates of brain cells by attaching electrodes to the scalp, or, occasionally, inserting them as needles beneath the scalp.
4. Alpha waves are rhythmic activity in the 6–13-Hz range on the EEG. They are most prominent at the back of the head, over the visual areas of the brain.
5. The basic premise of biofeedback is that using an electronic sensor to inform a person about the status of a physiological function that he or she normally has no way of feeling could promote voluntary control over that bodily process. Such control, if achievable, could obviously be useful for counteracting stress, assisting relaxation, and even alleviating certain medical conditions. Early predictions from the biofeedback community that they would soon have diabetics learning to secrete insulin, epileptics learning to inhibit seizures, and hypertensives learning to lower their blood pressure, have fallen prey to those cruellest of pruning devices, the control group and the demand for replicability of results (Simkins, 1982). In other cases, modest successes in learning to modify certain bodily functions with biofeedback have been achieved in the laboratory, but they have proved difficult to sustain in the rough-and-tumble of the outside world.
6. Operant conditioning, also known as "Skinnerian conditioning", after its best-known explicator, is essentially trial-and-error learning – that is, the probability that a candidate behaviour will recur is modified as a result of the good or bad consequences it provokes when it is "tried out" in the environment. Behaviours that are rewarded by attainment of desired goals are thereby made more probable when future opportunities arise, whereas the likelihood of those that are punished by resulting frustration or pain is diminished. There is no doubt that voluntary responses involving the skeletal nervous system are acquired in this way. It remains controversial, however, as to whether bodily functions controlled by the autonomic nervous system can be conditioned in the same manner. Even where it may appear that this has been achieved, critics maintain that the apparent control of autonomic functions is mediated by voluntary responses of the skeletal nervous system.
7. Alpha conditioning was supposed to teach people to produce alpha waves in the EEG while their eyes remained open, something most people cannot do spontaneously – because they cannot refrain from attending to the barrage of stimuli entering through their open eyes.

Whatever else trained meditators may have achieved, many seem to have acquired the ability to avoid attending to this train of stimulation and thereby maintain their production of alpha activity.

8. Transcendental Meditation (TM) has been, by far, the most successful marketing organization following this approach (Forem, 1973). The criticisms in this section, though mostly usually directed at TM specifically, apply to meditation claims in general. Based on the teachings of the Indian swami, Maharishi Maheshi Yogi, TM is one of the quasi-secularized self-help schemes that tries to appeal to a broader audience by downplaying its mystical origins and adopting a supposedly scientific front (Woodrum, 1978). TM has even spawned its own political party, The Natural Law Party, that has contested national elections in Europe and North America. Despite the TM organization's self-professed scientific orientation, most objective observers remain deeply sceptical of most of its claims. A clue to the organization's real level of scientific sophistication can be seen in the fact that it continues to be one of the major disseminators of the myth that we only use 10% of our brains (see my critique of this hoary falsehood in Chapter 1).

9. Subliminal messages are presented visually or auditorily, but so briefly and/or weakly that they are not perceived. The claim is, however, that they none the less reprogram "the subconscious" to cancel bad habits, engender new skills, improve health, and enhance well-being, motivation, social skills, etc. Breast and penis enlargement through the use of subliminal audiotapes is widely advertised, but my personal favourite is a strongly promoted subliminal audiotape that claims to cue deafness! There is, of course, no scientific evidence that these products work as advertised (Greenwald et al., 1991).

10. When the editors of the journal *Science* took their opposite numbers at the popular science magazines to task for helping to peddle this kind of self-improvement pseudoscience, Paul Hoffman, the editor of *Discover*, wrote to the editors of *Science* (2 February 1990): "It made me sad to see you sniping at *Discover* magazine in your 1 December issue . . . Yes, there are ads we carry, generally toward the back of the magazine, that tout products and services we would never endorse in our editorial pages. And the reason we do so should be obvious to anyone who works in publishing. It is an economic necessity." This necessity had prompted *Discover* to run advertisements for, among other things, Scientology and get-rich-quick books, as well as Zygon's "brain-booster", a "brain Supercharger/Subliminal Mindscripting System" that will, for only $49.95, "zap stress, boost your brain power and unleash awesome creative and intuitive powers". If that were not enough, Zygon boasts that the device "turns fat people thin and office clerks into mental millionnaires".

11. In susceptible individuals (estimated to be around 1 in 10 000 in the general population), this kind of flickering stimulation is ideal for provoking epileptic seizures, though one would never learn this fact from the braintuners' promotional materials. At one time, the Monroe Institute even recommended its Hemi-Sync machines as a *treatment* for epileptics (Beyerstein, 1990). As I write, news stories are pouring in, describing an epidemic of seizures in Japanese children. The attacks were triggered by flashing lights emanating from the eyes of a popular television cartoon character. Over 700 children were sent for emergency medical treatment following seizures they experienced while watching the cartoon serial *Pokemon*, a derivative of the Nintendo game, "Pocket Monsters" (Smillie and Strauss, 1997). Of those affected, 120 required hospitalization for more than 24 hours ("Cartoon sparks convulsions", 1997). Back in the 1970s when strobe lights were popular in dance halls, similar bouts of "disco epilepsy" were reported. I am pleased to note that since I warned about this potential hazard of the brain tuner machines in my 1990 review, at least a few of the Web sites devoted to selling such devices on the Internet have now begun to mention that they might not be suitable for anyone who thinks that they could be susceptible to seizures. Despite this small progress, though, a visit to the Monroe Institute's homepage shows, with depressing predictability, that, in the same interval, AIDS relief has been added to the marvels supposedly achievable with the Hemi-Sync machine.

12. "Set" refers to the beliefs, values, expectations and predispositions of the user, and "setting" refers to the cultural, social, psychological and physical environment in which the usage takes place.

13. Research has shown that malnutrition harms mental abilities if it occurs prenatally or during early childhood when the brain is undergoing its most rapid growth spurts (Winick, 1976). Attempts at later remediation through dietary supplementation greatly alleviate, but do not

always erase entirely, the intellectual deficits caused by early malnutrition. Similar nutritional deprivation in healthy adults, however, produces negligible effects, so the question is, ''Will augmenting an already balanced diet with these building blocks of neurochemistry produce any additional benefits in ordinary people?'' In patients suffering from certain degenerative brain diseases, studies have found that particular nutritional supplements and drugs derived from herbal sources might alleviate some symptoms or slow the progress of the disease (LeBars et al., 1997). It should be remembered, however, that the improvements seen in these instances are quite modest and that they are seen in people who have been debilitated by serious brain diseases. This study of demented patients treated with ginkgo extract for 6 months to a year found that 27% of the treated patients improved by at least four points on a test of mental function, as opposed to 14% of those patients given a placebo. Obviously, the majority of patients treated with ginkgo obtained no relief. The relevance of these very modest effects to a non-impaired population is debatable. The few studies in the literature have been criticized for poor methodology and have generally not been replicated by other scientists.

14. All communication in the brain is achieved through release, reception and response to chemical agents known as neurotransmitters and neurohormones (Bradford, 1986). By regulating the electrical potentials maintained across cell membranes in all nerve cells, and by affecting various intracellular metabolic processes, these signalling molecules are responsible for everything we feel, think, or do. About 20 such transmitter substances have been well documented in the brain, but researchers have speculated that there may be as many as 100 or more (Rosenzweig, Leiman and Breedlove, 1996, p. 167). Modern psychobiology has attributed many of the mental abnormalities found in neurological disorders to specific shortages or excess activity of one or another of these neurochemicals. For instance, the memory deficits in people with Alzheimer's disease are largely attributable to depressed activity of cells containing the neurotransmitter acetylcholine. The movement disorders seen in people with Parkinson's disease are attributable to a shortage of dopamine in certain brain tracts, while excess dopamine activity in other parts of the brain seems to be responsible for some of the symptoms of schizophrenia. Similarly, severe forms of depression have been linked to underactivity in the tracts of the brain that are regulated by interactions among the transmitters serotonin, noradrenaline and dopamine. Modern pharmacotherapy for mental disorders is aimed at restoring the normal balance and communication in these brain tracts by use of chemicals that mimic or block these endogenous transmitter molecules. These molecules, which are involved in specialized physiological functions, are synthesized by enzymes in the brain from raw materials derived from the diet. It is therefore a reasonable speculation that if disorders stem from shortages of a given neurotransmitter, the symptoms might be alleviated by loading the diet with the precursor molecules that are ultimately turned into the neurotransmitter that is in short supply. For instance, in conditions where acetylcholine is scarce, relief might be obtained by increasing the intake of its precursor, choline. Likewise, where the effects of serotonin are lacking, a dietary increase in its precursor, tryptophan, might be beneficial. Or if there is a lack of dopamine, then bulking up on tyrosine could possibly help. There are some problems with this view, however, that make this simple solution less viable than it might seem at first glance. One of these has to do with whether oral doses of these precursor chemicals can produce high enough levels in the brain to affect synthesis of the desired transmitter in more than a trivial way. In sum, the idea of dietary effects on brain function is reasonable; there is some evidence in its favour (Wurtman, 1988), but at present, commercial applications must be considered highly speculative and well beyond the bounds of proven science. Consumers should also be aware that when these supplements, derived from plant products, are bought from herbalists and health food stores, there can be wide variations in the concentrations of the active ingredients. There have also been cases of contamination, causing serious illness. Herbalists have downplayed the issue of possible toxicity and side-effects, as well. Just because something is ''natural'' is no guarantee that it is safe. Strychnine and belladonna, virulent poisons, are also derived from wholly natural plants.

Section 2

THE TWILIGHT ZONE BETWEEN
LIFE AND DEATH

The physician Raymond Moody is credited with coining the term near-death experience (NDE) to describe the set of sensations and experiences felt by people who are resuscitated from almost fatal accidents. Blackmore (1993) and other professional sceptics (e.g. Shermer, 1997) dichotomized the debate surrounding NDE between the ''afterlife hypothesis'' and the ''dying brain hypothesis''. However, as is often the case, dichotomies are oversimplifications. Indeed, the two hypotheses above are not mutually exclusive, and maybe a more pertinent question would be ''how can arcane brain states be transcendentally fulfilling?'' (Marshall, 1997). Given its philosophical implications, the topic is far from new and has attracted the interest of reflective thinkers and scientists alike. Plato (1993) in *The Republic* told the story of a soldier, Er, son of Armenius of Pamphylia, who having fallen in battle, came back to tell of his NDE. On the twelfth day after his ''death'' he came to life as he was lying on the pyre. ''When he had revived, he told them what he had seen yonder. His soul, he said, departed from him, and journeyed along with a great company, until they arrived at a certain ghostly place where there were two openings in the earth side by side, and opposite them and above two openings in the heaven'' (614, c).

In his autobiography, Jung (1971, pp. 320–324) described his own NDE following his heart attack in 1944, during which he ''bathed in a glorious blue light'' and witnessed ''the whole phantasmagoria of earthly existence''. This episode perhaps tells us more about the critical thinking of psychoanalysis than about life after life. Yet Jung is not alone. According to a Gallup poll, some eight million Americans maintain they have had a NDE (Gordon, 1996), maybe prompted by several Hollywood film-makers' views on the matter (Petries's *Resurrection*, 1980; Shumacher's *Flatliners*, 1990).

Virtually every book which presents the phenomenon as a glimpse into after-death life achieves best-seller status (Ebbern, Mulligan and Beyerstein, 1996). The reason for this is simple: NDE appears to offer proof that humans have a soul and that it survives the death of the body (Dash, 1997). As Sir Walter Scott once said, ''hope is brighter when it dawns from fears''.

To describe the consequences of a severe brain injury, often the media uses interchangeably several terms which have very different meanings: first, coma, which defines a state of unconsciousness, usually transient (Plum and Posner, 1980); second locked-in syndrome, in which all movements, but those of the eyes, are abolished, but arousal and awareness are retained; third, brain death (or irreversible coma), which is irrevocable (Pallis and Harley, 1996); and fourth, vegetative state, in which patients breathe without mechanical support but do not show any response to the environment, being in a persistent vegetative state when recovery is very unlikely to occur (Zeman, 1997). This may cause some confusion, and give rise to legends such as the resuscitation from deep coma state thanks to some improbable stimulus. De Renzi tells us of the performance of Mr Berlusconi, media tycoon, head of the right-wing opposition in Italy, and president of the soccer team AC Milan, who miraculously awakened a teenager in a deep coma state after a motorcycle accident, sending him a tape with his own voice and that of the Milan players inviting the unfortunate youth to wake up. To avoid readers dismissing this event by attributing it to the notorious gullibility of Italian journalists, I would like to draw attention to the headline which appeared in the British Teletext on Saturday 11 January 1997: ''Coma boy wakes up to Wallace and Gromit''. The story went that Edward, 13, was hit by a car while rollerblading and lay in a coma for 2 weeks. Doctors believed that Edward would not get better, but one day his brother put on a video of his animated heroes. To everyone's amazement, Edward sat up in bed and started watching.

CHAPTER 5

Near-death Experiences and Ecstasy: a Product of the Organization of the Human Brain?

MICHAEL A. PERSINGER

"I SEE A TUNNEL....."

INTRODUCTION

The belief that the mind, a term wide enough to embrace both ''sense of self'' and ''soul'', maintains temporal continuity before and after the organic deterioration of the brain has been one of the most persistent in human history. The idea of a continuum between the mind and a cultural god or afterlife reduces the anxiety created by the anticipated dissolution of the self, hence reinforcing the saliency of this belief (Persinger, 1985). The personal accounts of those who have had a near-death experience (NDE) influence and reflect the nature (and details) of this belief.

DEFINITION OF NDE

NDE is a general label applied to the remembrance of subjective phenomena that occur when the person approaches neurophysiological limits after which death is highly probable. Although the general similarity of NDEs through human time and across human culture would be expected if the human mind existed as an independent entity, their common themes may emerge from a factor that has until recently eluded the purely egocentric references of personal experience. The similarities across various NDEs are also predictable because the gross structural patterns and neuroelectrical configurations of the billions of brains that define the continuum of our species were and still remain more congruent than discrepant (Persinger, 1987). The fact that similar dosages of hundreds of different pharmacological compounds can evoke very specific experiences in people cross-culturally and through time emphasizes the strength of this similarity.

PHENOMENOLOGICAL PATTERNS OF NDEs

That a person remembers a NDE indicates that the portions of the mesiobasal temporal lobes, specifically the hippocampus and amygdala (Figure 5.1), were functioning within normal limits. If the consequences of the trauma that generated the NDE were too extreme and the optimal patterns of hippocampal activity were exceeded, only dense amnesia would remain; there would be no representation of experience. NDEs should be more probable when the physiological boundaries of brain integrity are approached but not penetrated (Persinger, 1974).

There are multiple subtypes of human memory, each of which maximally involves statistically greater activity within different regions of the brain (Grafton, 1995; Ungerleider, 1995). Reports of NDEs require autobiographical memory (Fink et al., 1996), aspects of episodic memory, and autonoetic awareness (Wheeler, Stuss and Tulving, 1997). The ''memory'' of one's self in time and space is a reconstructional process involving arrangements (strongly influenced by contextual cues) and integrations of the neural representations of the past experiences mediated through words. Consequently, the report of an experience emphasizes the strong contribution of language and cultural expectations to this reconstructed ''memory''. The specific beliefs, in large part derived from the person's culture and reinforcement history, will be reflected in the details of the NDE.

For example, one of my patients who sustained a trauma to his right parietal lobe during a snowmobile accident reported his experience as follows:

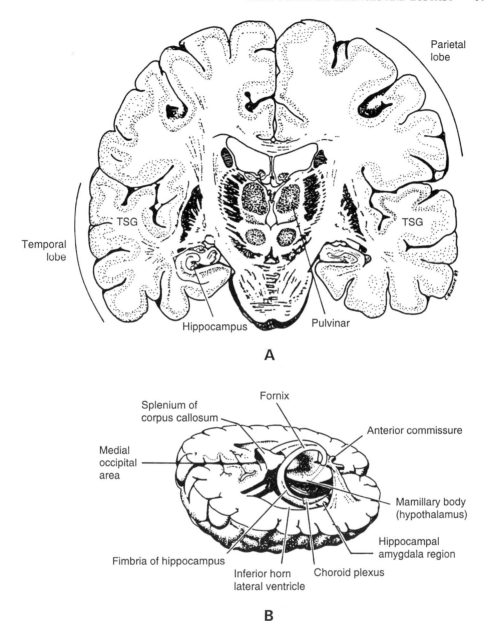

Figure 5.1   Diagram of human brain. (A) Coronal section (a cut from left to right across the cerebrum) showing the key structures. TSG refers to temporal superior gyrus. (B) Horizontal orientation (partial three-dimensional perspective from back, medial occipital area, to front).

I was suddenly sitting in the backseat of a white limousine travelling down a narrow road . . . everything was white around me . . . a kind of bright, blinding glowing light. I could see the back of the driver's head but I could not see his face. I could feel us moving forward through this narrow street . . . I could not see anything from the side windows, just movement up ahead. A red stop light suddenly appeared and the car stopped. The door opened and I figured I should get out when my grandmother poked in her head and said "you stay put, it's not your time". The next thing I recall I was in the hospital.

This patient was employed as a car mechanic and parts specialist; the grandmother, for whom he felt strong emotional bonds, had died about 6 months before and was his strongest association with personal death.

NEUROPROCESSES AND NEUROMECHANISMS INVOLVED IN NDE

At any given time those portions of the brain that are most metabolically active will determine experience. The basic themes of the NDE are consistent with the transiently electrical enhancement within aggregates of neurons from which the experiences are generated (Blackmore, 1993). Most of these neurons (Figure 5.1) are located within: (1) the medial portions of the occipital surface (with input from a deep brain nucleus called pulvinar) which contain the representations from the peripheral or perimacular visual fields from the retina; (2) the superior parietal lobes; (3) the medial and ventral portions of the temporal cortices that are associated with representations of human faces, colours and some vestibular inputs; and (4) the hippocampal–amygdaloid structures, which are supposed to be the gateway for the consolidation of autobiographical episodic memories and their "meaning" or emotional significance.

The blood supply (the primary source of oxygen and glucose) to most of these regions is provided by branches and sub-branches (spriglets) of the posterior cerebral arteries (PCAs). They are derived from the vertebral–basilar arteries, one of the two major arterial inputs into the brain. There is an artery for the left cerebral hemisphere and an artery for the right cerebral hemisphere. One would expect that even small discrepancies between the bloodflow in one of the two hemispheres, particularly the right because of its statistically greater flow rates, would dominate the general theme (spatial movement and experiences involving spatial referents) of the NDE. Ischaemia within some branches of the PCA can be produced even by some forms of heart dysfunction and can be influenced by gender or genetic factors (Bogousslavsky and Caplan, 1993).

Mechanical impacts to the skull or vascular insufficiency (from cardiovascular failure) frequently disrupt the normal function of the PCAs, and therefore these two conditions commonly precede NDEs. Inhibitory interneurons, the most numerous subtype of neurons within the cerebral cortex and limbic system, are particularly vulnerable to hypoxia, and interference with them would release the experiences processed by adjacent structures into awareness. As long as the electrical activity within the hippocampal formation can hold the representation of the experience until more permanent consolidation occurs, the experience can be "remembered".

Other stimuli could trigger activity within this neuronal matrix, without any requirement for the subject to be actually "near" physical death. They include: (1) metabolic hypoxia (due to starvation, insulin surges or even high altitude), which could selectively interfere with hippocampal activity; (2) specific surgical anaesthetics whose mechanisms involve reduction of consciousness by partial hypoxia; (3) ingestion of α_2 receptor agonists such as ketamine or some hallucinogens that can directly affect neurons or produce vasospasm within the blood vessels that supply those neurons; (4) patterns of applied electromagnetic fields whose complex sequences are resonant with the groups of limbic neurons activated by partial hypoxia; and (5) rituals that induce hypoxia, hypoglycaemia (starvation) or the release of endogenous opiates (nociceptive inputs or meditation).

The specific serial activation of these neuronal aggregates is thought to be the substrate for the temporal evolution of the personal NDE. Since metabolic changes brought about by a trauma often follow very similar sequences in the brain, the "unfolding" of the "average" NDE should be similar.

Under extreme oxygen failures, brain tissues surrounding the structures supplied by the PCA would be activated because they would be disinhibited by the marked reduction of neural input. The most frequent regions within this toroidal or penumbral field are the amygdala and hippocampus (Figure 5.1), portions of the nucleus accumbens, and cortical regions of the parietal lobes and the superior gyrus of the temporal lobes that mediate the body image and vestibular-visual sensations, respectively. Because the posterior choroidal arteries, which are derived from the PCA (and supply the portions of the midbrain associated with vision and hearing), interface and fuse with the anterior choroidal arteries (which supply the hippocampus and amygdala), vascular steal or shunting of blood from the anterior to the posterior system would induce a relative hypoxia within the hippocampal regions.

However, depending upon the region of transient hyperactivity, the NDE can be fragmented and very modality-specific. The experience would not reflect the progression of successive disinhibition of groups of neurons with different thresholds. A fragmented NDE would involve only one component of the potential theme of what would have been experienced had hypoxia emerged more slowly. For example, a 40-year-old bilingual left-handed man drank too much alcohol before driving his snowmobile. He struck an ice-break, was thrown from the machine, and hit his head on an outcrop of rocks; consciousness was suspended. As he awoke, he heard a voice say "stop drinking liquor you asshole". After this episode he gave up drinking and displayed an aversion to the smell and taste of ethanol.

A COMMON COURSE OF EXPERIENCES IN NDE

The first stage following a brain injury, induced by impact from mechanical energies (the most common cause), microvascular failure or alterations in ligand (neurotransmitter) binding, would be vestibular experiences that include vibrations, spinning, dizziness, displacement in space or "pulling by a force". For example, a 21-year-old woman who sustained a right parietal lobe trauma (and subsequent electrical activation of the anterior right insular orbitofrontal region) remembered her "self" suddenly looking down upon her body that was connected to a heart monitor. She did not feel as if she were floating but experienced a type of "constant vibration".

Depending upon the type of precipitating stimuli, the feeling of blissfulness occurs differentially over the duration of the NDE. Sudden mechanical impacts or vascular failures sufficient to produce immediate "falling" (hypotonia of the lower limbs) but maintenance of consciousness (a classic indicator of disruption in PCA circulation) could induce the release of the endogenous opiates and the activation of the amygdaloid neurons dominated by the subtype of receptors with which the experiences of euphoria and blissfulness are associated. Because the amygdala is associated with the meaningfulness of experiences, its optimal activation could also generate the feeling of profundity.

Additional mild disruption of bloodflow and enhanced electrical activity of neurons in the caudal structures within the thalamus or within the periaqueductal grey of the midbrain could also elicit experiences of pleasantness with characteristics of analgesia, lightness and floating.

A more pronounced hypoxia (such as drowning), which would preferentially affect the hippocampal formations (due to the unusual geometry of the blood supply and its specific neurochemistry), would increase the probability of disinhibition within these structures. The person would be inundated with images from his or her experiential repertoire; this sequence of firing would represent the "life review". The concomitant disruption of the mediodorsal thalamus or its major input from the amygdala would be associated with a marked distortion of subjective time. One's whole life could be "felt" to have occurred instantaneously.

As the neurons within the medial occipital cortices are activated transiently by insufficient blood supply (and then released from inhibition) and inhibitory interneurons begin to fail, the peripheral portion of the visual field becomes activated and the contrast between the central portion of the visual field (whose cortical neurons are supplied by spriglets of the middle cerebral artery) and the peripheral field is enhanced. The experience of a tunnel emerges. With the concomitant activation of neurons within the superior temporal lobe that subserve the experience of radial gradients (Duffy and Wurtz, 1997), the person experiences vestibular movement through the gradient which can be described as a "tunnel", "light shaft", "narrow valley", "vortex" or even "highway" or "road".

The "bright" light, which is not (and should not be) reported in all NDEs, would be an expected correlate of activation of the pulvinar or its connections with the occipital cortex. This association nucleus within the thalamus is differentially supplied by a spriglet of the PCA. The stronger foveal connections between the pulvinar and the occipital pole associated with the central field would contribute to the experience of a bright circular light at the end of the tube or tunnel.

However, NDEs also display themes which are clearly neocortical and involve language and experience. People who have had an NDE report various themes of the "sensed presence" which is later attributed to a dead relative, spirit, alien, or god. For example, the 21-year-old woman mentioned above, who reported herself "vibrating over her body" (but did not experience a tunnel), also stated that she "felt the presence of God" and she "knew that he was bigger, more powerful and more expansive than anyone had imagined".

OUT-OF-BODY EXPERIENCE

The occurrences of both detachment of the self and dreamy states with concomitant awareness of "another consciousness", regardless of the attribution to a spirit, god or "second self", are relatively frequent during spontaneous ictal periods for patients who display complex partial seizures with a limbic focus (Bancaud et al., 1994). Very similar experiences, described as identical to the "natural" experiences by the patients, can also be surgically induced by electrical stimulations that encourage interactions between the lateral temporal cortex, the hippocampal formation and the amygdala (Gloor et al., 1982, 1993). In fact every component of the themes of NDE – from the tunnel experience to blissfulness – has been reproduced or elicited by electrical stimulation of the epileptic brain.

Within the context of the NDE, the detachment is described as an out-of-body experience (OOBE). Although OOBEs can occur in the absence of a classical NDE or without obvious insult to the brain or body, the thematic pattern of the experiences is similar. The primary difference between OOBEs not associated or associated with NDEs is the emphasis within the latter upon death themes, inferences concerning non-dissolution of the self (immortality) and religious innuendo. During the one or two seconds of realization of imminent death, the continued activation of the left prefrontal cortex, lateral temporal cortices, hippocampal formation and amygdala would encode experiences according to the experient's *current* cognitive context (i.e. near-death).

As long as these experiences are maintained within the deep portions of the temporal and parietal lobes (the extrastriate regions), in a manner similar to dreams, they would be available for later reconstruction (within a few seconds) by the right prefrontal cortex when the person "regained consciousness". As in dreams, the decreased activation of the primary visual regions and the prefrontal areas during this transient state would suffuse the experiences generated *within* the person's brain with powerful emotions. Without the reality check carried out by prefrontal operations during this suffusion, the experiences would appear as real as waking sensations and would be accepted without challenge.

The feeling of a sense of self independent of the body is possibly the primary phenomenological basis for the belief in mind–body dualism. During dream states, normal human beings can "see" themselves from "outside" of their body as well as be aware of this observation from "within" their body. There is some evidence suggesting that the capacity to detach and to experience the sensed presence is essentially determined by the existence of mild variations in the microstructure and neuroelectrical coding of experience within the left and right cerebral hemispheres.

Recently I have proposed a hypothesis based on the above-mentioned hemispheric imbalance, which I called vectorial hemisphericity (Persinger, 1993a). According to this hypothesis, the sense of self is fundamentally a linguistic process (which should be experimentally accessible by the appropriate neuroelectromagnetic patterns) with a slight but statistically greater representation within the left hemisphere. A right-hemisphere homologue to the left hemisphere sense of self was also postulated. When this right-hemisphere homologue is stimulated and the resultant electrical patterns intrude into left-hemispheric awareness, the person will experience the sensed presence (Cook and Persinger, 1997) which, depending upon the concomitant limbic affect of unpleasant or pleasant, is attributed to demons or to gods, respectively. However, when the integrity of the left-hemisphere activity is preserved and is represented together with its right-hemisphere homologue, the sense of self is maintained but the experience of being detached or out of the body will be reported.

Although we have supported this hypothesis with experimental data and the general trend is replicable experimentally, there are still confounding variables, such as the specific modulatory role played by different regions within the right prefrontal cortex. They influence the "format" or the linguistic structure by which the neuroelectrical patterns, maintained during altered states of consciousness, are organized. At present, our experimental results are consistent with the interpretation that relative activation of left-hemisphere processes in conjunction with right-hemisphere deactivation, following a brief period of marked vigilance (right-hemisphere activation), increases the probability of an OOBE. As the right-hemisphere activity compensates and the person's physiological status returns to normal, the sense of a presence and the auditory experiences are more likely to be reported. Within the classic NDE the sensed presence is enhanced towards the end of the sequence and is often associated with a short auditory sequence, which is interpreted by the experient as "a message", "an instruction", or "special information". As normal neuroelectrical interaction and the required reciprocal inhibition between the left and right hemisphere returns, the subjective experience is a "return to the body" (Persinger, 1995).

FREQUENT QUESTIONS ABOUT NDE

Are NDEs Always Reported to be Pleasant?

Considering the likely neural substrates of NDEs, they will always be personally profound and meaningful. However, they will not always be pleasant. About 7% of people who reported NDEs (Persinger, 1974) before the contemporary enthusiasm to report only the more positive components of these natural phenomena (Eadie, 1992) stated that their mood was negative, aversive or hellish. The details were congruent with the mood.

If one considers the functional organization of the amygdala, this proportion would be expected. In fact, the amygdala and related neural groups that mediate reward and punishment are organized intrastructurally with areas of subjectively pleasant experiences (ecstasy to orgasm) surrounded by inhibitory areas of negative or unpleasant experiences. As shown in several mammalian species, including humans (Grossman, 1967), small electrical currents induced within limbic regions of the brain are associated with positive experiences as defined by approach behaviour. However, as the amplitude of these electrical currents increases and their consequences (recruitment of larger and larger populations of neurons) spread through the surrounding inhibitory areas, negative experiences emerge; this is inferred from the observed avoidance behaviour in non-human animals and marked "fear" or "affective painfulness' in humans.

If the electrical lability of the neurons begins to approach the values sufficient to generate negative experiences, then disruptions or distortions of memory consolidation within the hippocampal–amygdaloid formations are also likely. Consequently, the small percentage of people (7%) that report the experiences of hellish NDEs would have been at the borderline of having *not* recalled any experiences because their existence within fragile neuroelectrical patterns and their representation within hippocampal activity would have been disrupted.

Why do Young Children Experience NDEs?

The essential themes of NDEs for young children do not differ appreciably from those of adults. However, the structures that mediate NDEs are functionally organized by the time language is sufficient to communicate with adults. The neuroelectrical integrity of the left hemisphere, more associated with language than the right in most human beings, asymptotes by age 5, while the same activity in the right hemisphere asymptotes by age 10. Autonoetic memory has clearly emerged by 4 years of age (Wheeler, Stuss and Tulving, 1997). Consequently, the argument that the "innocence" of the young brain supports the purity of the NDE is not valid because the metabolic activity and primary function of these structures are comparable in children and adults. Because many of the children whose

NDEs have been investigated were also dying, the subtle yet powerful contribution from the beliefs and incidental comments from parents and medical personnel to the specific details of the child's NDE cannot be overemphasized.

Why do People "Change" After an NDE?

The change in behaviour, often attributed to a "different" personality, after an NDE has been considered a positive consequence of the phenomenon. The reduction in anxiety concerning personal death would be expected if the experient infers that the NDE was real and therefore concludes that "there is something beyond death" or "the self exists independently of the body". Considering the importance of death anxiety to the sense of self, any profound experience – real or not – that reduces anxiety would shift the polarity of future perspectives from negative to positive.

However, many of the stimuli that initiate the NDE sequence also evoke excitotoxic death within some neurons. About 50% of all cerebral neurons survive at the hypoxic threshold. Small microinfarcts or periods of hypoxia can produce immediate necrosis or prompt apoptosis (programmed cell death). The loss of a small percentage of neurons within most structures would not be discernible by objective examination or subjective experience for most normal, healthy people because of the marked redundancy of neurons within neuromatrices associated with any given behaviour or experience. For example, at least 50% of the neurons in the portion of the midbrain that modulates motor movement must be lost before overt symptoms of Parkinsonism become obvious.

The loss of a small number of neurons, particularly within the hippocampus, would promote neuroplasticity and activate synaptogenesis (Houser, 1992). New connections would be made between neurons which were typically not associated. If we accept the dogma that structure dictates function, it becomes clear why these individuals may display different experiences and appear as different people. They may also perceive relationships between environmental stimuli that would elude the normal brain or their own brain before the event. The moderate likelihood of neuroelectrical kindling and the evoked and progressive alternation in synaptic organization due to this intermittent paroxysmal activity would encourage a gradual "evolution" of the "different person" for decades.

One characteristic that frequently emerges from the same biochemical insult that produces the NDE is temporal lobe lability or limbic sensitivity as inferred from an inventory designed to quantify the epileptic spectrum disorder (Roberts et al., 1992). Individuals who display this profile are normal people with no psychiatric symptoms who excel in the fields of music, art, poetry, creative writing and creative science. These individuals are more likely to employ intuition to solve problems and to report that they have, for example: (1) heard someone call their names before falling asleep; (2) become aware of intense smells from nowhere; and (3) become aware of the sense of the presence of a cosmic consciousness. Many of these normal individuals have sustained mild brain traumas or periods of hypoxia whose consequences would have escaped a neurological examination.

About 10% of head injury patients (mostly motor vehicle incidents) referred to us for clinical neuropsychological assessment, report a NDE. After mild brain injuries associated with NDEs, these individuals are more likely to report more psi or parapsychological experiences. Belief in parapsychological phenomena often increases and may become a secular replacement for traditional religious attributions. The widened affect experienced by these people often allows association between stimuli, especially odd or novel stimuli, that others would consider non-consequential.

This clinical subgroup, as well as many other clinical groups who have sustained mild trauma that is followed by an enhancement of subjective experiences that suggests elevated limbic activity, are also more likely to become deeply "philosophical" (or religious) and to feel as if they have been selected personally to proselytize about their beliefs or experiences (Bear, 1979). The profile is similar to, although less intense than, that shown by patients who ultimately develop a clinically diagnosable form of limbic epilepsy or complex partial epilepsy with a focus within the temporal lobes (Persinger and Makarec, 1993).

Does Paranormal Validity Confirm the Literal Interpretation of the NDE?

There are some empirical and experimental data suggesting that remote viewing or psi experiences regarding events with strong affective components can be discerned through mechanisms not known to date. The most frequent experiments that produce weak but replicable effects involve conditions such as dream (Ullman, Krippner and Vaughn, 1989) and other stimulus procedures that encourage temporal lobe lability and input from right-hemispheric patterns (Puthoff and Targ, 1976). Cognitive styles, particularly those linked with persistent experiences associated with temporal lobe and limbic activity, increase the probability of accuracy (Bem and Honorton, 1994; Radin, 1997).

During many NDEs the experient feels as if he or she is detached from the body and in another place or dimension (Table 5.1). Information about distant events or people or events that may later occur can be "experienced". During experiments associated with OOBE, the person may actually visualize detachment and detection of target stimuli such as a series of numbers hidden on the top of a high shelf. However, the experience of the accurate detection of the target stimuli is not necessarily valid or logical. The same neurocognitive process that produced the experience (and by definition illusion) of "leaving the body" would be the one that resulted in the acquisition of the information. The conclusion that the OOBE was the cause of obtaining the accurate information would be analogous to concluding that precise information about the time of day obtained by the angles of the shadows from a sundial was due to the sun rotating around the earth. Details can be correct while their attribution or explanation is incorrect.

EXPERIMENTAL SIMULATION OF NDEs

A theory is not very fruitful unless it can generate hypotheses which allow us to devise methods and measurements that are internally consistent and can systematically and accurately predict a given phenomenon. During the last 15 years we have been discerning the effects of transcerebral application of weak, complex magnetic fields upon human experiences. Our approach has emphasized the isolation of the neuroelectrical patterns and regions of the brain that generate NDEs rather than the attempts to refute or support their validity. Obviously, the two issues are not necessarily mutually exclusive. Our testing procedure will be briefly described below.

A normal individual is seated in a comfortable chair within a darkened, acoustic chamber. The individual's eyes are covered with opaque goggles. Complex sequences of weak

Table 5.1   General categories of reported experience before, during and after the termination of out-of-body-experiences (derived from 50 cases) (Persinger, 1974).

1. Antecedent condition
    (a) Normal sleep, 14%
    (b) Anaesthesia, 18%
    (c) Excessive fatigue, 24%
    (d) Crisis/near-death, 34%
    (e) Nothing unusual, 10%

2. Initial sensations
    (a) Tingling or strange feeling, 10%
    (b) "Nothingness", 8%
    (c) "Spinning", moving through space, 16%
    (d) "Heard sweet music or 'name'", 8%
    (e) Paralysis or pain, 12%
    (f) Thinking about OOBE, 8%

3. Detachment
    (a) Saw body while "consciousness looked down", 44%
    (b) No detection of "body", 46%

4. Experience of finding self in "another place", 66%
    (same place but independent of body, 33%)
    (a) Another place, but earth, 33%
    (b) Another place, but not earth, 67%

5. If not earth
    (a) A dark abyss or valley, 27%
    (b) A bright, luminous light appearing at distance of blackness and approaching experient, 45%
    (c) Colourful meadows landscape, 27%

6. A sensed presence, 80%
    (a) Voices, identified as angel, god or dead person saying "go back", 73%
    (b) Sight of dead people (related to experient), 24%

7. Before the end of the experience
    (a) Voice says "go back", 36%
    (b) No obvious indicator, 52%
    (c) Fear, 8%
    (d) A coercive force, 4%

magnetic fields are applied through the brain by solenoids within containers that are attached by velcro along the scalp or by clusters of solenoids that were embedded within a helmet which is worn by the participant. The rationale for this procedure is that the sudden removal of visual and auditory input allowed the estimated several millions of neurons, normally involved with this routine surveillance of the environment, to be recruited into the weak neuronal ensembles induced by the complex magnetic fields. Consequently, the weak experiential correlates of these experimentally induced neuropatterns could be amplified into "conscious" awareness and hence could be reported by the experient (Persinger, Richards and Koren, 1994; Persinger and Richards, 1995). The intensity of the magnetic fields are in the order of 0.1 to 1 microTesla (1–10 milligauss). Our assumption was that complexity and information within the computer-generated patterns were more biologically relevant than their magnitude, given the amplifying capacity (stochastic resonance) of endogenous neural networks. Consequently, the incremental voltages, digitally to analog converted, can involve between 200 and 10 000 sequences (or lines) of code whose graphic representation could range from the simplistic sign wave to the complex equivalent of the spoken word.

We have assumed, as have Edelman (1989), Crick and Koch (1990) and Eccles (1992), that the phenomena of consciousness and self-awareness exist within a narrow band of weak neuroelectrical interactions within fields generated by the entire cerebral cortex. The frequency band for this "binding" or "cohesion" factor is approximately 40 Hz as measured by contemporary electroencephalographic techniques. If the experience of waking consciousness and "dream states" is recreated every 20–25 ms as reported by Llinas and Ribary (1993), then subtle complex magnetic fields that induce interference patterns in the cerebral field may be as effective in producing NDEs as more traditional stimuli. Consequently, the isolation and understanding of (1) the precise duration of the pixels that generate the applied elecromagnetic fields, (2) the specific timing of those pixel series and (3) the time between packages of these pixels that affect the "binding factor" could also allow the reproduction of altered states, including the NDE.

Table 5.2 shows the percentages of volunteers who have reported the classic types of experiences associated with these experiments. These items were contained in a "debriefing questionnaire" that was completed by the participant at the end of the experiment (which takes between 15 and 30 min). This was only one procedure by which the experiences were monitored. Because this method of monitoring experience was limited by potential amnesia and by the bias of reconstructing the experiences due to the syntax of the items, other methods of measurements have also been employed in our experiments. All subjects were told that the experiments were involved with relaxation and that they may or may not have involved exposure to weak magnetic fields whose intensities were less than that associated with a hair-dryer. Experiments were usually conducted according to a double-blind

Table 5.2   Proportions of 91 volunteers (tested in 1995) reporting specific experiences (not graded for frequency) during application of complex weak magnetic fields across the temporoparietal lobes with co-stimulation of the limbic regions

Debriefing questionnaire item	Percentage reporting yes
1. I felt dizzy or odd	73
2. I felt the presence of someone	24
3. There were tingling sensations	70
4. There were visual sensations	55
5. There were pleasant vibrations moving through my body	54
6. I felt as if I left my body	26
7. I heard an inner voice calling my name	3
8. I experienced anger	18
9. I experienced sadness	43
10. The experiences did not come from my mind	15
11. I heard a ticking sound	31
12. There were odd smells	10
13. I experienced terror or fear	35
14. There were odd tastes in my mouth	11
15. I felt as if I were somewhere else	41
16. I experienced thoughts from childhood	51
17. The same idea kept occurring	69
18. I felt as if I were spinning around	27
19. There were images from a dream I've had	31

procedure: neither the subject nor the experimenter (usually a graduate student or under-graduate thesis student) were familiar with the primary hypothesis being tested.

As can be seen from Table 5.2, which contains the results of several different experiments, the experiences of being detached from the body and leaving the body as well as the sense of presence were reported by about 25% of the participants in this series. The hemisphere over which the magnetic fields were applied (resulting in anistropic resonance within groups of neurons within either the left or right cerebrum) strongly affected the occurrences of specific types of experiences. Application of complex, pulsed magnetic fields over the right hemisphere or both hemispheres evoked a "sensed presence" in about 70% of all participants, while application of the same field patterns over the left hemisphere rarely evoked these experiences. When the sensed presence occurred, both the feeling and the correlative experiences were reported to have profound personal and emotional significance (even in a laboratory context).

Factor analyses of the responses for the items (for each item possible scores were: 0 = never, 1 = at least once, 2 = several times), based upon about 200 participants, revealed shared sources of variance that were influenced by the person's "temporal lobe sensitivity", as inferred from their scores on the complex partial epileptic-like sign indicator (Persinger and Makarec, 1993) and by gender. Whereas a factor that was positively loaded by experiences of dizziness, sensed presence, OOBE and "being somewhere else" was characteristic of right-handed women, right-handed men displayed greater scores for a factor loaded positively by reports of a sensed presence, the conviction that the experience was ego-alien (not from one's own mind) and the feeling of being somewhere else.

Experiments in which participants were requested to speak during the exposure allow narrative text to be analysed. However, the act of introspection during the field exposures shifts the regions of cerebral activity that potentially interact with the applied magnetic fields. This procedure has both advantages and disadvantages. One example of the type of free narrative detail that was reported by a subject who received stimulation by a 1 microTesla pulsed wave containing 200 sequential points whose pixel durations were 3ms, and which was presented every 3000 ms for 20 min, is shown in Table 5.3.

Table 5.3 Specific immediately reported experiences of a male experient who received stimulation bilaterally over the temporal–parietal–occipital interface from 20 min.

Time	Experience
0:30	There is a tingling in my head
0.56	I feel like I am pulsing . . . strange pumps
1:00	I am being pulled down from my legs
2.38	There are vague images . . . water in a river . . . horses . . . just saw an image of a snake
9:00	I see a ladder . . . a rope . . . it's black and I'm going into it
9:20	The lights are spinning . . . light is splitting . . . dark centre with bright edges
9:25	I am flying . . .
9:30	Something is going up like a vortex, an inverted tornado
9:40	I'm spinning rapidly
10:00	I see a light . . . a flashlight at the end shining at me
10:10	I feel something to my left . . . there is something there . . . a shadow of someone to my right
10:30	I see trees . . . a cotton grove . . . see green . . .
10:55	Something is spinning around me . . . the word "lateral" keeps occurring . . . there's a hand on a lever moving back and forth
11:30	I see cartoons . . . like Walt Disney characters

The themes that evolved over the exposure time were dizziness, a pulling force, variations of a tunnel-like perception, spinning and flying, a light at the end of this tunnel (attributed to a flashlight), a peaceful forest scene, an intrusive word "lateral", and humanoid equivalents (cartoons). Because the experiences were generated within an experimental context and were not preceded by a crisis or potential death, the details would be expected to be, and were, more mundane.

Table 5.4 contains the narrative (explicatives and non-verbal sounds, e.g. "uhs", deleted) of a woman who received stimulation over the right caudal hemisphere by a different pulsed field generated by 500 pixels (1 ms in duration) presented every 330 ms. The dizziness and detachment experiences were reported first. The predicted and frequent reports of a feeling of fear (associated with right-hemispheric stimulation) and a bright light then occurred. The dream-like experiences, often attributed in this context to childhood memories, followed. Stimulation of the right hemisphere, as shown in this case, was primarily associated with a left-lateralized feeling of a presence and somatic (twitching, touch) sensation. A subjective experience of an "interactive" relationship with the presence, e.g. "it moves when I think about it", often encourages the explanation that the phenomenon responded to the "thought". Finally, the experience of "someone saying something" and being with a group of friends, not present, was reported.

Table 5.4 Serial narrative of a woman who received right-hemispheric stimulation for 15 min. Each experience occurred for approximately 20 s to 1 min.

1. I feel dizzy . . . like spinning
2. My foot . . . feet aren't right . . . they feel small . . . not here
3. I feel I'm not here . . . not in my body . . . I can't feel it.
4. There are lights . . . greenish . . . purple . . . I see a tube in front of me . . . darkish . . . soft tube
5. I'm kind of afraid . . . moving head forward into it. I feel I'm looking straight ahead and not down at the floor.
6. I see my mother . . . she's [unintelligible]
7. There's a bright white light everywhere . . . I'm floating around in this big white light . . . it seems to swallow me
8. Images . . . lots of images . . . like a dream . . . this is weird
9. I feel someone . . . when I say something he goes away . . . I'm warm . . . my left side is twitching
10. It moves from left to right when I think about it . . . I feel close to him . . .
11. Somebody's saying something to me . . . I'm not here . . . with my friends . . . I see them
12. I'm relaxed . . . there a triangle . . . that stupid triangle keeps turning

Taken together, the results of the research by the Laurentian University Neuroscience Research Group (Cook and Persinger, 1997; Healey, Persinger and Koren, 1996; Persinger, 1996; Persinger, Richards and Koren, 1994; Tiller and Persinger, 1994) have indicated that all major themes associated with natural NDEs have occurred within our experimental setting (Persinger, 1993b). The specific sequence of the temporal evolution of these experiences within the experimental setting has been less integrated than natural NDEs and the details are more context (laboratory) dependent. Even the most subtle innuendo or expectancy can affect the details (hence the employment of double-blind procedures). However, both our ethics and methods inhibit us from exposing the volunteers to the type of sequence that would stimulate the vascular correlates of the limits that approach physiological termination.

CONCLUSION

The themes of NDEs are alike historically and cross-culturally. These "common phenomenological themes" are extremely similar to the known patterns of experiences correlated with enhanced, transient electrical activity within the regions of the brain supplied or influenced by the posterior cerebral artery. Although transient vascular insufficiency would be a central source of stimulation, other stimuli that affect the networks associated with these structures and simulate the neuroelectromagnetic patterns that are generated during these more extreme physiological states, would also activate the continuum of NDE. The details of the experiences would be influenced by the person's cultural beliefs and the individual reinforcement history.

There is not a single component of the themes within the NDEs that has not been evoked by surgical stimulation of the temporal lobes or mesiobsal structures (the hippocampus–amygdala) of complex partial epileptic patients or by application of weak complex magnetic fields through the cerebral hemispheres of normal, non-dying individuals. Because ethical restrictions prevent the application of forces sufficient to exactly reproduce the sequence of metabolic challenge that occurs during actual near-death events, the experimental simulations involve more limited sequences whose details are affected by the context. For an experienced near-death event to be remembered requires that the stimulus (insult) does not evoke electrical disruption within the hippocampal formation during the consolidation of the experience.

The mind is likely to be the neurocognitive equivalent of the prescientific concept of the "substance" phlogiston which emerged as an explanation for "why things burn". With the growth of the measurements and concepts of modern chemistry, the quantitative data could be analysed externally to the singular perspective of egocentric perception. The idea of phlogiston was no longer required. Paper still burned but the mechanism and process were neither mysterious nor implicitly non-physical. People still experience the phenomenon of an entity labelled "the mind", but it, like phlogiston, is no longer required as the only explanation for experiences.

ACKNOWLEDGEMENTS

My thanks go to Sandra Tiller, Rodney O'Connor, Pauline Richards, Charles Cook, Stanley Koren (the electronics technologist and design engineer who constructed all the equipment) and Dr Katherine Makarec for their contributions to the research during this decade.

CHAPTER 6

Lazarus' Syndrome

ENNIO DE RENZI

In this chapter I will discuss two popular beliefs which are upheld by the hope that severe coma and even death are reversible events. The first concerns the resuscitation of people who were apparently dead, and the second the benefit that comatose patients can obtain from emotionally charged messages delivered by a relative or a spouse.

A GLIMPSE INTO THE AFTERWORLD?

The problem of death has always been a mainspring of myths, built up in an attempt to seek an alternative to the agonizing prospect that all the links we have established with the world will suddenly cease and that life will end in nothing. The traditional answer that humankind has provided to this *horror vacui* has been the development of religious beliefs, centred on God's promise of an afterlife. Religions, however, are grounded more on faith than empirical evidence, and believers have always felt the need to strengthen the cogency of their arguments with more tangible phenomena, such as miracles, that attest to the presence of divine or supernatural powers. Unfortunately, miracles are becoming rarer and rather outmoded, possibly because they jar with the rationalistic approach that characterizes modern civilization. Thus they have been substituted by reports of events which provide evidence of a life after death, but do not imply the violation of natural laws. Returning to life after death is conceived of as a possible, albeit rare, biological phenomenon, providing us with a unique opportunity to discover what happens when we die. It is the interpretation of such phenomena within the frame of natural facts that legitimizes an analysis in terms of their internal consistency and agreement with current knowledge on the biology of life. To make this point clearer, it may be instructive to begin their assessment by drawing a comparison between returns to life and miracles of the same import.

There is little doubt that Lazarus' resurrection was the greatest miracle allegedly performed by Jesus Christ and that it is also the one that most defies any attempt at explanation in terms of natural laws. The description in the gospel of John is clear-cut and straightforward.

When Jesus came to the tomb where Lazarus lay, he asked for the stone across the entrance to be taken away. "But, Lord" said Martha, the sister of the dead man, "by this time there is a bad odour for he has been there four days." Then Jesus said "Did I not tell you that if you believed, you would see the glory of God?" And so they removed the stone. Then Jesus looked up and spoke to God. When he had finished he called out in a loud voice, "Lazarus come out!" The dead man came out, his hands and feet wrapped with strips of linen and a cloth around his face. Jesus said to them "Take off the grave clothes and let him go." Return to life was not a fleeting event, because, as John tells us, when a few days later Jesus came back to Bethany, "a dinner was given in Jesus' honour. Martha served, while Lazarus was among those reclining at the table with him."

This story can either be accepted as proof of Jesus's supernatural powers or rejected, questioning the historical validity of the gospel testimony. For instance, it could be pointed out that not even the slightest mention of such an extraordinary miracle can be found in the gospels of Mark, Matthew and Luke.[1] However, what disbelievers cannot do is to broach an account in naturalistic terms, arguing, for instance, that Lazarus' death was only apparent (hysterical loss of consciousness, transient coma from toxic substances, or accidental poisoning) and that there had been no true interruption of life during the 4 days of burial. This is far too long a period of time to be compatible with a diagnosis of apparent death.

Thus it has to be acknowledged that the description of Lazarus' resurrection is internally consistent and that, if one believes that the gospel of John is trustworthy, only a miracle – the suspension of natural laws – can bring back to life a man who has lain in the grave for 4 days.

Compared with Lazarus' resurrection, the reports of people alleged to have returned to life after death appear more contradictory. Their basic assumption is that, after death, the soul leaves the body to begin its journey in the afterlife, having experiences that can be recorded and passed on to other people, when the soul rejoins the body. These reports are not usually written by the patients themselves, but by the person who interviews them after their recovery. Their content tends to be rather stereotypical, a feature often taken as evidence that they are not the fruit of the patients' imagination, but reflect the real sequence of events. Subjects have the feeling that they are walking along a dark passage and that they are hearing a sound. They then become aware of having left their own body and of looking at it from outside, while souls of dead acquaintances gather round to welcome them. At this point an extremely bright light appears and establishes a mental contact with the patients, asking them whether they feel ready to die and to take stock of their lives. Subjects are driven to recapitulate their lives and experience a feeling of beatitude, until suddenly they are called back to the real world.

For the time being, we will assume that these reports are a truthful record of what subjects say and are not influenced by the interviewer's expectations. But what inferences can we draw from these accounts? One hypothesis is that the patients really died and that their souls left the body and entered the afterworld, although, after a while, the process of death was interrupted and their souls rejoined their bodies. However, this contention clashes with all the available evidence on the biological correlates of death, which indicate that it is an irreversible process that, once started, cannot be stopped or reversed. Thus the only possible interpretation of the patients' return to life is that the border between life and death had not been crossed, and the soul had not deserted the body. It might also be argued that the idea that the soul can buy a return ticket to the hereafter sounds odd and hardly in keeping with the sacredness attributed to the afterworld by believers. An alternative hypothesis is that the patients still retained a life potential and were in the condition known as "apparent death". This term is applied to patients who are taken for dead, but who are in fact still alive and can, under certain circumstances, recover their vital functions. Strictly speaking, the term "minimal life" would be more appropriate, in that the process of death had not yet begun. There is a wealth of anecdotal evidence bolstering the belief that apparent death can occur and result in the untimely burial of the unfortunate person. In days gone by, the horrifying prospect of being buried alive and waking up in the grave without any possibility of establishing a contact with the external world used to be a recurrent nightmare for many people. Doctors, in turn, were understandably concerned about the harmful consequences that not only the patients but also they themselves might suffer as a result of an untimely diagnosis of death. These are highlighted by the aftermath of the blunder made by the famous anatomist Vesalius, when he was in Spain at the Court of Philip II. While he was dissecting the body of a Spanish gentleman, he discovered to his unspeakable horror that the patient's heart was still beating. The fate of the gentleman has not been handed down to posterity, but that of Vesalius was grim. Brought to the Court of Inquisition, he was sentenced to death. Though the sentence was subsequently commuted to an expiatory journey to the Holy Land, his destiny was marked by that experience. During the voyage, the ship carrying him was wrecked by a storm, and Vesalius barely saved himself by swimming towards a remote Greek island, where he died a few days later.

Nowadays, cases of apparent death are virtually unheard of, thanks to the improved diagnostic abilities of doctors and to laws which demand a 24–48-h interval before the corpse can be buried or cremated. The term is, however, still used to refer to the condition of patients whose cardiac and respiratory activities are interrupted for a few minutes, but can be restored, if resuscitative efforts are begun immediately. It might be argued that some of the patients reported to have come back to life belonged to this category. Could it be that while in the state of apparent death they caught a glimpse of the afterlife? We must beware of not becoming entrapped by an imprecise use of words. If vital functions were reduced, but not abolished, and patients were not in fact dead, how could the door that leads to the afterworld remain ajar long enough to let in some light from it? Moreover, even conceding, for the sake of argument, that their condition allowed them to catch a glimpse of what lay beyond the door, they would have been unable to exploit this possibility, because the extreme slowing down of circulatory and respiratory functions associated with apparent death would have resulted in cerebral anoxia, i.e. a severe reduction of oxygen uptake by the brain. This condition is incompatible with the integrity of consciousness and, if it lasts longer than a few minutes, causes damage to the brain areas subserving memory functions. Thus the patients would be unable to perceive and keep a record of the experiences they were having in the afterworld or to retrieve them once they had returned to life.

In short, these patients never died and so never had the opportunity to know what happens in the afterlife. Even supposing that apparent death can be equated with true death, they would have been unable to register their experience, let alone retrieve it. What they claim to recall is but a confabulatory reconstruction of what they or the people reporting their story thought must happen in the afterworld.

RECOVERY FROM COMA

Coma is one of the most shocking manifestations of the breakdown of nervous functions. Unless the patient recovers within a few minutes, as occurs following epileptic fits or syncopal states, coma is a sign of severe cerebral disease. The patients who have lost consciousness are totally unresponsive to external stimuli and unaware of themselves and the environment. To a casual observer coma may present some superficial resemblance to sleep, but the difference is readily detected, because the sleeping subject can be promptly awakened by sensory stimulation, while the comatose patient is impervious to any kind of stimulus. The social consequences of coma are comparable to those of death, since both isolate the patients from any form of communication with their fellow men.

Understandably, this dramatic condition has a profound impact on relatives and friends, who perceive the patient's inability to maintain a communicative link with them as the end of his or her psychic presence. It is natural for them to believe that stimuli that are familiar and welcome to the subject will arouse his or her interest and stir emotional reactions that may help to bring him or her back into contact with the environment. This idea finds apparent support in the stories of patients who regain consciousness after hearing favourite songs or messages from loved persons. The auditory modality is ob-viously preferred, since it is assumed to be more viable in patients who keep their eyes closed. In a report of a successful attempt at reawakening a patient from coma in this way, an Italian newspaper summarized the cases published by the press over the last few years. A 9-year-old girl recovered from the coma, into which she had sunk following anaesthesia for a minor operation, on hearing her mother and favourite doll's voice. An 11-year-old boy, who was comatose for 2 months, regained consciousness and sang a few notes, while listening to the songs of his favourite singer. On his way home from the football ground where he had watched a soccer match, a 30-year-old man was involved in a car accident in which he suffered a head injury with a loss of consciousness. The patient recovered from coma when he heard the tape-recording of songs and cheers of the fans of his favourite team. A recent case, which got massive media coverage because of its obvious political implications, concerned a young supporter of the AC Milan football team, who awoke from a prolonged vegetative state on hearing the encouraging voice of his team's president. The all-important particular was that this president (Silvio Berlusconi) happened to be the leader of the opposition party and the proprietor of a number of private television stations. Unsurprisingly, he did not miss out on the opportunity to make numerous television appearances with the patient, the implicit message being that, if his thaumaturgic powers were such as to heal a man who trusted him, they could also be expected to be effective in the management of public affairs and the recovery of the sick Italian economy.[2]

Everybody rejoices at good news, especially when it reinforces our confidence in mechanisms we already believe in. This is true for the deep-rooted idea that the course of pathological events is sensitive to the influence of psychological factors. Generally speaking, it cannot be denied that there are several strands of evidence to support this assumption, which underpins the flourishing of psychosomatic medicine which investigates the relationship between psychic events and somatic diseases. Thus, it is little wonder that people have thought of songs and emotionally loaded messages as effective means of breaking through the curtain that isolates a comatose patient from the environment. Music and songs can do no harm and so there is no objection to their bedside use. But whether the rationale underlying this procedure and the evidence provided in its support meet the minimal requirements needed to recommend its application is quite another matter.

Perhaps the first point to make is that the media rarely give enough information on these events for us to formulate even an approximate judgement on their reliability. Too many important facts are left out, e.g. the severity of the coma, the level of recovery attained following treatment and its persistence over time. Even more crucially, we are rarely told anything of the professional competence of people who witnessed the awakening and whether they were in any way involved in the outcome of the trial. To understand the potential impact of these factors, consider the rigorous constraints set out in the double-blind paradigm that has become the gold standard for assessing the effectiveness of a new drug. By way of an example, doctors participating in the trial must not be informed whether the patients are taking the drug or an inert substance (placebo), because the mere knowledge that the patient is being treated with a drug has been repeatedly found to bias the observer's judgement, independently of his or her will (see Chapter 13).

Strict compliance with methodological constraints takes on an even greater importance if one considers that what we know about the mechanism of consciousness and its disruption contradicts the assumption that meaningful messages can influence the outcome of coma. Consciousness results from the integrated activity of two cerebral structures, the reticular formation, located deep within the brain, and the cortex, which covers its surface. Their activation is essential for the processing of sensory information. The stimuli gathered by peripheral receptors, located in the retina, inner ear, skin, muscles, etc., are transmitted to the cortical analyzers through pathways, which ascend in the white matter of the brainstem, make connections in the thalamus (a structure located deep in the hemisphere) and end up in sensory-specific cortical areas. Here a two-stage process takes place. In the first stage, the physical features of the object are analysed and combined to form a global percept. In the second stage, the perceptual output is compared with the memory traces that previous experiences with the same object have left in the brain. The whole process involves discrete, hierarchically organized areas and its outcome is stimulus recognition. There is, however, a second system which participates in the modulation of cortical activity, increasing the readiness of cortical neurons to respond to incoming stimuli. It involves the ascending reticular formation and its projections. The reticular formation is a network of neurons, extending in the brainstem from the caudal medulla to the mesencephalon, which receives input from the collaterals of the sensory pathways. Its upper part is connected with neuron populations of the thalamus that are called *non-specific* thalamic nuclei, to distinguish them from the nuclei which receive *specific* (i.e. visual, auditory, somatosensory) pathways. They in turn project to the whole cortex (Figure 6.1). Thus the cortex receives two types of input, one of which is transmitted by sensory pathways and the other by the non-specific system originating from the reticular formation. The latter has been found to be the source of synchronous cortical wave activity and to play a crucial role in sustaining vigilance and the fine-tuning of conscious states. In a way, it can be described as being involved in monitoring the tone of cortical neurons. Under physiological conditions, the reticular formation is active while we are awake and depressed while we sleep. Its pathological deactivation leaves the cortex unable to respond to stimuli of any kind and is the case of coma.

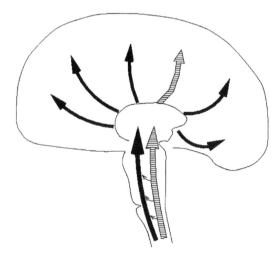

Figure 6.1   A schematic drawing of the lateral view of the brain. The pathway transmitting somatosensory information (striped arrows) ascends in the brainstem, makes connections in the thalamus and then projects to the parietal cortex. In the brainstem it sends collaterals to the ascending reticular formation (black arrows), which makes connections in non-specific thalamic nuclei and then projects to the whole cortex.

It follows that coma can result from damage to two distinct structures. There can be either diffuse cortical damage (cerebral anoxia, encephalitis, meningitis, etc.), which disrupts the processing of sensory input and makes consciousness similar to a blank blackboard where no trace is registered, or damage to the reticular formation, which interrupts the flow of input that maintains the tone of cortical neurons. The cause of reticular formation impairment may be a direct injury, compression by a hemispheric lesion bulging downwards or the depressant effects of drugs and toxic substances on its cell metabolism.

Like any other biological event, coma is not an all-or-nothing phenomenon, and different stages of severity can be distinguished in its evolution and regression. Clouding of consciousness and obtundation define increasing degrees of impaired alertness, revealed by the patients' delay and inaccuracy in answering basic questions and their tendency to fall asleep when left alone. At a deeper stage, they can only be roused by strong sensory or painful stimulation (*stupor*) or become totally unresponsive (*coma*) and lie with their eyes closed. Pupil and eye movements and breathing disorders are sensitive markers of the deepening of coma and must be careful monitored, because they indicate the progressive deterioration of brainstem activity. When bulbar centres are damaged, vital functions, such as respiration and circulation, fail and coma becomes irreversible unless artificial means are applied. This stage is known as *brain death*, to emphasize the fact that the patient has reached a point of no return, from where consciousness can no longer be regained, even though the peripheral organs are still functioning. Within days the circulatory system breaks down and the patient dies. The definition of brain death has recently assumed great importance and is subject to very strict rules, because it defines the interval in which organ transplantation can be successfully performed.

Recovery from coma also passes through distinct stages, which on the whole parallel those seen as it deepens. Of particular importance is the *persistent vegetative state*, in which patients are apparently awake, keep their eyes open and move them towards an unexpected stimulus, display normal sleep and wakefulness rhythms, but neither answer questions nor manifest any sign of psychic life either verbally or through facial expressions. Its pathological correlate is thought to be diffuse damage to the hemispheres and a relatively intact brainstem. The vegetative state may be a transient stage, through which the patient passes on the way to recovery from coma, but, if it lasts more than 2 weeks, it is associated with a poor outcome in terms of the restitution of conscious activity and often also of life. It is only at first glance that this condition can be mistaken with the *locked-in syndrome*, in which consciousness is intact, though the communication of its contents is prevented by the concomitant paresis of oral and limb movements.

The main determinant of coma prognosis is the nature and evolution of the underlying disease. Inoperable tumours have an intrinsic tendency to grow over time and are, therefore, associated with a progressive deterioration of function. Vascular and traumatic diseases, on the contrary, reach a plateau of severity in the early days, but, if this critical phase has passed, tend to improve. Other factors influencing the outcome of coma are the extent of damage and its localization with respect to the structures subserving vital functions. For instance, a lesion encroaching upon the brainstem, a small space where the centres controlling respiration, circulation, etc. are concentrated, portends more ominous consequences than a lesion of the same size located in a hemisphere. In the early days of disease, the effect of anatomical damage is further aggravated by transient phenomena that enlarge the area of dysfunction, such as oedema, penumbra and diaschisis. *Oedema* results from the leakage of plasma through the walls of capillaries. The swelling of the surrounding tissue extends the dysfunctional area beyond the boundaries of the lesion and may cause brain hernia, i.e. a protrusion of the expanding hemisphere. When downward herniation occurs, the outlook is particularly serious, because it results in brainstem compression and directly interferes with the activity of structures subserving consciousness. *Penumbra* is a term used to define the diminished blood supply in the area which lies at the periphery of an infarct. Insofar as its energy metabolism is depressed, but not abolished, the tissue, though functionally impaired, is potentially salvageable. *Diaschisis* refers to a loss of function in a cortical region due to a localized injury in another region with which it is connected. The lack of input from the damaged region results in hypometabolism of the disconnected region. In the early days of disease, the net result of all these phenomena is a clinical picture of a far greater severity than might be expected from the extension of anatomical damage. Their regression over time tends to tip the scales favourably with respect to the prognostic outcome. A positive factor is also the development of compensatory mechanisms, which shift functions originally performed by the injured neurons to the healthy tissue. They are, however, more involved in the regression of neurological and cognitive deficits than in the recovery of consciousness, since the structures that underpin it can be barely compensated.

The features of coma, particularly its severity and duration, have proved useful for predictions of outcome. A number of studies agree that, when loss of consciousness was short-lasting, recovery was the rule. In one study, when the period of coma lasted more than 6 h, 50% of the patients were dead at a 6-month follow-up and 35% of those who survived were in a vegetative state. In another study, none of the patients who were still in a vegetative state 1 month after the accident recovered physical or psychic independence in daily life. As with all biological phenomena, there are exceptions to the rule. Two patients have been reported who began to react to stimuli after being in a vegetative state for 8 months and 3 years, respectively. From then on they continued to improve and eventually regained the ability to read a newspaper, watch television and respond to questions promptly and correctly. These reports remind us that single cases of delayed restitution of function can occur, even if most experts would agree that, after the first 6 months of disease, there is little hope of improvement. It is against this background that the efficacy of stimulation techniques must be assessed. Some authors advocate the use of a massive sensory bombardment as a means of helping patient to awake from coma, on the assumption that it prevents sensory deprivation, encourages responsiveness to external input and monitors the cognitive status. The philosophy underlying this procedure is reminiscent of that recommending massages and passive exercise to prevent muscular atrophy in patients who cannot move their limbs, due to a paresis or bone fracture. There is, however, an important difference. In the latter case the treatment is aimed at remediating the muscular atrophy caused by the inactivity of a basically healthy limb, whereas in the comatose patient stimulation purports to improve the function of the diseased tissue. The rationale underlying this procedure is questionable. The patient's unresponsiveness is not a manifestation of laziness or ill will, but reflects the disruption of the biological mechanisms subserving vigilance and, in a sense, it must be respected. Luria warned against increasing the excitation of cells that are already in a state of impaired metabolism and whose recovery would benefit from rest. To suggest that it would be enough to trigger the firing of a cell assembly to ensure the recovery of its function seems rather an oversimplification, if one considers the complex interaction between the activating and inhibitory patterns of input that modulates nervous responses.

These theoretical considerations apart, the crucial point is that advocates of the "sensory bombardment" treatment have never provided empirical evidence that it improves coma evolution, beyond the level attained by spontaneous recovery. This brings us to a problem common to the assessment of every therapeutic proposal, namely, the need to demonstrate that the treated group fares better than a control group, matched for age, aetiology, severity of symptoms, and so forth. If the results of this comparison are not available, any claim about the improvement caused by the treatment is a matter of faith that must be evaluated with a healthy dose of scepticism. Regrettably, no systematic trial comparing the evolution of treated and untreated pa-tients has ever been carried out to verify whether sensory stimulation results in any significant improvement. The existing evidence is at best circumstantial, limited to single cases and lacking in detail.

Even more questionable is the idea that recovery of consciousness can be aided specifically by messages of a sentimental value for the patients, because they have the potential to capture their attention and to encourage them to react to the environment. Does this idea make sense? Let us consider the sequence of neurocognitive events supposedly triggered by Berlusconi's encouraging message. To begin with, its acoustic features must be processed by the auditory cortex and its output transmitted to Wer-nicke's area, where its linguistic content is decoded. To become meaningful and endowed with an emotional value, this information must activate the neural structures that mediate the retrieval of the general and personal memories from the sites where they are stored (who Berlusconi is, what Milan soccer team represents, etc.). However simple, such a performance demands sustained attention and involves the co-ordinated and interactive participation of the whole associative cortex. It is hard to see how this result could be achieved by a comatose patient, whose cortex is either directly damaged or deactivated by the lesion and does not respond even to strong sensory or painful stimuli. Nor is the issue solved by limiting the treatment to patients no longer in coma, but in a vegetative or simply stuporous state, because they too are unable to focus attention or engage them-selves in any prolonged mental activity. Another point to consider is that as the message is repeated it loses its novelty features and induces habituation, i.e. non-responsiveness, even in normal subjects. Hoping to obtain a lasting improvement in the patient's vigilance is like hoping to wake a person sleeping in an inner room of a castle by gently knocking on its external walls.

A sceptical evaluation of stimulation techniques does not mean that we must wait passively for the spontaneous evolution of coma, refraining from taking active therapeutic measures. Apart from the specific intervention required by the nature of disease, in the early days of coma we must keep the airways patent, assist respiration, support circulation, regulate the cardiac rate and rhythm and fight intervening infec-tions. Oedema is a deleterious, though transient, worsening factor, which can some-times be reduced by hyperosmolar agents and steroids. In short, our efforts should be directed towards treating the underlying disease rather than the coma *per se*. Only when improvement has reached a level that permits patients' co-operation can we attempt to rehabilitate cognitive skills. It is at this stage that rehabilitative techniques can take advantage of stimuli that arouse the patients' interest and activate their attentional resources.

NOTES

1. Luke (VII, 41–56) does report a resuscitation miracle, but it concerns a different person and is far less impressive. Jairus, a ruler of the synagogue, pleaded with Jesus to come to his house, because his 12-year-old daughter was dying. Jesus agreed, but had to delay his visit, because a woman who had been subject to bleeding for 12 years was beseeching his aid. While he was engaged with her, a man arrived and announced that Jairus' daughter was dead. Then Jesus went to Jairus' house and when he saw the girl, he said "She is not dead but asleep" and took her by the hand and said "My child, get up. Her spirit returned and at once she stood up." Clearly, the circumstances of this resuscitation do not dispel doubts about the real death of the girl.

2. A few irreverent souls argued that, given Berlusconi's well-known tendency not to stop speaking once he takes the floor, recovery from coma was the only way the patient could shut him up. Although one must be open-minded about these things, I would not think this likely in the case of a comatose patient.

Section 3

MYTHS ABOUT MEMORY AND CREATIVE THINKING

Elizabeth Loftus is known for reporting a series of experiments aimed at demonstrating the fallacy of eyewitness testimony (Loftus, 1996). In these experiments the participants, who were tested in absolutely normal circumstances, maintained that they remembered seeing something that they in fact never saw. Probably the most relevant experiment is that in which she cogently demonstrated that it was possible to dramatically modify the witness's recollection of an event by adding subtle information during questioning. Maybe we should be asked to "tell the untruth, a whole fabrication, and nothing but invention". These spurious recollections are by no means rare. We experience them frequently in our daily life. Sagan (1996) reminds us of the story of Ronald Reagan who "spent World War Two in Hollywood" and nevertheless during his presidential campaign "vividly described his own role in liberating Nazi concentration camp victims" (p. 132), borrowing several details from the black-and-white film with Don Ameche called *Wing and a Prayer*, directed by H. Hathaway in 1944, which must have had some impact on him when he was younger.

Several studies have been recently published providing strong evidence that false memories can be reliably induced using standard experimental procedures both in healthy volunteers (e.g. Payne et al., 1996) and amnesic patients (Schacter, Verfaellie and Pradere, 1996; Schacter, Verfaellie and Anes, 1997). Indeed, García Márquez (1994, p. xiii) reminded us that often "true memories seem like phantoms, while false memories are so convincing that they replace reality".

Of course, the false memory syndrome is not the only myth concerning memory. Just think how often you have seen serious textbooks reporting, as hard evidence, the alleged discovery that untrained flatworms can learn a task by eating other, trained, worms. In the second chapter dedicated to memory myths, we will discuss in some detail the issue of learning without effort.

Finally, we will be taken by Ken Gilhooly through the territory of creative thinking.

CHAPTER 7

Lie Down and Let Me Tell You About Your Childhood

MARYANNE GARRY, SUSAN FRAME and ELIZABETH F. LOFTUS

NOW.... LET ME TELL YOU ABOUT YOUR CHILDHOOD MEMORIES

INTRODUCTION

The present time might well be the time of personal entertainment technology; of realistic, interactive worlds available on demand. Nintendo is a necessity, virtual reality is looming on the horizon, and the *Star Trek* holodeck gives us a window into a possible future world not so far away. Did you go through childhood wanting to be a professional football player, a Jedi Knight or a rock star? Depending on what kind of technology you have access to, you can fire up your Nintendo, or put on your goggles and data gloves, and give Michael Jordan a go. As personal entertainment technology progresses, these kinds of pseudo-experiences promise to put a whole new twist on what we mean by "mind games". But in these last years, already, we have witnessed the disasters that result when some well-meaning professionals engage in their own mind games, deliberately digging into the dark recesses of human memories. Today, many families stand accused of perpetrating the most horrific, sustained sexual abuse on their children, who in turn repressed memories of the events, only to recover them years later. Recently we have learned all we need to create seemingly authentic experiences is a little imagination.

AUTOBIOGRAPHICAL MEMORY

What do we remember about our own life? This kind of memory is what cognitive psychologists call *autobiographical memory*. Why do we remember events from our own lives? That is a different question entirely. Neisser (1984) proposed that memory is not a way of faithfully recording life events so much as a means of capturing information about their continuing and constant aspects, such as people and relationships, a way of maintaining support for the sense-making processes that are the core of human experience.

Most adults do not recall specific memories earlier than about the age of 3, a deficit known as *childhood amnesia*. Although one study (Usher and Neisser, 1993) suggests that some information about the birth of a younger sibling or a hospitalization may be remembered if the event occurred before age 3, this relatively new finding has been subject to alternative interpretations (Loftus, 1993). As Neisser (1993) notes, young children have no sense of their own timeline; they do not sit around the sandbox and swap tales from their past, or wonder if Social Security will be around when they retire. A functional explanation of childhood amnesia may be that early childhood events tend not to be remembered because, from the child's perspective, they simply do not mean the same thing as they do in later years. We remember the essence of an event, not the specifics, and we cannot go back and get more detail than what we were aware of originally during the event.

Of course, in this chapter we are not talking about adults recalling their childhood sandbox conversations, or even the birth of their little brother. To some clinicians, an "especially significant event" might invoke a much stronger form of memory in which a unique detail-preserving mechanism squirrels away information about the event, storing it in the dark reaches of the unconscious. But cognitive psychologists have been asking if there truly are special detail-preserving mechanisms, if repression is possible; indeed, if the unconscious does anything particularly clever at all. Although we have seen great progress in our research, we have also been witness to the increasing political polarization among the psychological community. The political agenda has replaced the research programme, and too many people spin conclusions rather than draw them. The repressed memory controversy has caused chaos in the neat, orderly world of academic research. Fairly staid, academic conferences these days are a forum for mental health professionals who produce tapes of clients recovering memories *live on video*, and who decorate their poster presentations with photographs of abused children and their abusers-who-look-like-deceptively-like-nice-men ("and this man lived right around the corner from these girls, in a nice, white, upper middle-class neighbourhood").

But it gets worse, and more bizarre. The psychologist Cory Hammond has said that people sceptical of those with memories of, for example, satanic abuse are either un-trained, naive, or intellectualizing. And then, in a truly weird McCarthy-like twist, he revealed

> they're cult people themselves and I can assure that there are people who are in that position . . . There are people who are physicians, who are mental health professionals who are in the cults, who are raising trans-generational cults . . . (2 March 1991 hypnosis workshop at Parkwood Hospital, Atlanta)

Recently, Hammond (1997) spoke to a conference, and expanded upon his warnings with a clinical call-to-arms:

> In closing, I want to say that I'm an academic, and a clinician. I'm a full professor. But you know, it's been open season on clinicians with the false memory movement. I think it's time somebody called for an open season on academicians and researchers. In the United States and Canada in particular, things have become so extreme with academics supporting extreme false memory positions, so I think it's time for clinicians to begin bringing ethics charges for scientific malpractice against researchers, and journal editors – most of whom, I would point out, don't have malpractice coverage – when they grossly over-generalize, overstate, and selectively review research. And it's time to begin bringing ethics charges and bringing them before the APA, state associations, and any other organization's ethics committees that they belong to, and holding them accountable for their behavior, and some of the over-generalizations and extreme things that they say. False memory extremists must not dictate the directions of the field of clinical hypnosis.

Then he ends his speech by saying:

> You know, this week I've actually heard an academic make what I consider a very extreme statement: that all clinicians using hypnosis should videotape and save all their hypnosis sessions to document and control for bias. Well then, I think we ought to ask all researchers to videotape every experimental session, every pre- and post-hypnotic experimental session with every one of their subjects and save them for seven years to document the kind of uncontrolled bias that is occurring in the laboratory. Thank you.

And Herman and Harvey (1993) wonder if there's a "social backlash" against *clinicians*?

PSYCHOLOGY: THE DYSFUNCTIONAL FAMILY

Although psychologists argue in the literature, they can often find quite a big patch of common theoretical ground. The repressed memory fray tends to revolve around the primary disagreements over the nature and authenticity of recovered memories, but psy-chologists are also dealing with the realization that, among some of its branches, there is no common base of knowledge. With these trauma memory issues in particular, our different perspectives and belief systems sometimes render our discussions as effective as shouting at each other across a canyon. By and large, cognitive psychologists and clinicians have a fundamentally different approach to understanding memory. In some sense, we don't even speak the same language.

Take, for example, the concept of repression. Whether or not there is any evidence of repression in the literature depends completely on how it is defined. Just what is meant by repression runs along a very broad continuum. Erdelyi's (1990) historical review of Freud's use of "*repression*" shows him introducing it in 1895, and using different phrases synonomously over the years to describe the rejection of a thought from consciousness. In Erdelyi's analysis, Freud was not committed to the idea of repression as an inevitably unconscious process, and the concept retained an ambiguity that seems to persist. More recently, Crews (1995) has presented a damning (and witty) analysis of Freud and his influence today. Not one to mince words, Crews has argued that today's recovered memory therapy is nothing more than psychological snake oil, and today's Freudians are carrying on the work of an egomaniacal guru who tweaked his results to advance his career (Miller, 1995).

However, it almost does not matter what Freud actually thought about repression, so much as it matters how the term is used today. In the modern literature, repression runs the gamut from forgetting any part of an experience for any period of time to banishing repetitive traumatic events from awareness for decades. At the extreme end of the definition, Fredrickson (1992, p. 15) claims that people commonly block "frightening episodes of abuse, years of their life, or their entire childhood". Given this wide variance in an operational definition, it is virtually impossible for any one repression study to be equated with any other.

What a sorry state medicine would be in if physicians accepted the same imprecision in their diagnostic and treatment procedures. Suppose Dave makes an appointment to see his doctor, complaining of lethargy and dizziness. His physician runs a few tests and says, "Mr Harper, I think you have this brain *thing*, although I'm not sure where it is, or how far down it's buried. Call it a professional hunch based on my experience. Now, I'm pretty sure it's the root cause of your problems, and I'd like to operate, dig around a bit in your brain and see if I can't find it." Yet some clinicians seem unconcerned that the diagnostic criteria for repression are fast and loose, and instead appear to find vindication in its sheer popularity. It is as though the exponential rise in recovered memory cases validates the concept.

THE ACCURACY OF RECOVERED MEMORIES

It would be one thing if clients who recover memories of childhood abuse made a link between the past abuse and current dysfunction and then went on with their lives. Unfortunately, newly recovered memories have formed the basis for criminal and civil law suits. A frightening number of women (and some men) have left therapy bearing freshly retrieved memories of abuse. Sometimes they sue for damages instead of filing criminal complaints, because criminal charges are often too difficult to prove (Davis, 1991). Recently, some courts have rejected claims made with repressed memories, so some plaintiffs are claiming that they remembered being abused all along, and merely sharpened their memories in therapy. Even when people don't sue, they still believe, and often accuse, other people of perpetrating the most horrifying acts long ago. Now we have spawned a whole cottage industry in which there are support groups for the people who have recovered sexual abuse memories, support groups for the family members who have been accused, lawyers who specialize in recovered memory cases, and workshops for mental health professionals who do the uncovering. Accused parents, lawyers, judges and juries seek explanations from clinicians and researchers, but what they want to know most of all is: *are these memories authentic?*

One of the problems with gauging authenticity is that not all clinicians think it to be an important issue. Take, for instance, John Briere, a respected research clinician. Briere (1992) has treated numerous adults who were molested as children, and his opinion of recovered childhood trauma memories is as follows: "It is my clinical impression that these memories are relatively accurate" (Ritter, 1991, p. A10). To be fair, Briere has since retreated a bit from his earlier position. Recently he described recovered memory therapy as a kind of mental liposuction and said "it was a bad idea, bad therapy and I don't recommend it" (1998). Some clinicians do attempt to corroborate trauma memories, and one of the most frequently cited studies was done by Herman and Schatzow (1987). They claimed that about 75% of women involved in therapy groups were able to find some confirmation of the sexual abuse from another source. However, confirmation was not made independently, and the published paper does not say whether those labelled as having severe memory deficits were ever able to find corroborating evidence. Furthermore, the corroboration criteria were never outlined in the paper; Herman and Schatzow never examined the corroborating evidence, relying instead on each woman's description of that evidence, so we do not really know what corroboration meant for the purposes of this study. Finally, the cases that Herman and Schatzow describe in some detail in their paper aren't really cases at all. They are composite cases; a kind of impressionistic representation of data. They are the psychological equivalent of an ideal gas.

Linda Williams is another researcher whose 1994 study is frequently used as evidence of repression. She interviewed women who, 17 years earlier, had been taken to a hospital for examination and treatment following a sexual assault. At the time, these women were between infancy and 12 years old. Williams showed that 38% of the adult women did not recall the target abuse episode when interviewed, or at least they chose not to report it. What is even more interesting about this study is how it has taken on almost mythical status in the clinical community. For a few years before it was even published in a refereed scientific journal, it was cited and miscited and misrepresented. Williams herself was quite careful and straightforward in stating her results, simply noting that some of the women did not recall their childhood sexual abuse (CSA) experiences. But others were not so careful. Wylie (1993), for instance, said that 38% of the women in Linda Williams's study "reported they had not been abused" (pp. 42–43). Terr (1994) went even further, saying that the Williams study showed either repression or some kind of defensive forgetting. But what does the Williams study actually demonstrate? Repression? Amnesia? Defensive forgetting? There's no need to dress up an utterly common phenomenon in fancy clothes; perhaps the simplest answer is the best – they just do not remember.

THE CREATION OF FALSE MEMORIES

As much as cognitive psychologists debate the creation of false memories of CSA, and argue about the theoretical underpinnings of the slippery concepts of repression and recovered memory, in our heart we like to do experiments. The venerable tradition of the scientific method is how we approach a problem. Of course, we cannot simulate child abuse, nor suggest to subjects that they are repressing memories. However, we can talk about some traumatic situations. Ultimately, we can make memories.

Since the mid-1970s at least, investigations have been done into the creation of false memories through exposure to misleading post-event information. Now, nearly two decades later, hundreds of studies support a high degree of memory distortion. People have remembered seeing non-existent small objects, large objects, and even mustachioed men (Loftus and Ketcham, 1991). This new information often becomes part of a person's memory, riddling it with distortions. Understanding how we can recall seeing things that never were is central to understanding how some people can remember experiencing things they never did. However, critics often charge that laboratory research on memory distortion only changes trivial details (Darton, 1991; Herman and Harvey, 1993). There is no relevant evidence, they allege, that you can tinker with memories of real traumatic events or that you can inject whole memories of trauma into the mind if it never happened.

More often than not, proponents of special trauma memory mechanisms believe that these events are virtually branded on the brain; for example, ''traumatic events create lasting visual images . . . burned-in visual impressions'' (Terr, 1988, p. 103); ''memory imprints are indelible, they do not erase'' (Kantor, 1980, p. 1963). But there are myriad reasons to believe that there is no privileged class of memories. Rather, memory is malleable even for life's most traumatic experiences. As the singer-songwriter Jackson Browne wrote, ''While the future's there for anyone to change, Still you know it seems, it would be easier sometimes to change the past.''

Case reports provide unusually dramatic evidence that a traumatic event itself was actually experienced and yet the memory radically changed.

Let us consider two such examples. The first comes from Robert Caro's 1990 book on Lyndon Johnson (Caro, 1990). Caro describes how LBJ's accounts of action in World War II grew more incredible over time, noting that ''always the details became richer, more vivid'' as time went by (Caro, 1990, p. 48). Now, anyone with a relative who fought in a war knows that war stories can be like fish stories, getting larger than life over the years. However, Caro says that Johnson's war stories were beyond simple exaggeration; they were outright lies, but he believed them, and repeated them over and over – even embellishing his lies – even after the lies were detected. ''But most significant of all was Lyndon Johnson's own attitude toward his war story: he was coming to believe that it was true'' (Caro, 1990, p. 51). For instance, when Johnson was awarded the Silver Star for patently political reasons, he said publicly that he would never wear it, because he did not deserve it. In a letter refusing the medal, he said that his service was very brief, and did not compare to what other men did and the sacrifices other men made. But he never sent the letter; he simply filed it away. In the end, Johnson received the Silver Star in a public ceremony; not once, but a few times, each time as though he were receiving the honour for the first time. But it did not stop there: he began wearing a smaller version of the medal on his lapel, and began referring to it in his speeches. And then, astonishingly, Johnson began to believe that he deserved much more than the Silver Star, and began to complain that he had ''only got the Silver Star'' (Caro, 1990, p. 52).

Some may question the value of this example by charging that perhaps Johnson didn't believe what he was saying, and thus, Caro describes not a distortion of autobiographical memory, but nothing more interesting than a politician's outright lies. The second example describes a false memory that developed with no apparent reason to lie. It involves the political cartoonist Garry Trudeau and his own Vietnam draft experiences.

Shortly after the inconsistencies in President Clinton's draft saga caused a stir in the press, Trudeau wrote two letters to the *New York Times* Op-Ed page. In the first letter, Trudeau describes his recollection of drawing a low number in the draft lottery (Trudeau, 1992a). He describes his original student deferment status, hours of emotional phone calls with friends and family that night, and the steps he took to obtain another deferment. He applied at the National Guard, and was interviewed at his local draft board ("for which I received a memorable haircut"). He eventually went home, and his physician father diagnosed evidence of an ulcer, sent the film to a New Hampshire physician, and obtained a permanent deferment. At the bottom of the letter Trudeau wrote, "This account was prepared without benefit of consultation of existing records."

For the second letter, Trudeau sought external means of corroborating his memory of the draft, which he noted had been "recounted in unvarying language for more than 20 years" (Trudeau, 1990b). After examining his records and talking with relatives, Trudeau was in for a surprise. He discovered that his original student deferment lasted 1 year, not 3; he did not speak to any friends or relatives on the night of the lottery. In fact, he now thinks he went out for beers. Trudeau also misremembered (by several months) when he applied to the National Guard, and to how many units he applied. He never got his memorable haircut. Finally, Trudeau was not a resident of New Hampshire, and by law was not eligible to be examined by a physician there. He says, "I must have known a resident who was willing to lend me his address."

Anecdotes are interesting in their own right, but scientists prefer more rigorous, empirical investigations of evidence of flaws in personally experienced traumatic memories. For example, one study examined people's recollections of how they heard the news of the 1986 explosion of the space shuttle Challenger (Neisser and Harsch, 1992). These subjects were questioned on the morning after the explosion, and again nearly 3 years later. Most participants described their memories as "vivid", but none of them was entirely correct and over a third were extremely inaccurate. For example, one subject actually was on the telephone having a business discussion when her best friend interrupted the call with the news. Three years later she remembered that she heard the news in class, and at first thought it was a joke. She later walked into a television lounge and saw the news, and then reacted to the disaster.

These anecdotes and experimental examples suggest that false memories of traumatic events can be created, and details of genuinely experienced traumatic events can change over time. Drawing on what appears to be this sort of naturally occurring phenomenon, it seems the logical next step was to simulate this kind of memory-making in the psychology laboratory.

MYTHICAL MEMORIES IN THE LABORATORY

Can false traumatic memories be created out of mere suggestion? Recent scientific evidence suggests that they can. Loftus and Pickrell (1995) described how false childhood memories could be created by using close relatives as the source of both true and false suggestions. Subjects were asked to recall events that were described by the relative. Three of the events were true, but one was false. The false event was always about the subject getting lost in a shopping mall or other public place at the age of 5, crying, being found and helped by an elderly woman, and reunited with the family. They read the suggested events in booklets, wrote down what they remembered, and were interviewed twice, with a week or two between interviews. About a quarter of the subjects (29%) remembered at least some of the suggested false events. Here is just one example, of a woman who came to believe that she had been lost at the Hillsdale shopping mall. During the second interview, she said:

> I vaguely, vague, I mean this is very vague, remember the lady helping me and Tim and my mom doing something else, but I don't remember crying. I mean I can remember a hundred times crying . . . I just remember bits and pieces of it. I remember being with the lady. I remember going shopping. I don't think I, I don't remember the sunglasses part.

After she was debriefed, the memory still persisted a bit: "I totally remember walking around in those dressing rooms and my mom not being in the section she said she'd be in. You know what I mean?"

Loftus and Pickrell (1995) rightfully note that this study does not speak to the prevalence of false autobiographical memories in the population, but it is an existence of proof showing that false, mildly traumatic memories can be created. Hyman, Husband and Billings (1995) have demonstrated similar results with events that were far more unusual. By the end of their three-interview procedure, 25% of subjects remembered a childhood event in which they were running around at a wedding reception and accidentally spilled a punchbowl on the parents of the bride.

Pezdek, Finger and Hodge (1997) question the "appropriateness" of Loftus and Pickrell's (1995) generalizing their findings to situations in which adults recover memories of childhood sexual abuse (p. 441). In their view, being lost in a shopping mall is quite a plausible event. On the other hand, childhood sexual abuse is not. Their hypothesis was that it should be easier to implant a false memory of a plausible event than one of a less plausible one. To support their claim, they conducted two experiments in which they varied plausibility and script knowledge. In the first event, Catholic and Jewish high-school students were read descriptions of some true and some false events that purportedly happened when they were 8 years old. One of the false events was a Catholic ritual (Communion), and the other was a Jewish ritual (Shabbot). Pezdek et al. predicted that Jewish subjects would be less likely to remember Communion, and Catholic subjects would be less likely to remember participating in Shabbot prayers. About 22% of subjects "recalled" one false event, a figure in line with Loftus and Pickrell's results. Unsurprisingly, Pezdek et al.'s subjects were far more likely to "recall" the plausible event than the less plausible event.

How should we make sense of these results? Pezdek, Finger and Hodge (1997) would have us believe that subjects were unable to generate enough information about the less plausible event to have it seem real. Thus they were unable to falsely recall the event. Are there other reasons why they might not have falsely remembered? A thought experiment might help us at this point.

Suppose we take a group of New Zealand high-school students and a group of US high-school students, and suggest to them some true and false events that purportedly happened when they were 8 years old. Both false events have to do with Christmas celebrations. One false event describes a northern hemisphere winter ritual, making a snowman, and the other false event describes a southern hemisphere summer ritual, having a barbecue on the beach. Now suppose that 25% of the Americans falsely recall that when they were making the snowman's nose, the carrot poked them in the eye and they had to go to the hospital. Meanwhile, in New Zealand, 25% of our subjects falsely remember tossing a frisbee on the beach, knocking over the flaming barbecue on their leg, and having to go to the hospital. Nobody in either group remembers the event from the opposite hemisphere. These results would not be surprising. Our American subjects can reject the idea of romping on the beach at Christmastime. Similarly, our New Zealand subjects can dismiss the notion of making a snowman, simply because there are no snowmen around during New Zealand's warm Christmases. But false memories can be created precisely because they are not entirely false. They are made up of some true things and some false things combined together to make a false event. They are not spun out of whole cloth so much as woven from the idiosyncracies of our lives. So our New Zealand subjects find no truth at all in the notion of a white Christmas, let alone making a snowman. In other words, Pezdek, Finger and Hodge (1997) have succeeded only in demonstrating that it's hard to get an apple to remember being an orange.

In a second experiment, they used the Loftus and Pickrell (1995) procedure to try and induce memories of two other false events: the plausible "getting lost in the shopping mall", and a less plausible invasive painful procedure, a rectal enema. Pezdek, Finger and Hodge (1997) explained their selection of the enema event by asserting that "like sexual abuse, being given a rectal enema is shameful and embarrassing and involves discomfort in a private part of the body" (p. 439). Three out of 18 subjects remembered having been lost, but none remembered the enema. By analogy, Pezdek, Finger and Hodge argue that their results support the idea that false memories of sexual abuse would be difficult to implant because sexual abuse is implausible, shameful, embarrassing and uncomfortable. But let us look at this analogy more closely.

Is CSA really all that implausible? Krivacska (1993) notes that child sexual abuse prevention (CSAP) programmes have mushroomed in North America since the mid-1980s. Children as young as 2 or 3 learn the difference between a "good touch" and a "bad touch". Meanwhile, parents see photos of missing children on milk cartons, and the whole family can tune into any talk show and hear yet another presentation of the prevalence of CSA. After decades of ignoring CSA, it is good that we are finally dealing with the horrors of it. But in the meantime, have we swung too far the other way, so that we now think every man in the park is a child molester, and every male teacher is a sex offender? Such a phenomenon may be nothing more than an expression of Tverskey and Kahneman's (1973) idea of cognitive availability, in that when we talk about CSA and think about CSA and wonder about CSA, we think it is more likely to happen. We think CSA is more plausible.

Is CSA shameful, embarrassing and uncomfortable? Some child psychologists who work with sexually abused children say that because sexual acts often feel good, they must deal with children who masturbate or engage other children in an effort to try and duplicate the good feeling (Isherwood, personal communication). Moreover, shame and embarrassment may well come later, as the child matures and begins to comprehend the abuse in many different ways. So, as horrific as it is, CSA may not be a physically unpleasant experience.

To sum up, the generalization of Pezdek, Finger and Hodge (1997) is only as strong as the similarity between an enema and CSA. But there is no necessary parallel between these two events, no definitive shared set of features. Perhaps the results of Pezdek, Finger and Hodge tell us that they're not very good at implanting false memories.

In more recent research, we have developed a far less laborious procedure, in which we rely on the power of imagination to increase confidence that specific childhood events actually happened (Garry *et al.*, 1996; Garry, Manning and Loftus, 1997). The basic procedure uses a three-stage, pretest/post-test design.

First, we pretest subjects on how confident they were that a number of childhood events happened on them before the age of 10. This "Life Events Inventory" asked subjects to consider how certain they were that each event (or a very similar one) had or had not happened to them before the age of 10 (e.g. "Broke a window with your hand", or "Got in trouble for cutting a playmate's hair", with anchors "1 = definitely did not happen" and "8 = definitely did happen"). They responded by circling the appropriate point on an 8-point scale. In the second stage, weeks later, we asked them to imagine some of those events, for a seemingly unrelated project. For instance, one target involves playing in the house and breaking a window. For that event, subjects are instructed to

> Imagine that it's after school and you are at playing in the house. You hear a strange noise outside, so you run to the window to see what made the noise. As you are running, your feet catch on something and you trip and fall. As you're falling you reach out to catch yourself and your hand goes through the window. As the window breaks you get cut and there's some blood.

Sometimes subjects write down what they imagine, and sometimes they merely imagine. In the third stage (either later that session after a filler task, or a week later), we gather new confidence measures. Figure 7.1 shows the typical result: we find that subjects consistently become more confident that imagined events actually happened to them before age 10.

In more recent research, we ask people to imagine the event happening to *other* people. Still, they become more confident that the event happened to *them*, not to the other person. This increased confidence – which we call *imagination inflation* – occurs when the subjects closely identify with the other protagonist, and even when they don't.

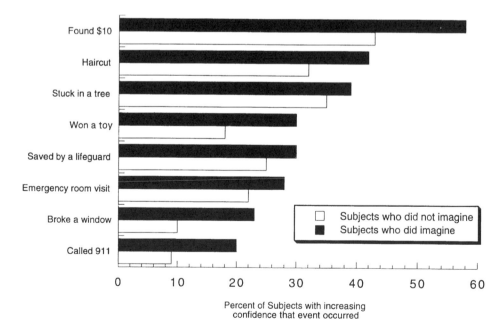

Figure 7.1   Imagination inflation by event.

For example, here is what one subject wrote about when asked to imagine someone other than herself getting in trouble for cutting a playmate's hair:

> Miss Piggy, Miss Horsey and Mrs Horsey were at playgroup, where you tell the class what you want to be when you grow up. Miss Piggy said she wanted to be a hairdresser, so cut off Miss Horsey's mane in front of everyone in playgroup. Mrs Horsey, Miss Horsey's mum was so upset she called the hair police, who gave Miss Horsey immediate extensions. Miss Piggy was charged with misuse of scissors and intent to embarrass.

Put another way, this more recent research suggests that even if you imagine Miss Piggy getting in trouble for cutting Miss Horsey's hair, you might still become more confident that you got in trouble for cutting a childhood playmate's hair. In short, our participants were easily led, by the most innocuous of procedures, to become more confident that childhood events they imagined actually happened.

But surely a simple, one-time imagination or imagination/writing task is nowhere near as powerful as the extended, repeated, deliberate exercises we might imagine to occur between some clients and clinicians. It is commonly acknowledged that much of the information in human conversation is non-verbal. Glances, gestures and facial expressions all serve as powerful sources of information in addition to the literal content of the written or spoken words. Investigating the power of a more authentic setting is what Hembrooke and Ceci (1997) had in mind when they created a long-term supportive environment in which subjects with a history of recurring physical pain could try to remember the child-hood event that had manifested itself as their pain.

Like Loftus and Pickrell (1995), and Garry et al. (1996), Hembrooke and Ceci (1997) worked with false childhood memories. But instead of suggesting that a specific, traumatic childhood event had occurred – indeed, without even mentioning a specific childhood event – participants were asked to remember a certain kind of episode, relying on informa-tion from their own idiosyncratic experiences and imaginings. To help them remember, participants used a variety of techniques, such as imaging, journalling, and self-suggestion. Participants also attended "support groups" populated with confederates. After 6 weeks, five (half) of the participants had developed a total of seven "memories", only two of which were corroborated by their parents. Of the remaining five memories, four were remembered by subjects who had been led to believe that their ongoing headaches might be traced to some early head injury (more specifically, to the left side of their head). The fifth memory was in line with the suggestion that chronic adulthood kidney dysfunction may be caused by difficult childhood toilet training.

Hembrooke and Ceci noted that where other research has succeeded in implanting an entire specific event, the important contribution of their study is that

> the participants actually develop the entire memory themselves. From beginning to end, all the details are the product of the participant's imagination, history and previous experiences, prompted only by the global suggestion.

CONCLUSION

It comes down to this: cognitive psychologists who question the idea of repressed and recovered memories want some evidence. What we are getting instead is the duck test. The duck test became popular during the Reagan–Bush era in response to the euphemistic way in which new taxes were labelled "revenue enhancers". "If it looks like a duck, and quacks like a duck, it's a duck," charged the critics, who insisted a tax by any other name was just as ugly. Unfortunately, death and taxes remain the only certainties in life. We cannot add memories to that list, and we can't use the same standard of proof. Still, the legions of women who remember too much (and the therapists who make them) claim that if it *feels* like a real memory and *sounds* like a real memory, it's a real memory.

There is one difference, however, between saying a thing is a duck and saying, without hesitation, that a recovered memory is accurate: ducks can be verified. At present, we have no good way to tell if memories are real unless we have corroborating data. This is, of course, the reason why we do laboratory experiments, so that we have external means of verifying a memory, and psychologists have to approach the issue of authenticity by developing multiple hypotheses about where the memories might have come from.

And what is meant by this slippery term repression? By repression do we mean that an experience is wholly shrouded in protective cloth and buried until some time later, when together the therapist and client roll the stone away? Or at the other end of the spectrum, does it mean simply, "I forgot"? The comedian Steve Martin was obviously ahead of his time when he suggested years ago a surefire defence for committing crimes. Just tell them, "I forgot!" he said. "I forgot murder was a capital offense," or "I forgot to pay my taxes!" By some definitions, the defence would be a legitimate instance of repression, and why not? Isn't one way of conceptualizing the phenomenon of "forgetting" to think of it as "delayed discovery?" Nearly twenty years ago, this Steve Martin gag was outrageously funny; but in the 1990s, as life imitates art, it is just sad.

Today we already have very simple, low-technology methods of creating false but seemingly authentic experiences. Yet we are increasingly fascinated with the hype of virtual reality, and the promise that today's Game Boys and *Star Trek* episodes are glimpses into a world not so far away when every home has a holodeck. In that future, three-dimensional, interactive and eerily real virtual worlds will be available on command. And if our basketball fan finds a game of one-on-one with Michael Jordan's a little too frightening, well, that's what the stop button is for. Nobody gets hurt in the holodeck, but imagining too much can do a lot of harm.

ACKNOWLEDGEMENTS

Our thanks to Leonard Newman, University of Illinois at Chicago, for telling us about Robert Caro's book.

CHAPTER 8

Repetita (non) Iuvant

ROBERT H. LOGIE AND SERGIO DELLA SALA

According to Greek mythology, Mnemosyne was the mother of all the Muses, *id est* (*i.e.* – that is) the Arts. Mnemosyne also gave her name to mnemonics and to memory, in recognition that human arts and skills arise from learning and retrieval from memory. Memory acquires and retains skills such as riding a bicycle, typing, and reading music; it also acquires and retains knowledge and experiences during our lifetime. The knowledge might be fact or fantasy and it is intriguing how memory, which owes its name to Greek mythology, can itself be peppered with myths as to its own nature and function. As with many human experiences, there are popular misconceptions about memory. These misconceptions arise largely because each of us feels that we have insight into how our own mind works. This makes the study of memory difficult – the researchers have their own misconceptions about memory, and the skill lies in separating a personal impression from the findings of impartial and thorough investigation. Many popular views are seen as either true or false, whereas science is largely probabilistic, *id est* what is likely to be true or likely to be false based on available systematic evidence. Moreover, the probabilistic conclusions of science often do not match our intuitive views, making the science difficult to accept. Memory is no exception. However, the reality of science can often be just as intriguing as human intuition, once it frees itself from the quagmire of popular myths. This is not to say that intuition cannot be used to generate questions. It is more that personal experience and observation should not be taken as fact, but as the start of an investigation that capitalizes on the availability of scientific methods. In doing so we are in a better position to avoid personal biases, mistaken beliefs and prejudices, or the influence of the illusions of introspection. From Chapter 7, it is clear that we can be convinced of the reality of events that are merely implanted in our memory. There are other popular myths about memory, some of which will be addressed in this chapter. For example, does repetition lead to learning? The answer is, no and yes. Can we learn while asleep? The answer is assuredly not. Can we learn without being aware of learning? Yes – sort of, but it will not help much in learning a new language or the methods of science.

MEMORY ESCHEWS REPEATED EVENTS

Crawl through the web of memories in your mind and try to recall the appearance of an everyday object such as a stamp, a coin, the style of spectacle frame of people you know well, or frequency of your favourite radio channel. Despite having seen these items many thousands of times in our lives, few people can recall such details. *Exempli gratia* (e.g. – for example) how many UK readers could recall the number of sides or the direction of the queen's gaze on a 50-pence piece (which is correct in Figure 8.1), and how many US readers could recall the position of E *Pluribus Unum* (Unity from a Multitude) on a one-cent coin (Figure 8.2)?

It is a popular myth that repeated experience leads to learning, but systematic investigations have shown that this is simply not the case. In 1979 two American researchers asked US citizens to draw a one-cent coin from memory or to recognize which of several drawings showed the correct features such as E *Pluribus Unum* in the correct positions on the coin (Nickerson and Adams, 1979). Surprisingly few people could do so with any accuracy, demonstrating that even an item that has been used many thousands of times in the lifetime of the individuals concerned is not stored accurately in their memory. One of the most common mistakes was in the direction of Lincoln's gaze on the coin (Rubin

Figure 8.1   Two views of a UK 50-pence piece. Which is correct?

Figure 8.2   The US one-cent piece showing the correct position of E *Pluribus Unum*.

Figure 8.3   The US one-cent piece. Which is the correct direction of gaze for Lincoln?

and Kontis, 1983) – Lincoln's head faces to the right (Figure 8.3). Similar confusions about directions of gaze have been shown for the Queen's head on UK coins (*exempli gratia* Jones, 1990; Richardson, 1992).

To show that this failing of memory is not peculiar to coins, in 1980 Debra Bekerian and Alan Baddeley investigated memory for radio frequencies. This experiment was carried out at a time when the BBC was changing the frequencies for its radio broadcasts, and for several months leading up to the change it mounted a saturation advertising campaign including jingles and repeated broadcasts informing listeners about the new frequencies. Bekerian and Baddeley recruited a group of volunteers who spent much of their time at home with the radio tuned in to their favourite station. On the basis of information from the BBC, these volunteers would have heard the new frequencies several hundreds of times in the lead-up to the day of the change-over. Bekerian and Baddeley found that their volunteers had a reasonable idea of when the change was due to take place, but fewer than 3 in 10 people had a clue as to what the new frequencies were going to be. Again, repeated exposure, even several hundred times over, clearly does not lead to learning.

Finally, Morton (1967) reported an experiment with memory for the details of the telephone dial that was in common use in the UK at the time. The circular dial showed both letters and numbers, and over 200 volunteers were asked to recall the position of the letters. Not one of these individuals succeeded in doing so, including some experienced users of the telephone who frequently used the letters for calls.

One possible explanation for this poor memory is that people simply do not attend to the details of a coin or ignore repetitive and tedious radio messages. It is sufficient to discriminate between different types of coin and this can be done in most cases simply by noting its colour or shape. It was sufficient to know when the radio frequencies were being changed, and to re-tune by trial and error or by reference to the newspapers on the day. Few people, other than numismatists or radio enthusiasts, would examine the details closely.

In order to test this idea, in an experiment of our own, we sought the co-operation of members of an Episcopal church who regularly attend services at which elements of the liturgy are recited by all members of the congregation from the service book. One particular element of the service involves repeating in English the *Credo* (I believe).[2] This is repeated once in most services, and regular participants in the service would recite the *Credo* at least once a week, leading to, in many cases, several hundreds, and for older members, several thousand repetitions in their lives. It is common for the *Credo* to be read from the service book rather than recited from memory, and the congregation recites this together, so words forgotten by one individual might be recalled by a neighbour or vice versa – another example of E *Pluribus Unum*. We asked 10 members of one congregation individually to recall from memory the second sentence of the Nicene Creed which is a regular feature of the Sunday morning service. None of the attempted recalls took place in the church building. The ages of the members ranged from 44 to 59 (nine male, one female) and the number of repetitions of the Nicene Creed estimated by the participants ranged from 500 to 1200. None of the participants, including two clergymen, could recall the second sentence *verbatim* (word for word). Six could recall some of the first few words of the first sentence, and two others also recalled the second half of the first sentence but could go no further. One recalled a few of the words from the target (second) sentence, but not in the correct order. One could not recall more than the first four words in English, but could recall a few of the second-sentence words in Latin which he had regularly sung as a member of the choir in other parts of the service. In *nuce* (in essence or summarizing), repetition, even several hundreds of times, does not guarantee subsequent recall of the repeated material.

CONDITIONING MEMORY

Are there any circumstances under which repeated exposure works, *exempli gratia* the techniques used to train animals, often referred to as conditioning – a form of learning that also affects human beings? The person attributed with the discovery of so-called classical conditioning was a Russian physiologist named Ivan Pavlov, who was investigating the digestive system in dogs. He noticed that every time the dog saw or smelled meat, it began to salivate. On several occasions, the presentation of the meat was preceded by a bell, and eventually, presentation of the bell alone (without the food) resulted in salivation.[3] Similar effects can be demonstrated in human beings, such as the fear response. People exposed to frightening experiences can show a fear response when they encounter objects that were present at the time. *Exempli gratia*, people who witness shootings might subsequently respond with terror at the sight of toy guns that previously were viewed as children's playthings. While, fortunately, few people have such extreme experiences, unpleasant or frightening experiences can lead to fears carried into adulthood and throughout life. This may be the cause of many phobias, such as fear of snakes, sharp objects or hypodermic needles. *Idem* (likewise or similarly), pleasant experiences can give rise to happiness or excitement when objects or events are encountered that happened to occur at the time of the original experience. This latter fact has been used on occasion to treat phobias, by, for example, associating a pleasurable experience, relaxation, soothing music, a favourite food *et cetera* (etc. – and other things) with the gradual introduction of a feared object. In the case of snake phobias, the relaxing environment would first be accompanied by words related to snakes such as slithery, reptile, scaly, slimy, python, rattle, poison, serpent *et cetera*. Later there would be the pictures of snakes and then snakes in glass tanks, followed eventually by snakes sliding over the sufferer's arm. Note that the response will vary greatly from one individual to another. For some, the appearance of a snake evokes excitement, interest and perhaps a career in ophiology. There are at least two important points here. One is that the response is automatic – normally, we do not consciously invoke a fear response such as sweating palms, increase in breathing and irregularity in heart rate. The second is whether the learning requires conscious effort: is this a form of automatic learning through repetition? We can address the second point with reference to the first. *Id est*, the kind of learning that occurs cannot result in the acquisition of a new language (Chomsky, 1959; Green, 1975; Skinner, 1957) or a knowledge of psychology. It is an association between an event or object and an automatic response over which we have little, if any, conscious control. Experiences that do not require conscious effort can result in learning, but the learning is of a particular kind, namely that an automatic behaviour pattern is prompted by a previously unrelated event or object. One view of this is that the brain automatically monitors contingencies, and when a light, a bell, a toy gun or a spider appears there is an automatic expectation that some unpleasant experience will follow. In contrast, the appearance of an ice cream, a cheque or a holiday brochure gives rise to expectations of a forthcoming pleasant experience. Again, these emotional responses or mood states result from an automatic form of learning, and give rise to fear, sadness, happiness or ecstasy without a conscious decision about whether or not these are the appropriate emotional responses.

The phenomenon of learning by association, or conditioning as it is referred to within psychology, applies not only to seemingly irrational fears or simple pleasures. Daily in Western industrialized nations we are bombarded by advertisements for products or politics that bamboozle a credulous public. This attempt to deceive relies not just on a naive audience, but on a fundamental characteristic of human beings to learn associations between features of the environment that occur together, such as the freshness of a waterfall and a particular brand of toothpaste, the company of beautiful people and expensive cars, or a healthy lifestyle and brands of breakfast cereal (Gorn, 1982; Stuart, Shimp and Engle, 1987).

SCIENCE DEBUNKS SLEEP LEARNING

Another form of putative learning without awareness has been explored using so-called subliminal learning or by exploiting the largely mythical capacity for learning while asleep. On these points the British Psychological Society (1992) commissioned a report which drew the very firm conclusion that subliminal messages have a negligible effect on learning or on behaviour: "There is no evidence that people can learn while asleep. Learning can only occur if the sleeping person is partly awakened by the message." A comprehensive report of research on sleep learning, sometimes referred to as hypnopaedia, is contained in an edited collection by Rubin (1968). There are several reports of such research, primarily from the former USSR; for a review on the practice of hypnopaedia in the USSR, see Bliznitchenko (1968). However, attempts to replicate the results have largely failed when studies have included appropriate experimental controls and appropriate measures of whether or not the subjects were actually asleep during the crucial learning phase. Simon and Emmons (1955) provide a critical review of the main studies which were being used at that time as evidence for hypnopaedia. Of 10 studies that they considered, five were student thesis projects at BSc or MSc level, two were personal communications from the authors, and only the remaining three were formally published in sufficient detail to allow an evaluation. In none of the published studies did the researchers have an adequate measure of sleep, in one case giving no indication of how sleep was measured (LeShan, 1942), and in the other cases relying on observation as to whether or not the subjects were "restless during the night" (Leuba and Bateman, 1952) or whether the subject reported that they had awakened during the night (Fox and Robbins, 1952).

Despite the serious methodological problems with studies reporting successful hypnopaedia in the first half of the century (Simon and Emmons, 1955) and more recently (Aarons, 1977; Eich, 1990), the first report (Druckman and Swets, 1988) of the USA Committee on Techniques for the Enhancement of Human Performance did not dismiss the possibility of learning while asleep, even if there was no strong evidence in its favour. However, in later, better conducted studies the results have been almost invariably negative. *Exempli gratia*, Wood et al. (*et alia* – and others) (1992) examined learning during sleep of word pairs such as tortoise–hare in which one of the words had at least two legitimate forms of spelling (hare–hair). Notably, one form of the word (hair) is more common in everyday use than is the other (hare). Volunteer participants in these experiments were given these pairs either while asleep or while awake, with the pairs repeated five times.

Two minutes later the participants were first tested (the sleeping participants were awakened) on their ability to recall all the words that had been presented. Then they were shown a number of words, some of which had been presented and some of which had not, and given the task of identifying which words had been presented. Finally, they were asked to spell words that had been presented. Wood et al. found that subjects who were asleep during presentation showed no evidence of learning, and, when asked to spell the words, were more likely to give the common spelling (e.g. hair) than the correct spelling for the word that had been presented (hare–tortoise). Another group of control subjects who had been awake during the presentation showed clear evidence of learning and, in particular, gave the correct spelling for the word in the pair. In this experiment, sleep was defined in terms of well-established criteria based on readings taken from electrodes attached to the top and right and left sides of the head (electroencephalogram), to an area close to each eye (electro-oculogram), and to the area under the chin (electromyogram).

In the 1994 report of the Committee on Enhancing Human Performance (Druckman and Bjork, 1994), the committee stated, contrary to their earlier conclusion, that more recent evidence eschewed the possibility that learning can occur during sleep. It is fascinating to note that some of the early studies in this area referred to a book, *Cerebrophone, Inc.*, by Sherower published in 1948, in which an apparatus for sleep learning was described. However, Sherower's book was a science fiction novel, not a report of actual scientific evidence. In a brief history of hypnopaedia, Svyadoshch (1968) pointed out that one major claim for the success of hypnopaedia (Kulikov, 1964) referred to the first demonstration of the phenomenon as being reported in Aldous Huxley's 1932 science fiction novel *Brave New World*.[4] Indeed, Zabalova, Zukhar and Petrov (1964) based their belief as to the efficacy of hypnopaedia on an alleged experiment demonstrating that people are able to learn during sleep by means of earphones. Unfortunately, this "experiment" is "quoted" in another science fiction novel, *Ralph* 124C41, written by Hugo Gernsback in 1911, in which he describes people being able to do so in the year 2660. Perhaps we can wait until then, but in the meantime it is intriguing how suggestions from the imagination of science fiction writers can become incorporated in public views of how the mind works. Teleporting is not currently physically possible (Krauss, 1997), but how many people believe it to be so through the influence of *Star Trek* in its original form and its offspring?

OR DOES IT?

An apparent contradiction comes from research on learning under anaesthesia. *Exempli gratia*, a rather disturbing experiment reported by Levinson (1965) involved patients having surgery under a general anaesthetic. During the operation, a mock crisis was enacted in which the anaesthetist called out "Stop the operation. I don't like the patient's colour. His lips are much too blue. I'm going to give a little oxygen." Although all of the patients were in a state of clinically adequate anaesthesia at the time, 1 month later, under hypnosis, some of the patients could recall, almost *verbatim*, what the anaesthetist had said, and others could recall some of the words. This kind of procedure would nowadays most likely not meet ethical guidelines for experimentation, but at the time it was most probably assumed by the medical staff that because the patient was under anaesthesia, and *igitur* (therefore) not conscious, that he or she would not be aware of anything said in the operating room. Andrade (1995) provides a comprehensive review of this work, and it has

become clear that although patients are in a state of clinically induced anaesthesia it is possible for them to be aware, at the time, of events during the operation, but to forget after the operation that they have had this experience. It appears that there are several forms of anaesthetic state that can be induced, depending on the form of anaesthetic used and the dosage for an individual. A patient can be unable to move, but nevertheless be conscious and feel pain. They can also be unable to move, free of pain but able to hear and understand events that occur. Moreover, they may forget the experience but nevertheless show by indirect tests that they had learned something about events during the operation. This is not as strange as it sounds, because there are many facts that we can retrieve without remembering when or where we first acquired the information.

One example experiment demonstrates clearly the circumstances under which learning in anaesthesia might occur. Schwender et al. (1993) studied three groups of patients. Each group was given different forms of anaesthetic and the brain electrical activity (EEG) was measured via electrodes attached to the head of each patient. The EEG pattern showed that the three groups differed in their anaesthetic state corresponding to different levels of consciousness. While under anaesthetic, two of the groups of patients were played a tape of part of the story of Robinson Crusoe. Between 3 and 5 days after the operations, each patient was asked to free-associate to the word "Friday", that is to respond with the first word that came into their head. Among the group of 10 patients whose EEG patterns were closest to that found in the normal waking state, five responded with "Robinson Crusoe". However, in the other group, whose EEG activity was suppressed by the anaesthetic, only 1 of the 10 patients responded with the word "Robinson Crusoe". A third group of 15 patients was not played the tape during the operation and none of them responded "Robinson Crusoe" to the word "Friday". In an informal experiment of our own, each of 10 colleagues were asked to respond with the first word that came into their head in response to the word "Friday'. As far as we are aware, none had recently read the story of Robinson Crusoe, but only one responded with the related information that "it is a man's name". Therefore, we might expect that, just by chance, about 1 in 10 people would make this kind of response without having read or heard the story. You can try the experiment yourself, but only the part which does not require you to make your friends unconscious! The main message from this kind of experiment is that the only evidence of learning while under anaesthesia comes from situations in which it appears that the participant was conscious at the time of learning. The depth of anaesthesia is therefore crucial, and when the depth of anaesthesia is systematically altered, it directly affects the likelihood of retrieving information presented while in the anaesthetic state. A related manipulation involved giving the patient a mild electric shock while in a relatively deep level of anaesthesia, and this resulted in a higher likelihood of recalled information presented just after administration of the shock. All of this points again to conscious awareness being necessary for learning.

DO WE COVET WHAT WE DO NOT SEE?

A related claim is that audio tapes with repeated suggestions played to people while they are asleep can help them to give up smoking, stop drinking, think creatively, increase their confidence or make friends. These tapes simply have no effect, and tapes played while asleep that do not have these messages appear to lead to exactly the same outcome. That is, if you do end up smokeless, or with a new circle of friends, it is not because of the messages on the tape but because you were motivated anyway to stop smoking or to be more gregarious and this led to you buying the tapes. One well-publicized case was reported in 1957 by James Vicary, an advertising consultant (Pratkanis, 1996). The claim was that when the message "Eat Popcorn" or "Drink Coke" was flashed on a cinema screen too quickly for people to have been aware of its presence, subsequent sales increased for popcorn and Coca Cola. However, the claim turned out to be a complete hoax; Vicary had in fact collected little or no evidence for his claim, and later attempts have completely failed to demonstrate this effect. Similar claims about using subliminal messages to persuade people to adopt particular political views or ideas (Cousins, 1957), to start taking drugs or to commit suicide have also been shown to be completely false (Moore, 1982, 1995; Pratkanis, 1996; Rogers, 1993).

Tapes that claim to help improve memory through subliminal messages have been shown to lead to people *reporting* that their memory is better. One very attractive study involved giving people audio tapes that were labelled to indicate that they were for memory improvement but in fact were tapes intended for enhancing self-esteem. These tapes led to some people believing that their memory had improved, but when tested, their memory ability was no better than it was before (British Psychological Society, 1992). This was shown in studies by Pratkanis, Eskenazi and Greenwald (1990) and by Greenwald et al. (1991). *Idem* findings have been reported using self-help tapes for losing weight: people who were given the self-help "subliminal" tapes lost no more weight through dieting than did people who had also dieted but had not played the tapes (Merikle and Skanes, 1992).

Having made the commitment and the financial investment, the simple belief that the purchased tapes might work can be sufficient to change beliefs or even to change habits. This is the so-called "placebo" (I shall please) effect. Similar effects appear when people suffering from some illness appear to recover after being given a pill which they believe to offer a cure, even if the pill is in fact simply made of an inert white paste or of sugar (see Chapter 13). *Id est* (i.e. – in other words), claims reported in the popular media often reflect the attractiveness of the claims rather than their scientific credibility; hence the plethora of myths about memory. Sadly, too, when science is seen to undermine such claims, the scientific message is often seen as boring and unattractive, *igitur* less likely to be accepted. However, from the weight of evidence these tapes do not appear to deliver the service as advertised: if you want to buy tapes, then you might be better investing in some Mozart piano *concerti* (musical pieces for soloist and orchestra).

WHAT THE EYES IGNORE THE BRAIN PERCEIVES

It is important to be clear that the evidence strongly points to no effect on behaviour of subliminal messages. This does not mean that there is no unconscious processing of information in the brain. The human brain expends a great deal of energy on activities of which we are unaware, such as controlling the other organs of the body, *exempli gratia* the digestive system, or emotional reactions, including heart rate and sweating. Moreover, the brain can deal with cognitive activities non-consciously. This has been found in people who suffer from so-called "blindsight" or from "hemi-spatial neglect" as well as in normal cognition. Blindsight arises following damage to the areas of the brain responsible for making sense of what we see (Weiskrantz, 1996). People with this form of brain damage are virtually blind, although their eyes remain healthy. However, when shown movements, points of light, pictures or objects they can often "guess" what is being presented without being aware that they are accurate. For example, when presented with a small object, such patients deny being able to see anything but can form their hand into the appropriate shape for grasping the object; when shown a vertical or horizontal line, they can guess its orientation without being aware that a line is present. The conclusion from studying these patients is that there is more than one route into the brain from the eyes, and that one of the routes does not rely on the primary visual areas in the occipital cortex (at the back of the brain) that are damaged in blindsight patients. This alternative route does not give rise to conscious awareness, but does allow some processing of the visual information which is sufficient to support a plausible guess (Stoerig and Cowey, 1997).

Hemi-spatial neglect is a condition following brain damage in which the patient fails to detect or to respond to events, people or objects on one side of their body, normally on the left. Typically, it arises from damage to the right parietal lobe of the brain (about halfway down on the right side towards the rear). When asked to describe the layout of the room, such patients will omit details on their left side. As with blindsight, the difficulties in patients with neglect do not arise from damage to the eyes, but, unlike with blindsight, the areas of the brain devoted to vision may be spared, *id est* (i.e. the deficit is not one of vision. However, even although these patients seem unaware of information presented to their left, there is evidence that they can "implicitly" process some stimuli in the "neglected" field. *Exempli gratia*, Marshall and Halligan (1988) presented a patient affected by neglect with a series of outlines of two houses, one above the other. The two houses were identical except that one was drawn with flames coming from one side or the other. The patient was asked to decide whether the two houses were the same or different. When the flames were on the right, the patient could readily detect the difference, but when the flames were on the left, the patient maintained that the two houses were identical.

However, when asked in which of the two houses she would like to live, she tended to point to the one without the flames, without being able to say why that one was preferred. Several other examples have been reported of this kind of non-conscious processing of visual information in patients with hemi-spatial neglect. Although scientists are still debating the explanation for this phenomenon, there is general agreement that covert processing of information is perfectly possible.

Given that covert or non-conscious processing has been found in brain-damaged patients, can we find evidence of this in normal, healthy adults? There is some evidence that subliminal presentation of words and pictures can result in non-conscious processing, even if it does not affect overt behaviour. In our own laboratory (*exempli gratia* Ellis, Della Sala and Logie, 1996) we presented some healthy volunteers with pictures that were flashed up on a screen too quickly for normal perceptual awareness (less than 30 ms). The volunteers indeed reported that they were aware of a brief flash of light, but were not aware of what was displayed. Each picture represented a well-known proverb. *Exempli gratia*, the picture might depict a two-headed man. Following each subliminal presentation of a picture, we next presented a set of six alternative proverbs, only one of which would be associated with the immediately preceding picture, *id est* "Two heads are better than one." The volunteer had to guess which of the proverbs shown was linked with the picture. Although the volunteers were completely unaware of what had been shown, they nevertheless, on many occasions, could guess the correct proverb. That is, the picture, although presented too rapidly for conscious awareness, still permitted an awakening of related information in the brains of the volunteers, and this effect, although subtle, was

SEW HER UP AS BEST YOU CAN, NURSE,
I'M DUE ON THE TEE IN TEN MINUTES

sufficient to bias their guesses towards the correct response. This general principle of activating our stored knowledge is thought to be the means by which retrieval from memory occurs, but conscious retrieval results only when the extent of the activation of the memory exceeds some critical threshold. In nuce, subliminal presentation can be shown to have subtle effects on efficiency of access to related information stored away in our brains, but there is no evidence to suggest that it affects overt behaviour in normal, healthy adults.

How, then, does learning occur, and if repeated exposure, presentation while asleep or subliminal messages do not lead to acquiring knowledge, what does? Other techniques for improving memory *can* be beneficial. However, these schemes often involve a significant amount of mental effort to learn a technique, and once the technique is learned and applied, memory performance does indeed improve. The crucial point is that this improvement results from substantial mental effort to acquire and to apply; the techniques do not offer the "lazy person's way to a better memory". One way to pursue this is to invest fairly substantial amounts in purchasing memory improvement courses through newspaper advertisements. However, a more economical method of access to these mnemonic techniques is to purchase summary descriptions such as Baddeley's (1993), or Tony Buzan's books originally published by the BBC on memory improvement (*exempli gratia* Buzan, 1991). Many of these techniques can work if properly applied, although don't expect to become a professional mnemonist as a result. The university student might be helped by applying mnemonic methods in study, but these cannot substitute for understanding and intellectual effort, and nor will these techniques offer a cure for the brain diseases underlying memory failure.

CONCLUSION

In closing, it is worth mentioning that embedded in this chapter have been two experiments in which you as a reader have taken part. Before revealing the nature of these experiments, we should first collect the results. Those who are fluent in Latin need not participate. As you will all be aware, several expressions in everyday written English come from Latin, but people who use these expressions are often unaware of their original form. Without looking back at the text, can you write down the complete Latin expressions for which e.g., etc., i.e. and et al. are abbreviations? Now can you remember which of the following Latin expressions appeared in the text (not all of them did) and what the English translations are for those that did so?

- *a fortiori*
- *concerti*
- *credo*
- *curriculum vitae*
- *de facto*
- *et alia*
- *e pluribus unum*
- *et cetera*
- *exempli gratia*
- *honoris causa*
- *idem*

- *id est*
- *igitur*
- *in nuce*
- *vade mecum*
- *verbatim*

In the case of all the Latin expressions, your attention was drawn to the translation, and the expressions that did appear were repeated in the chapter. Also, the fact that Latin expressions appear in an English text and with some expressions shown in an unusual form (in full) would itself draw attention to the items. *Igitur*, unless you knew these expressions and their meaning before reading the chapter, any success you have had in recalling the expressions and their translations has come about because of repeated experiences of conscious attempts to understand the expressions when they are encountered, and not simply because the items appear repeatedly. The expressions varied in frequency in the text, with *exempli gratia* occurring 10 times and *verbatim* twice. The expressions also vary in the frequency with which they appear in English. However, each time you read the expressions and thought "why have they included the Latin words?", this constituted a separate learning experience. *Idem*, repeated attempts to learn do lead to better memory for the information being learned, whereas repeated exposure to the information without attempts to learn does not.

We have made the case throughout the chapter and tried to demonstrate experimentally that simple repetition does not lead to learning (*repetita non iuvant* – sheer repetition is not useful), whereas conscious repeated efforts to learn can be successful. We hope to have dispelled a few popular myths along the way and persuaded you of the value of evaluating evidence, a key feature of scientific methods. Myths can make our language and culture more colourful. They can inspire and have inspired art and poetry. At least in the case of memory, the crucial point is that there is some awareness of their use as metaphor and not as a genuine reflection of how the mind works.

> I therefore claim to show, not how men think in myths, but how myths operate in men's minds without their being aware of the fact. (Lévi-Strauss, 1970)

NOTES

1. We insert the qualifier "largely" because there are several discoveries of science where the weight of probabilistic evidence is to give the discovery the status of a fact. *Exempli gratia*, there is no longer any uncertainty that the earth is round (Cohen, 1994), or that thinking happens in the brain (Della Sala and Logie, 1998).
2. The text of the first two sentences of the Nicene Creed as used in this congregation are "We believe in one God, the Father, the almighty, maker of Heaven and Earth, of all that is, seen and unseen. We believe in one Lord, Jesus Christ, the only Son of God, eternally begotten of the Father, God from God, light from light, true God from true God, begotten, not made, of one substance with the Father."
3. The alternative from the point of view of the dog is suggested in the novel *Il Cane di Pavlov* (Pavlov's Dog) by Giorgio Prodi, in which the dog noted that every time it salivated then Pavlov smiled, showing a conditioned response in the scientist to the previously unconditioned stimulus of salivating generated by the dog.
4. In Chapter 2 of *Brave New World*, Aldous Huxley described rooms for Neo-Pavlovian Conditioning where the Director of Hatcheries and Conditioning was experimenting with hypnopaedia, but, even in this science fiction novel, hypnopaedia failed as an instrument of intellectual education.

CHAPTER 9

Creative Thinking: Myths and Misconceptions

K.J. GILHOOLY

INTRODUCTION

In ancient times, people were in considerable awe of the physical and biological world and invented many and various colourful myths to explain the creation of the world and its inhabitants. In modern times, most people, despite the claims of hyper-relativism, would accept that science is providing a sounder understanding of the origins of the universe, the earth and its creatures than did the myths of old. However, regarding the mental realm of ideas, there does seem to be some resistance to the notion that the creation of new ideas can be explained scientifically or even that such thinking *should* be explained. Any readers who strongly feel that creative thinking should not be explained (e.g. because such an explanation would knock the human kind from a last remaining pedestal) are free to stop reading this chapter now!

Just as there were pervasive myths concerning physical creation in ancient times, today there are common myths or misconceptions (Weisberg, 1986) about mental creativity. It is my belief that psychology will replace these myths about mental creation with more valid interpretations.

Some current myths that appear quite widespread are (1) that creativity is a mystery which cannot in principle be explained, (2) that creativity is heavily dependent on innate talents which one either has or not and, contrariwise, (3) that with some special tricks anyone can quickly become highly creative, i.e. there are "fast tracks" to creativity, such as "brainstorming" (Osborn, 1953) or "lateral thinking" (De Bono, 1976, 1983).

In this chapter I will be presenting evidence that runs counter to the myths of creativity. This evidence indicates that creativity involves rather everyday mental processes and so *is* explicable; that although innate factors may play a modest role, training, practice, extended knowledge acquisition and motivation are crucial; and that special tricks are likely to be of limited value in significant real-life creative activity.

Before outlining substantive results, let us attempt to clarify the key concepts under discussion.

DEFINITIONS

First, let us consider what is meant by the term "creative" and its associate "creativity". It is perhaps easiest to start by defining creative products. Creative products, whether they are poems, scientific theories, paintings or technological advances, are both *novel* and acknowledged to be *valuable* or useful in some way. Whether a product is novel or not is relatively easy to determine, although an element of judgement is involved, in that some products are more obviously derived from previous developments than others. It can also be argued that subjective novelty is what is important. Is the idea new to the individual rather than historically new, i.e. never thought of before by anyone (Boden, 1990)?

Objective measurement of novelty is possible in laboratory settings, since the same task can be given to a large number of people (e.g. "think of ways of improving a doorknob"), and the degree of novelty of proposed solutions can be readily assessed by counting their frequencies of occurrence. In real life, however, only the "creator" may be working on a given self-set problem (e.g. only one author may be tackling the self-set problem of representing the stream of consciousness of a Stone Age man, as in *The Inheritors* (Golding, 1955)), and so frequency of production is not always available as a creation. This discussion also raises the point that laboratory studies have used small-scale, externally set problems that can generally be "cracked" in 20 min or less, whereas real-life creativity tends to involve large-scale, self-set problems that occupy large tracts of time (months or years rather than minutes). Clearly, processes involved in laboratory-sized problems are likely to be different from those in real-life large-scale problems. Having said that, of course, everyday life does sometimes throw up small-scale problems that require novel thinking. (For example, a cassette tape got stuck in my car's cassette player; I thought of tweezers to remove it but did not have any in my pockets; but I had two very flat and thin car keys which I realized could be used as tweezers by holding a key in each hand, pressing one of them downward and one upward on the edges of the stuck cassette which were accessible and pulling the cassette back towards me. In this way, the problem was solved by a novel use of car keys. No doubt you can think of other examples from your own experience.)

When we turn to the quality of a product, subjective judgement looms still larger than in the case of judging novelty. In science and technology the criteria for quality are clearer than in the arts. A new theory can be seen to "work" if it covers more phenomena with no more assumptions than its predecessors (e.g. Einstein's theory compared to Newton's). A new device can be seen to work if it meets the function for which it was devised (e.g. the first telephone). Notoriously, there is usually less agreement about the merits of artistic productions, both at the time of their emergence and over history. Initial reactions may well be negative to artistic products that either depart too far from established styles or, at the other extreme, are too conventional. Later generations are more likely to appreciate the boldness of developments that their ancestors decried as "insane", e.g. Surrealism, Cubism, or Expressionism.

It may also be suggested that judgements of "novelty" or "unusualness" will relate to the degree to which the product can be fitted into an established style (in the arts) or "paradigm" (in the sciences). Highly creative products signal and exemplify a new style or paradigm (Boden, 1990). Subsequent work within a given style or paradigm would generally be regarded as less creative than the initial style-defining work.

The above comments should serve to indicate what is meant here by a creative product. What of "creative processes" and persons blessed with "creativity"? Although it is a starting point, it is not very informative to say that creative processes are those processes that result in creative products! Whatever the details, it may be noted that psychologists hold to the belief that creative processes are composed of similar ingredients to those entering into less exalted forms of thinking and that supernatural interventions in the form of "daemons" or "divine sparks" are ruled out. It is assumed that creative products result from many small steps carried out by limited-capacity cognitive systems that suffer from all the normal limitations of cramped working memory and imperfect retrieval from long-term memory.

Turning now to "creativity", this is an attribute ascribed to those individuals who show a long-term tendency to generate novel products that are also influential (Albert, 1975). With a few extremely rare exceptions (such as Leonardo Da Vinci), most "creatives" display their valued characteristic within a particular domain or speciality – but within that speciality they are marked for their combination of productivity and high quality of work (as indexed by its impact and influence). Of course, in real life, for someone to be acknowledged as displaying "creativity" involves social processes, as well as purely within-individual cognitive processes. To become known, creative individuals or agents acting on their behalf must "promote" their products and convince enough others who control the communication media that these products should be presented to a larger audience (Stein, 1974). Given that broader presentation, further social processes leading to widespread acceptance and influence on the one hand, or to apathy or rejection on the other hand, can begin. A similar point is made by Simonton (1988), who argues that creativity is a form of *leadership* in that it entails personal influence over others. Just as a leader must have followers to be classed as a leader, so a creator must have appreciators and disciples to be classed as an effective creator. Indeed, it has been suggested (Czikszentmihalyi, 1975; Gardner, 1994) that instead of asking "*What* is creativity" we should ask "*Where* is creativity?" Creativity emerges, it is proposed, out of a three-way interaction between an individual, his or her domain of work and the "audience" of knowledgeable peers and judges. Although a full account of creative processes must include consideration of the social context, as a psychologist I will focus on intra-individual cognitive processes which are essential ingredients in any creative work.

In the rest of this chapter, I will discuss some of the main findings that have arisen in the study of creative processes and consider these in relation to the prevailing myths and misconceptions. First, I will look at the role of individual differences. In what ways do individuals acknowledged to be creative differ in cognitive, personality or biographical characteristics from others? Second, we will consider personal accounts by artists and scientists of how creative processes seemed to them, and stage models for creative thinking. Third, we will then turn to specific fast-track approaches to stimulating idea production and seek to evaluate them. Fourth, we consider some theories about creative cognition and, finally, a summing-up is presented.

STUDIES OF CREATIVE INDIVIDUALS

It may be that highly creative individuals differ from less creative people in personality or biographical characteristics. If such differences exist and are crucial for creativity, then fast-track approaches to increasing creativity are likely to have little effect, as they cannot change personality or biographical characteristics. A number of studies have been made of people acknowledged to be creative (e.g. Roe (1952) on scientists, MacKinnon (1962) on architects, and Barron (1955) on writers and artists) with a view to uncovering any common background or personality characteristics in these groups of unusual people.

In one of the earliest investigations of its kind, Roe (1952) studied 64 US scientists who had been rated as particularly creative in their fields by expert panels. The 64 were roughly evenly split among physicists, biologists and social scientists. Each individual was subjected to long interviews, projective personality tests and a conventional intelligence test. On the basis of this investigation, Roe gave the following composite picture of the average eminent US scientist in the 1950s: he was a first-born son in a middle-class Protestant family, with a professional man as a father. He was likely to have often been ill in childhood or to have lost a parent early. He had a very high IQ and began reading avidly at an early age. He felt "lonely" and different from his schoolmates, did not have much interest in girls and married later than average. He usually decided on his career as a professional scientist as a result of a student project involving individual research. He worked hard and persistently, very often 7 days a week with few holidays.

Similar evidence was gathered by Cattell and his colleagues. Before actually testing any "live" scientists, Cattrell (1959) scanned the biographies of many famous creative scientists and noted that they seemed to be introverted and stable. Although introverted, they were generally independent and self-sufficient. They also tended to be solemn or restrained and rather dominant in personal relationships.

Cattell and Drevdahl (1955) selected groups of about 45 creative researchers in physics, biology and psychology and had them complete a well-established personality test (16 Personality Factors (PF) test). Compared with the general population, the creative researchers were more introverted, intelligent, dominant and inhibited; they were also more sensitive emotionally and more radical. These findings are in line with the suggestion of biographies and with the results of Roe's investigation.

Also of interest is Mitroff's (1974) study of scientists engaged in the analysis of lunar samples as part of the Apollo moon project. Mitroff noted a strong tendency towards a style of thinking often labelled "convergent" (Hudson, 1966). Any open-ended question put to the scientists would be quickly transformed into a narrower, more tightly defined one. This tendency fits in with Hudson's finding that secondary-level school pupils who performed better on convergent (one answer) test questions than on divergent items (multiple possible answers) tended to specialize in science subjects, while those who scored better on divergent items than on convergent items tended to specialize in the arts. It was also noted that the lunar scientists strongly identified with the traditionally conceived "masculine" characteristics. They believed in hard work, dedication and striving, and did not disapprove of a touch of ruthlessness. Intriguingly, Mitroff found evidence in his interviews of strongly aggressive tendencies. In discussing other scientists and rival groups, the desire to win glory at the expense of others and a fear of their rivals' overaggressive tactics (e.g. idea-stealing) were evident. Aggressiveness was also clear in their attitude to promoting their own ideas. As one scientist remarked, "if you want to get anybody to believe your hypothesis, you've got to beat them down with numbers: you've got to hit them again and again over the head with hard data until they're stupefied into believing it" (Mitroff, 1974, p. 144).

Mitroff suggested that the scientists were somewhat one-sided in emotional expression, and he found that they were far less free in displaying soft emotions as against harsh or aggressive ones. The notion that science is an aggressive activity was also expressed in Freud's self-description. He wrote: "I am not really a man of science, not an observer, not an experimenter, and not a thinker. I am nothing but by temperament a conquistador – an adventurer, . . . with the curiosity, the boldness, and the tenacity that belong to that type of being" (Jones, 1961, p. 227).

A study of artists and writers (Drevdahl and Cattell, 1958) using Cattell's 16 PF test yielded a profile rather similar to that of the scientists (Cattell and Drevdahl, 1955). The artistic group scored more highly on scales of emotional sensitivity and inner tension than did the scientists, but were otherwise similar.

More recent studies have pointed to a "dark side" of artistic creativity, reflected in a higher than normal incidence of manic-depressive and depressive pathology (Jamison, 1995; Andreasen, 1987; Ludwig, 1992) in creative artists. Jamison reports studies of acknowledged creative writers and artists, which have found rates of depression 8–10 times, of manic-depression 10–20 times and of suicide up to 18 times those of the general population. Although the association should not be overinterpreted – not all artists and writers display pathology and not all sufferers from depression/manic-depression are highly creative – none the less a statistical association is present. Could such mood disorders conceivably be of help in artistic endeavours? Mania and especially its mild form, hypomania, do have features that are plausibly conducive to creative thinking. Indeed, one of the diagnostic criteria for hypomania is "sharpened and unusually creative thinking and increased productivity". Hypomanic individuals tend to use rhyme, other sound associations and unusual words in their speech far more than do normals. Also, hypomanics are markedly faster at giving synonyms and word associations than normals. The condition, then, seems to involve a speeding of thought and a tendency to use uncommon associations and ideas. These tendencies could well be helpful in bringing together unusual combinations of ideas. During manic periods the person tends to be extremely confident and energetic, which would facilitate the pushing through of creative work to a conclusion and the promotion of the work to possibly sceptical recipients.

While little overt progress is normally made during periods of pathological depression, it is conceivable that experience of such states gives a broader range of contrasting experiences to draw on in normal periods than would be available otherwise.

Some interesting points emerge from studies of the ages at which creative accomplishments tend to occur in different domains. Data gathered by Lehman (1953) reveal that in many fields the most highly regarded contributions are produced between 30 and 40 years of age. The average age is younger in some domains; for example, in chemistry it is at 25–30 and it is older in others such as psychology, philosophy, novel writing and architecture. Although these age trends were detectable, it should be noted that good work was evident in all fields at a very wide range of ages. Declines from peak productivity tend to be gradual, and productivity tends to remain well above initial levels even late in life.

It seems from the above reports that there are good grounds for the view that there are some personality characteristics (e.g. introversion, dominance, aggressiveness) associated with creativity. Also, there are some associations between manic-depression and creativity in the arts. Of course, these links between creativity and personality are ambiguous in terms of causal direction. Being recognized as having done creative work might alter personality! Assuming, as is usually done, that the causal path is from personality to creative production rather than vice versa, these results do not bode well for fast-track methods of boosting creativity. Personality factors cannot be readily affected by simple training in shortcut tricks. Further, there is biographical evidence that in all fields a considerable degree of background knowledge has to be built up before peak creativity is reached. In the more formal domains such as mathematics, at least 10 years of training seems to be required (Ericsson and Charness, 1994), and in less structured domains of knowledge many more years are required before sufficient mastery is achieved to permit creative advances to be made. These considerations point to the importance of accumulated knowledge and so count against fast-track approaches.

Regarding the view that innate "talent" is vital for creative work, it is relevant to note that knowledge of complex domains, which is a prerequisite of creative work, is clearly not innate. Arguably, the ability to acquire knowledge (which ability is at least part of what is generally meant by intelligence) may have innate components and there is evidence that highly creative individuals tend to have measured intelligence scores above average but not necessarily in the extremely high ranges (Eysenck, 1994). Although the extent of the genetic contribution to measured intelligence is hotly debated (e.g. Howe, 1996), it is clear that environmental factors will govern access to appropriate learning experiences and opportunities and are of undoubted importance (Gardner, 1994). Evidence for *specific* innate cognitive talents (as against broader personality characteristics or general intelligence) relevant to superior performance in music (e.g. "absolute pitch") and the arts, for example, is very weak, while the evidence for a major role of practice and motivation is very strong (Howe, Davidson and Sloboda, 1998; Ericsson, Krampe and Tesch-Rohmer, 1993).

However, proponents of fast-track approaches to creativity could claim that there are crucial cognitive processes which could be specifically trained for and then used to good effect in creative work by those with the requisite background knowledge of their domain of work. How could we find out about these processes? A popular answer has been to ask people acknowledged to be creative to tell us how they did it. Although such accounts may be viewed sceptically because they are generally gathered long after the event (Ericsson and Simon, 1993), they are none the less intriguing, and common patterns have tended to emerge.

We will examine some of these personal reports in the next section.

PERSONAL ACCOUNTS OF CREATIVE PROBLEM-SOLVING, STAGES AND INCUBATION

Many scientists and artists have provided accounts for their experiences in solving complex problems (e.g. Ghiselin, 1952; Koestler, 1964; Vernon, 1970; Gardner, 1994). These personal accounts are of interest for evidence they may contain about features common to the creative process in a wide range of difficult tasks. Fairly consistent patterns do seem to emerge and these patterns have served as the bases for various analyses of stages of both creative thinking and more routine problem-solving.

It is worth noting that some well-known thinkers have disclaimed any ability to tell us how they solved problems or thought creatively. For example, Bertrand Russell was once asked to contribute to a book on how to think clearly. He replied that he could not help because, for him, thinking was instinctive, like digestion. He said that he simply filled up with relevant information, went about his business, doing other things, and later, with time and good luck, he found that the work had been done. Perhaps Russell was too modest on this occasion. His brief account broadly matches those of others who have tried to be more detailed. Consider now two reports; one by Poincaré and one by Helmholtz.

Poincaré's Account

Henri Poincaré was a prominent French mathematician of the 19th century. He reported (Poincaré, 1908) once struggling for a long time to prove a certain theorem without getting any results. One evening he drank black coffee before going to bed and it seemed to him that ideas of possible ways of solving the problem combined and recombined in one way after another before he finally got to sleep. In the morning, he clearly saw how the problem was to be solved, and after 2 h had completed the detailed proof. The solution to the initial problem raised further problems, and Poincaré noted that these problems were solved as a result of ideas that occurred while he was not actively engaged on them, e.g. while riding in a bus, or walking along a street or beach.

Helmholtz's Account

The 19th-century scientist Herman Helmholtz, who contributed to physics, neurology and psychology, volunteered the following report of his problem-solving experience in a speech made at a dinner in honour of his 70th birthday in 1896 (Woodworth and Schlosberg, 1954, p. 838).

> So far as my experience goes, "happy thoughts" never came to a fatigued brain and never at the writing desk. It was always necessary, first of all, that I should have turned my problem over on all sides to such an extent that I had all its angles and complexities "in my head" and could run through them freely without writing. To bring the matter to that point is usually impossible without long preliminary labour. Then, after the fatigue resulting from this labour had passed away, there must come an hour of complete physical freshness and quiet well being, before the good ideas arrived. Often they were there in the morning when I awoke, just according to Goethe's oft cited verses, and as Gauss also once noted. But they especially liked to make their appearance while I was taking an easy walk over wooded hills in sunny weather.

On the basis of reports such as those of Poincaré, Helmholtz and others, Wallas (1926) proposed a four-stage analysis of creative problem-solving in a very influential book (*The Art of Thought*).

Preparation

In this stage, the problem-solver familiarizes himself with his problem and engages in conscious, effortful, systematic and usually fruitless work on the problem. Although this stage may well not lead to solution in itself, it is widely believed to be very important in influencing the likelihood that the next stage will result in a useful idea. Much personal testimony indicates that inspiration will not be forthcoming without this preliminary labour or, as Edison, the prolific inventor, is reported to have said, "No inspiration without perspiration."

Incubation

This is a period during which the task is set aside. No conscious work is done on the problem during this stage. Poincaré and others have hypothesized that unconscious work is carried out during this phase. On the other hand, it may be that this is simply a necessary rest period which enables a later period of conscious work to proceed more effectively than it would have without the break.

Illumination or inspiration

This is the point when a fruitful idea, or "happy thought" in Helmholtz's phrase, occurs to us. The inspiration is not usually a complete solution to the problem but points in the direction in which the complete solution may be found.

Verification

This stage is much like preparation, in that conscious work must be done in order to develop and test the inspiration.

The above four stages appear to be visible in the personal reports of Helmholtz, Poincaré and others.

Wallas's stage analysis suggests that "inspiration" can be facilitated by taking an incubation break, which is a pain-free method; however, the personal accounts suggest that considerable preparation and extensive problem knowledge is needed before incubation will be effective. So stage analysis offers the hope that one rather passive tip, i.e. "Incubate", could be useful, in conjunction with the longer haul of extensive preparation activity. Most people, I am sure, would feel that incubation is a real phenomenon which they have experienced. However, it has not proven easy to establish "incubation" as a reliable phenomenon in the laboratory.

Murray and Denny (1969) investigated the effects of incubation opportunity on subjects who had been divided into those of high and low problem-solving ability by a prior test. Subjects were given a rather complicated problem devised by Saugstad, in which the subject is given a nail, pliers, a length of string, a pulley, some elastic bands and several newspapers. Eight feet from the subject was a glass containing metal balls and standing on a movable frame. Next to the glass was a steel cylinder. The subject had to find a way of transferring the steel balls from the glass to the cylinder without going nearer than 8 feet to the glass or the cylinder.

The solution involves two stages. First, bend the nail into a hook, attach the hook to the string and throw it into the frame. The frame can then be dragged back to the line and the balls removed. The second stage is to construct a long, hollow tube by rolling up the newspapers and connecting them telescope fashion by elastic bands, and then roll the balls down the tube to the steel cylinder.

Control subjects were given 20 min continuously to solve the problem. The experimental subjects worked for 5 min on the task, and then had 5 min on an unrelated pencil and paper task. They were then given a further 15 min on the main task.

Neither incubation nor ability level significantly affected the frequency of solutions, but there was a significant interaction, in that high-ability solvers were hindered by incubation opportunity, while low-ability solvers were aided by an incubation opportunity. Murray and Denny interpreted these results by suggesting that low-ability subjects quickly became set or fixated on one line of approach to the problem, and incubation allowed their inappropriate sets to weaken, while the high-ability subjects may have been working more systematically through various possibilities, without fixation, but this orderly process was disrupted by an incubation opportunity.

Murray and Denny suggest, then, that incubation will be most effective when the problem is very difficult for the solver – as for their low-ability subjects tackling the tube and balls problem and, presumably, for famous scientists and artists tackling major problems and projects.

However, incubation effects appear to be difficult to obtain in the laboratory. Dominowski and Jenrick (1972) carried out a follow-up of Murray and Denny using a different problem involving manipulation of objects but found no significant effect of incubation. However, on a divergent task, where subjects had to think of many unusual uses for familiar objects, Fulgosi and Guilford (1968) found significant effects of 20 min of incubation on the quantity of solutions provided, but no effect on the quality of solutions. Clearly, research remains to be done, e.g. varying problem types, preparation time and length of incubation period. Olton and Johnson (1976) examined possible incubation effects on the solving of chess problems by expert players. Thus, the problems were realistic and familiar for the subjects (unlike the situation in previous studies that used unfamiliar puzzles). However, the chess-playing subjects given an incubation opportunity showed no advantage over subjects who worked continuously on the task.

Given the intuitive appeal of incubation as an aid to creativity, it is surprising that laboratory studies have not yet yielded a reliable procedure by which incubation effects can be demonstrated and explored. The relatively short duration of laboratory problem-solving tasks and the low level of knowledge required in such problems may be relevant factors. The real-life examples reported by acknowledged creative individuals generally involved large-scale problems of considerable complexity which have been a focus of the person's work over long periods. The method of incubation may only work, if at all, after a considerable prior period of familiarization with the problem domain.

ACTIVE FAST-TRACK METHODS

Just as most people would like to become richer, healthier, more attractive and thinner, preferably with no effort or expense, so most people would like to become more "creative", ideally through some quick and painless method. Where there is a need or desire, the market will provide (alleged) remedies and, just as there are many schemes for sale which promise rapid increases in physical and financial well-being, so there are schemes promising to boost creativity quickly and easily.

Let us now consider some proposed fast-track schemes to greater creativity which are more active than merely "incubating" and assess how plausible these schemes are. Fast-track schemes, such as brainstorming (Osborn, 1953) and lateral thinking (De Bono, 1983), offer very general methods that are claimed to bring great benefits to creative work in all fields with but little effort. The contrasting long-haul view argues that, sadly, there is no substitute for the laborious business of developing expert knowledge in a given domain and that creative results are largely brought about by extensive and time-consuming trial-and-error search (Weisberg, 1986).

Numerous proposals have been put forward for stimulating the idea-production stage of creative thinking. Probably the most famous, and certainly the most researched, such method is that known as "brainstorming".

Brainstorming

In the 1940s and 1950s a practical businessman, Alex Osborn, developed a package of recommendations known as the brainstorming method. This was intended mainly for use in group problem-solving and as a means of increasing idea production. The method can be adapted for individual use and is described in Osborn's (1953) book *Applied Imagination*. Brainstorming has been taken up quite widely in a variety of organizations and has also been extensively investigated in laboratory settings.

Osborn adopts the standard view that problem-solving and creative thinking involve (1) problem formulation, (2) idea-finding and (3) evaluation of ideas to find a likely solution. Brainstorming aims at facilitating the middle, idea-finding, stage and it can be summarized as involving two main principles and four rules.

Principles:

1. Deferment of judgement.
2. Quantity breeds quality.

Rules:

1. Criticism is ruled out.

2. Freewheeling is welcomed.
3. Quantity is wanted.
4. Combination and improvement are sought.

The "deferment of judgement" principle meant that evaluation of ideas was to be postponed until a set period of idea production had elapsed. The untutored thinker will tend to evaluate each idea as it is produced. Osborn suggests that this can be inhibiting and may lead to premature abandonment of ideas that, although not useful in themselves, may lead on to possible solutions. The "quantity breeds quality" principle states that the more ideas produced, the larger the absolute number of useful ones there are likely to be, even if the proportion is very low. The rules listed above remind "brainstormers" not to criticize their own ideas or those of others, to free-associate to ideas already produced, to aim for quantity and to combine and improve already generated suggestions.

The method was originally devised for group use but can be adapted for individual applications. A number of questions arise, e.g. does the method lead to better productivity (a) for groups and (b) for individuals, and does group brainstorming lead to better results than would be obtained by pooling the ideas produced by the appropriate number of individual brainstormers?

Numerous studies support the hypothesis that groups using brainstorming produce more ideas than similar groups working along conventional lines. Brainstorming instructions strongly affect the quantity of ideas produced, and although effects on average quality are not so evident, reports of more high-quality ideas have been obtained (as would be expected by virtue of the "quantity effect"). An example study is the following, by Meadow, Parnes and Reese (1959). They compared the effects of group brainstorming instructions with the effects of instructions that stressed the quality of ideas produced. The subjects were to think of as many uses as they could for (1) a broom and (2) a coathanger. Ideas were rated independently for uniqueness (the degree to which the suggested use differed from normal use) and for value (social, economic or aesthetic). "Good" ideas were defined as those rated highly on both uniqueness and value. The results indicated that significantly more good ideas were produced by groups with brainstorming instructions than with non-brainstorming instructions. Favourable results on individual brainstorming have also been reported by Parnes and Meadow (1963).

Given that both individual and group brainstorming seem to be effective, the question arises of whether brainstorming in a group produces better results than would be obtained by pooling results from individual brainstormers. It could be argued either that the group procedure would lead to beneficial mutual stimulation or, alternatively, that participants would be inhibited by fear of implicit criticism even although overt criticism is not permitted. Perhaps surprisingly a number of studies (Taylor, Berry and Block, 1958; Dunnette, Campbell and Jaastad, 1963; Bouchard and Hare, 1970; Dillon, Graham and Aidells, 1972) found that group participation in brainstorming inhibited creative thinking relative to individual brainstorming. That is, more different ideas resulted from N people working individually, using brainstorming rules, than were obtained from N people working in subgroups. Why should this be so? It may be that individuals fear implicit criticism even when open criticism is not permitted and consequently inhibit overt production of more eccentric ideas. Also, individuals working in a group or more likely to develop the same set or direction in their thinking than the same number of individuals working alone, thus producing fewer different responses. Individuals working alone will probably develop "sets" but these sets are likely to differ from person to person.

Checklists and Morphological Synthesis

The brainstorming technique was not very explicit on how to actually generate ideas, apart from urging free association. Warren and Davis (1969) compared three more specific methods that are suitable for individual use. Subjects were set the task of thinking of ideas for changing or improving a particular object, e.g. a doorknob. One group of subjects was given a short checklist of general 'idea-spurring'' suggestions (e.g. add something; sub-tract something; change colour; change materials). A second group was given a long checklist of 73 idea-spurring questions organized into nine categories (e.g. magnify (add what?, time frequency, strength)? modify (meaning, colour, motion)?). The third group was instructed in a technique known as morphological synthesis (Zwicky, 1969). This technique requires the problem-solver to list ideas for one aspect of the object in question along one axis and ideas for another aspect of the problem along a second axis. Novel ideas would then be found in the matrix formed by combining the two axes. For example, if the problem was to invent a new type of vehicle, this could be tackled by creating a matrix with ideas for power sources along one dimension (axis) and ideas for the medium of transport along the other dimension. See Figure 9.1 for a possible morphological synthesis of the "new vehicle" problem.

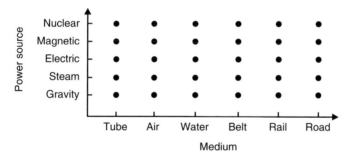

Figure 9.1   Morphological synthesis applied to new vehicle task.

Each point in the matrix (Figure 9.1) represents some combination of power source and medium. Some are familiar, and some impossible; but others may be new and useful. Evidently, the number of combinations increases rapidly with the number of ideas per dimension. More than two dimensions may be used, leading to further increases in the number of combinations.

A fourth, control, group was given no particular instructions in problem-solving methods. Of the four groups, the short-checklist and morphological synthesis groups produced the highest number of ideas and the greatest number of high-quality ideas. Surprisingly, perhaps, the long checklist produced no improvement over the control conditions. The morphological synthesis instructions produced the greatest number of ideas and had the highest rate of production; and so, when time is taken into account, this method appeared to be the most effective of those studied.

Lateral Thinking

De Bono (1983) has popularized the notion of lateral thinking as an aid to effective creativity and has developed instructional materials aimed at teaching lateral thinking skills. Lateral thinking involves re-representing or "restructuring" a problem while, in contrast, normal ("vertical") thinking involves working within a given problem representation. Vertical thinking is seen as logical, sequential, predictable and habit-bound, while lateral thinking would be characterized by the opposite attributes. De Bono has devised a set of instructional materials known as the CoRT programme (named after de Bono's Cognitive Research Trust). These materials are intended to increase individuals' skills in lateral thinking. The programme involves six units each consisting of ten 35-min lessons. The six units are outlined in De Bono (1983) and may be summarized as follows: CoRT 1, "Breadth", stresses thinking about problems in different ways; CoRT 2, "Organization", aims at effective control of attention; CoRT 3, "Interaction", focuses on questions of evidence and arguments; CoRT 4, "Creativity", provides strategies for producing unusual ideas; CoRT 5, "Information and feeling", considers affective factors related to thinking; and CoRT 6, "Action", presents a general framework for tackling problems. De Bono suggests that CoRT 1 should be taught first, after which the other units can be used in any order. Broadly speaking, the CoRT lessons involve using "operators" which are given to help students retrieve and apply the operators when needed. Sample operators are "consider all factors" or "CAF", and "positive, negative and interesting points", or "PNI".

De Bono (1976) reports studies in which students who had received CoRT instructions produced more ideas than control groups. This certainly suggests a "quantity" effect; whether average quality was improved is unclear. The test questions were similar to the exercises in the training material and so the extent of transfer of training is also unclear. Edwards and Baldauf (1983) carried out an instructional study using CoRT 1 and found that various measures of quantity and quality of divergent thinking improved after the CoRT 1 course. Transfer of training in CoRT 1 to performance in high-school physics was investigated, but no clear indication of transfer emerged.

Rather stronger evidence supporting the CoRT programme comes from a large-scale study carried out under the auspices of the Venezuelan Ministry of Education (Herrnstein et al., 1986). Large groups of children received training in a version of the CoRT programme for periods of 1–3 years. Control subjects of similar background did not receive these lessons. Pre- and post-tests with divergent problems similar to those used in training showed significantly larger gains on quantity and quality measures for the experimental subjects than for the controls.

Although some of the results, particularly those of the Venezuelan study, are quite encouraging for the CoRT programme, questions regarding transfer to dissimilar tasks and long-term beneficial effects remain open.

Overall Comments on Fast-track Methods

While the effects of incubation seem uncertain, brainstorming, morphological synthesis, short checklists and lateral thinking show some signs of beneficial effects, at least with small-scale puzzles and rather artificial divergent-thinking tasks. Brainstorming versus conventional approaches appears to produce benefits largely though a "quantity" effect of increasing the sheer number of proposals made, thus increasing the number of good proposals (at the cost of a lot of poor proposals). Morphological synthesis again shows marked quantity effects. Lateral thinking methods have not shown convincing transfer beyond the training materials used. In all cases the tasks used have been small scale and have not depended on extensive domain knowledge. Overall, whether these methods are really useful in large-scale real-life creative problem-solving, as found in the arts, sciences and technology, is as yet "not proven".

THEORETICAL APPROACHES

In this section I will consider some attempts to explain creative processes within the frameworks of theoretical approaches established in other areas of cognitive psychology. The approaches discussed here draw on associative, Piagetian and information-processing theory, and serve to indicate that creativity could indeed be explained in terms of everyday cognitive processes.

Simonton's Chance-configuration Theory

Simonton (1988) builds on Campbell's (1960) earlier blind-variation and selective-retention model of creative processes. Campbell's model involved the following three basic propositions:

1. The solution of novel problems requires some means of generating *ideational variation*. This process is "blind" in that the problem-tackler cannot know in advance of testing a new idea whether it will help or not.
2. The idea variations are subject to a fixed *selection process* that retains advances and rejects non-advances.
3. The selected variations must be *retained*.

Campbell's model of idea generation, selection and retention is clearly analogous to Darwinian evolutionary theory. Simonton builds on this model in his chance-configuration theory by introducing concepts of (a) the chance permutation of mental elements, (b) the formation of stable configurations, and (c) the communication and acceptance of those configurations.

Simonton proposes that the creative process operates on mental elements which are unitary ideas that are free to enter into combinations with other elements. The basic mechanism is *chance permutation* of these elements. The use of the term "permutation" (rather than the more often used term "combination") draws attention to the order in which elements are combined. The same elements (e.g. musical notes) will have very different effects depending on the order in which they are combined. Once a chance permutation has occurred, some selection must be introduced. Most chance permutations are unstable in that the elements do not cohere; the few that form an interrelated whole are highly stable, and Simonton labels these *configurations*. Stable configurations are retained and become new "chunks" which function as a single element and can thus enter into further permutations. Hierarchical combining of configurations (as in taxonomies) is an especially useful mode of combination for cognitive efficiency and is pervasive across many domains.

A new configuration which seems useful has to be further developed into a *communication configuration* before the creative process is complete. The initial chance configuration, then, is a starting point, e.g. a sketch, an outline, or a germinal idea, which must be the basis for a publicly available product, e.g. a painting, a symphony, a scientific paper and so on. Finally, the product must be perceived as meeting a need of an audience.

Simonton draws support for the chance-configuration theory from data on the distribution of creative productivity over contributors to particular fields, the relation between age and creativity, and the quantity–quality relationship. In many fields the distribution of outputs is such that a few contributors account for a majority of products. Dennis (1955) found that the top 10% produced around 50% of contributions, while the bottom 50% produced about 15% of the contributions over many disciplines. Thus, the distribution of number of products per contributor is highly skewed (Lotka, 1926). Simonton (1988) argues that even if the number of mental elements (n) available for chance permutation is normally distributed, as seems plausible, the number of possible chance permutations (e to the power n) is a highly skewed distribution. Thus, those contributors with more elements will produce disproportionately more configurations, and so the observed productivity distributions are consistent with the chance-configuration theory.

The relationships between age and output reported by Lehman (1953) have been supported by more recent research (Simonton, 1984). The main patterns are that productivity in all fields tends to increase initially with age, reach a peak and then decline more slowly than the initial rise; the onset, peak and rate of decline vary from field to field; and, finally, exceptional output is associated with precocity, longevity and high productivity rates. Simonton (1988) argues that the typical age–productivity curve reflects the operation of two processes, i.e. production of chance configurations (ideation) and elaboration of chance configurations into creative communications (communication configurations). Ideation is held to occur at a rate proportional to the size of the set of free mental elements which have not yet been combined, while elaboration rate depends in a similar way on the quantity of ideations awaiting conversion into communicable form. Simonton shows that by varying these two rates, the typical age–productivity curves can be produced. In relatively formal disciplines (e.g. mathematics), the rates of ideation and elaboration are high, leading to early peaks; but in less formalized domains (e.g. history), the rates of ideation and elaboration are low, leading to late peaks and slow declines. Total productivity should be governed by the total number of possible chance configurations of the mental elements which a person brings to the domain. On Simonton's model it can be shown that the greater the number of such combinations that are theoretically possible, the earlier the person will begin to contribute (precocity) and the higher the rate of production will be. The longer the lifespan (longevity), the greater the total contribution (assuming reasonable health).

There appears to be a fairly consistent link between quantity and quality in that the longer the list of products a person has contributed, generally the longer will be that person's list of high-quality products. Over a creator's working life, the quality ratio of major to minor works tends to be constant (Simonton, 1977). The "constant-probability-of-success" rule follows from Campbell's blind-variation model and from Simonton's chance-configuration theory. The stability of creative reputations may partly depend on the existence of multiple high-quality products which can support the reputation even when individual products' perceived worth may fluctuate with time. Equally, it is notable that high creatives often have a "tail" of work which is less highly regarded than the best work of their generally lower-ranked contemporaries. As W. H. Auden said, "the major poet will write more bad poems than the minor", but only because the major poet will tend to write much more than the minor poet (Bennett, 1980).

Overall, Simonton's theory is consistent with a broad range of historical data on productivity and is applicable very broadly over a range of artistic and scientific areas. However, as with Darwin's original theory of evolution, further specification of the means of variation and retention are needed to complete the chance-configuration theory.

Gruber's Evolving-systems Approach

Gruber (1980) has painstakingly analysed the case of Charles Darwin's development of evolutionary theory in terms of evolving systems of ideas. To understand the evolution of ideas, Gruber has drawn on Piagetian theory, which is, of course, mainly concerned with the development of concepts (e.g. that of the conservation of mass) in children; however, Gruber shows that the approach can be usefully applied to conceptual growth in adults. Gruber points to the long time periods involved in developing significant new ideas. The emphasis on "acts of creation" and "moments of insight" has, perhaps, been misleading and diverted attention from the long-term growth-like processes in which moments of insight are embedded. Analysis of Darwin's notebooks indicates a series of changes in his "system of ideas" concerning the relationship of biological and geological phenomena. Initially, the dominant conceptual scheme was that the physical world and the species inhabiting it were fixed at creation. However, evidence from geology more and more indicated a changing physical world. This led to a conceptual conflict. How could species fixed at creation remain adapted to changing environments? Darwin's first theory – the monad theory – suggested that simple living forms (monads) appeared through spontaneous generation from inanimate matter and then evolved to match the environment. This was fairly quickly abandoned, and Darwin then sought other ways in which species could change. Hybridization seemed possible and led Darwin to a study of plant and animal breeding which increased his knowledge of artificial selection. The transmission of acquired characteristics was another possible solution and led Darwin into a study of mental processes and behaviour in animals and humans. Although this approach did not produce the desired answer to the question of heritable variation, it produced much evidence that would influence the final theory. Studying the evolution of mental processes also raised forcibly the issue of materialism. This was a somewhat suspect and dangerous idea at the time, and Darwin expressed fear of persecution on account of his materialist notions. After many years of prior study and experience, Darwin read Malthus' *Essay on Population* on 28 September 1838, and this seems to have led him to realize that natural selection could work in favour of variants that were better suited to their environment than their ancestors had been. The idea of natural selection as a "conservative" force, weeding out weak or maladapted variants, was well known, but the positive aspects of natural selection, favouring the best-adapted variants, had not been emphasized before Darwin's insight.

Darwin was not quite satisfied with the theory because it did not explain variation but rather took variation and heredity as unexplained assumptions. A further 20 years of work and the stimulus of Wallace's independent conception of "evolution by natural selection" were required before Darwin finally published his evolutionary theory.

Gruber emphasizes the slowness of the changes in Darwin's system of ideas and he interprets the process of change in terms of Piaget's notions of "assimilation" and "accommodation". "Assimilation" involves the incorporation of new information into existing conceptual structures, while "accommodation" involves changes in conceptual structure brought about by new information. Gruber argues that what appear to be dramatic breaks with the past can also be seen as the culmination of numerous small changes. This approach, then, places "moments of insight" within their long-term context and would suggest that little understanding of high-order creativity will result from laboratory studies of small-scale problem-solving.

Gruber and his colleagues (e.g. Gruber and Davis, 1988) have applied their evolving-systems approach to case studies of the work of a number of other creative individuals in addition to Darwin, in a range of domains, including the scientist Benjamin Franklin, psychologist William James, philosopher John Locke, novelist Dorothy Richardson, and poet William Wordsworth. Overall, these studies have supported the view that creative work in real life takes a very long time – months, years or even decades. The spread of work over long time periods means that considerable organization of effort is needed. Subgoals and sub-subgoals must be set up and integrated into the overall effort; delays, tangents and false starts proliferate. Initial sketches, rough drafts and early notebooks play a crucial role in shaping and guiding projects. For example, Picasso's famous painting *Guernica* began as a sketch which underwent successive elaborations and transformations over a month to yield the final product (Arnheim, 1962). Often, the creative individual has a network of related projects, some of which are relatively active and some relatively dormant at any one time. These interrelated projects influence each other and can offer useful analogies from one project to another and general linking themes. For example, Darwin worked on geological, zoological, psychological and botanical projects; a linking theme which he developed in all areas was that of *gradualism* ("nature makes no jumps"). Gruber and Davis also argue that multiple projects enable the creative individual to continue good work even when experiencing a blockage on one project; an alternative project is taken up until perhaps an accidental stimulus offers a way of dealing with the impasse in the first project. Finally, intrinsic motivation to work in the domain concerned for its own sake seems to be essential and underlies the high activity levels of creative individuals.

Boden: Improbabilist and Impossibilist Creativity

Boden (1990, 1994) has argued that there are two broad types of creativity, which she labels "improbabilist" and "impossibilist". These in turn can both be divided into psychological/personal and historical creativity. Improbabilist creativity involves generating new and valued products while working within an established rule-system which defines a conceptual space of possibilities; impossibilist creativity involves the transformation of conceptual spaces so that new ideas arise which were impossible within pre-transformation spaces. Psychological/personal creativity involves production of ideas new to the individual (though they may have been produced by many others), while historical creativity involves producing ideas which have never been produced by anyone before. Boden points out that historical creativity is a subset of psychological/personal creativity, and she focuses on impossibilist psychological/personal creativity. To transform a conceptual space, Boden argues that one must be able to map and explore the space. She points to developmental evidence that children become ever more flexible by using "representational redescriptions" of lower-level skills (Karmiloff-Smith, 1993). Initially, children develop basic schemas for drawing a man. These schemas are quite rigid, and 4-year-olds cannot spontaneously draw a one-legged man because that is outside the schema (or conceptual space). They have difficulty copying out-of-schema figures also. By 10 years of age, most children can distort, repeat and omit parts and have greatly transformed their earlier schemas. These transformations develop in a fixed order. Normally, children can change the size or shape of an arm before they can insert an extra arm and well before they can draw a man with wings instead of arms.

Larger-scale examples may be found in the history of music and mathematics. Post-Renaissance music in the West involved explorations of tonal harmony. Atonal music (e.g. Schoenberg) represents a marked transformation of the original tonal space into the atonal space. The transformation fundamentally consisted of dropping the requirement that a piece of music must have a "home key" from which it starts and to which it must return. Schoenberg dropped this constraint and added new ones (e.g. using every note in the chromatic scale). A similar case of dropping constraints to develop a new space is found in the move from Euclidean to non-Euclidean geometry which arose from dropping Euclid's fifth axiom.

What type of cognitive system might support impossibilist creativity? Boden suggests a hybrid serial–parallel system. On this view, long-term knowledge is stored in a connectionist network which can throw up unusual associations, combinations and analogies, while the serial part steadily searches through problem spaces. The network may suggest new problem spaces through associations and analogies retrieved in response to the task. There are echoes here of the traditional view that the unconscious (the network) is the source of inspiration and the conscious (the serial system) carries out the more routine work of preparation and verification (Wallas, 1926).

CONCLUDING COMMENTS

Overall, the data and theories outlined here indicate, contrary to the myths set out in the introduction,(1) that large-scale real-life creativity is explicable in terms of normal everyday cognitive processes marshalled in a goal-directed way over long periods, (2) that knowledge acquisition is a key process in providing the starting points and ingredients for creative work, (3) that innate cognitive talents do not feature strongly, and finally (4) that fast-track methods are of limited use in large-scale real-life creative problem-solving, compared with extensive trial-and-error search.

Section 4

CONTROVERSIAL ISSUES: CLONES, AGEING, AND HYPNOSIS

HAPPY, GRUMPY, SNEEZY,
DOC, BASHFUL, SLEEPY,
DOPEY.
AND AS FOR TODAY,
NO AGEING BRAIN....

Since the time on a warm night in July 1996 (Kolata, 1997), when Dolly, the second most famous lamb in history, was born, the media has been struck by the upsurge in debate on the rights and wrongs of cloning, a controversy not unlike that about the so-called preformationism, the idea that in each sperm there is a minuscule homunculus (Eisenberg, 1976), which excited Seneca and Aristotle.

The debate in the media has been little concerned with the technicalities or the potential outcome of the cloning methods, such as the implications it might have for cancer research. Rather, it has focused on the matter of human cloning, concentrating in particular on the frightful idea of reproducing evil people (could Hitler live again?), thus reducing the whole debate to a science fiction script.

Leave the my-opinion-on-everything media-ethicists wrestling on large white television armchairs, and let us try to understand why clones would never be exact replicas of each other (Changeux, 1983; Pennisi, 1997).

The following two chapters deal with similarly controversial issues: the analysis of the performance of the elderly and hypnosis.

CHAPTER 10

The Myth of the Clonable Human Brain

GIOVANNI BERLUCCHI

CLONING AND THE BRAVE NEW WORLD

The recent announcement (Wilmut et al., 1997) of the successful production of a viable, apparently normal lamb from an oocite whose nucleus had been replaced with the nucleus of a cell derived from an adult mammary gland has generated a heated debate about the envisionable horrors of the possible application of this technology to the cloning of human beings. Biological and psychological individuality is part and parcel of human nature, and most human values are corollaries of the concept that each person is unique and identical to himself or herself through space and time. Men, women and children are all marked and set apart not only by the characteristics of their bodily structures, but also by the idiosyncrasies of their minds as determined by the unique organization of their brains. Among the several reasons why the cloning of a human being appears repugnant to most people, pre-eminent is the conviction that this kind of genetic manipulation may interfere with biological and psychological diversity, and therefore with the distinctiveness and autonomy of the individual. A visionary anticipation of this hypothetical shocking scenario can be found in Aldous Huxley's novel *Brave New World* (Huxley, 1932), an articulate depiction of a scientific dictatorship in which a foolproof system of genetic control, specifically designed to standardize the human product, was used to reduce the bewildering diversity of human nature to some kind of manageable uniformity. At the Central London Hatchery and Conditioning Centre fictionalized by Huxley, human eggs fertilized and nurtured in vitro were submitted to a procedure by which each egg would repeatedly bud, split and develop into up to 96 genetically identical embryos and eventually into as many phenotypically identical adults, intended to constitute homogeneous and unvarying castes. Socially desirable behaviour appropriate to each caste was ensured by combining the process of genetic and embryonic treatment with infant conditioning, hypnopaedia and chemically induced euphoria as a substitute for the satisfaction of mastering one's own life. In short, social stability was achieved by granting a largely homogenized humankind a state of physical well-being without conscious experience of suffering and deprivation, but also without freedom, beauty and creativity, and ultimately without the feeling of a unique personal existence.

THE NATURAL CLONES

Nature has, of course, been producing genetically identical humans from time immemorial, though not in scores at once as in Huxley's fable, but usually in trifling pairs of monozygotic twins, and even less frequently in batches of monozygotic triplets, quadruplets or at most quintuplets. If there are moral arguments for opposing the possibility of full human cloning – and there are many – they should not include the suspected potential annihilation of personal identity by this technology, for nothing of what we know about the genetically identical products of nature challenges the facts of individual diversity and uniqueness. More specifically, studies of monozygotic twins provide enough information for debunking the myth that since identical genes appear to make identical bodies, they also make identical brains and, by implication, identical minds. It is true, of course, that monozygotic twins not only look alike, but also seem to think and feel alike. Even when raised in different families, they are undoubtedly quite similar in many psychological traits, to the point of choosing the same occupation, showing preferences for the same brands of hair tonics, toothpaste or cigarettes, and performing the same peculiar antics (Bouchard, 1997). A favourite anecdote which finds its way into most books on evolutionary psychology is that of the female monozygotic twins raised apart who used to enter the ocean backward and just up to their knees (e.g. Pinker, 1997). But the psychological differences between monozygotic twins, whether raised together or apart, are at least as important as the identities. The 19th-century monozygotic men from Siam who, being conjoined at the abdomen, performed in the Barnum circus and gave origin to the term Siamese twins, had quite different destinies in spite of their forced cohabitation, because one became morose and alcoholic, while the other remained benignly cheerful and teetotal (Gould, 1997). The genetically identical Dionne quintuplets born in Canada in the early 1930s were no more alike in their lives than might have been expected of five unrelated girls raised at that time in that social environment (Lewontin, 1997). More quantitative and less anecdotal evidence indicates that the concordance on various personality traits is about 50% between genetically identical monozygotic twins, as opposed to 25% between dizygotic twins (who have shared the maternal uterus but have only half of their genes in common), 11% between siblings, who also share half of their genes, and virtually 0% between randomly chosen unrelated individuals. The concordance between monozygotic twins on intelligence tests is even higher, reaching 70% as opposed to 40% or less in dizygotic twins (Bouchard, 1997; McClearn et al., 1997). There is thus little doubt that genetics has a strong influence on the mind, but an even more interesting point is that the 30–50% non-genetic psychological variation between monozygotic twins can hardly be regarded as a bona fide effect of the environment. Indeed, the concordance on cognitive and personality measures found between monozygotic twins reared apart is only minimally smaller than that found in monozygotic twins living together (Bouchard, 1997).

BIOLOGICAL FACTORS OF INDIVIDUAL DIVERSITY: BETWEEN GENES AND ENVIRONMENT

What, then, are the causes of psychological variation between monozygotic twins that cannot be accounted for by the overall influence of their family environment, and what are the neural underpinnings of the similarities and differences between their mental processes? One interpretation ascribes non-genetic psychological differences between monozygotic twins to unique non-shared personal experiences that are bound to occur even under strict cohabitation conditions, such as being chased by a dog or receiving an occasional individual reward or punishment from a teacher or parent (Gazzaniga, 1992; Pinker, 1997). There seems to be no way to gather direct objective evidence to support this interpretation. Another, alternative view can be traced back to the original suggestion of Hebb (1966) that growth of the embryonic and fetal brain and behavioural development alike are bound to be significantly affected by the varying physiological conditions existing in the prenatal uterine environment. With twins, factors such as variations in the position of the fetuses in the womb, in the exchanges between maternal blood and fetal blood, and in the amount of head trauma associated with parturition, may all account for mental and cerebral differences which occur in spite of identical genomes. But I think that there is now ample evidence that the cerebral and mental uniqueness of each monozygotic twin owes more to quite subtle but powerful prenatal epigenetic factors than to the above gross intrauterine influences. As lucidly argued by Changeux (1983) several years ago, the complexity of the nervous system is such that already at birth it is virtually impossible for genetically identical twins to possess exactly the same cerebral organization down to the level of the trillions of single synapses that occur in the human brain. He called attention to the experiments of Macagno, Lopresti and Levinthal (1973) on the crustacean *Daphnia magnia* and by Levinthal, Macagno and Levinthal (1976) on the fish *Poecilia formosa*, showing that in the relatively simple nervous systems of these species, isogenic animals born by parthenogenesis were distinguishable on the basis of the fine details of the branching of presynaptic terminals in corresponding neural sites, though not in terms of number of neurons and major selective interneuronal connections. In considering the development of the nervous system, one has to keep in mind that in addition to cellular differentiation, migration and aggregation processes that apply to the rest of the body, the orderly growth of neuronal axons and dendrites and the formation of highly organized and selective systems of synaptic connections are enormously more complex than the events involved in the genesis of all non-nervous organs. Such complexity greatly expands the fringe of nervous system traits that are not subject to a strict genetic determinism and are there-fore open to a more or less pronounced phenotypic variability. Molecules of various types (growth factors, hormones, neurotransmitters, netrins, semaphorins, adhesion molecules, etc.), whether residing in the extracellular matrix or anchored to cell membranes, are essential for directing growing axons and dendrites along appropriate paths to the appro-priate targets with which they are to form functioning synaptic relations (Levitan and Kaczmarek, 1997). The combinatorial explosion in the number of synaptic connections between several billions of neurons in the large human brain makes it likely that the fringe of non-genetic variability in neural development attains an unsurpassed extent. More specifically, the brains of human neonates are bound to differ with respect to a number of discrete, functionally important features of the pattern of synaptic connections within a shared, species-specific general plan of brain organization which has remained unchanged since the appearance of *Homo sapiens* at least 100 000 years ago. This is true not only of genetically different individuals, where brain differences are at least partly determined by different genes, but also of genetically identical twins, where genes alone cannot specify the innumerable intimate details of the overall individual pattern of neuronal interconnec-tions. That major changes in this organization can and do occur postnatally as a result of experience and general environmental influences is, of course, another story. The message here is that if it were possible to bring a newborn baby back to the condition of a fertilized egg in the maternal womb, its non-neural organs would probably form much in the same way, whereas at least some details of the development of its brain would be sufficiently altered to give rise to a perhaps slightly but no doubt significantly different neural machin-ery for mental activity and behavioural control.

MACROSCOPIC DIFFERENCES BETWEEN THE BRAINS OF MONOZYGOTIC TWINS

The non-invasive magnetic resonance imaging technique has made it possible to examine and compare the brains of monozygotic twins in vivo. Oppenheim et al. (1989) reported a much greater similarity in the appearance of the corpus callosum between the members of each of five pairs of monozygotic twins than between unrelated individuals, yet subtle intrapair differences in callosal morphology could also be detected. In the members of nine pairs of right-handed monozygotic twins, Steinmetz et al. (1995) found the typically human side asymmetry whereby the left planum temporale is larger than the right, but only in four pairs was the magnitude of this difference consistent between twins. In an additional exceptional pair, one twin showed an inverse difference in favour of the right side. In another sample of 10 pairs of monozygotic twins who were discordant for manual dominance, the intrapair variability in the planum temporale asymmetry was even more remarkable, since most of the left-handed individuals showed an inverse or no asymmetry (Steinmetz et al., 1995). In a more recent imaging study, Bartley, Jones and Weinberger (1997) analysed various aspects of brain morphology in 10 pairs of monozygotic twins and nine pairs of sex-matched dizygotic twins. There was a highly significant 94% intrapair concordance in brain volume in the monozygotic sample, compared to an insignificant 34% intrapair concordance in the dizygotic sample, suggesting that, like body size, brain size is under strict genetic control. By contrast, statistical evidence for heritability of the overall external configuration of the cerebral cortex was low and ill-defined, given the remarkably imperfect concordance in the pattern of cortical sulci and gyri between monozygotic twins, in spite of a greater apparent similarity than in dizygotic twins. All in all, it seems easier to distinguish identical twins by looking at their brains than by looking at their faces. According to Van Essen (1997), the characteristic folding of the cerebral cortex can be explained by the non-random action of tension along axons in the white matter, and therefore by implication it reflects the connectivity and topology of the underlying neural circuitry. To the extent that individual mental and behavioural characteristics depend on unique specific properties of brain organization, the observed differences in cortical configuration between the brains of monozygotic twins can reasonably be assumed to be major factors of the demonstrable differences in their psychological make-ups. It can, of course, be argued that since all the above imaging studies were performed in adults, any observed difference in brain morphology between monozygotic twins may well be the result of postnatal environment actions. However, this possibility seems quite unlikely, since macroscopic brain features such as the right–left asymmetry of the planum temporale (Chi, Dooling and Gilles, 1977) and the overall pattern of cortical folding (Armstrong et al., 1995) are determined before birth. In attributing differences in cortical configuration between monozygotic twins to postnatal environmental influences, Bartley, Jones and Weinberger (1997) misinterpreted Armstrong et al.'s (1995) findings about the ontogeny of human cortex gyrification. Contrary to their statement, between birth and adulthood the degree of cortical folding does not double, but rather remains virtually constant in spite of a threefold increase in brain size (Armstrong et al., 1995).

THE BRAIN AS A SOCIAL CONSTRUCT

There are two senses in which the brain can be regarded as a social construct (Eisenberg, 1995). One is that the individual's social environment moulds the anatomo-functional organization of the individual's brain. The other is that in any given historical period, ideas and beliefs about the brain reflect the culture of that period. The current prevailing view of the brain is that the genes predispose a structure of the nervous system which, throughout the entire individual's life, is partly maintained and partly modified and adjusted by personal experiences and interactions with the environment. I see in this view a failure to recognize the contribution of the chance events occurring in the ontogenesis of each nervous system to the prenatal production of unique brains, each of which will interact with the environment in its own idiosyncratic manner. The idea that genetic manipulation may allow a brain and the mind associated with it to be replicated is preposterous, not only because of the sheer impossibility of recreating the detailed vicissitudes of an individual existence, but also because of the uncontrollable nature of the chance events in the formation of the brain circuitries. If nuclear genetic material were available to make a clone of Leonardo da Vinci, and it were possible to reproduce the conditions in which he grew up and lived, it would be unduly optimistic to foresee that the clone would unfold into a polymath and an artistic genius, and absurd to expect him to paint La Gioconda. For all we know, he may not even turn out to be left-handed, as Leonardo was, because left-handedness appears to be a chance phenotypic expression in the absence of a gene that biases the direction of handedness towards the right (Corballis, 1997). Individuals lacking the gene and, as a result, the right bias, may develop as either right- or left-handers, which may explain why monozygotic twins can be discordant for handedness (Steinmetz et al., 1995). It has long been recognized that biological evolution by natural selection is predicated on the uniqueness of the biological make-up of the individual and the resulting variability among individuals in sexually reproducing populations. I suggest it is time to acknowledge that a non-genetic inborn variability between the brains of different individuals may in turn help the cultural evolution of the species by the chance production of the cerebral primordia of exceptionally gifted minds, to be nurtured and developed in appropriate environments.

CHAPTER 11

When Age is In, the Wit is Out?

PAT RABBITT

Old age has a bad press which has generated gloomy stereotypes; in later life, like La Rochefoucauld, few of us expect much fun ("old age is a tyrant who forbids, under pain of life, all the pleasures of youth") or achievement ("There are few people who, in the first decline of old age, do not give evidence in what respect their body and mind must fall away"). At best we wryly agree with Groucho Marx that "growing old is what you do if you are lucky". Nevertheless, cheerful counter-examples abound.

At 70, Churchill was able to announce that the military, industrial and diplomatic effort that he had brilliantly co-ordinated over the last 5 years had been successful. At 75, Nicholas Hawkesmoor completed designs for the towers of Westminster Abbey, John Nash designed Carlton House Terrace and Monteverdi completed "L'incoronazione di Poppea", arguably his most daring and influential work. It is not recorded that Henry Ford managed any remarkable intellectual achievement at any age, but eye-witnesses testify that at 75 he could still do handstands and enter convertibles by leaping over their doors. At 80, Justice Roger Brook Taney gave an historically significant judgement on the Dred Scott case and continued as Chief Justice of the US Supreme court until he died at 87. Lord Dearing was still Master of the Rolls at 80 when he published a notable book *The Discipline of the Law*. At 85, Gladstone at last retired as Prime Minister to work on his translation of Horace's odes; Joan Miro was, simultaneously, busy with commissions for a sculpture for the city of Chicago, murals for Barcelona and a tapestry for the National Gallery at Washington DC, and Karl Boehm continued as the star conductor of the Salzburg Festival and chief conductor of the Vienna Philharmonic. At the age of 90, Will and Ariel Durant published the eleventh and last volume of their history of the world *The Story of Civilisation*, Georgia O'Keefe continued to produce excellent paintings; Leopold Stockowski began to record his last 20 albums and Havergal Brian began to compose the first of seven symphonies that occupied him for the next 6 years. It is also nice to know that for the age of 90 the men's track records are 19.9 s for 100 m, 49.2 s for 200 m, held by Duncan McLean, who did not take up competitive running until his 60s, and for 800 m 8 min 54.2 s, held by Robert Willis. At 90, Teischi Igarishi made the first of his six, successive, annual ascents of 12 385-foot Mt Fuji.

Are these outstanding achievements merely statistical anomalies that tell us little about the potential of the majority of humans? If cognitive decline in old age is inevitable, how soon does it start and how rapidly does it continue? Does old age spare some cognitive skills while eroding others, or do all mental abilities change at the same, coupled, rate? Finally, and most interestingly, can we do anything to slow cognitive change?

HOW COMMON ARE NOTABLE ACHIEVEMENTS IN OLD AGE? ARE LATE ACHIEVEMENTS MORE COMMON IN SOME FIELDS THAN IN OTHERS?

The first systematic attempts to answer these questions were made by Lehmann (1953), who compiled statistics on the ages of peak achievement of Olympic athletes and professional sports people, as well as the ages at which remarkable individuals made their most notable intellectual achievements and at which they made their largest numbers of professional contributions. Lehmann's statistics on winners of the Olympic games have been updated by Schultz and Curnow (1988), who analysed records from the first modern Olympics in 1886 through to 1980. They found that for swimming events of most distances (e.g. 100-m, 400-m and 1500-m freestyle), winners' ages fall into a very narrow range between 19.94 and 21.42 years. For running, mean ages of winners increase regularly with distance: from 22.85 years for 100 m to 28.4 years for 1500 m. For long-distance events (5000 m, 100 000 m and marathon), the mean ages of record holders are between 27.20 and 27.85 years. Because Smith and Curnow analysed statistics over a period of 100 years, they were also able to ask whether the ages of peak achievement have changed with the striking improvements in records due to developments in training methods and the increased demands of modern Olympic competition. Comparing averages for the games between 1986–1936 and 1948–1980, they found that, in spite of the marked improvements in all records between these periods, the average ages of Olympic gold medal swimmers, for all distances, have reduced by only about 12 months; the average ages of winners of two of the three long-distance running events have increased by about 3 years and the average ages of short- and middle-distance runners have remained remarkably constant.

Ericssen (1990) made a broader analysis of the ages of the best performances by runners from seven countries in sprint, middle-distance and long-distance events. He found a steady increase from about 23 for 100 m and 400 m, through 25 and 25 respectively for 1500 m, to just under 26 for 5000 m and 10 000 m. It does indeed seem that running and swimming are young persons' sports. This confirms an earlier analysis by Letzelter, Jungermann and Frietag (1986), who computed the annual averages and fastest times for breaststroke, backstroke, butterfly and freestyle achieved by professional swimmers in each age-decade from 20 to 70. They found an almost linear increase in average times with age for all styles. It might be argued that these increases in mean times for groups of swimmers occur because some individuals show very marked deterioration in performance while others are hardly affected. Ericcsen (1990) addresses this point by plotting the best achievements by individual athletes during successive years of their lives, finding for 5000-m and 10 000-m races peaks at 27 with subsequent steady declines until 38 (Pavlo Nurmi); for the hammer throw a peak at 26, followed by a near-plateau until well past the age of 55 (Karl Hein); and, for the javelin, a peak at 28 followed by a near-plateau sustained until the early 30s (Matti Jarvinen). While it does seem that declines over the lifespan are general and regular, Ericcsen's plots make the important point that although all these great athletes did show some decline after reaching relatively early peaks, they were all capable of quite exceptional performances until late in their lives. Even in middle age some sportsmen maintained much higher levels of performance than those they had managed some years before they reached their lifetime peaks. This finding is a neglected key to analysis of biographical statistics. Although talented individuals' lifetime *best* performances may occur early in their lives, they seem to be able to continue to maintain levels of achievement beyond the reach of most of humankind well into middle age and older. There is every reason to suppose that what is true of exceptional individuals is also true of the less gifted majority who, having achieved some modest success, can continue to surpass mediocrity.

Lehmann (1953, 1954, 1957) also pioneered studies of levels of cognitive achievements over the lifespan. Most later surveys confirm his findings that at disciplines such as mathematics, physics and chemistry, which are recognized to be exceptionally demanding of intellectual power and ability to find novel solutions to difficult abstract problems, outstanding practitioners reach their peaks between their mid-20s and mid-30s. In contrast, historians and novelists who may need many years to master large amounts of information, or to acquire a rich life experience, often produce their best work in their 50s or later. There appears to be no upper age limit to outstanding achievements by graphic artists, architects, musical composers and executants. Although Lehmann accurately analysed the data available to him, his conclusions do not tell the whole story. A first limitation is that he considers only the single "glory years" in which exceptional individuals produced work that experts agree to be their "lifetime best", and the single years in which they attained the maximum numbers of achievements of any kind. This omits achievements which are marginally "lesser" only in the contexts of brilliant careers but which are still extraordinarily impressive in relation to those attainable by most humans. Many of Lehmann's intellectually distinguished people lived during the 18th and 19th centuries when life-expectancy was much shorter than it is today. In consequence, his data are skewed by many, prematurely curtailed, careers. This is, perhaps, one of the reasons why Stern (1978), analysing the careers of mathematicians using much more recent citation indices, found no evidence of particularly early "peaks" either in terms of age at which the most outstanding achievements occurred, or the age at which the largest number of publications appeared. He concluded that any changes in productivity by distinguished mathematicians after the ages of 45–49 might be explained by the onset of administrative and family responsibilities as their careers progressed. This difficulty of separating the possible effects of cognitive ageing from the demands of career structures has also been emphasized by Dennis (1956, 1958b, 1966). For example, until quite late in the 19th century it was quite common for even distinguished young academics to set aside scholarship in their late 20s or early 30s in order to follow more lucrative, and perhaps more prestigious, professions. It is naive not to recognize that most scientists are not entirely motivated by pure intellectual curiosity and so are most strongly impelled to produce quantities of excellent original work while they are young and still need to gain recognition. Besides entailing administrative distractions in middle age, an established career may well blunt hunger for further achievements. Differences in the conclusion reached by analysts often reflect the fact that biographical data have been pooled across very different historical periods during which current career structures, and the resources now available to older scientists, did not exist.

Conclusions from biographical data are tentative even when we consider such apparently "pure" cases as the tournament records of distinguished chess players who, because the game is their major source of income, have often been forced to try to support themselves by competing in tournaments for as long as possible. While Elo's (1965) classic analyses of tournament records do show early peaks (20–40) followed by slow but inexorable declines, age is not the only factor involved. For example, Alekhine, one of the most brilliant players whose lifetime record Elo analyses, was also remarkable for the duration and steadily mounting intensity of the alcoholism that eventually killed him. Such tragic cases highlight the problem that, as their lives unfold, people do not just grow old but also accumulate an increasing toll of pathologies and of "negative biological life events". Because the 18th- and 19th-century biographies that have contributed to the statistics analysed by Lehmann and others were, by modern standards, not only relatively short but also unhealthy, they do not provide useful data from which to extrapolate current or future expectations. Recent advances in clinical treatment and preventative medicine have not only greatly increased life-expectancy but have also ensured that people remain much healthier for a much greater proportion of their lifespans. It is plausible that during the next decades most of us will follow our modest early peaks with plateaux which last into a healthy old age.

This raises a central question in cognitive gerontology: whether changes in mental abilities in old age are mainly, or entirely, driven by the lifetime accumulation and steadily increasing incidence of pathologies, or whether the change we observe is mainly driven by much less well understood processes that we may term "normal" or "usual" ageing.

LIMITING CASES OF MODELS FOR THE AETIOLOGY AND TIME COURSE OF COGNITIVE AGEING

In cognitive gerontology, as in all of the other neurosciences, the problem is to find ways of using incomplete data to guide our choices between alternative models for functional processes. The developmental trajectory of the central nervous system (CNS) is a useful starting point, because it is axiomatic that all mental abilities depend on its functional integrity. Nearly all of the cells of which our bodies are composed live for only 5–7 years. If they did not reproduce themselves before they died, this would be the brief limit of our lives. On the other hand, if they could successfully and indefinitely reproduce and replace themselves, we should, barring accidents, be effectively immortal. We are not, because there is a limit, named after its discoverer Hayflick, of between 7 and 15 successful cell reproductions. It follows that because most tissues in our bodies are completely renewed on a roughly 7-year cycle we, like all other animals, have physical continuity only as dynamic patterns imposed by our genetic programmes on a constantly changing collection of matter rather than as static arrangements of unchanging stuff like boulders or books. Unlike most of our other body cells our neurons do not reproduce, so that the ones we are born with must serve us through our entire lives into old age. Because our neurons continue to die throughout our lives, and because the rate of this attrition accelerates in old age, we may pessimistically infer that because the number of functional units in our brains steadily declines throughout our lifespans, our powers of mental computation are correspondingly enfeebled. (It may be some comfort to reflect that although we may feel that this arrangement is sub-optimal, it is probably more convenient than would be the continual death and renewal of our entire central nervous systems on a 7-year cycle. This might better preserve our maximum possible computing power but, in the process, might also continuously erase all of the information and useful skills that we manage to acquire.) It is also crucial to note that while there must be some gross relationship between the number of neurons in a brain and its "computing power", this is unlikely to be straightforward. Although the total volume of the brain is less than 2 litres, it contains, on average, over 10^{12} neurons. This vast number certainly guarantees impressive redundancy of function, as is shown by the fact that the period of most rapid and substantial neuronal death occurs during infancy while we make our most remarkable and rapid gains in cognitive computing power. We may speculate that this is because the brains of infants are engaged in the process of self-programming their neural "wetware" and that those units that do not rapidly become incorporated into functionally useful assemblies soon die. A rapid increase in mental ability during childhood and adolescence is accompanied by a reduced, but still detectable, rate of neuronal death that continues through middle age and accelerates during the sixth, seventh and eighth decades, so that men who manage to live to 70 will, on average, have lost 10% of their young adult cortical mass (women do somewhat better).

This global loss of brain tissue seems to be most marked in the frontal and temporal lobes and is often also accompanied by depletion of neurotransmitter systems, in particular of the cholinergic and dopaminergic systems (e.g. Haug et al., 1983; Mittenberg et al., 1989; Petit, 1982; Veroff, 1980; West, 1986; Whelihan and Lesher, 1985). This suggests that while ageing must affect all functional systems of the brain, and so all mental abilities, skills that are mediated by the frontal and temporal cortex may be particularly vulnerable. The ranges of variation between individuals in the time course and extent of these changes are still unknown so that, as for all the other physiological concomitants of ageing, it is hard to draw clear distinctions between "natural" or "usual" and "patholog- ical" changes. It is evident that there is a marked increase, with age, in the incidence of conditions such as atherosclerosis, respiratory disorders such as emphysema and car- diovascular problems that affect supply of oxygen and nutrients to the brain and so must accelerate changes (Rabbit, Bent and McInnes, 1997). The incidence of these conditions is also known to be related to occupation, socio-economic advantage and choice of life- style, so that we might expect that socio-economic disadvantage, which clearly reduces life-expectancy, must also accelerate the rate of cognitive ageing. Apart from environmen- tal factors, it is also clear that individuals do, very markedly, differ in what may be termed their basic, genetically programmed, rates of physiological, neurological and so, inferen- tially, cognitive ageing.

Thus the neurophysiological evidence suggests that we must all decline, though perhaps at very different rates that are determined by complex interactions between our genetic inheritance, "biological life events" and socio-economic conditions. This would be more discouraging if we supposed that there must be a very direct relationship between brain mass and cognitive function. However, as we have seen, within each individual's lifespan this relationship paradoxically reverses during infancy. The speculation that this happens be- cause nerve nets are "self-programmed" to exchange initially massive redundancy for greater efficiency can, just as reasonably, be extended to the much slower declines in neuronal redundancy accompanied by continued acquisition of cognitive skills in middle and later life. It remains a plausible speculation that lifelong learning may also entail lifelong "self-programming" of the brain with consequent, progressive, reduction of redundancy.

Comparisons between animals species do indeed reveal a general, positive relationship between their average brain mass and their "intelligence" (Jerison, 1982) but there are striking exceptions to this trend, and factors such as density of neuronal packing, and degrees of neuronal connectivity, seem to be crucially important. If we compare humans of the same ages, evidence for a one-to-one relationship between brain size and cognitive ability is certainly lacking. Assertions that the brain volumes of different races, or of different individuals, directly determine corresponding differences in their cognitive abil- ities have been shown to be a "neuromyth" based on careless misreading or even deliber- ate misrepresentation of evidence (see Gould, 1981; Howe, 1997). Recent claims of direct correlations between brain volume and cognitive ability across individuals and, in particu- lar, the suggestion that women, who tend to have smaller heads, are, for that reason, less gifted on average that men (Lynn, keynote address at Spearman symposium 1995), are based on poor evidence and bad logic and seem to be pursued with a curious and distasteful stridency.

It is certain that brain integrity must affect cognitive performance and it is also certain that loss of brain integrity must account for many of the phenomena of cognitive ageing; however, it is equally clear that, in healthy individuals, this relationship is neither very direct nor at all simple. It is also clear that because any relationships that do exist must be strongly modified by a wide range of genetic, physiological, psychological and socio-economic variables, they offer only a weak and partial description of extremely complex, and still cryptic, interactions.

It is helpful to contrast limiting cases of possible descriptive models for the trajectory of cognitive changes across the lifespan. Since no behaviour of any kind has ever been elicited from a newly fertilized ovum or from a corpse, it is wise to assume that, in spite of some claims to the contrary, mental ability at conception and after death is zero. This sets limits for the alternative lifespan profiles of cognitive change illustrated in Figure 11.1. Most middle-aged people would be very happy to accept the implications of Figure 11.1A that, after a very rapid and asymptotic initial rise, cognitive abilities remain at a plateau, declining little until sharply reduced by rapidly impending death. This has become known as the "terminal-drop" model of cognitive ageing (Kleemeir, 1962). The alternative limiting case is that after an asymptotic rise through infancy and adolescence, all cognitive abilities begin to suffer an initially gradual but steadily accelerating decline. This "continuous-decline" model is illustrated in Figure 11.1B.

These descriptions offer other interesting predictions of what we may observe when we collect data on performance on cognitive tests from large populations of people of different ages. The continuous-decline model easily incorporates the idea that individuals may attain very different early peaks of cognitive ability and may also decline from these peaks at different rates. This raises the question, which we shall consider later, of whether the heights of the initial peaks that individuals attain determine the rates of their subsequent declines. The idiosyncratic lifetime cognitive profiles of individuals will be determined both by their genetic inheritance and by their lifetime health status, education and experiences. As a result, trajectories of cognitive ageing will tend to vary markedly between individuals so that, especially if there is a very strong and direct relationship between initial peak attainment and subsequent rate of decline, the extent of this variation will become increasingly pronounced as increasingly elderly groups are sampled. The "terminal-drop" model also predicts that as a population ages, the average level of ability will decline and the difference in ability between its least and most able members will increase. This is because, as everyday observation suggests, it is quite rare for individuals to decline from competence to desuetude over a period of only a few weeks or months. Pathologies terminating in death more usually reduce competence over a period of at least some years so that, as increasingly old cohorts are sampled, the numbers of individuals who still maintain their performance plateaux are likely to steadily reduce and the numbers of those experiencing their "terminal drops" will, correspondingly, rise. Thus both models predict that as populations age their average ability will decline but the variance in ability between their members will increase.

Many large cross-sectional studies since that by Jones and Conrad (1933) have found some age-related decline in average scores on intelligence tests between groups in their 20s and 30s, but these early changes are slight, and only gradually accelerate to become marked between 65 and 75 years. Findings that as a population ages so variance in levels of performance between its members increases are supported by meta-analyses of data from laboratory studies such as that by Morse (1983). This picture is also found in data gathered in our laboratory from 2600 residents of Newcastle-upon-Tyne whose ages ranged from 50 to 86 years. On all of the tests of mental ability that they were given, while scores for the most able individuals show little decline between successive age groups, the gap between the most and least able individuals, and so also the variance of scores between individuals, steadily increases with cohort age.

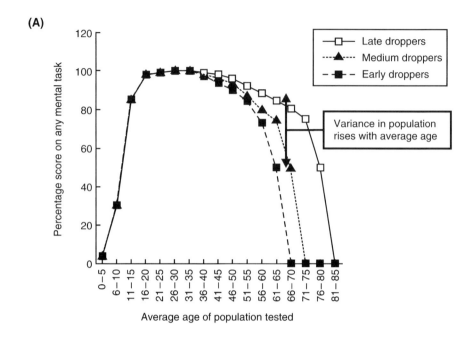

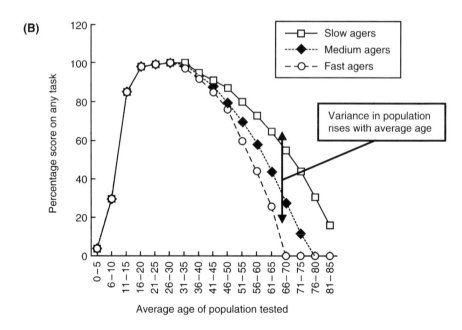

Figure 11.1 (A) Dummy data showing continuous-decline model. (B) Dummy data illustrating terminal-drop model.

Like all cross-sectional data yet available, these are illustrative rather than definitive, because the older the group sampled, the fewer people in it will be sufficiently fit or motivated to volunteer for screening. As cohort age increases, so increasing numbers of the least able individuals are not surveyed, and data tend to be increasingly based on "elite" survivors (Lachman, Lachman and Taylor, 1982). Another problem with cross-sectional comparisons is that we do not know whether the most able individuals in the oldest groups are maintaining performance plateaux or whether they have declined from some even more impressive pinnacles of attainment. This raises the further question of whether people of initially high ability decline at the same rate as, or less rapidly than, those of initially more modest attainment.

It might seem that the direct way to resolve these questions is to carry out longitudinal studies during which the same individuals are repeatedly tested over many years. Unfortunately, longitudinal studies also suffer from the problem of selective recruitment, with the additional difficulty of progressive selective attrition that occurs because only the fittest, ablest and best-motivated individuals are willing to continue with very long, tedious investigations (Lachman, Lachman and Taylor, 1982; Rabbitt et al., 1994). For these reasons, it is probably fair to say that no analysis of longitudinal data from large populations has yet clearly answered the question of whether people who attain different levels of ability as young adults decline at different rates, or whether the "continuous-decline" or the "terminal-drop" model provides the best description of population ageing. However, meticulous and insightful studies of single cases by Jarvik (1983) have shown that particular, lucky, individuals have shown remarkably little cognitive change until just before they have died in their late 70s or early 80s.

The author and his associates have studied over 6400 residents of Manchester and Newcastle-upon-Tyne who were aged between 50 and 86 years when they were first screened between 1982 and 1985. Over the last 15 years there have been measurable drops in *average* scores on most cognitive tests as age increases. However, the crucial finding is that these changes have been very slight indeed, and are very much less than might have been expected from earlier, smaller and shorter, studies. While we find, as we expected, that during the course of our study this decline has been more marked and rapid in initially older than in initially younger volunteers, it is also the case that, as in Jarvik's studies of particular individuals, some fortunate individuals have shown little or no detectable change as they have moved from their mid-60s through their 70s into their early 80s. The key question is what factors make these people so much luckier than their co-evals. When our longitudinal data have been completely analysed, they will tell us whether level of initial ability is one of the factors that determines the rate and extent of subsequent change and will also identify other factors that show or accelerate decline. At the moment, cross-sectional comparisons between groups of different ages offer only provisional answers to these questions. One obvious question has been whether the rate of cognitive change is determined by level of socio-economic advantage. Affluent individuals have enjoyed longer than average education, have worked all their lives in intellectually demanding jobs, have experienced better diet and living conditions, and less risk of industrial toxicity and accidents, and have had better access to medical treatment and to information about health care. Because all of these factors are known to markedly affect life-expectancy it is a reasonable speculation that they are also likely to affect the rate of cognitive change before death. To test this, we plotted scores on tests of cognitive function against group age for samples of individuals categorized in terms of the HM

Registrar General's taxonomy of occupational status (Office of Population Censuses and Surveys, 1980). Figure 11.2 shows average scores for these groups on the Heim (1970) AH 4 (1) intelligence test obtained from 2500 residents of Newcastle-upon-Tyne aged between 50 and 85 years.

As expected, for all socio-economic categories average scores decline slightly, but significantly, with group age. It is also not surprising that in all age groups less advantaged individuals who have had shorter and poorer education and less opportunity for lifelong intellectual engagement also had correspondingly lower AH 4 (1) scores. However, the rates of decline in average scores across age groups were the same for all socio-economic categories, so that these data give no evidence that the rates of decline of test scores across age groups differ with socio-economic advantage.

Other studies, such as the Berlin longitudinal study of ageing (Dr Margaret Baltes, personal communication), have found similar results. Because all epidemiological studied agree that both mortality and incidence of pathologies increase sharply with socio-economic disadvantage, these findings probably reflect strong selection biases rather than the operation of natural justice. Particularly in the oldest age groups, only individuals who still maintain a certain level of general health, mobility and competence will agree to join, or to continue with arduous longitudinal studies. The higher risk of pathologies and of consequently reduced cognitive ability for the majority of the socially disadvantaged may not be apparent in such self-selected samples. Further, as analysis of the Manchester/Newcastle data has shown, drop-out rates are significantly higher for less advantaged socio-economic groups (Rabbitt et al., 1994), and those who drop out of studies for reasons of illness or loss of motivation have significantly lower initial scores than those who continue.

However, it is precisely because selection bias prevents us from estimating the extent to which socio-economic advantage affects the rate of cognitive change that these data allow us to ask whether level of peak attainment affects amount of subsequent change. In

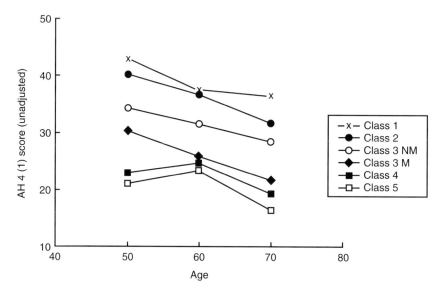

Figure 11.2   AH 4 (1) scores by age and social class.

groups that are "elite" in terms of their general health and level of motivation, peoples' mental abilities appear to decline at the same rates, irrespective of differences in the peak levels of performance that they reached as young adults. When health and motivation are held constant by self-selection, there is no evidence that marked differences in mental attainment in young adult life, subsequent years of education or type of profession practised over a lifetime affect the rate of cognitive change in old age. A second point is that, in these atypically healthy and motivated people, although differences between age groups are statistically reliable they are so small in absolute terms that it is unlikely that they can have any real effect on people's abilities to manage their everyday lives.

These suggestions that individuals decline at the same rates whatever their levels of ability as young adults and whatever their subsequent intellectual experience await confirmation by analyses of longitudinal data. However, it is also possible to approach the question in another way by using the well-established finding that not all mental abilities change with age. A number of studies have replicated findings by Birren (1956, 1974) and Birren and Williams (1980) that while average levels of performance on intelligence tests that require rapid solution of problems decline with the ages of the populations sampled, scores on vocabulary tests remain constant, or may even increase, up to age 80 and beyond. These findings have been interpreted by Horn and his associates (Horn, 1982; Horn and Cattell, 1967) as evidence that while "fluid" mental abilities such as solving novel problems, mental speed, learning rate and short-term memory span decline with age, complex bodies of information, skills and procedures that are learned over a lifetime and continue to be used in old age become "crystallized" and are relatively unaffected by ageing or, indeed, by other pathologies, conditions and insults that may be expected to reduce the efficiency of the brain and central nervous system. This difference between "fluid" and "crystallized" abilities is central to our theme and will be discussed in greater detail below. For the moment, the fact that in our data, consistent with early findings by Birren (1956, 1974) and Horn (1982), scores on tests of recognition vocabulary such as the WAIS and Mill Hill do not change with age offers another way to test whether the levels of ability that individuals attain as young adults affect the rate at which they subsequently decline as they grow old.

Data from the Manchester/Newcastle sample show that individuals in their 50s and late 70s and 80s differ in terms of their average levels of performance on tests of "fluid" intelligence, of memory and learning and of information-processing ability, but not on the Mill Hill and WAIS vocabulary tests. It is well established that in samples of adolescents and young adults Mill Hill vocabulary scores strongly correlate with scores on the AH 4 (1) test of general fluid ability ($r = 0.75$ or higher). In our sample, since Mill Hill scores do not change between the ages of 50 and 80 we can assume that individuals of all ages who currently have similar Mill Hill scores also had similar AH 4 (1) scores when they were young adults. This allows us to select, from our entire volunteer panel, subgroups of people who are currently in their 50s, 60s and 70s but have the same Mill Hill scores. We further subdivided these groups into relatively "high", "medium" and "low" Mill Hill scorers. Figure 11.3 shows average AH 4 (1) scores for all these groups.

Thus Figure 11.3 shows that AH 4 (1) intelligence test scores decline consistently, but modestly, as group ages increase. The rate of this decline is identical for high, medium and low Mill Hill scorers. This comparison gives us no evidence that the maximum levels of ability that people attain in middle age, or as young adults, affect the rate at which they subsequently change as they grow old. Similar analyses found that age-related declines in

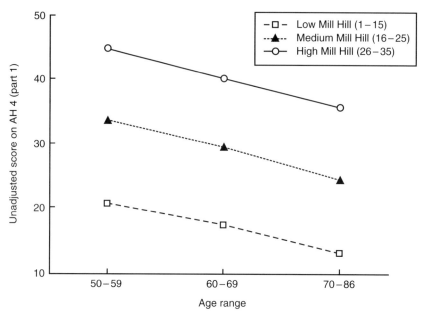

Figure 11.3 Changes in average AH 4 (1) IQ test scores between decade samples aged 50–59, 60–69 and 70–86 years, stratified by Mill Hill (A) vocabulary score bands.

scores on all of the tests of memory and of information-processing speed in our batteries were also identical for high, medium and low Mill Hill groups.

There are problems of interpretation. One is that we have compared rates of decline in average scores across successive age groups in absolute rather than in relative terms; that is, as in the case illustrated in Figure 11.3, in terms of unadjusted scores on intelligence tests, or in terms of numbers of items learned or remembered in memory tests, or in terms of milliseconds increase in decision times. Comparisons of change in absolute levels of scores may not be the most meaningful way to ask whether levels of youthful ability affect rates of subsequent change. For example, if Figure 11.3 were re-plotted to show changes as proportions (e.g. percentages) of initial values, the higher Mill Hill scorers would show very slight, and the lower Mill Hill scorers quite marked, declines from middle-aged base-lines. This procedure might be defended on the grounds that the small absolute drops in intelligence test scores that we observed do not imply any significance change in the everyday competence of the most able individuals. In contrast, for those whose compet-ence has already been marginal in middle age, even these slight declines may imply increased risk of dependency. There are good theoretical arguments for computing age-related changes in cognitive performance in either absolute or in proportional terms, depending on the particular question that we hope to address. A second problem of interpretation is that absolute comparisons are informative only if we can be certain that our indices of measurement represent points on an equal-interval scale. When, as with intelligence test scores, we have good reason to believe that differences in scores at the uppermost and lowest ends of the scale are very much less meaningful than, and so are incommensurable with, numerically equivalent differences in its middle region, neither absolute nor proportional comparisons unambiguously answer our questions.

A more useful way to approach the question of the amount and significance of change is to ask how the effects of age compare with those of all of the other, very powerful, factors that contribute to individual differences in competence, whether age affects all mental abilities to the same extent or whether it affects some cognitive skills more than others, and what are the most effective steps that we can take to slow or arrest change.

HOW DO THE EFFECTS OF OLD AGE COMPARE WITH THOSE OF ALL OTHER SOURCES OF INDIVIDUAL DIFFERENCES IN MENTAL ABILITIES?

Perhaps the most meaningful way to ask this question is to compare simple rank-order correlations between peoples' ages and their scores on each of the tests on which they have been assessed. Table 11.1 lists correlations between scores on a variety of different cognitive tests and age between 50 and 90 years for 2500 members of the Newcastle volunteer sample. For all measures, except for the Mill Hill and WAIS vocabulary tests, correlations with age are negative and statistically reliable. This simply confirms that between 50 and 90 years, recognition vocabulary is unaffected by age, while, in contrast, scores on all measures of "fluid" abilities, such as intelligence test scores, memory test scores and tests of information-processing speed, do show some decline. The squares of correlation coefficients give the proportions of the total variance in text scores between individuals that are accounted for by differences in their ages. That is to say, if we consider the sum of all of the effects of all of the factors that help to make individuals' test scores different from each other as 100%, the squares of correlations between test scores and age provide estimates of the proportion of this total variance which is attributable to differences in age between 50 and 90 years. Table 11.1 shows that although the proportions of individual differences which are attributable to age are statistically significant, they are small, ranging from less than 8% (immediate free recall of a list of 30 words) to a maximum of 18% (unadjusted scores on the AH 4 (2) intelligence test). Even well-designed and validated intelligence tests are, rightly, controversial as comprehensive measures of human ability (Gould, 1981; Howe, 1997). However, such tests are still the best practical

Table 11.1   Correlations with age for scores on a variety of cognitive tests, with proportions of total variance in scores between individuals which is accounted for by age.

Test	Correlation coefficient (R)	Age as percentage total variance
AH 4 (1) IQ test	0.42	17.6
AH 4 (2) IQ test	0.45	20.25
Cattell "Culture Fair"	0.48	23.04
Free recall of 30 words	0.32	10.24
Recall of information about people	0.15	2.3
Cumulative recall	0.39	15.21
Letter/letter coding	0.39	15.21
"Stroop" interference condition	0.39	15.21
Visual search	0.19	3.6
Mill Hill 'A' vocabulary	0.01	–
WAIS vocabulary	0.11	1.0

predictors of peoples' mental competence in everyday life that we have. We note from Table 11.1 that not more than 20% of individual variation in test scores between these individuals is associated with their ages.

Correlation analyses also allow us to compare the relative effects of age with those of other factors that also alter cognitive competence, e.g. with the effects of illnesses such as late-onset diabetes that become increasingly common in old age, or with measures of general fitness, such as aerobic efficiency, which tend to reduce as age advances. Rabbitt, Bent and McInnes (1997) discuss a variety of such comparisons in which they used multiple regression analyses to estimate what proportions of variance in mental ability between individuals were attributable to differences in their general health and aerobic efficiency after variance attributable to age has been partialled out and vice versa.

Rabbitt et al. (1993) summarize the evidence from the Manchester/Newcastle longitudinal study. A first, counter-intuitive, finding is that although individuals' cognitive performance significantly declines as the number of pathologies from which they suffer increases, and although particular pathologies such as non-insulin-dependent diabetes do significantly impair mental ability, their effects are surprisingly small. After the variation associated with differences in age between 50 and 90 years had been taken into account, even pathologies that subsequently terminated in death within 5, or between 6 and 11 years, from point of assessment accounted for no more than 3% of the total variance between individuals. New techniques of regression analysis pioneered by Baltes and Lindenberger (1997) and Lindenberger and Baltes (1994) also allow us to ask the better question how much of that small proportion of variance (i.e. in the case of intelligence test scores about 20%) that is associated with individuals' ages can be explained as the consequence of declining health, and of the lifetime accumulation of pathologies and "biological life events". Preliminary computations from the Manchester/Newcastle data suggest that no more than 10–15% of age-related variance in intelligence test scores can be related to general health status – at least as indexed by self-reports on questionnaires such as the "Cornell Medical Questionnaire". That is to say, of the 100% of variation between individuals that arises from all of the factors that make people different from each other, only 20% was associated with differences in their ages and, of this 20%, at most 11% was associated with differences in self-reported pathology.

This illustrates two points: the first is that, at any time of life, mental ability is determined by a very wide range of different factors. Genetic inheritance is known to be a very powerful determinant of general mental ability and attainment (Bouchard, 1983, 1992), but so are education, motivation and lifetime intellectual involvement. In later life, differences in age and health status also significantly affect ability. However, in contrast to the major determinants of individual differences (there is, for example, convincing evidence that genetic inheritance accounts for between 40% and 80% of variation between individuals), the effects of age and general health status seem to be surprisingly small. The second point is that, at least in the relatively "elite" and healthy Manchester/Newcastle sample, the effects of age and of differences in general health seem to be different from and, to a large extent, independent of each other. It will be noted that these findings provide no support for a "terminal-drop" model of cognitive decline with age such as is illustrated in Figure 11.1B. While cognitive decline does, indeed, seem to accelerate towards the end of life, the changes that we have observed are much less severe than has been supposed and, perhaps counter-intuitively, cannot be explained as the effects of pathologies, even those that result in death within 5 years (Rabbitt et al., 1997).

DOES AGE AFFECT ALL MENTAL ABILITIES TO THE SAME EXTENT, OR DOES IT AFFECT SOME EARLIER, AND MORE SEVERELY THAN OTHERS?

It has proved surprisingly hard to answer this apparently simple question. Everyday language makes definite, and intuitively satisfying, distinctions between different mental abilities such as "attention", "memory" "problem-solving" and "mental speed". It might seem that simply by comparing younger and older people it would be easy to discover whether these abilities change at different rates. One problem is that it is very hard to design "pure" tasks that evaluate one single mental ability and no others. In particular, complex skills such as "problem-solving ability", as evaluated by intelligence tests, depend on a variety of sub-skills to which we would have to give quite distinct common-language descriptions such as "mental quickness", the maximum number of different items of information that can simultaneously be held in memory so as to be assessed in relation to each other ("working memory capacity"), the ability to focus and maintain attention on critical and to ignore irrelevant information, or the ability rapidly and accurately to retrieve necessary information from long-term memory. Neuropsychological models also predict that these different abilities are supported by different, functionally discrete, brain subsystems that can be affected by age at different rates (e.g. Verhoff, 1980). In this context, intelligence test scores are very gross measures that do not distinguish between localized losses of functionality that may affect some mental abilities but not others.

A second, and more pervasive, problem has been that common-language labels such as "mental speed", "memory efficiency" or "problem-solving ability" describe the *demands* that tasks make but not the underlying *functional processes* by means of which these demands are met. Even as a descriptive terminology for task demands, everyday language is arbitrary, inconsistent and tentative in the extent to which it can operationally distinguish particular demands from others. Semantic confusions between the imprecisely specified demands of particular tasks, and the inferred functional processes by means of which these demands are met, has been responsible for much confusion as to whether different functional processes change at different rates as old age advances (Rabbitt, 1993a). One extreme proposal has been that slowing of information-processing speed in old age is the unique functional change that, by its 'knock-on" effects, reduces the efficiency of all other mental abilities. The argument is that as processing speed becomes slower, so attentional selectivity must also become less efficient, short-term memory capacity must reduce because material cannot be so rapidly or frequently rehearsed, learning must slow because useful associations cannot be so rapidly formed, and the time taken to retrieve items from long-term memory also increases so that acquired information is less efficiently available (Salthouse, 1985, 1991, 1995).

There are many problems with the idea that changes in all cognitive skills are "knock-on" effects of changes in a single master functional performance characteristic of the central nervous system such as "information-processing rate". One is that the only performance indices that we can actually measure from any behavioural task are speed and accuracy and, further, because performance on any task must, necessarily, take place in time, rate and duration are intrinsic to all of the task performance indices that we can obtain and compare, so that it is merely tautologous to point out that speed is likely to emerge as a very strong mediator of correlations between all task performance indices. It is also misleading to confuse the *performance indices* that we can measure in behavioural experiments with the *characteristics of the functional processes* in the brain and central nervous system by means of which the tasks are carried out.

Another form of the "single-change" argument is that even though reaction times, as measured in laboratory experiments, are not equivalent to functional processes in the brain, it is nevertheless the case that age differences in reaction times are, statistically speaking, uniquely good predictors of the extent of age-related changes in all other tasks (Salthouse, 1985, 1991, 1996) and, indeed, of individual differences in performance of all cognitive tasks in adults and children of all ages (Anderson, 1995; Jensen, 1980, 1985 1987; Eysenck, 1986).

This direct statement of the hypothesis allows empirical tests. Large numbers of people of different ages can be given a variety of tasks. Some of these, like choice reaction time (CRT) tasks make minimal demands on memory because they only require participants to answer the ignition of signal lamps by pressing keys as fast as they can. Others, such as tests of memory and of learning rate in unpaced tasks, index the efficiency with which information can be acquired and retained while making minimal demands on information-processing speed. If both CRT tasks and memory tasks are given to large numbers of younger and older people, statistical techniques such as principal components analyses, confirmatory factor analysis and logistic regression analysis can be used to ask whether individual differences in speed do, in fact, account for *all* individual differences in memory and learning efficiency. When this is done it is usually found that differences in information-processing speed do account for substantial amounts of age-related variance in tests of memory and learning. Indeed, when the techniques of regression analysis pioneered by Lindenberger and Baltes are used, it appears that up to 70% of age-related variance in scores on memory tests can be accounted for by individual differences in information-processing speed measured on tasks with little or no memory load. However, it is also clear that by no means *all* age-related variance in memory tests can be accounted for by variance in information-processing speed, and it is also clear that we cannot completely account for age-related variance in scores on memory tests unless we also use as predictors scores on other, different, memory tests (Rabbitt and Yang, 1996; Robbins et al., 1994). In other words, although information-processing speed is certainly a good predictor of performance on a wide range of memory tasks, in order to explain *all* of the changes in memory efficiency that occur we also have to include scores on tasks that make demands on functional processes whose efficiency is not adequately indexed in terms of decision speed or information-processing rate.

It is useful to consider this issue in another way. The limiting-case models are that as a population ages all of its members change in the same way to a greater or lesser degree, or alternatively that while many individuals change little or not at all, there is a steady increase with age in the incidence of individuals who do experience marked change. In either case we may speculate that while individuals experience little change from young adult performance, the levels of correlation between their performances on different tasks will also remain unaltered. On these assumptions, it is only after age-related changes begin that some mental abilities will change faster than others so that disassociations between performances on different tasks will begin to be observed. Given these assumptions, both the "continuous-decline" and the "terminal-drop" models of cognitive ageing predict that the older the sample of a population that we test, the more likely it is that we shall find disassociations between efficiency on different cognitive tasks.

Because all volunteers in the Manchester/Newcastle samples have been given both intelligence tests and memory tests, it is possible to identify individuals whose performance on memory tests is very much worse (i.e. 2 or more standard deviations below) than expected from their intelligence test scores. The incidence of such individuals increased markedly with the age of the sample tested. In other words, age increases the probability that individuals' performance on memory tests will fall markedly below what is expected from their intelligence test scores. When these "memory-poor" individuals are identified and further examined, it emerges that the strength of the relationship between their intelligence test scores and their information-processing speeds is no different from that found in groups of people of any age. Further, while "memory-normal" individuals show significant and robust correlations between information-processing speed and scores on memory tests, for these exceptionally "memory-poor" individuals correlations between information-processing speed and scores on memory tests are zero. In other words, it seems that the functional changes that have reduced these individuals' memory efficiency well below what is expected from their intelligence test scores are not attributable to changes in the maximum speed with which they can process information. This answers the question with which we began: there is indeed evidence that ageing of the brain can affect some functional processes, such as those involved in memory and learning, more severely than others, such as those involved in making fast decisions or in rapidly solving intelligence test problems.

It seems that while measures of age-related slowing of information-processing rate in simple laboratory tasks are generally good predictors of decline in performance on other tasks, it is misleading to describe cognitive changes in old age as the results of a "global" change in a single system performance parameter which can be identified as "mental speed". Some performance parameters, notably those involved in learning and remembering new information, can change independently of, and more radically than, others. This is consistent with the idea that because some areas of the cortex suffer more marked loss of tissue in old age than others, changes in cognitive function are likely to reflect the patterns of these differential losses and so to be "local" rather than "global" in nature.

Evidence that losses of memory efficiency can be disproportionately greater than losses of the more "global" cognitive skills that are measured by intelligence tests is consistent with evidence from post-mortems and scans that loss of cortical tissue with age is relatively marked in the temporal lobes, whose integrity is known to be necessary for efficient memory and learning. It is a natural hypothesis that functions mediated by the frontal lobes, which also suffer relatively severe tissue loss in old age, should also decline disproportionately to other mental abilities. However, in spite of considerable research, the evidence on this point remains unclear – perhaps mainly because we do not yet seem to have any reliable or convincingly validated tests of frontal function which can clearly be shown to measure abilities distinct from those assessed by "intelligence tests" (see Burgess, 1977; Duncan, 1995; Duncan, Burgess and Emslie, 1995). At this moment, the best guess is that changes in mental abilities in old age will eventually be shown to be "local" and related to the differential rates of changes in different parts of the brain rather than "global" in the sense that they are all driven by changes in a single, "master" performance parameter of the human cognitive system.

Horn and his associates (e.g. Horn, 1982; Horn and Cattell, 1967) proposed that bodies of information about the world, and problem-solving skills which have been acquired over a lifetime, can be termed "crystallized" abilities and may be robustly preserved in old age, but "fluid" abilities such as the ability to solve novel problems, to hold substantial amounts of information in working memory, to process information rapidly and to learn and remember new information, all steadily decline. A useful analogy for Horn's distinction between "crystallized" and "fluid" abilities is the distinction between the processing capacity of a computer and the integrity of the data and programs available to it. Data, and programs to manage particular data, can be indefinitely maintained on floppy disks or other storage media. However, the "processing capacity" of a machine on which these data can be handled and these programs run may degrade independently of well-preserved data and procedures. In terms of this analogy, information about the world and techniques for solving problems that have been acquired during a long lifetime may be robustly maintained in memory by continual use into old age; however, changes in the brain may affect the efficiency of systems that are necessary to process new information, or even to retrieve learned information from memory and to manage long-acquired problem-solving routines. In old age we cease to be able to make use of the information and problem-solving procedures that we have learned in our youth. In terms of the computer analogy, we no longer have the functional capacity to run elaborate problem-solving routines that we have built up over many years and which may still, theoretically, remain accessible to us. An alternative possibility is that the computer analogy is misleading and Horn's distinction is not absolute, because a lifetime of practice, carried on into old age, may not only maintain the information about the world and the problem-solving techniques that we have acquired over a lifetime but may also preserve the particular structures that allow us to use this particular information and these particular techniques. In Horn's terminology this would mean that "fluid" abilities can also be maintained by continued practice, though possibly only in very situation-specific contexts. A lifetime's practice may allow us not only to maintain particular familiar information and procedures, but also to continue to use this information and to implement these procedures much faster and more accurately than we can acquire new information or carry out other, novel, tasks.

TO WHAT EXTENT ARE MENTAL ABILITIES PRESERVED BY A LIFETIME'S PRACTICE?

Many studies in our laboratory have replicated previously well-documented findings that the levels of performance that older individuals can attain on simple skills is determined at least as much by the level of practice that they are given as by differences in their "fluid" intellectual ability as indexed by their scores on intelligence tests (Rabbitt, 1993b). Young adults need less practice to get to their limiting levels of performance and, when both old and young adults are practised to limiting levels, the young continue to perform better than the old. However, this misses the important point that, if they are given sufficient practice, elderly people can attain impressive levels of performance that are often more than an order of magnitude greater than those attainable by untrained individuals of any age (Rabbit, 1993b). In old age, as at any time of life, there is everything to play for and, given sufficient practice, remarkable levels of performance are still possible. A different question is the extent to which practice on one skill can improve and maintain performance on other, similar, skills.

Some laboratory studies provide partial answers. Winder (1993) compared expert elderly cryptic crossword puzzle solvers with controls who were less good at crossword puzzles but who had been individually and exactly matched for age and gender, and who had identical scores on intelligence tests. It is, of course, not surprising that the expert solvers completed puzzles much faster and more accurately than their novice controls. More interesting was the finding that, because of individual matching, intelligence test scores declined with age at the same rate for both groups. To put this another way, the crossword puzzle-solving ability of older experts was markedly better than what was expected from their relatively reduced performance on intelligence tests. In contrast, the crossword puzzle-solving abilities of novices were well predicted by their intelligence test scores. There was no evidence that the experts' ability at crossword puzzle solving had declined as they aged, but there was also no evidence that their maintenance of skill at crossword puzzles also preserved the more general abilities that are assessed by intelligence tests. Practice maintained a particular, very complex, intellectual skill in spite of a decline in intelligence test scores that reflected age-related changes on other mental abilities.

Like the skill of solving intelligence test problems, crossword puzzle solving can be "decomposed" into many different, clearly identifiable, "component skills" such as the ability rapidly to find the appropriate words from vague or deliberately misleading definitions, to find sets of words that match incomplete letter strings, to solve anagrams and so on. All these simple component skills involve what Horn and his associates have defined as "fluid" abilities; in particular, the ability rapidly to process information so as to quickly generate and compare alternative solutions and the ability simultaneously to hold alternative procedures and information in working memory so that, by comparing them against the demands of the clue and any letters that may be available, the best alternative can be selected. Since elderly experts maintained performance at the entire complex skill of crossword puzzle solving, we may assume that they also maintained performance on these "fluid" abilities of decision speed and working memory capacity. The question is whether this preservation of "fluid" abilities was "dedicated" in the sense that it extended only to the particular procedures and materials used in solving crossword puzzles, or whether it was more general, and extended to many other skills with words. A finding that practice can preserve "fluid" abilities, even in highly restricted domains, would indicate that the borderline between age-liable "fluid" and age-stable "crystallized" abilities is less clear-cut than has been thought.

To explore this, Forshaw (1994) recruited crossword puzzle solvers of a wide range of ages and levels of expertise, established their relative competence on tests of puzzle solution, and then gave them a variety of other tests such as the speed with which they could distinguish words from non-words, the speed and accuracy with which they could solve anagrams or find legal words that matched incomplete letter strings, and the speed and accuracy with which they could recognize homonyms and homophones. Apart from these tests of the ability to do a variety of different things with words, he also gave them tests which measured their information-processing speed and working memory capacity with different, non-verbal, materials. He found that the speed and efficiency with which non-experts "did things with words" was well predicted by their ages, by their intelligence test scores and by their speed and efficiency at similar tasks involving non-verbal material. For these relatively unpractised novices it was a plausible assumption that levels of performance on all tasks was determined by "global" changes that could be accurately indexed by their intelligence test scores and by their speed and memory capacity. The speed with which "expert" crossword puzzle solvers could make decisions about non-verbal material, and their working memory capacities for non-verbal material, were also well predicted by their ages and by their intelligence test scores. However, experts' decision speeds and working memory capacities for verbal material were much greater than would be predicted by their ages and intelligence test scores, and were also much faster and greater than would be predicted by their decision speeds and memory capacity for non-verbal material. Evidently, prolonged practice, maintained into old age, cannot only maintain particular information and procedures, but also the efficiency with which this information and these particular procedures can be used. However, these procedures are "dedicated", or "domain specific", so that while they can be carried out very efficiently, other, logically similar, procedures involving novel material become increasingly slow and unreliable.

CONCLUSIONS

Biographical evidence suggests that although outstanding individuals are more likely to attain their most remarkable achievements when they are young, they can still maintain, until surprisingly late in life, levels of ability at their sports or at intellectual pursuits that are much greater than they could reach shortly before they reached their peaks, and which remain inaccessible to most humans of any age. The age at which peak achievements at different intellectual disciplines occur varies with the particular mental demands that they entail. Major achievements and periods of greatest productivity tend to occur in the 20s or early 30s in mathematics, chemistry, physics or lyric poetry, all of which demand the ability to come up with novel and unexpected solutions and ideas. Achievements in other disciplines such as history, philosophy or literature, which demand the acquisition of very large amounts of information or life experience, tend to peak in middle age or even later. Remarkable achievements in the graphic arts, architecture and music have often been accomplished in later life, even in the 70s and 80s. These conclusions are interesting, but remain tentative because they are partly based on the careers of individuals who lived in the 19th century and much earlier. During the present century, the social and career resources available to middle-aged and elderly people have greatly improved; more particularly, lifespans have greatly extended and people not only live longer but remain healthier throughout their lives. Given this picture, it seems that while lifetime peak achievements in athletics and many intellectual pursuits may occur early in life, very high levels of achievement can be maintained in middle age and perhaps beyond.

  Laboratory studies also suggest some decline in performance on simple tasks. Although these changes are statistically detectable they are very small indeed in absolute terms. In large groups of volunteers who have been recruited for prolonged longitudinal studies, differences in cohort age between 50 and 86 years account for no more than 20% of the total cognitive variance between individuals. Even comparatively late in life, up to 80% of the variance in cognitive ability between individuals seems to be due to factors other than their ages. Age-related changes occur significantly earlier, and faster, in some individuals than in others. This means that, in demographic terms, age-related cognitive change is best modelled as the increase in incidence, with age, in the numbers of individuals who have experienced marked change. Lucky individuals may show little change until very late in life. The appearances of cognitive changes in later life are certainly partly due to increasing prevalence of particular pathologies such as late-onset diabetes or cardiovascular problems, which are known to reduce cognitive function. There are also cumulative effects of all pathologies and "negative biological life events" experienced during the lifespan. However, within large populations the cognitive effects of particular pathologies account for surprisingly small proportions (5% of less) of the total variance in cognitive ability between individuals and, as best as we can determine, for only 10% of that 20% of the total variance between individuals that is associated with differences in their ages between 50 and 90 years (Rabbitt et al., 1997). Our current best guess is that the bulk of cognitive change in old age is accounted for by processes of "normal" or "usual" ageing (Ricklefs and Finch, 1995) which are not identified by clinicians as treatable pathologies.

Age does not affect all mental abilities to the same extent. Much of the change observed in laboratory tasks and in the ability to solve intelligence test problems is related to a "global" slowing of information-processing rate. More careful examination shows that in some individuals memory is impaired disproportionately early and more severely than performance on "intelligence tests" or information-processing speed. Cognitive skills that depend on the gradual acquisition of information about the world, and the discovery and learning of problem-solving procedures and which continue to be practised throughout the lifespan, tend to be well preserved in old age. These have been termed "crystallized" abilities, in contrast to the "fluid" abilities which are indexed by intelligence tests, such as information-processing speed, the ability to find solutions to novel problems, the ability simultaneously to hold many items of information in "working memory" and the ability rapidly to access previously learned information. However, it seems that this distinction is not entirely satisfactory because retention of highly practised "crystallized" skills can also imply the retention of "fluid" abilities such as decision speed and working memory capacity which are "dedicated" or "domain specific" to particular, highly practised bodies of information and procedures.

Moreover, even in tasks in which performance is directly assessed in terms of decision speed, working memory capacity or problem-solving ability, if elderly people are given sufficient practice they can achieve and maintain remarkable levels of performance, greatly superior to those possible for young adults who have had less training. In old age everything is still to be played for and, even if the game does become steadily harder, the rewards continue to be both accessible and satisfying.

CHAPTER 12

Hypnosis

GRAHAM F. WAGSTAFF

THE TRADITIONAL VIEW OF HYPNOSIS

To most people, the traditional view of hypnosis is instantly recognizable and can be summarized as follows:

1. There is a special sleep-like state, or trance, which is qualitatively, and probably quantitatively, different from the normal waking state. It is not the same as ordinary sleep, though it may be related to sleepwalking (indeed, the term "hypnosis" itself derives from the Greek *hypnos*, or sleep, and hypnotized individuals are sometimes referred to as "somnambules"). This state is generally called a "hypnotic trance".
2. This trance can occur spontaneously but is normally brought about by certain induction rituals; these can include eye fixation, rubbing the scalp and other parts of the body, making passes over the body, and giving vocal suggestions for sleep and relaxation.
3. When a person is in this trance, he or she will have certain experiences that can be used as indicators of the presence of this state; these include a loss of awareness, a loss of control and volition, increased suggestibility, amnesia, an extraordinary susceptibility to delusions and hallucinations, and an increased capacity to perform perceptual and motor tasks, including the production of anaesthesia. Moreover, the "deeper" the trance, the more these phenomena will be experienced.
4. The hypnotic trance is not a momentary condition, but lasts a period of time. The subject is typically brought out of it by a command from the hypnotist such as "wake up", or a predetermined signal such as clicking the fingers, or counting down from 20 to 1.
5. Even after the termination of the trance, if the subject has been given a post-hypnotic suggestion, he or she may still, involuntarily, and sometimes without awareness, respond to the commands of the hypnotist.

Survey research indicates that this view of hypnosis is still widely held by the general public (Wagstaff, 1993); however, in recent decades, there have been efforts by both academic and clinical researchers to move away from many aspects of this tradition, and to dispel what many experts believe to be public misconceptions of hypnosis (e.g. Perry, 1992). The move away from the traditional stereotype of hypnosis has largely been as a response to experimental research stimulated by what is often called the "state versus non-state debate".

THE STATE VERSUS NON-STATE DEBATE

Although the term "hypnotic trance" is now rarely used by academic researchers, a number of modern researchers and theorists continue to refer to hypnosis as an "altered state" or "condition" of consciousness (e.g. Barber, 1991; Bowers, 1983; Hilgard, 1978, 1986; Nash, 1991; Spiegel, 1994). Perhaps the most popular modern version of the "state" approach is Hilgard's "neodissociation" theory (Hilgard, 1985, 1986, 1991). Basing his ideas on the early dissociationists, Hilgard argues that there exist in the mind multiple systems of control, or "parts" of the mind, that are not all conscious at the same time. Normally, these cognitive control systems are under the influence of a central control structure, or "executive-ego", that controls and monitors the other systems; but when the subjects enter the hypnotic state, subjects surrender to the hypnotist some of their normal control and monitoring such that, for example, in response to suggestion, motor movements (such as arm lowering) can be experienced as involuntary (because the part responding to the hypnotist and actually controlling the movement is "dissociated" from awareness), pain can be reduced or eliminated (because the painful sensations are dissociated from awareness) and memory and perception can be distorted such that, for instance, suggested reversible amnesia is experienced (because the forgotten information is temporarily dissociated from awareness).

However, a growing number of researchers have now rejected the whole concept of hypnosis as an altered state. The supporters of the non-state view of hypnosis (variously described as the "social psychological", 'cognitive-behavioural" or "sociocognitive" view), the notion of hypnosis as an altered state of consciousness is misleading and inaccurate (Barber, 1969; Coe and Sarbin, 1991; Sarbin and Coe, 1972; Kirsch, 1991; Lynn and Rhue, 1991a; Spanos, 1982, 1986, 1991; Spanos and Chaves, 1989; Wagstaff, 1981, 1986, 1991a). Non-state theorists argue that various hypnotic phenomena are more readily explicable in terms of interactions between more mundane psychological processes such as imagination, relaxation, role-enactment, compliance, conformity, attention, attitudes and expectancies.

Non-state theorists see hypnosis as primarily a strategic role enactment. In other words, "susceptible" hypnotic subjects enact the role of a "hypnotized" person as defined by cultural expectations and cues provided by the immediate situation. This role-enactment is largely accomplished by the use of strategies aimed at making hypnotic suggestions come about; for example, to experience a suggestion for arm lowering ("your arm is getting heavier"), subjects may try to imagine that their arms are heavy; when asked to "hallucinate" an object ("there is a cat in your lap"), subjects may try to vividly imagine such an object; and to experience hypnotic "amnesia", or analgesia, subjects may focus attention away from the target items or the pain. The degree to which they take on the role also depends on whether they possess appropriate attitudes and expectancies; or, as Barber and his associates put it, "Subjects carry out so-called 'hypnotic' behaviours when they have positive attitudes, motivations, and expectations toward the test situation which lead to a willingness to think and imagine with the themes that are suggested" (Barber, Spanos and Chaves, 1974, p. 4).

Barber's particular position has been conceptualized as in Figure 12.1. According to this model, whether subjects respond will depend not only on the wording of suggestions (some suggestions may be worded in such a way that they seem impossible to perform, or they put people off), but also on subjects' general attitudes, expectancies and motivations. Subjects will be unlikely to respond, for instance, if they are worried about loss of control, or being manipulated; also, subjects will not respond to certain suggestions if they are unable to use their imaginations to think up ways of generating the required responses.

Another variable that has been associated with hypnotic responding by Barber and others is "involvement or absorption in imaginings or fantasy"; the central idea being that, even with all the other factors present, subjects will not be able to respond to hypnotic suggestions unless they are prepared to become actively absorbed in them. Thus, although some may eventually feel "carried away" by the role involvement, if subjects passively expect things to happen to them, and are not prepared to involve

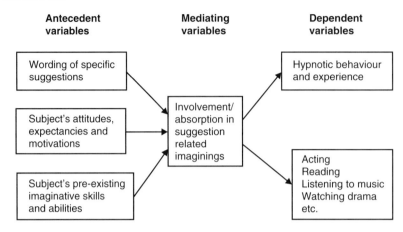

Figure 12.1   Barber's alternative view of hypnosis (from Fellows, 1986).

themselves, nothing will happen (Lynn and Rhue, 1991a). In this way, certain aspects of hypnotic responding can be seen as equivalent to involvement in activities such as acting, reading and watching a play.

However, according to some non-state theorists, hypnosis can also include a degree of "behavioural compliance", or "acting out suggestions" without the suggested subjective experiences, especially in response to suggestions for some of the more unusual and extreme hypnotic phenomena (Coe, 1989; Perlini, Spanos and Jones, 1996; Spanos, 1991, 1992; Wagstaff, 1981, 1986, 1991a, 1996). It is important to emphasize, however, that non-state theorists do not argue that all hypnotic behaviours are "faked", or "just acting". According to the non-state viewpoint, many of the strategies and expectancy effects may be very successful in bringing about the suggested phenomena, and some subjects may genuinely believe they are or have been in a "hypnotic state" because, in context, this seems to be an appropriate way to label their experiences. So, for example, according to the present author's version of the non-state view, hypnosis is best conceptualized as a three-stage process. Thus, when subjects enter a situation defined as one of 'hypnosis'', they do the following (Wagstaff, 1981, 1986, 1991a, 1996):

1. They work out what is appropriate to the role.
2. They apply "normal" cognitive strategies to make the experiences veridical or "believable" in line with expectations and what is explicitly or implicitly demanded in the suggestions.
3. If the application of "normal" strategies fails, is not possible, or is deemed inappropriate in the context, they may stop responding, or behaviourally comply and exaggerate.

In effect, then, to non-state theorists, terms such as "hypnosis" and "hypnotic" are simply labels that refer to situations defined by participants or observers as such (because, for example, the situations contain what are called "hypnotic induction" rituals). Put simply, "hypnosis" is any set of instructions or procedures that invite the subject to enact the role of someone who is "hypnotized' as they understand the term; it does not assume the existence of some kind of unique brain state or process.

But on what evidence have the non-state theorists based their claim that the notion of a hypnotic state is misleading and inaccurate?

THE PHYSIOLOGY OF HYPNOSIS

If there were an identifiable brain state that we could associate with the term "hypnosis", it would be useful to have some identifying physiological marker. Unfortunately, however, research on the physiology of hypnosis has been dogged by methodological difficulties. Hypnotic procedures typically include a number of instructions that have obvious physiological consequences independently of any assumption about the existence of a hypnotic state. For example, there are often fairly definable patterns of physiological responses related to fairly mundane activities such as eye closure, relaxation, concentration, and attention, all of which can be involved in the behaviour of hypnotic subjects. The physiological responses of a person seated, relaxing, and concentrating with eyes closed, may be markedly different from those of someone alert and simply staring around the room, yet could not be considered evidence for a special "hypnotic state".

The physiological evidence suggests that the subject who is responsive to hypnotic suggestions is not asleep or sleepwalking (Barber, Spanos and Chaves, 1974); nevertheless, hypnotic subjects often display the physiological concomitants of being relaxed. Indeed, Edmonston (1991) has argued that what he terms "neutral hypnosis" is just a state of relaxation. The difficulty is, however, that hypnotically susceptible subjects seem to be just as responsive to suggestions when involved in strenuous, "non-relaxing", activities such as pedalling an exercise bike; this has been termed "alert" hypnosis (Banyai and Hilgard, 1976; Malott, 1984). Of course, there may be other forms of relaxation, such as the sort of "cognitive relaxation" sometimes reported by athletes, but we are left with the difficulty of finding a set of definable physiological correlates that will relate "relaxed" and "alert" hypnosis. We are also left with the problem of what exactly it is about "relaxation" that is supposed to generate the various phenomena we associate with hypnosis.

Particular problems in assessing physiological correlates of hypnosis arise when subjects classified as highly susceptible to hypnosis ("highs") are compared with subjects, given identical instructions, who are classed as not susceptible to hypnosis ("lows"). Subjects who are classified as "lows" can illustrate what is known as a "negative subject effect"; that is, "lows", because they do not wish to give the appearance of being susceptible to hypnosis, may actually reject or perform counter to the suggestions given to them; in other words, when placed in a context defined as hypnosis, "lows" fail to carry out the instructions (Jones and Spanos, 1982; Lynn, 1992). Appropriately instructed independent control subjects are therefore essential for meaningful research in this area, and there now seems to be fairly wide agreement among researchers of both state and non-state persuasions that, when appropriate controls are applied, there is no definitive evidence for a unique physiological marker that can tell us whether or not someone is "hypnotized" (Davies, 1988; Sarbin and Slagle, 1979; Jones and Flynn, 1989; Spanos, 1982; Wagstaff, 1981).

The search continues, but all that really seems to emerge is evidence consistent with the non-state "strategic-enactment" view of hypnosis. For instance, if subjects are trying actively to respond to hypnotic suggestions, we might expect them to be constantly shifting their focus of attention; and, accordingly, data from a number of physiological studies are consistent with the view that "highs" are more likely to engage in attention-shifting strategies than "lows" in response to hypnotic suggestions (Crawford, 1996).

Some have tried to argue that hypnosis is a "right-hemisphere" brain activity, but as Crawford (1996) comments, "there is growing evidence that hypnotic phenomena selectively involve cortical and subcortical processes of either hemisphere, dependent upon the nature of the task" (p. 272). Again, Crawford's observations fit well with the strategic-enactment view; for if "highs" are continually trying to think and imagine along with suggestions, we should expect the physiological correlates of hypnotic responding to vary according to the particular task. Consistent with this, Gruzelier (1988) has found that, during a standard hypnotic induction, "highs" and "lows" tend to show a different pattern of responding. "Highs" start off showing left-hemisphere dominance, but as the induction continues, the electrical activity shifts to the right hemisphere. However, these are the responses that might be expected from two groups of individuals, some (the "highs") "thinking and imagining" along with the induction, and others (the "lows") not, or less so. The standard hypnotic induction first requires you to concentrate on the words of the hypnotist. This form of analytical processing might be considered typical of left-hemisphere function. After a while, however, the words of the induction typically shift towards the idea of concentrating on one's feelings, or internal states; that is, "holistic" activity, argued by some to be more associated with the right hemisphere (Springer and Deutsch, 1981). In contrast, "lows", who for the reasons stated earlier fail to carry out instructions, would be less likely to show these laterality shifts.

The finding that the physiological measures show changes that correspond to the tasks assigned is also well illustrated in a study by Saletu (1975), in which it was found, not surprisingly, that, with a standard induction procedure, EEG patterns of hypnotics showed responses associated with relaxation and drowsiness; however, these soon disappeared when the subjects were given an analgesia suggestion in response to electric shocks.

In sum, although there is no evidence for a fixed set of physiological indicators that can indicate the presence of a "hypnotic state", not surprisingly, the physiological correlates of hypnotic responding vary according to the nature of the task, the strategies involved, and the degree to which individuals engage in these activities.

HYPNOSIS AND THE ENHANCEMENT OF PERFORMANCE

One of the most popular conceptions of hypnosis is that it somehow enables one to tran-scend normal performance; and this, in itself, has been seen by some as evidence itself for existence of a special hypnotic state. Once again, however, methodological problems have hampered research in this area. For example, it has been shown that if the same subjects are tested in both hypnotic and non-hypnotic situations, subjects will sometimes show what has been termed a "holding back" effect in the non-hypnotic control situation; that is, they will underperform in the control trials, so that their performance appears "boosted" in the hypnotic trials (Wagstaff, 1981). Another problem is that hypnotic procedures and instructions may simply serve to motivate subjects. When appropriate methodological controls are applied, however, there seems to be no evidence that hypnotic subjects perform better than suitably motivated control subjects on a wide range of tasks, including appearing deaf, blind and colour-blind, acting like a child and recalling events from childhood, lifting weights and other athletic tasks (including performing as a "human plank" suspended between two chairs), and showing improvements in eyesight (Barber, 1969; Barber, Spanos and Chaves, 1974; Jacobs and Gotthelf, 1986; Jones and Flynn, 1989; Wagstaff, 1981).

Studies in this area can have important practical implications. For example, publicity has recently been given to the view that hypnosis can be a useful technique for facilitating the memories of witnesses in police investigations. The empirical evidence strongly suggests, however, that hypnosis does not magically improve memory to a level above that achievable by suitably instructed non-hypnotic control groups; instead, when it makes a difference, it seems only to encourage subjects to adopt a more lax criterion for report (that is, report things about which the subject may previously have been unsure). Hence, if any new information is produced, it is usually accompanied by an increase in incorrect information and an inflated level of confidence (reviews: Anderton, 1986; Erdelyi, 1994; Smith, 1983; Wagstaff, 1984, 1989, 1993).

As a response to findings of this kind, there has been a tendency among some involved in research on hypnosis and memory to change their emphasis; hence, instead of viewing hypnosis as a potentially valuable tool for uncovering accurate memories, they consider it to be a liability in that it increases the probability of inaccurate reporting (Diamond, 1980; Orne, 1979). However, other research suggests that hypnotically induced inaccuracies may often reflect reporting biases rather than genuine irreversible memory distortions (that is, subjects report false information because they think the situation requires it of them, rather than because their memories are impaired). Thus hypnotically created pseudomemories and false confidence effects can be significantly reversed if "hypnotized" subjects are told, for example, that a "hidden part" of them can describe their "real" memories, or are cross-examined under oath, or are given a financial incentive for accurate reporting, or are given an opportunity to deny being in a "trance". Under these circumstances, errors are not completely eliminated, but the errors that accompany hypnotic procedures are no greater than those produced by non-hypnotic procedures (Murray, Cross and Whipple, 1992; Spanos and McLean, 1986; Spanos et al., 1989, 1991; Wagstaff and Frost, 1996).

But, even so, "reporting biases" will still presumably present problems in police investigations, so, given all of these considerations, how can we explain claims that hypnosis has been successful in helping the police? One obvious point is that, in real-life investigations, what is known as "hypnotic interviewing" may possess advantages over routine police interviewing; for example, the instructions and suggestions may help to relax the witness, and provide imaginal cues to help them remember through "context reinstatement". But it is not necessary to postulate a "hypnotic state" to explain the effectiveness of these factors; indeed, similar techniques have been incorporated into non-hypnotic interview techniques such as the "cognitive interview" (Fisher and Geiselman, 1992; Wagstaff, 1982b, 1993).

As most of the alleged advantages of hypnosis as an interview procedure can be achieved with a non-hypnotic cognitive interview, but without the same disadvantages of possible distortions in reporting, many hypnosis experts are now attempting to dissuade the police from using hypnosis.

THE PROBLEM OF COMPLIANCE

Although most modern theorists seem to reject the idea that hypnosis enables one to transcend one's normal non-hypnotic capacities, nevertheless, a feature of modern state/dissociationist views of hypnosis is that they still appear to give credence to some phenomena which, in any other psychological context, might be treated with scepticism. For instance, one of the most dramatic alleged hypnotic effects is the "negative hallucination''. Thus, in response to suggestion, some hypnotic subjects will claim that they cannot see someone or something, such as a person, or chair, set before their eyes. One dissociationist interpretation is that, although the material is not seen by the "aware" part of the mind, it is somehow "seen" by another part of the mind, outside awareness. But if true, such an interpretation would seem to defy any mainstream psychological theory of perception. An alternative view, however, is that subjects may be using deliberate strategies to bring the suggested effect about, such as looking away, or closing or defocusing their eyes. It is also possible that subjects may try to visualize an image that will "blot out" the material that is not supposed to be seen (Spiegel, Bierre and Rootenberg, 1989; Spiegel et al., 1985).

However, even though all of these strategies may to some extent be successful, it is still debatable whether any would enable a subject to selectively yet fully obliterate part of the visual field. Indeed, two studies have shown that virtually all subjects who claim to have seen nothing in response to a negative hallucination suggestion are subsequently able to report what was presented to them if they are told that there is another "hidden part" of the mind that actually saw what was presented (Zamansky and Bartis, 1985; Spanos, Flynn and Gwynn, 1988). These studies suggest that strategies such as attempting to blot out the visual field cannot adequately account for reports of negative hallucinations. So how do we explain these reports? Of course, it could be argued that there really is another dissociated "part of the mind" that saw what happened. This seems a rather unlikely explanation, however, given that subjects will even report a reversal of a previously "unseen" number (such as 81 instead of 18) if they are led to believe that the "hidden part of the mind" sees a reversed version of the stimulus! A further, and perhaps more parsimonious, explanation, therefore, is that so-called negative hallucinations are primarily manifestations of behavioural compliance; that is, subjects simply pretend that they cannot see something (Spanos, 1992; Perlini, Spanos and Jones, 1996; Wagstaff, 1981, 1991a).

The issue of the extent to which hypnotic subjects may be exaggerating or lying has long been contentious, even among non-state theorists (Council, Kirsch and Grant, 1996; Kirsch, 1991), and some remain unconvinced that compliance plays a significant role in hypnotic responding. Indeed, in one study using a skin conductance measure as a "lie detector", Kinnunen, Zamansky and Block (1994) reported that a group of seven highly susceptible hypnotic subjects met the criterion for truthfulness for 89% of the time when asked about their experiences in response to a number of suggestions, whereas six subjects instructed to simulate hypnosis met the criterion for only 35% of the time. This study, however, suffers from some serious methodological problems.[1]

Supporters of the compliance viewpoint can, nevertheless, point to classic examples in the hypnosis literature (Wagstaff, 1996). For example, Pattie (1935) reports the case of a woman who claimed that, under hypnosis, she was blind in one eye, and she passed a number of tests that seemed to indicate that her blindness was genuine. However, subsequently she failed a more complex test. It was then discovered that she had managed to achieve the appearance of blindness in one eye on the earlier tests by practising at home with a friend. Sometimes it seems that compliant hypnotic subjects can be caught out fairly easily. For instance, Barber, Spanos and Chaves (1974) report that when, having received a suggestion for hypnotic deafness, subjects were asked "Can you hear me?", a number of subjects said "No I can't." (Of course, a dissociationist might argue it was "another part of consciousness" speaking; though if it were, perhaps it should be saying "Yes, I can hear you"!)

Most notable, however, is some recent work using an experimental design developed by Spanos and his associates that appears to strongly implicate compliance in hypnotic responding (Spanos, 1992; Perlini, Spanos and Jones, 1996). For example, Spanos and his colleagues have demonstrated that highly susceptible subjects will tend to report that various suggestions were effective, or not effective, depending on whether, afterwards, the experimenter conveys to them that they had "drifted into hypnosis" when the suggestions were presented. This suggests that "highs" deliberately bias their reports to comply with experimental demands. It could be argued, however, that the suggestion to "highs" that they had "drifted into hypnosis" affected their memories of what they had experienced; they reinterpreted what they experienced to fit in with experimental demands or expectancies, and believed in these reinterpretations (Council, Kirsch and Grant, 1996).

In another study, however, Spanos et al. gave subjects a negative hallucination suggestion that they would not see a number "8" that was presented clearly in front of them. Some subjects subsequently claimed they had seen nothing. These same subjects were then told that "reals", unlike "fakers", do see the number for a short period, but then it fades. Having been given this information, virtually all of these subjects confirmed they had seen the number. It is obviously more difficult to explain this result solely in terms of "reinterpretation of memory"; instead, it seems to indicate strongly that the subjects were lying when they originally claimed they could not see the number. Significantly, Spanos and his associates found that those who complied on this task tended to be the sort of highly susceptible subjects who perform well on other "difficult" hypnotic tasks, such as seeing a stimulus in a different colour (Spanos, 1992; Perlini, Spanos and Jones, 1996). Hence Perlini, Spanos and Jones (1996) conclude that "compliance is a central component of hypnotic responding" (p. 206).

The issue of compliance figures again in discussions of another famous hypnotic phenomenon, hypnotic amnesia.

HYPNOTIC AMNESIA

Contrary to popular belief, it is unusual for subjects to claim unsuggested "spontaneous amnesia" following a session of hypnosis. Thus, unless subjects are actually led to expect that spontaneous amnesia will follow hypnosis, they typically remember what has transpired, subject to the constraints of normal forgetting. Suggested amnesia, however, is another matter. In a typical demonstration of suggested hypnotic amnesia, "hypnotized" subjects are given a series of tasks to perform, or a list of items to remember; this is followed by a suggestion that they will find it difficult to remember what has happened, until they hear a reversal cue such as, "now you can remember everything" (in the case of post-hypnotic amnesia, the suggestion and reversal are purportedly enacted after subjects "wake up" from hypnosis). In general, experimental results show that many subjects will show an initial decrement in recall and recognition which is subsequently dissipated by the reversal cue; moreover, this "amnesia reversal" is not simply a consequence of repeated attempts to remember. Thus, as Bowers (1983) has emphasized, "one of the distinguishing characteristics of suggested hypnotic amnesia is that it is reversible; the person can recover the forgotten material" (p. 41).

According to the state/dissociationist interpretation, reversible post-hypnotic amnesia occurs because when subjects enter the hypnotic state they relinquish to the hypnotist at least part of the control they normally have over their memory processes. As a result, their memories are dissociated from awareness behind an "amnesic barrier", and cannot be accessed until the hypnotist issues the signal for normal control to be resumed (Bowers, 1983; Hilgard, 1986). However, the sociocognitive or cognitive-behavioural view is that hypnotic amnesia is primarily a consequence of deliberate strategies in response to task demands. According to this interpretation, hypnotic subjects have a strong investment in presenting themselves as "hypnotized"; thus, when hypnotic subjects respond to the amnesia suggestion, they engage in strategies such as distraction, inattention, and voluntarily withholding responses (compliance), to give the appearance of amnesia until the experimental demands (the reversal cue) indicate otherwise (Coe, 1989; Coe and Sarbin, 1991; Spanos, 1986, 1991; Wagstaff, 1977a, b, 1981, 1986, 1991a).

However, if reversible hypnotic amnesia is indeed a volitional response to situational demands, then one might expect that exhortations to be honest and try hard to remember might be successful in breaching the "amnesia". It is notable, therefore, that attempts to breach amnesia in this way have only been partially successful, and leave a significant proportion of subjects maintaining amnesia until the reversal cue is given (Coe, 1989; Kihlstrom et al., 1980; Kunzendorf, 1990). In response, however, sociocognitive theorists have argued that amnesia is maintained in such cases because some subjects find that breaching in response to such instructions is inconsistent with their previous denials of access to the material (Spanos, 1991; Spanos, Radtke and Bertrand, 1984; Wagstaff, 1981, 1986, 1991a). What is necessary, therefore, is a breaching instruction that will either put such extreme pressure on subjects to remember that they will cease to employ strategies that give the appearance of amnesia, or one that will enable them to remember the material without "losing face".

A number of studies support this idea; for instance, post-hypnotic amnesia can be breached almost entirely by using a package that involves exhorting subjects to be honest and not to lie, presenting them with a videotape of their actions, and rigging them up to a lie detector (Coe, 1989). Other successful "face-saving" breaching techniques include suggesting to subjects that the different materials can be made available by contacting different hemispheres of the brain (Spanos, Radtke and Bertrand, 1984), requesting subjects to "trust their imaginary memories" (Kuzendorf, 1990), and suggesting to them that memory can be recovered in "deep hypnosis" (Silva and Kirsch, 1987). Perhaps most definitively, however, it seems that hypnotic amnesia can be eliminated entirely if subjects are given an opportunity to say they were "role-playing" rather than in a "trance", before being tested for amnesia, i.e. before committing themselves to appearing amnesic (Wagstaff, 1977a; Wagstaff and Frost, 1996).

Nevertheless, standard measures of hypnotic amnesia are, as one might expect, easy to simulate, and consequently researchers have looked for some rather more subtle measures of amnesia. According to some, one such measure is "source amnesia" (Evans, 1979). It has been argued that, after a session of hypnosis, some "real" hypnotic subjects will sometimes recall novel information given to them while they were "hypnotized", but will be unable to say how they came by this information. Subjects instructed to simulate hypnosis, however, tend not to do this. Another measure that has been alleged to differentiate between "reals" and simulators is "disorganized retrieval"; thus it has been contended that hypnotically amnesic subjects who remember a few items tend to remember them in a fairly random, disorganized way, whereas simulators tend not to do this (Evans and Kihlstrom, 1973; Kihlstrom and Wilson, 1984).

However, these kinds of comparison again highlight one of the major problems with what is known as the "real-simulator" design in hypnosis. In this design, simulators are typically told to behave like "excellent" hypnotic subjects, and when they do this the result is often an "overplay effect". That is, simulators behave as if "extremely hypnotized" (just like some, but not all, of the "reals") and display *total* amnesia for both the information and the source; consequently, both source amnesia and "disorganized retrieval" are impossible to demonstrate (Wagstaff, 1981). What are necessary, therefore, are non-hypnotic control groups instructed to simulate *partial* amnesia; and there is now evidence to suggest that, when such controls are applied, non-hypnotic subjects will indeed display "source amnesia". Also in line with the non-state position, disorganized recall effects have been shown by non-hypnotic subjects who have been instructed simply to "pretend to forget", or "attend away" from the material (Coe, 1989; Spanos, 1986; Wagstaff, 1977b, 1982a; Wagstaff and Carroll, 1987).

The role of compliance in hypnotic amnesia is again a contentious issue, but undeniably it is present; indeed, research has shown that a large proportion of subjects (as many as 60%) will subsequently confess on questioning that they deliberately suppressed their reports so that they might appear "amnesic" (Coe, 1989). As Coe asks, "Perhaps we should wonder how many did not confess?" (Coe, 1989, p. 118). But in any case, as yet there seems to be little in the hypnosis literature that either supports the idea of, or requires the postulation of, a special "hypnotic" state of consciousness, or special dissociative condition, to explain reports of hypnotic amnesia.

REPORTS OF NON-VOLITION WITH HYPNOSIS

Another characteristic of the traditional view is that hypnotic behaviours are experienced as "involuntary". On first consideration, this would seem to contradict the view held by many non-state sociocognitive theorists that hypnotic subjects maintain control over their behaviour, and strategically alter it to fit task demands. However, to non-state theorists there is no necessary contradiction between the view that subjects employ strategies, and actively think and imagine along with suggestions to bring about hypnotic effects, and the idea that some effects may be experienced as involuntary (Gorassini, 1997; Lynn, 1992; Lynn and Rhue, 1991a; Lynn, Rhue and Weekes, 1990; Spanos, 1991). For example, if I deliberately move my arm while deliberately focusing my attention on something else, eventually I may feel that the arm is moving by itself.

Moreover, as the hypnotic role itself demands that suggestions may be experienced as involuntary, hypnotic subjects may deliberately attempt to convince themselves that they have partially lost some control. So, for example, if I deliberately try to keep my arm stiff, concentrate only on this, and do not make a conscious effort to switch my attention so that I can bend it, I might be able to state with some conviction that I cannot bend it (this is somewhat like trying to stand up and sit down at the same time). Significantly, some research suggests that even some low susceptibles will show gains in hypnotic susceptibility and report that at least some of their responses are involuntary if they are instructed to deliberately try to make their responses feel automatic, rather than passively wait for something to happen (Gorassini, 1996). These findings fit in with others which suggest that if techniques are used to inculcate in subjects those attitudes, expectancies and strategies that non-state theorists believe are responsible for producing hypnotic effects, then considerable success is possible in turning low susceptibles into high susceptibles (Bertrand, 1989; Spanos, 1991; Spanos et al., 1995).

Although state/dissociation theorists have tended to reject this strategic-enactment account of the role of volition in hypnotic responding (Bowers and Davidson, 1991), the sociocognitive and dissociationist perspectives are not actually as discrepant on this issue as it might at first appear. For example, modern dissociationists adopt the position that hypnotic suggestions are experienced as involuntary because some control over action is given up to the hypnotist and dissociated from awareness; nevertheless, the act of allowing the hypnotist to control one's actions could still be seen as a deliberate act (such as the act of allowing a doctor or lecturer, or family member, or game-presenter, to dictate one's behaviour). Hence, even from a dissociationist perspective, it could be argued that although some subjects may subsequently experience their behaviours as involuntary (because control is "dissociated" from awareness), they have not actually "lost control" of their actions and experiences in the sense of becoming automata in the hands of the hypnotist (Nash, 1991).

This point is exemplified by the fact that, no matter what their theoretical persuasion, most modern researchers and theorists now indeed seem to reject claims that hypnosis can turn people into helpless automata (Lynn and Rhue, 1991b, p. 606). This has obvious implications for claims that hypnosis can impel people to commit self-injurious and antisocial acts of which they would not normally be capable. Indeed, reports that people have unwittingly been "hypnotized" into committing criminal acts are not only rare but have generally been treated with scepticism (Barber, 1969; Conn, 1972; Gibson, 1992; Laurence and Perry, 1988; Udolf, 1983; Wolberg, 1972). A few early experiments did seem to confirm that "hypnotized" persons can be made to perform acts that are immoral or harmful, either to themselves or others; such acts have included indecent exposure, picking up a dangerous snake, throwing acid at the experimenter, minor thefts, and verbal attacks (Wagstaff, 1989, 1991b, 1993). However, a number of reviewers of these studies have concluded that the notion of a hypnotic state is not necessary to explain the results. Instead, they can be explained primarily in terms of subjects (1) wanting to help the hypnotist/experimenter, (2) thinking that their actions were actually safe, and/or (3) making assumptions that someone else would take responsibility for the consequences of the acts (Barber, 1969; Coe, Kobayashi and Howard, 1972, 1973; Orne and Evans, 1965; Udolf, 1983).

For example, early studies by Rowland (1939) and Young (1952) found that a majority of "deeply hypnotized" subjects would attempt to pick up a dangerous snake and throw acid at the experimenter; subjects generally refused to do this in the "waking" state. However, Orne and Evans (1965) found that both hypnotic subjects *and* non-hypnotic subjects would attempt to pick up a dangerous snake, plunge their hands into a beaker of concentrated nitric acid, and throw the acid at the experimenter, when given emphatic suggestions to do so. Further studies have shown that non-hypnotic subjects are just as likely as (and sometimes slightly more likely than) hypnotic subjects to perform a variety of antisocial or repugnant acts that have included mutilating the Bible, cutting up the national flag, and even heroin dealing (Coe, Kobayashi and Howard, 1973; Levitt et al., 1975; O'Brien and Rabuck, 1976).

Further endorsing the point that hypnosis does not turn subjects into helpless automata, Wagstaff, Green and Somers (1997) showed that a significant proportion of subjects who had no experience of hypnosis were prepared to accept a plea of hypnotic "automatism" as an excuse for committing a crime (that is, because he was "hypnotized" the defendant did not know what he was doing); however, subjects who had experienced a hypnotic induction procedure, and rated themselves as having been "hypnotized", unanimously rejected such a plea.

Finally, there seems to be little evidence for the involuntary persistence of hypnotic behaviours after the termination of the hypnosis session. Thus Orne, Sheehan and Evans (1968) found that some hypnotic subjects continued to respond to a post-hypnotic suggestion (to touch their foreheads on hearing the word "experiment") even when the hypnotist was not present, whereas simulators stopped responding in the absence of the hypnotist. However, in this study, the post-hypnotic response was tested by someone obviously known to the experimenter. Thus, while a non-response would have been perfectly compatible with the roll of a simulator who, as part of the same experiment, had been explicitly instructed to simulate, it would not have been compatible with the role of a "hypnotized" individual (Wagstaff, 1981). To assess this interpretation, Spanos et al. (1987) tested for post-hypnotic responding using someone who ostensibly had nothing to do with the experiment; they found that post-hypnotic responses disappeared entirely.

TRANCE LOGIC

Some of the most controversial studies in hypnosis have concerned claims that "hypnotized" subjects display a certain type of thinking, or "trance logic" that differs from normal "waking" thought. The term "trance logic" was first devised by Orne (1959, 1979) to refer to the observation that, unlike simulators, some "hypnotized" individuals appear to be able to tolerate illogical inconsistencies. For instance, if instructed (1) to look at a person, and (2) see (hallucinate) that person standing in a different place, simulators tend to report a single hallucinated image; however, some hypnotic subjects may report seeing *both* the image of a hallucinated person, and the actual person; this has been labelled the "double-hallucination response". Also, simulators tend to report opaque hallucinations, whereas some hypnotic subjects may report seeing "transparent" hallucinations. And when responding to suggestions for age regression, some hypnotic subjects may say that they feel both like a child *and* an adult ("duality"), and correctly write a complex sentence that no child could write ("incongruous writing"), whereas simulators will tend to say that they felt like a child all of the time, and write a complex sentence incorrectly (Orne, 1959; Nogrady et al., 1983; de Groot and Gwynn, 1989). Although attempts to replicate real-simulator differences on the so-called 'double-hallucination" response have been unsuccessful, the other "trance-logical" phenomena have been replicated (de Groot and Gwynn, 1989).

However, it could be argued as before that, acting as "excellent" hypnotic subjects, simulators may again simply be overplaying their role and exhibiting extreme responses, and that so-called "trance-logical" hypnotic subjects may simply be exercising their imaginations, or offering less complete or extreme responses (Wagstaff, 1981). To test this view, some researchers have used control groups who have been instructed to *imagine* rather than fake the various effects, or have been given equivalent instructions without hypnotic induction. Such groups have successfully reproduced the "trance-logic" effects (Spanos, 1986; de Groot and Gwynn, 1989). Of course, it could still be argued that just because the effects can be replicated by appropriately instructed controls, it does not necessarily follow that hypnotic subjects are behaving in the same way for the same reason. Nevertheless, these studies suggest that there is a perfectly rational and mundane explanation for these effects that does not require invoking the idea of some special hypnotic thought process that operates during hypnosis (Wagstaff, 1981; Spanos, 1986; Lynn and Rhue, 1991a).

CLINICAL HYPNOSIS

Hypnosis has allegedly been useful in the treatment of a variety of clinical problems, including insomnia, obesity, mild phobias, smoking, skin complaints and dental stress. However, another common misconception about hypnosis is that if one rejects the idea that hypnosis involves some special state, one also has to reject the idea that hypnotic procedures can have therapeutic benefits. In fact, although non-state theorists have argued that some of the therapeutic benefits of hypnosis have been exaggerated (Stam, 1989; Wagstaff, 1981), few would deny that what are described as hypnotic procedures seem to have been successful in the treatment of a number of complaints, especially when compared with no treatment at all (Heap and Dryden, 1991; Kirsch, Montgomery and Sapirstein, 1995; Spanos and Chaves, 1989; Wadden and Anderton, 1982; Wagstaff, 1981). Thus, in such cases, the issue is not so much whether hypnosis "works", but compared to what, and why?

A major problem is that hypnotic techniques usually involve a variety of factors that are not unique to hypnosis and that might account for improvements without the necessity of postulating the intervention of a "hypnotic state". Such factors include social support, relaxation, covert modelling, placebo effects and even social compliance (Wadden and Anderton, 1982; Wagstaff, 1981, 1987). Indeed, clinicians are often at pains to point out that hypnosis *per se*, in the sense of the administration of a hypnotic induction procedure, is not used as a therapy in itself; instead, hypnosis is an adjunct to some other therapeutic intervention. However, Kirsch, Montgomery and Sapirstein (1995) examined 18 studies in which cognitive-behavioural therapy was compared with the same therapy augmented by the addition of something described as "hypnosis"; their results showed that the average client receiving the extra "hypnosis" showed greater improvement than 75% of those receiving the same treatment without this ritual. But also, in about half of the studies the only salient difference between the hypnotic and "non-hypnotic" treatments was the fact that the treatment was described as "hypnosis"; yet the effect size for the treatment was the same. As Kirsch notes, the latter finding suggests that it was not the induction ritual itself that was responsible for the improvement, but the increased positive expectancy, or placebo effect, generated by labelling the situation as one of "hypnosis".

Similarly, in a study on the treatment of nail-biting, Wagstaff and Royce (1984) found that suggestions were significantly more effective when preceded by a hypnotic induction procedure. However, further analyses showed that the best predictor of whether the treatment was effective was the patient's *belief* or expectancy that the treatment would be effective, not whether they had been assigned to the hypnotic or non-hypnotic treatment conditions. In other words, it could be argued that labelling the procedure as "hypnosis" produced benefits, not through the induction of a special brain state, but principally by encouraging the clients to believe that the treatment would be effective (Johnson, 1989).

HYPNOTIC ANALGESIA

And so we come to the phenomenon that to many people provides the most convincing evidence for the existence of some special state; that is, the ability of hypnotic subjects to endure or eliminate surgical pain.

According to the state/dissociationist position, hypnotic analgesia works because, in the hypnotic state, pain is dissociated from awareness (Bowers, 1983; Hilgard, 1986; Hilgard and Hilgard, 1983; Miller and Bowers, 1993). However, again, non-state theorists argue that it is possible to explain this phenomenon without invoking the concept of a hypnotic state. They point out, for example, that cases of surgery with hypnosis are comparatively rare, and that procedures for hypnotic analgesia usually involve a variety of non-specific pain-coping strategies that are potent pain relievers; these include suggestions for pain relief (numbness, coldness, etc.), relaxation and distraction, and preoperative preparation to alleviate fear and anxiety (Barber, Spanos and Chaves, 1974; Chaves, 1989). But obviously it is difficult to conduct controlled experiments on surgical pain to test these ideas, so researchers have turned to laboratory methods to study hypnotic analgesia. (In laboratory studies, the pain-inducing procedure usually involves placing the subject's arm in ice water, or using a pressure stimulus. Both methods can induce severe pain without any permanent damage.)

One would think that an obvious method for testing the validity of reports of hypnotic analgesia would be to use physiological measures associated with pain. However, the interpretation of studies employing this method has proved difficult. For instance, some studies have found that, although hypnotic subjects do report reduced sensations of pain following suggestions for analgesia, the physiological concomitants of pain (such as increased heart rate and blood pressure) appear to contradict these reports. This might suggest that some hypnotic subjects report less pain than they actually feel (Wagstaff, 1981). A number of state theorists, however, believe that this finding can be explained in terms of dissociation. To demonstrate this, they have applied what has been termed the "hidden observer" procedure.

To demonstrate the hidden observer during a hypnosis session, the hypnotist suggests that when he or she touches the shoulder of the hypnotic subject, the hypnotist will be able to contact another "part" of consciousness (a hidden observer) that is more aware of what is happening. When using this procedure, some researchers have found that although the usual "hypnotized" subject will often report a decrease in pain in response to a noxious stimulus, when the hidden observer is contacted (which allegedly represents a dissociated part of consciousness), pain is reported as "normal" (Bowers, 1983; Hilgard, 1986; Knox, Morgan and Hilgard, 1974). This finding has been used to support the idea that during hypnotic analgesia pain is "felt" outside awareness, and thus explains the apparent contradiction between verbal reports and physiological indices. Non-state theorists, however, suggest that two other factors may be involved in this effect, both of which represent subjects' attempts to accord with experimental demands; first, the hypnotic subject may simply be exhibiting compliance and reporting in the hidden observer condition what he or she *really* feels (pain), and second, the subject may be using pain-coping strategies in the "normal" hypnosis condition, but switching away from these in the hidden observer condition. In support of the latter idea, there is a variety of evidence to indicate that non-hypnotic pain-reducing strategies can be as effective as hypnotic ones (Spanos, 1986, 1989).

Other experiments by Spanos and his associates appear to lend further support for the non-state sociocognitive view. For example, they found that when experimental instructions are used that imply that the same, less or greater pain will be felt during the hidden observer condition, then the hidden observers of hypnotic subjects report the same, less or greater pain accordingly (Spanos, 1986, 1989). They also found that, if "highs" were subjected to a painful stimulus but without any mention of hypnosis, they subsequently reported that they experienced analgesia if, but only if, the experimental instructions given afterwards implied that they were "hypnotized" at the time when they were receiving the pain-inducing stimulus (Spanos et al., 1990). Further studies have implicated both placebo-responding and possible behavioural compliance effects in the production of hypnotic analgesia (Baker and Kirsch, 1993; Spanos et al., 1990; Wagstaff, 1981). Together, these results suggest that reports of hypnotic analgesia may represent a mixture of "real" effects, mainly due to positive expectancies and the use of pain-coping strategies, and response bias effects, which arise as subjects attempt to conform to task demands.

Naturally, some state/dissociation theorists continue to oppose these interpretations. For example, it has been argued that during hypnotic analgesia there is evidence of true dissociation (Bowers and Davidson, 1991; Miller and Bowers, 1993). Thus Miller and Bowers (1983) found that during hypnotic analgesia, highly susceptible hypnotic subjects performed well on a competing ("dissociated") cognitive task, whereas subjects instructed to use non-hypnotic cognitive strategies to reduce pain performed less well on the competing cognitive task. Bowers and his associates argue that this occurred because subjects using cognitive strategies expended effort that interfered with performance on the competing task; in contrast, the hypnotic susceptibles, under hypnosis, did not expend any effort in attempting to produce analgesia, because they were able to dissociate the control of pain from awareness.

However, even if we rule out the possibility that the "highs" were complying, and exaggerating their reports of analgesia, there are alternative explanations for this finding. For instance, in the absence of specific instructions to use cognitive strategies, the highly hypnotically susceptible subjects might simply have switched their concentration to the competing task instead. As a result, they could simultaneously do better on the competing task and reduce pain through shifting attention away from the pain to the cognitive task. This interpretation fits rather better with other evidence that suggests that hypnotic subjects do *not* necessarily perform better than controls on dissociated competing tasks; if anything, they do worse (Stevenson, 1976; Wagstaff, 1981). Moreover, at a physiological level, it has been argued that some data appear to be consistent with the view that "highs", more than "lows", use cognitive effort to bring about suggested effects (Crawford, 1996). Another possibility is that cognitive effort is not in any case a very reliable index of using a pain-coping strategy; for instance, Spanos (1991) has argued that perhaps what counts most in hypnotic analgesia is a capacity and willingness to reinterpret the sensory activity as painless.

But even if we were to accept a dissociationist explanation for hypnotic analgesia, it would still be unnecessary to invoke the concept of a special hypnotic state to explain the effect. It does not follow that because some individuals possess an ability to dissociate pain from awareness, they need to be in a special hypnotic trance state in order to do it. However, this draws attention to another issue; why do some people appear to be more hypnotically susceptible than others?

INDIVIDUAL DIFFERENCES IN HYPNOTIC SUSCEPTIBILITY

Studies have shown a number of dimensions to correlate with hypnotic susceptibility, though typically the correlations tend to be small. These dimensions include positive attitudes and expectancies regarding hypnosis, a tendency to be prone to fantasy and to become absorbed in imaginings, a capacity to act, a tendency to report dissociative experiences and even a tendency to conform and comply (de Groh, 1989; Hilgard, 1970; Sarbin and Coe, 1972; Spanos, 1991; Wagstaff, 1981, 1991a; Wilson and Barber, 1982). However, research suggests that relationships between variables such as fantasy proneness, imagination, dissociative experiences and hypnotic susceptibility may be inflated by context effects; that is, sometimes they only correlate significantly when measured in the same context as hypnosis. Results tend to be mixed, though attempts to relate hypnotic susceptibility to measures of dissociative experiences seem to be particularly prone to this problem (Faith and Ray, 1994; Council, Kirsch and Grant, 1996).

Thus although there seems to be no single characteristic that can identify a person who will be susceptible to hypnotic suggestions, it may be possible to build up a picture of the "ideal hypnotic subject"; this will be a person who has positive attitudes towards experiencing hypnotic phenomena, is prone to fantasy and reporting strange experiences, likes to become immersed in imaginings, enjoys acting, is willing to go along with suggestions and try to experience them, generally does what he or she is told, and is willing to adopt a rather lax criterion for reporting hypnotic experiences!

CONCLUSION

So what can we conclude from the huge amount of research that has been conducted in the area of hypnosis?

First, no matter what theoretical stance one takes, it is evident that the procedures we associate with hypnosis can produce effects of considerable psychological significance. Research into hypnosis has enabled us to gather a wealth of information about the capacities, skills and vulnerabilities of ordinary people.

Second, it is clear that a number of key issues remain unresolved; for example, the meaning and usefulness of the concept of "dissociation" in the explanation of hypnotic phenomena is a continuing topic of debate, as is the extent to which hypnotic phenomena can be attributed to behavioural compliance.

Third, however, there does seem to be one substantial issue on which most professional researchers and theorists are now very much agreed; the 19th-century notion of hypnosis as some mysterious unitary altered brain state in which subjects become automata possessed of supernormal powers, is outmoded, inaccurate, and more or less defunct; for although some researchers continue to consider the term "hypnotic state" to be useful, what they have in mind is something more akin to "focused attention" or "imaginative involvement". Hypnotic subjects are thus to be construed fundamentally as active, sentient, cognizing agents, not passive respondents who lose control of their behaviour and mechanically respond to the whims of the hypnotist. It is notable in this respect that the idea of hypnosis as an altered state or trance is not central to the new definition of hypnosis released by the American Psychological Association (1994);

moreover, this definition of hypnosis has been widely endorsed by members of the British Society of Experimental and Clinical Hypnosis (Fellows, 1994).

Despite these developments, however, survey evidence also suggests that the public conception of hypnosis, bolstered by a media ever willing to sensationalize, remains firmly rooted in its more extravagant past. The research literature on hypnosis may be voluminous; however, the process of communicating the findings to the general public has really yet to begin.

NOTES

1. One difficulty with this type of study is that, as a lie detection measure, skin conductance works on the assumption that untruthful responses are accompanied by a degree of anxiety (Ney, 1988). This is problematical in that in the study by Kinnunen et al. (1994) during the critical hypnosis experiment, subjects were misled and were not told that the skin conductance measures were there to detect lies; thus the subjects selected to be "real" hypnotic subjects would have had little reason to be anxious, for not only had they a history of being able to display hypnotic suggestions successfully, but they also were given no reason to assume that any attempt was being made to "catch them out". In contrast, as in many hypnosis experiments, subjects chosen as simulators were those who had previously been unsuccessful at responding to hypnotic suggestions (some experimenters tend to choose "lows" as simulators to stop them "accidentally" falling into "hypnosis"), and they were given simulating instructions that might have sensitized them to, and made them feel anxious about, being "found out".

Section 5

THE MULTIFARIOUS ASPECTS OF DECEPTION

Placebo is the Latin for "I shall please". It is also the *incipit* of the Vespers for the Dead, which were referred to as "placebos".

The topic is unpopular because it is often confused with quackery and is conceived as mockery (Wall, 1993). However, it is very contemporary and has an impact on health purchasing policies. About one-third of adults in the industrialized Western world use unconventional medicine (Eisenberg et al. (1993), but see also the relevant correspondence in *The New England Journal of Medicine* of 14 October 1993, pp. 1200–1204), the efficacy of which has never been demonstrated. Not dissimilarly, "official" medicine also ascribes therapeutic power to scientifically unsound treatments; for instance, think about the widespread use of antibiotics (invaluable weapons against bacteria) to treat the viral common cold, or the unlimited untested exercises proposed by physiotherapists to remedy the effects of strokes (Della Sala, 1997b), or, indeed, the frequency with which general practitioners and consultants alike, more in some than other countries (Garattini and Garattini, 1993), prescribe drugs of uncertain efficacy. Indeed, several studies have suggested that only one out of five commonly used treatments and remedies has been scientifically proved to be really effective (e.g. Brown, 1998).

The Lourdes Medical Bureau has certified 64 miraculous cures since the apparition of the Madonna in 1858 (Nickell, 1993). For the sake of argument, let us accept that these cases were "medically inexplicable" (but see West, 1957; Randi, 1982; Rogo, 1991; Nickell, 1993). Even the less perspicacious believer should concede that, given the number of visitors per year, this figure cannot be really considered an outstanding result, being just less than the chances of winning the national lottery (Sagan, 1996). Of these 64 spontaneous remissions, three were from a diagnosed cancer. The estimated probability of spontaneous remission of cancer (independently of type or severity, and without a trip to Lourdes) is between $1/10\,000$ and $1/100\,000$. Therefore, the probability of being cured from "untreatable" cancer seems higher if the patient stays at home reading love poems. Of course, this extraordinary phenomenon is not limited to Christians: Islamic pilgrims are cured in the waters of the river Zamzam, near Mecca, while Brahmins treat their ailments in the Ganges.

A common myth about placebo treatment is that if a given condition improves with placebos, than it must have been "all in the head". The next chapter presents an alternative view. Those readers interested in finding out more about the mysteries of the placebo effect will find additional information in the comprehensive volumes by White et al. (1985), Frank and Frank (1991), Hartwick (1996) and Harrington (1997), or in the recent thorough reviews by Skrabanek and McCormick (1989), Wall (1993), Chaput de Saintonge and Herxheimer (1994) and Brown (1998).

The following two chapters are written by two magicians. They have taught me that the capacity for self-delusion, even among scientists, should never be underestimated (Wolpert, 1993, p. 141). Taylor (1976), professor of mathematics in London, who later would change his mind completely (Milton, 1994), maintained that Uri Geller's sleight-of-hand, "posed a serious challenge for modern scientists". Credulity is not limited to the layperson, and it suffices to remind ourselves that Conan Doyle believed in fairies and that Nancy Reagan, the US First Lady, was prone to the advice of the San Francisco astrologer Joan Quigley (Regan, 1988). Indeed, there is a growing interest in the neurology and psychology of deception and self-deception (Drake, 1995; Myslobodsky, 1997). In our experiments, we should all be aware of the dangers of the dogma of the immaculate investigation (Eco, 1997). Of course, this is not to say that magicians are exempt from self-delusion. The great Harry Houdini was fooled by the special effects he saw in the film *The Lost World* by Willis O'Brien (1925), and believed he was watching real dinosaurs (*Radio Times*, 25 April 1998).

To say that blind belief is blank and boring does not mean that all scientists are thorough and all science enticing (Cerf and Navasky, 1984; Kohn, 1986). The final chapter of this section demonstrates with a few examples the irony of hasty science. Leafhead and Kopelman follow the steps of Sacks (1995, p. 151) in pointing out that much too often in neuroscience publications, there is "a historical or cultural scotoma". To paraphrase Calvino (1991, p. 19), who was trying to convince us of the need to read classic literature, I would say that to read the originals is better than not reading them.

CHAPTER 13

I Shall Please: the Mysterious Power of Placebos

EDZARD ERNST and NEIL C. ABBOT

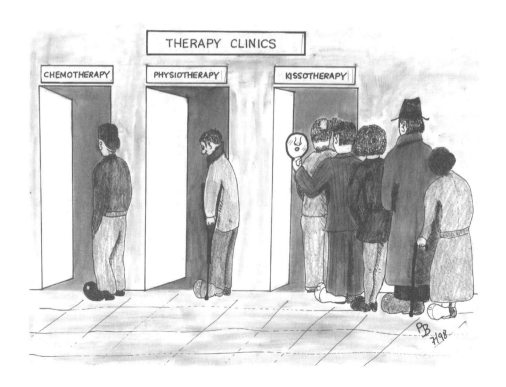

Physicians use it more than any other "therapy", yet they feel uncomfortable when discussing it, often admit that they do not really understand it and rarely conduct focused research into it. We are, of course, speaking about placebos and the power they have to effect clinical improvement.

Before developments in science made powerful and effective drugs available, doctors relied for their success almost entirely on the placebo effect; most therapies did not have a direct effect on the target disease. Any therapeutic success was falsely attributed to the "specific" actions of their prescriptions. The fact that placebo effects are an inherent part of the response to virtually any treatment was ignored, for to knowingly give placebos to patients was equated with quackery. This mixture of ignorance and embarrassment barred the systematic investigation of placebo until relatively recently.

Placebo is Latin for "I shall please", but in the past it has also been described as "make-believe medicine" or "medicine of convenience". Today there are numerous elaborate definitions of the placebo effect. It can be described simply as the effect due to the treatment process which includes the many non-specific effects of therapy (NHI Conference on Placebo, 1996). Yet placebo effects can exist with or without obvious placebos (such as pills, injections, etc.) or, indeed, any overt therapy at all; the mere intention to treat, to talk or to attempt a diagnosis of a patient will usually result in some sort of "placebo effect".

It is not always easy to tell what falls under the umbrella term "placebo" and what does not. Most experts would agree that the placebo effect is by no means a single entity but is like a colourful bunch of flowers. Depending on which single flower we pick, we will get rather different impressions. This may be why the whole subject seems confusing at first and why views of experts can differ widely. There is even some doubt about whether placebo effects exist at all, since most studies which point to their existence are methodologically flawed in one way or another (Kienle, 1995). I would argue that, with similar reasons, one could probably doubt the analgesic effect of aspirin.

Most practising physicians have some stories to tell about the placebo. In my own medical school days, I (E.E.) had been taught to "wire up" patients for electrocardiograms, a diagnostic procedure to diagnose heart disease. One of my first patients, an elderly lady, said to me after the procedure, "That was great, I feel much better, my chest pain has completely gone." I was utterly speechless! This was my first lesson in the mystery and power of the placebo.

THE DETERMINANTS

It would be fascinating and extremely valuable to define why placebo effects are sometimes powerful and on other occasions so weak that we can hardly detect them. In part this seems to depend on the way that treatment is given (Turner et al., 1994). An invasive procedure, or one which involves a panoply of medical techniques, is likely to induce stronger effects than, say, swallowing a simple pill. Surgery is a good example: it comes with the potential for a powerful placebo response. In one study, sham surgery (opening the skin without doing the actual operation) brought relief to nearly 100% of the patients (Dimond, Kittle and Crockett, 1960). Acupuncture is another good example: it is invasive (sometimes even painful) because it entails puncturing the skin. In one trial, nearly 100% of pain sufferers benefited from a "sham acupuncture" in which needles were inserted into non-acupuncture points (Taub et al., 1979). Other studies have shown that the size and the colour of a dummy pill can influence the effect it has on volunteers (Craen et al., 1996). My patient was obviously impressed with the "high-tech" atmosphere of being wired up to a sophisticated piece of equipment. This created strong expectations resulting in a therapeutic effect even though no treatment was administered.

Furthermore, the response will crucially depend on the patient. There are some preliminary data suggesting that Asians have stronger placebo responses than Caucasians (Johnson and Din, 1997). The elderly lady in my story was open to the possibility of symptom relief – indeed, hoping for it – and therefore experienced a positive result. Involving the patient in the therapy is also likely to enhance the placebo effect. We have, for instance, shown that a placebo pill is less beneficial than a placebo cream (Saradeth, Resch and Ernst, 1994), and it may be that the active involvement of the patient by rubbing the skin with cream yields a better outcome.

The attitude of the doctor or therapist is similarly crucial, as it determines the patient involvement with treatment and so influences the therapeutic success. When I did the electrocardiogram, I certainly tried to make up with kindness and understanding what I lacked in experience. Doctors who believe in a given remedy are likely to have more successful patient outcomes than those who are more sceptical (Gracely et al., 1985). Similarly, a positive, warm and empathic encounter with the patient can increase therapeutic success (Lasagna et al., 1954).

The nature of the condition being treated is another potentially important factor in the placebo effect. It is sometimes believed that placebos can influence only subjective experiences or potentially imagined complaints such as pain, anxiety or well-being. This is not quite true. Objective variables such as the results of blood tests, postoperative tissue swelling, body temperature or the healing of wounds are also placebo-prone (Ernst, 1992). None the less, there can be little doubt that certain conditions tend to respond better than others – premenstrual tension, depression, sleeplessness, migraine or other types of pain are complaints that usually respond well. However, there is hardly any disease or symptom that yields no response at all.

At present we do not fully understand all the influences on the placebo response or their possible, complex interactions. There are simply too many variables. One large multicentre study, aimed at pinpointing them more closely, showed that the most important determinant was "the centre" (Tangrea, Adrianza and Helsel, 1994). In other words, even within one single trial there are remarkable geographical variations, and we cannot define exactly why these differences occur.

MYTHS ABOUT PLACEBO EFFECTS

Beecher in 1955 analysed those placebo-controlled trials which had been published at that stage. His paper was to become most influential but was to mislead researchers for decades. Beecher concluded that, on average, about one-third of all patients responded to placebo therapy (Beecher, 1955). This led to the misunderstanding that placebo effects contribute about one-third to the total therapeutic response. We now know that this is not true. Beecher's figure was an average of trials published, but the possible range of responses spans all the way from 0% to 100%.

Some researchers have also postulated that there is a certain type of personality which can be called a "placebo responder". False again! Research over the last decades has failed to identify psychological traits characterizing responders as opposed to non-responders (Richardson, 1994). The individual who today shows a placebo response may, under different (or even the same) circumstances, not show one tomorrow and vice versa. It is simply not possible to identify "placebo responders" as a distinct species. If certain characteristics exist which differentiate responders from non-responders, they remain undiscovered.

A further misunderstanding is that placebo effects are "all in the mind", i.e. are imaginary and somehow unreal. This view fails to appreciate the ultimate connection between mind and body: the one influences the other in deep and subtle ways that we do not yet fully understand. In fact, pharmacologically, placebos behave much like drugs; they elicit dose- and time-dependent effects, and can have cumulative effects just like "real" drugs (Rosenzweig, Brohier and Zipfel, 1995). Moreover, placebos also affect objective signs – anything from cholesterol levels to hair loss (Ernst, 1992; Richardson, 1994).

One might be misled into assuming that placebos can do no harm. However, adverse reactions to placebo, often termed nocebo effects, are well known (Dhume, Agshiker and Diniz, 1975). On average, some 20% of healthy volunteers and 35% of patients report side-effects after placebo pills (Rosenzweig, Borhier and Zipfel, 1995) but the variation between studies is large. Many placebo-controlled drug trials show that the nocebo effects, seen in placebo-treated patients, appear in parallel with the side-effects of those receiving the experimental treatment. If, in one trial, a drug is tested that causes headache, the placebo group too will frequently report headache. If, in another trial, the experimental drug causes loss of appetite, the same symptom will be prevalent in the placebo group. We cannot be sure at present why this is so – possibly there is some (non-verbal?) communication between these groups. But other factors may be involved as well. The notion that nocebo effects are always mild and therefore not really important is refuted by those who view voodoo deaths as a strong nocebo reaction!

MECHANISM OF ACTION

Psychologists, physicians and other professions have repeatedly tried to identify the mechanism by which placebos work. Several theories have been developed (Richardson, 1994). One postulates changes in levels of endorphins (naturally occurring, opiate-like substances produced by the brain) and, interestingly, this theory finds some support from rare cases of "placebo addiction" that have been described (Richardson, 1994). Another sees the placebo effect mainly as an example of a classical conditioning response, first described by Pavlov in salivating dogs, and this is also plausible, since past experience of success of treatment is something we all carry with us. To date, these theories remain unproven and we cannot really tell how exactly placebos work. Common sense tells us, however, that expectation and suggestion are important.

THE RESEARCH AGENDA

After a flurry of interest in the 1950s, research into placebo became almost an exotic sideline of medical research, tainted with the suspicion of quackery (Wall, 1993). Most researchers saw the placebo effect as the "background noise" in a clinical experiment, a nuisance that was not to be researched in its own right but accounted for through adequate study designs and controls. This attitude is now changing. Some physicians remember just how beneficial the placebo effect has been in their daily practice and aim at optimizing rather than suppressing it. If a doctor doesn't elicit a powerful placebo response, they say, he or she has chosen the wrong profession. Indeed, there is a strong case for choosing medical students on the basis of innate empathy rather than proper qualifications. Although some physicians fear that knowingly prescribing placebos is being dishonest with the patient, surveys have shown that placebos are popular; around 80% of nurses, for instance, state that they have used them at some time or other (Gray and Flynn, 1981).

The area of placebos and placebo effects is still grossly under-researched. This is due partly to the failure of researchers and clinicians to recognize its importance, but also to the sheer breadth of its scope and, of course, lack of funding – which drugs firm would sponsor research into placebo effects?

Placebo effects are seen with almost all medical interventions – drugs, biofeedback techniques, surgery and even diagnostic tests (Voudouris, Peck and Coleman, 1990). They thus have a role in all interventions between patient and therapist in primary, secondary and tertiary care. The problem is *not* finding an aspect of the placebo response to research but rather choosing which of its myriad manifestations to start with.

Investigations to date have concentrated largely on the published medical literature (e.g. Turner et al., 1994). They bring together what is known about the effect from the comparatively few experimental studies done on it. The real need is for well-designed rigorous experimental studies focusing on a specified aspect of the phenomenon. To continue the flower analogy mentioned previously, the early history of plant physiology, which focused on very specific mechanisms of growth, development and decay, was a necessary stage for later understanding of the determinants of the bloom. Similarly rigorous, targeted studies are required to *understand* the placebo effect (though not to appreciate its wonder).

CONCLUSIONS

The totality of the evidence available today leaves no doubt that placebo effects help many patients every day. They are "powerful tools in expert hands to relieve patients of misery and are a substantial therapeutic approach in primitive medicine" (Sannita, 1995). They are complementary with virtually every medical treatment we may receive or administer. Instead of ignoring the phenomenon, taking it for granted or feeling embarrassed about "placebo quackery", therapists, physicians and scientists should consider finding out more about the phenomenon in order to better serve the patient – after all, placebo means "I shall please".

CHAPTER 14

The Magicians' Best-kept Secrets

JAMES RANDI

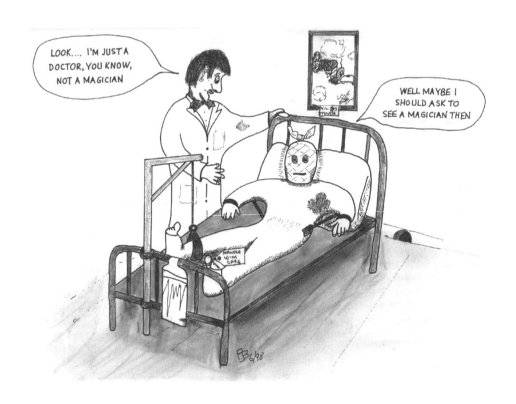

I'm a magician. Much more correctly, I'm a conjurer, but US readers will not recognize that term as readily as others do. I conjure in the sense that I use trickery, psychological as well as physical, to produce the effects that could be brought about by real magic. The definition of "magic" that I use is "changing the course of nature by means of spells and incantations, invoking spirits and other supernatural beings and forces to do so". Believe me when I tell you that, from a purely practical point of view, spells and incantations won't do; trickery is the way to go. It's all done for purposes of entertainment, and not as a swindle, except when the conjurer goes "bad" and tries to tell his audience that he actually possesses magical powers. These renegades are known as psychics. The profession abhors them.

Let's look at some of the psychological methods that the conjurer uses to achieve his illusions. I can reveal some of these without in any way invoking the wrath of professionals in the field, since I will not equip my readers here with anything more than a very rudimentary knowledge of the art, and there should be no presumption that my reader will be able to sit in David Copperfield's audience and smugly solve the wonders he presents. I might add that my reader certainly does not want such an ability, though the contrary may be expected; one loss suffered by the experienced performer is the ability to be swept away by the illusion in the same way that the uninformed viewer hopefully is. We sit before the conjuror and celebrate the subtle skills that are not seen or noticed by the lay person. It is little compensation for losing the thrill of surprise that others will enjoy.

I will not reveal to you the physical side of conjuring. The sliding panels, wires, chemicals, dextrous hand movements, mirrors and other mechanical aspects are perhaps only 30% of the total illusion, though absolutely essential to the final effect. It's the other 70% that is supplied by the performer, the part that doesn't come in the booklet of instructions or blueprints, that will concern me here.

THE EMPTY BOX PLOY

A primary rule of the conjuring art is, "Don't tell them what's so, let them decide for themselves." Suppose I enter upon the stage bearing a cardboard box. I want my audience to believe that the box is empty. (It may or may not be empty. That's beside the point.) I obviously have several ways of accomplishing this. The very worst is to tell them that it's empty. Consider: those folks are seated before me knowing full well that I'm there to deceive them. They're ready, or they think they are, to catch me in any misrepresentation that might lead them to a wrong conclusion. They will tend to disbelieve any assertion that I make, and nothing short of stripping that box down to the floor will convince them that it's empty, if I *tell* them it's empty. How, then, do I accomplish my need?

Brevity and simplicity have much value in conjuring. The conjuror who "doth protest too much" loses any trust the audience may have in him. To accomplish the task of convincing the audience that the box is empty, the conjuror will simply handle it casually, call no attention to it, and toss it down. The audience members see what appears to be an empty box, see it hit the stage, hear the sound of an empty box hitting the stage and come to the conclusion that they've seen an empty box tossed onto the stage. It's that simple. They have had sensory input via sight and sound, and they trust those senses. No one has tried to sell them on anything. They've sold themselves. And anything they decide upon, independently, they will believe.

"I known it's true. I saw it with my own eyes." Naivety was never better expressed, and the conjuror makes full use of this weakness.

ESTABLISH MANNERISMS

I remember many years ago in Canada, when I worked with a carnival, that a chap we only knew as "Jack" imparted to me a few subtleties of deception that I have often used since. I watched him playing cards with other carnies one evening when we were rained out. He repeatedly pinched and pulled on his nose as he thoughtfully perused the hand he'd been dealt, and by the end of the evening, he'd come out somewhat ahead of his fellow players. At an all-night diner following the game, I remarked to him that he'd done a lot of manipulation of his proboscis, and he confided in me that there'd been a reason for this gesture. "Nose oil!" he announced. "Good old nose oil, which I daresay has added to the coffers of many a cardsharp!" He explained that in order to surreptitiously identify certain desirable cards in the pack, he was using what card cheats call "daub". This can be in the form of colouring matter (lipstick and eye-shadow are used) or any substance that can be applied to the edge or back of a card and later easily removed. Jack was using "nose oil".

The sebaceous glands of the nose give out oil. That substance can be applied to the back of a playing card by means of a thumb, and later spotted by observing a reflection off the card back from a convenient light source. Jack had positioned himself so that a midway light glanced off the dealt-down cards and could be spotted.

But Jack had certainly fingered his nose far more than necessary. He had clutched that organ every time he looked over his cards, and I asked him about that anomaly. "Establish your gestures," he told me. "Get the suckers into accepting your little mannerisms and twitches. They may think you're eccentric, but they'll ignore it after a while. Then, when you need to use that gimmick, it's acceptable and they don't even notice."

The conjurer uses this ploy. He establishes certain gestures and mannerisms that may (or may not!) serve him at certain moments in the routine. Sticking his hand in a pocket, holding the edge of his vest while speaking, or resting both hands on a table from time to time, could all be parts of this process. Even looking offstage at imaginary persons, as if sharing a private joke with them, can be used.

A boyhood chum of mine, T. K. Lawson, once illustrated this method for me in an unforgettable fashion. I was acting as his behind-stage assistant at a Christmas party for some children. To our mutual horror, he discovered that a prop he had on stage was lacking a large wooden block that was essential to the trick. And I was standing by the edge of the stage, holding that block. Lawson stopped, looked startled, and exclaimed that he thought he'd seen Santa at the back of the auditorium. Every head turned for an instant, and we both knew what the next move was. Lawson carried on with another miracle he was presenting, and as his audience applauded, he glanced at me, nodded, and pointed to the back of the auditorium with a great shout. "There he is, boys and girls! Santa!" And as the heads once again turned, I did a Sandy Koufax with the wooden block, Lawson did a Johnny Bench and deftly slipped it into the proper place. The show went on.

DON'T EVER BLINK

I recently watched a young conjuror doing an impromptu card-manipulation routine for his peers at an NYC magic shop. The routine, while not flawless, showed great promise. But I was struck by his "twitch" wherein he closed his eyes every time the "instant of truth" arrived. It was as if he felt that if he couldn't see the "move", no one would. Ostriches, take note.

This is common among budding conjurors. They blot out the sight of the actual move by blinking or closing their eyes. Even John Scarne, the very famous card magician and gambling expert, in his later years developed a 'blink'' that consisted of emitting a short nasal sniff at the second he performed a second-deal or top-change. (I'll leave those definitions to your imagination.) It's hard to get away from.

Observe Lance Burton, today's most consummate performer, in my opinion, as he plucks living doves, lit candles and playing cards out of the charmed air through which he moves. Nary a blink, though he goes through a rapid sequence of deft and highly skilled moves that you just never perceive, though they're right there for you to see. Slick is not the word to describe it.

Bottom line: be cool. Any unusual movement or unexpected variation in what the observer will expect can give you away.

MAKE IT FIT, EVEN IF IT DOESN'T

I've a very favourite card trick I do, in which the spectator handles the deck, shuffles it, deals it out, and ends up with a most astounding result. He goes away with the impression that what happens is quite impossible, because of circumstances that he recalls, circumstances that did not in fact exist. It's all done by retrofitting.

This is the art of falsely reconstructing the account of an event so that the victim convinces himself that your reconstruction is correct. The "police psychics" do this with great skill. These are the people who purport to assist in solving crimes. Their technique is to give an enormous amount of non-specific data, and then, after the facts of the case develop, go back over the data and pick out "hits", no matter how insignificant they may be. All attention is concentrated on those few successes, and the other blatant misses are ignored. Lawyers are not exactly ignorant of this process, either. I've served as an expert witness enough times to have seen this ploy put to powerful use.

LET THE VICTIM FIND THE PROOF

This method echoes the first one described here, but it's far advanced and can be used only by the experienced player. I'm often asked by neophytes, "What do I do if the spectator grabs my hand?" or "How do I handle a heckler?" Those questions are not easy to answer. Those problems should not arise, and won't arise, when you've developed the authority. The performer must be in charge. This "authority" problem is, in my opinion, one reason that women have – until recently – been in the great minority in professional conjuring.

So, if you're authoritative enough, you can use a gimmick that I have employed with great success: let the spectator discover further proof of your skill, by himself, well after you've left the scene. An example will illustrate my point.

As a teenager, I invented a method for determining the identity of one card which has been removed from a full deck, simply by examining the other 51 cards. It's simple to do. I added up all the "values" of the cards in a full deck, aces being "1" and the court cards (Jack, Queen and King) being 11, 12 and 13, respectively. This comes to a total of 364. Now, if you run through the deck and add up all the values, and come to a total of 362, you know that the removed card is a two, right? Adding the actual total is rather tough, so I add up to 50, then start over again, getting seven clumps of 50, and allowing a remainder of 14 from which I can easily subtract to arrive at the identity of the removed card. Simple.

But the suit of that card is still a mystery, so I comment that I hate to make a fool of myself, and I'd like to check, quickly, if I'm right. I run through the deck very fast, looking only for the ones that match my determination, and as soon as I've seen three of them I know what the missing card is.

That's what we might call an ''okay'' trick, but not a prizewinner. The spectator, believing that I'm perhaps memorizing the deck as I go through it, will be moderately impressed when I announce the identity of the only card that's not there. But there's a ''convincer'' needed, a ''shot'' to emphasize my genius. And it uses the ploy we're discussing here.

After I've gone through the deck, I look puzzled and ask the spectator, ''Did you take *two* cards? Because, there are two missing!'' The spectator assures me he took only one card, and I announce the identities of the two cards I've found to be missing, one of which is his selected card. Then, and this is the delicious part, I depart and anticipate a phone call telling me that the other missing card was found behind the couch or under the newspaper, where I placed it, unseen by the victim, before I performed. I simply made allowance for that card when I was doing my adding-up. The fact that the spectator found the evidence of my stunning ability cements the impact and validity of my feat . . .

BLEND INTO THE SCENERY

This ploy has little to do with the conjuring art, except in very special circumstances. I learned it many, many years ago, from a reporter friend in the UK who specialized in covering murder scenes. He had ways of staying on the scene when other members of the press were shooed away. Dressed in a nondescript manner, appearing to be a particularly colourless person, he developed techniques whereby he could remain just outside the site of a crime until the suspects and/or officials emerged and he could approach them. One such technique involved measuring. He carried a clipboard and a tape-measure. He would set about measuring fire-hydrants, paving blocks, staircases, steps, or property frontages, in great detail, and writing down his results with painstaking accuracy. His glasses always needed cleaning, there was quite often a stone in his shoe that had to be removed, and his dramatic nose-blowing and coughing fits made him capable of standing his ground. Frequently he ''accidentally'' spilled a large mass of coins from his pocket when removing a handkerchief, and had to get down on hands-and-knees to recover it. The presiding officer might assist this incompetent fumbler, and thus present himself for casual questioning by the change-dropper. The ''Do tell!'' and ''You don't say!'' comments could have encouraged further information from the beguiled officer, and often did.

Years ago, as an escape-artist, I had great need to ''case'' a jail prior to attempting to break out of it. I found that night-officers on the desk of a small-town jail were happy to have any attention that might be offered them. More than once, I would call by at one o'clock in the morning, ostensibly to ask directions and to consult a street-map, but actually to ''scope out'' the terrain. Looking around me, I would comment on the lovely old/new building, and ask about its history and that of the officer himself. I'd drop a comment that I loved old locks, and I'd aver that there were probably some old locks, maybe even handcuffs and legirons, to be seen in this place! In one small town in Nova

Scotia, an elderly officer not only took me on a tour of the lockup, but showed me a drawer full of old irons and padlocks that had accumulated for years. It will not surprise you to learn that 2 days later, prepared for the cell locks I'd been shown as well as the antique manacles, I made a sensational and widely publicized escape from that jail. My sponsors, a local service club, raised a tidy sum for good works, and I was well paid for the show I gave. Since he worked the night shift, the officer who had unwittingly provided me with such valuable information probably never knew of how helpful he'd been. To ease any guilt he might have felt, I made sure that he received a bottle of strong spirits from Canada's finest distillery, as a surprise gift.

Well, there you have six of the professional deceivers' secret ploys, secret no more. Again, I will tell you that these revelations will bring you no sudden ability to solve the conjurors' secrets, but will only let you peek behind the curtain a bit. Remember that the Wizard of Oz told Dorothy and her friends. ''Pay no attention to that man behind the curtain!''

You've been warned

CHAPTER 15

It's All in the Mind: On the Mechanisms of Deception in Psychic Fraud

MASSIMO POLIDORO

It frequently happens that the media introduces to the public extraordinary people who claim to possess some fantastic psychic ability. They may read minds, move objects only by thinking, read newspapers with their fingertips, levitate or perform other marvels. Often, in such cases, the psychic is accompanied by some sort of scientific validation, which means that one or more scientists have observed him or her under scientific conditions and have reached the conclusion that his or her powers are genuine.

A problem arises when one examines the last 130 years in the history of psychical research. A striking fact that emerges, in fact, is that there are countless examples of cases in which scientists, even celebrated ones, have been duped by some clever trickster (Houdini, 1926; Mulholland, 1979; Randi, 1975, 1982; Gardner, 1981; Brandon, 1984; Hall, 1984a, b; Polidoro, 1995; Polidoro, 1998). The obvious question, then, is the following: are scientists always the best-suited persons to conduct investigations in the area of psychical research?

They most certainly are, but they should not work alone in this field, especially when they deal with subjects apparently gifted with some fantastic ability. As Gardner (1981, p. 92) clearly pointed out: "scientists are the easiest persons in the world to fool. It's not hard to understand why. In their laboratories the equipment is just what it seems. There are no hidden mirrors or secret compartments or concealed magnets. If an assistant puts chemical A in a beaker he does not (usually) surreptitiously switch it for chemical B. The thinking of a scientist is rational, based on a lifetime of experience with a rational world. But the methods of magic are irrational and totally outside a scientist's experience."

For this reason, scientists involved in the examination of psychics should seek the advice of those expert in the techniques and psychology of deception, who, usually, are competent magicians.

The aim of this chapter is to help the reader to get better acquainted with the many psychological stratagems used by fake psychics to convince their audience that they really possess psychic powers.

To begin with, we will consider an account of a session with a fictional self-proclaimed psychic, Turi Sneller. Although Sneller does not exist in reality, the account is based on the various similar accounts of actual psychic sessions – sometimes, the descriptions have been reported word for word. This exercise will make it possible to dissect the account, with the aim of understanding what often happens during such "experiments".

A SESSION WITH A PSYCHIC

Turi Sneller is a 28-year-old Italian who achieved quite a success a few years ago by demonstrating his psychic abilities in telepathy and psychokinesis. He appeared to be able to accomplish extraordinary feats: move objects without touching them, bend forks and nails, read messages sealed in boxes, dematerialize his body, and so on.

In an experimental session for a group of scientists in Pavia, Italy, Sneller recently gave some examples of his powers. After stating that he was tired, thus excusing himself in case something did not work, he explained that how well his powers work depends on the mental attitude of his audience. If people are with him, he said, all sorts of things happen; if they are not with him, nothing happens.

Sneller claims that he first noticed his strange abilities after experiencing a severe electric shock as a child. He kept his powers to himself, but continued practising them and finally decided he should use them to make his living. Inevitably, he started to attract the attention of parapsychologists, interested in studying his singular abilities.

Sneller asked for metal objects, like keys, cutlery, pens and so on. He gathered many such objects on a tray, and started to pick up one or another, and then selected a key. He held the key in his fist and concentrated hard. After a couple of minutes he opened his hand but nothing had happened. He was encouraged by the experimenters and agreed to try a different experiment. He asked a researcher to make a simple drawing on a pad, while he turned his back to her. He also asked the others present in the room to look at her drawing and concentrate on it without whispering what it was.

When the drawing was finished, he asked for the pad to be turned face down and then he turned back again. He closed his eyes, concentrated and drew on his pad a simple geometric house. The researcher turned up her drawing, which also showed a simple house. Sneller appeared to be enthusiastic about his success and the researchers also were impressed by it.

A new telepathic test was suggested. A previously prepared drawing, sealed in an envelope, was presented to Sneller. Would he be able to guess it? He drew a simple sun, but then cancelled the test when he noticed that the drawing (a sun, in fact) could be seen through the envelope. His honesty was, nonetheless, appreciated.

Finding a pack of cards lying around, he asked someone to shuffle them, since he said he was not very good at this sort of thing. He then asked the researcher to try to divide the pack of cards into two piles: red and black, but without looking at them. At that moment, he stood up, as if he felt something. He turned to the tray with the metal objects and looked through it to check if something had happened to the keys. But nothing had.

The card experiment was resumed. The cards were dealt in two piles, face down. However, when turned over, it could be seen that they were almost perfectly divided into blacks and reds. Sneller congratulated the researcher who had dealt the cards since, he felt, he must have strong psychic abilities too.

He then looked again at the tray and appeared to be surprised. A couple of keys and a spoon in it were bent. Sneller explained that sometimes things happen even when he is not paying attention. Probably, he said, some kind of "energy" liberated during the successful experiment with the cards influenced the keys somehow. As the nature of his powers, he could not say exactly, but felt they came from "an outside source", "some kind of external intelligence".

He then tried again to bend a spoon but without success. This, he said, showed that it was not a trick, which would always work. He asked for some metal object to be put close to the spoon and then tried again. This time, the spoon bent upwards. He then took a fork which melted into two pieces. The experimenters were quite impressed by what they had seen.

Sneller repeated that he was genuine and asked anyone present to search him, in case someone thought he had some hidden instrument with which he could cause the bendings. Before he left, a last phenomenon occurred. A noise was heard: a small toy had fallen onto the floor, apparently out of nowhere. One of the researchers recognized it as a toy, long thought lost, belonging to his child.

BEHIND THE SCENES

There have already been various attempts to describe the psychological stratagems used by charlatans to convince experimenters that they really have psychic powers (Fuller, 1975;

1980; Randi, 1975, 1982b; Marks and Kamman, 1980; Harris, 1985; Wiseman, 1994). This chapter, then, will attempt to summarize and, when possible, amplify all these previous works in a single list of psychological stratagems. There are at least 26 different strategies, divided into five main processes: (1) how to be believable; (2) how to limit and thwart the controls; (3) how to perform seeming miracles; (4) what to do in case something goes wrong; and (5) how to distort memories.

How to be Believable

The psychic creates a believable claim

To avoid arousing too many doubts in the observers, the psychic usually tries to present a claim that, although being paranormal, can be considered true by those ready to believe in this sort of thing. For example, in a telepathy test, where the psychic has to guess the identity of hidden cards, it is considered to be a success if the psychic correctly indicates a number of cards slightly above that expected from chance. Thus, a pseudopsychic, who finds a way to gain information on the cards by normal means, may decide to correctly identify a number of cards above that expected from chance but never all of the cards, since this might look too suspicious. In the example above, Turi Sneller had a researcher divide a pack of cards into two piles. This is a standard magic trick by which a person other than the performer can divide the cards into blacks and reds without realizing how he did it. To make it believable as a psychic demonstration, however, Sneller had to mess up the demonstration a bit, by having some wrong cards appear in the two piles.

The powers come from a force outside the psychic

Usually, psychics claim that the powers they possess are given to them by supernatural forces that are not under their control. Mediums usually say that it is the spirits that guide them and that suggest the ideal conditions for their manifestations (namely, sitting still in a dark room). Astrologer Jean Dixon claimed that her prophecies came from God; self-styled psychic Uri Geller stated that his powers came from a flying saucer called "Spectra". In this way, tricksters, like Turi Sneller, can impose their conditions on the tests without appearing to be artificial: "*They* want it so", they explain. Also, this allows prophets for example, to make any kind of wild prophecy without worrying too much about it being correct or not. As Randi (1990, p. 35) pointed out, one of the "rules" of astrologers and the like is the following: "Credit God with your success, and blame yourself for any incorrect interpretations of his divine messages. This way, detractors have to fight God."

The psychic appears modest and humble

His voice sounds sincere and he constantly apologizes "if nothing works". This inevitably makes the audience watching him want him to succeed. In this way, as in the Sneller example, an experimenter may feel motivated to help him and inadvertently overlook one control or another.

The psychic pretends to be amazed by his own powers

This is one of the best ways to lend authenticity to a demonstration. At the beginning of the test the psychic appears unsure of his success in a certain experiment. He may claim to be tired, like Sneller. This is a direct consequence of the second strategy; since his powers come from a force outside him, the psychic does not know if they always work. However, when the experiment works, the obvious reaction is to be amazed and thrilled by the results.

The consistency of the phenomenon with previously reported ones appears as strong evidence of its genuineness

In the heyday of Spiritualism, it frequently happened that "materialized figures" were discovered to be the same mediums, or their accomplices, dressed up as ghosts. Instead of dismissing materializations as mere tricks, every time a new medium was caught being disguised as a "ghost" believers considered it a further proof of the authenticity of the phenomenon. "Since this always happens," spiritualists reasoned, "there must be a reason for it". A theory was then put forward according to which, when a spirit wants to materialize, "he needs to borrow organic matter from the material world, and thus he takes it from the medium" (Holms, 1969).

The psychic may produce a claim that the individual wants to believe

A psychic may exploit people's physical and emotional needs. Wiseman (1994) notes, for example, how a pseudopsychic may claim to possess psychic healing powers, in the hope of motivating an individual needing to recover from an illness to believe in him. Also, mediums may exploit the need for comfort of individuals who have recently suffered a bereavement, by promising some form of communication with deceased friends and relatives.

Participants are credited with paranormal powers

Another strong way to involve participants and make them feel motivated is for the psychic to claim that they too possess paranormal powers. He can accomplish this by presenting a demonstration in which the participant appears to be in charge of the results while, in reality, it is the psychic who controls the game. An Italian psychic, Gustavo A. Rol, used to present a demonstration with playing cards, in which a spectator appeared to be able to separate black cards from red ones without looking (it is the same demonstration described in the Sneller story above). This is one of the classics of magic. It is a trick, invented by magician Paul Curry, called "Out of this world", in which the performer only has to briefly touch the cards in a very natural way for it to work. People who witness this trick inevitably go away convinced that they were the only ones who handled the cards and got the astonishing result. Randi (1982b, p. 196) comments, "Bear in mind that people so flattered are apt to get a bit gushy and relax just a mite more than ordinarily. Blame for a failure can be assigned to them by the same token."

How to Limit and Thwart the Controls

The result of a demonstration is not stated in advance

This is one of the oldest rules of magicians: never say in advance what you are going to do. How useful to a fake psychic this rule can be is very clear. If an audience does not know what is going to happen, they do not know what to look for, and this makes it impossible to apply useful controls or postulate possible normal solutions until the demonstration is over – when, usually, it is too late.

The original goal is switched and the new goal is accepted

Whenever the experimenter knows what kind of demonstration the psychic is going to present, the psychic can still escape the controls by presenting a slightly different demonstration from the one intended. An experimenter, for example, may ask a psychic to break a spoon with his powers (a feat which the latter is known for) and hand him a checked spoon; the psychic, however, bends the spoon, instead of breaking it. This switch of goal can be accepted by the experimenter, since the phenomenon is quite similar. The breaking of a spoon, however, requires a specially "gaffed" spoon, while the bending of it only requires special manipulatory skills but can be accomplished almost instantaneously.

The psychic creates chaos

This is a golden rule, which allows the psychic to divert attention away from the requested test. The psychic may: start an experiment, and then stop it because he lacks the needed "concentration"; start a different demonstration, and then stop for a while to "recharge" and talk a lot; then return again to the original one; and so on. In the Sneller story, this ruse is quite evident. The psychic starts an experiment with cards, but suddenly stands up for no apparent reason and examines the cutlery on a tray: nothing has happened. Then he returns to the cards and, later, it is discovered that some of the spoons on the tray have bent. By making use of actions or suggestions intended to relax observation of the original intended action, then, the psychic may be able to divert the attention of the observers. In this way, he can perform the so-called "dirty work" (that is, the trick) for a demonstration, while the attention of the participants is concentrated on a different feat. At the other extreme, still with the object of distracting the observers' attention, the psychic can make use of a strategy labelled "monotony" (Fitzkee, 1945): in brief, he takes a very long time before attempting any form of trickery, thus lessening the individual's vigilance.

The psychic exploits controls applied at inappropriate times

Very often, the psychic may be able to prepare the trick for a fake demonstration long before the experiment starts. For example, he may be invited onto a television show where he knows he will be asked to duplicate the drawing sealed in an envelope. By getting to the television station early, he may be able to get close to the envelope (even only for a few seconds) and, by means of various techniques available to magicians, get access to its content. In this case, even before the show starts, the psychic already knows what drawing is in the envelope and, when he is on the air, he only has to act the role of the uncertain psychic, who attempts a guess, and then acts excited when the envelope is opened and the drawings are seen to correspond. In the story of Turi Sneller, the materialization from nowhere of the toy could have been accomplished by similar means. For example, the psychic may be picked up and taken to the laboratory by an experimenter who uses his own car; in this case, the psychic only has to reach under the seats of the car, while unseen, and may often find lost objects, like earrings or toys. Only a long time after this ride, the psychic (or his accomplice) may throw in the air the object, while people are distracted, and claim it is an "apport" (Fuller, 1980).

The psychic exploits ineffective or removable controls

During the 1970s, when pseudopsychic Uri Geller became famous, there were many imitators, especially children, who claimed that they too could bend metal objects with the power of their minds. A common test used by parapsychologists in such cases was to present the child with a test-tube, inside which was inserted a piece of metal; the tube was usually closed (not sealed) with a cork. It was very easy for the children to take advantage of a moment of distraction of the experimenter to remove the cork, bend the metal and close the tube: it only takes a few seconds. It should be noted that no one has ever been able to bend a piece of metal (or anything else) inside a properly sealed test-tube.

The subject is allowed to suggest tests and conditions for tests

By suggesting test conditions, the psychic can set limits within which he can operate. In the 1870s the celebrated medium Daniel Douglas Home became very popular for his spectacular feats and for the fact that, as was claimed, he was never caught cheating (as opposed to all of his colleagues). This should not surprise us much, once the kind of conditions in which Home operated are known. He did not subject himself to any kind of restraint or control (although, sometimes, he made it appear that he did – instead, it was him who dictated the conditions; he could choose the participants in his séances, and could turn away those he felt were too sceptical; he decided what was going to happen and in what kind of light; and, of course, he justified his impositions with the fact that it was the spirits who wanted it so (Hall, 1984a; Polidoro, 1995).

How to Perform Seeming Miracles

The psychic appears incapable of fraud

To induce in the observers the idea that a psychic is performing real miracles, he first needs to convince his audience that he cannot and, above all, would not want to cheat. Some experts of the paranormal are convinced that fakers possess a sort of "physique du role". A faker, according to such experts, should be: adult, extremely intelligent and well educated; if he does not fit this idea of a trickster, then he must be real. There have been countless cases in which children, peasants or uneducated people have been credited with real psychic powers only because it was thought that they could not possibly be able to fool a cultured person. The truth is quite different, as psychical history shows. It may be sufficient to remind the reader that the whole Spiritualism movement was started by two little girls, Margaret and Kate Fox, who snapped their toes, creating noises that were quickly attributed to spirits. It was only after 40 years, when Spiritualism had gathered millions of followers, that the Fox sisters revealed the hoax and, as expected, very few acknowledged that they had been fooled by such simple tricks (Brandon, 1983; Polidoro, 1995).

The psychic fails to pass tests designed to determine if the necessary skill is present

Randi (1982b, p. 37) gives a clear example of this: "In France, recently, Jean-Pierre Girard was tested for strength by his mentor, Charles Crussard, to see if he could physically bend the bars that he seemed to be bending psychically. Crussard reported that Girard was not able to do so, no matter how hard he tried!" The subject's failure to pass a test should prove him honest to the experimenter. In passing, it may be noted that later Girard was proved to be a fraud.

The psychic appears to have no motivation to deceive

A common belief among certain parapsychologists is that a person may decide to become a fake psychic because he seeks money or fame. No other motivation is considered to be sufficient. Thus, if the psychic does not ask for money, and does not look for fame, the fact is presented as strong proof of genuineness of his powers. In Italy, the already named Rol never asked for money for his performances, and did not look for publicity in the media. The fact that he was already rich and that, thanks to his demonstrations, he had become very powerful and almost a cult figure among various artists, intellectuals and scientists (Federico Fellini, for example, was said to be one of his best friends) does not seem a sufficient motivation for cheating to Italian experts in the paranormal.

The psychic uses familiar objects

The use of everyday objects, sometimes borrowed, greatly enhances the impact of an effect, as illustrated in the Sneller episode: first, because an everyday object, better if borrowed, easily convinces an audience that it is authentic, and not a gimmick; and second, because the audience can identify with an everyday object and automatically assume that the item is free from deception. As Harris (1985, p. 11) notes, "many magicians use gimmicked apparatus for certain effects. Because the apparatus used consists of natural looking objects, handled every day by most of us, we do not suspect that there could be gimmickery involved. To further enhance this psychological subtlety all the magician needs to do is borrow his gimmicked wares from an accomplice planted in the audience."

The psychic uses simple methods

The best way for a psychic never to be caught cheating is to avoid using gimmicks (i.e. special apparatus that allows some kind of trickery). Instead, it is better to rely on simple methods, better if based only on psychological deceptions. For this reason, mediums who were caught hiding cheesecloth (generally used to fake ectoplasm) in their clothes or luggage had a hard time justifying themselves, while mental mediums, who relied on psychological techniques like "cold reading" (Hyman, 1977), were far better off. A very famous trick, used by some psychics to convince an audience that they can read minds, relies on this kind of psychological deception. The psychic asks the audience to think of a simple geometrical figure and then to think of a second simple geometrical figure inside it: he then draws what he "receives" from the audience and, most of the time, he is correct. The trick lies in the fact that, given this kind of instruction, most of the time people will think of a circle inside a triangle or vice versa.

The psychic never uses the same method to fabricate the same kind of phenomenon

This is an old dodge of conjurors: "never repeat a trick; or, if you do, use a different method". The reason is that when someone watches a trick for the first time he does not know what to look for and is easily deceived. This advantage is lost, however, if the trick is performed a second time. The only solution, in this case, is to use a different method to accomplish the same result. It is generally not known that there are, for example, many different ways to move a table or to bend a spoon, each one suitable for certain kinds of conditions.

The great fake psychics are improvisers

This means that a really good pseudopsychic is able to produce phenomena in almost any situation. A quick mind and a good knowledge of the techniques and psychology of deception are all that is needed. Sometimes, only a quick mind is sufficient. In one of the early tests of telepathy, in 1882, fake psychic G. A. Smith, and his accomplice Douglas Blackburn, were able to fool some researchers of the Society for Psychical Research. In a later confession, Blackburn (1911) described how they had to think fast and frequently invent new ways for faking telepathy demonstrations. Once, for example, Smith had been swathed in blankets to avoid the exchange of signals between him and Blackburn. Smith had to guess the identity of a drawing and Blackburn secretly drew it on a cigarette paper. When Smith exclaimed "I have it", and projected his right hand from beneath the blanket. Blackburn was ready. He had transferred the cigarette paper to the tube of the brass projector on the pencil he was using and, when Smith asked for a pencil, he gave him his. Under the blanket, Smith had concealed a luminous painted slate, which in the dense darkness gave sufficient light to show the figure on the cigarette paper, and only needed to copy the drawing.

Talking about fraud detection, magician Harry Houdini (Houdini, 1924, p. 245) noted, "It is manifestly impossible to detect and duplicate all the feats attributed to fraudulent mediums who do not scruple at outraging propriety and even decency to gain their ends . . . Again, many of the effects produced by them are impulsive, spasmodic, done on the spur of the moment, inspired or promoted by attending circumstances, and could not be duplicated by themselves."

What to Do in Case Something Goes Wrong

Failure is proof of genuine paranormal powers

It is a general conviction among some psychic researchers that "if it is a trick it always works". Thanks to this false belief, a pseudopsychic not only is excused when something in his demonstration does not work, but is also credited with real psychic powers *because* it did not work. It is claimed, in fact, that his kind of phenomena only work in a sporadic and unpredictable fashion, and the subject cannot produce them on command or on a regular basis. A pseudopsychic, then, has a great advantage over a straight magician; the latter has to perform and always obtain "miracles", to avoid being booed off stage; the former, instead, is allowed to "pass" when conditions are not ideal or an audience is too sceptical.

Sceptics produce "negative vibrations"

The subject does not do well when persons with a sceptical attitude are nearby (see Figure 15.1). As a consequence of this, phenomena are inhibited unless the sceptics can be turned

CONTROLS

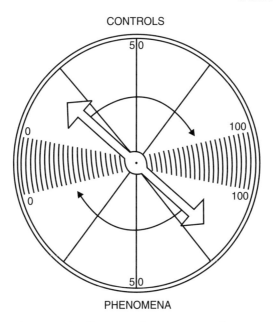

PHENOMENA

Figure 15.1 The "control meter". This illustration shows a very significant aspect of parapsychological research: when the controls decrease (0), the phenomena increase (100); however, when the controls increase (100), the phenomena decrease (0) (Angela, 1978).

away. Thus people who could watch a demonstration and not be biased towards belief are turned away. As has frequently been shown (Jones and Russell, 1980; Wiseman and Morris, 1995), believers tend to distort their memories of a psychic demonstration, while sceptics tend to correctly recall a demonstration, even when it appears to support the existence of paranormal powers.

Any trickery detected may be attributed to the subject's desire to please

One of the greatest mediums that ever lived, Eusapia Palladino, was also, possibly, the one most often caught at cheating (Polidoro and Rinaldi, 1998). However, her experimenters were quick to explain that she could not help herself, and the fault rested on the observers who did not prevent her from doing so. Of course, this is an immensely powerful tool in the stock of a fake psychic. Put in other words, it means that when he or she is not caught cheating, the phenomenon must be real. However, when he or she is caught it is not his or her fault, since he or she has a "compulsion to cheat", to please the observers. Some other psychic researchers, in trying to explain undoubted fraud by a psychic, instead of admitting the unreliability of said psychic, and thus reject all the previous work done with him, prefer to believe that the psychic acted "unconsciously".

Any trickery detected may be considered proof of genuine powers

Sometimes, an experimenter notices, in a test with a medium or psychic, some quite suspicious movement or action that could help the psychic to perform his feats by normal means. However, in such cases, many experimenters decide that this is further proof of the reality of the phenomenon. They simply explain that, since the ruse appeared too crude for it to be mistaken (i.e. there was no doubt that it was a move used to fake a demonstration), the psychic must have made it involuntarily, since it would have been too easy to spot it.

How to Distort Memories

Many researchers have shown that eyewitness testimony, in relation to psychic demonstrations, is generally unreliable and can lead to wrong conclusions. There are many factors that can influence the reliability of eyewitness testimony (Wiseman, 1996), and the pseudopsychic can take advantage of this situation.

The psychic is elusive

The claims are always vague and never specific in advance of a demonstration. As said above, this makes it impossible for the observer to know what to look for and, furthermore, after the demonstration it will be impossible to remember exactly what went on, especially if the demonstrations took place in "well-designed chaos" (see above).

The psychic recapitulates often what happened to alter memories

If the psychic declares that he never touched a key when it bent, that's what people will remember (Fuller, 1975). It will be completely forgotten, for example, that the psychic moved the key from one spot to another, because that movement is considered insignificant, while in reality that may be the moment when the trick took place. Also, a psychic may perform the same demonstration several times with the use of a different technique each time. Diaconis (1985, p. 572), in explaining the "bundle of sticks phenomenon", noted: "the weak points of one performance are ruled out because they were clearly not present during other performances. The bundle of sticks is stronger than any single stick."

CONCLUSIONS

After this review of the various strategies used by fake psychics to simulate real paranormal powers, you may feel better defended against psychic fraud. However, you should not think now that you are immune to fraud, since this is not possible and even great experts in psychic deception are not totally immune to this kind of fraud. What you can do, however, is to use this knowledge in a useful way to examine mysterious stories of psychic demonstrations. As a start, you could begin by reading again the account of the experiments with the fictional Turi Sneller and see if you can spot his methods; after this, you could direct your attention to real descriptions of claimed psychic feats: this kind of material will probably be seen with different eyes, now, and many previously overlooked details may assume a new meaning.

ACKNOWLEDGEMENTS

The author would like to thank Dr Luigi Garlaschelli for his kind help and assistance.

CHAPTER 16

Recent Advances in Moving Backwards

KATHARINE M. LEAFHEAD and MICHAEL D. KOPELMAN

INTRODUCTION

''I disapprove of what you say, but I will defend to the death your right to say it.'' So goes the oft-quoted Voltaire saying purporting to defend free speech. Except that he didn't say it. It was Evelyn Beatrice Hall, writing under the alias S. G. Tallentyre (1906) in her book *Friends of Voltaire* (Tallentyre, 1906), who wrote the now-famous words when summarizing Voltaire's general attitude after the public burning of Helvétuis' book, *De l'Esprit*. It is not clear whether she was quoting him or paraphrasing him, since she says '' 'I disapprove of what you say but I will defend to the death your right to say it' was his attitude now.'' We cannot now tell whether he ever did utter the more elegant phrase usually attributed to him. What we do know he actually said about the burning of Helvétuis' book was ''What a fuss over an omelette''.

Misquotation is not confined to Voltaire. On the contrary, the astute clinical observations of 19th-century writers, such as Capgras, Cotard, Korsakoff and Kraepelin, have commonly been caricatured and condensed, such that the original clinical richness of their descriptions is lost, and may even be misinterpreted.

In this chapter, we intend to illustrate how at least two leading clinicians over a century ago pre-empted much of what is being written today on their respective topics. Until recently, much of what they said had seemed to be largely forgotten, but advances in research and modern experimental evidence are confirming early clinical insights.

THE COTARD DELUSION

> Stating that she was no longer anything, the patient begged for her veins to be opened, her arms and legs to be cut off, and her body to be opened up, so that it could be seen that she had no more blood and that her organs no longer existed.
>
> Cotard (1882, 1974), Case 6
>
> I feel as though I have died . . . I believe I have died . . . I can't breathe . . . I have died.
>
> (Young, Leafhead and Szulecka, 1994)

It is now more than a century since Jules Cotard, a French psychiatrist, published a number of case reports (Cotard, 1882) in which the central feature was what he termed nihilistic delusions (*le délire de négation*). Cotard noted that these nihilistic delusions could range in severity both between and within individuals, varying from a mild form, in which the characteristic features were self-deprecation and feelings of despair, to their most extreme form, in which there was a total denial of the self and the external world. Hence, some of Cotard's patients began by expressing hypochondriacal delusions, in which, for example, the patient ''imagined that her throat was contracted and her heart displaced'' (Cotard, 1882, 1974, p. 364). This was accompanied by guilt at having supposedly caused suffering to others. Patients then went on to describe all manner of negativistic thoughts that Cotard saw as essential to the disorder. For example, some patients would imagine that they were going to be tortured for their supposed wrongdoings or would lament repeatedly, claiming to be damned, while others claimed that parts of their insides were putrefying. One patient (Cotard, 1882, Case 1) even believed herself to be dead, a feature which Cotard saw only in extreme cases, rather than as a defining feature.

Many authors have caricatured Cotard's description as referring simply to a single delusion that the body, or a part of the body, is dead (e.g. Drake, 1988; Campbell, Volow and Cavenar, 1981; Förstl and Beats, 1992; Malone and Malone, 1992). Moreover, the word "syndrome" is commonly used, although this is misleading because clusters of symptoms are not generally described in these case descriptions (Young and Leafhead, 1996). Indeed, it is simply the single belief that one is dead which distinguishes the "Cotard syndrome" from other aspects of depression in many case descriptions. Cotard viewed *le délire de négation* as being a distinct subtype of depression, and it was characterized by what he called anxious melancholia (Cotard, 1882; Hirsch and Shepherd, 1974). We now know that the delusion can be associated with a variety of psychopathological disorders, including schizophrenia and organic disorders as well as depression (e.g. Campbell et al. 1981; Joseph, 1986). Although the delusion can be seen in disorders other than depression, depressed mood is almost invariably present.

Young and Leafhead (1996) analysed 17 case reports available in English. In comparing these cases with Cotard's (1882) eight original cases, they noted some important differences. Cotard observed that half of his cases suffered from general nihilistic delusions, while neither negation of other people nor of the environment were remarked upon in any of the 17 subsequent case reports. Most striking was the fact that the delusional belief that one is dead was noted in only one of Cotard's cases, compared with 13 of the 17 later cases. Also noteworthy is the fact that while all of Cotard's patients suffered from self-deprecatory depressive delusions of one form or another, these were only found in five of the subsequent case reports. To sum up, all eight of the "pure" cases described by Cotard displayed self-deprecatory delusions, but only one believed she was dead and around half showed some of the symptoms (e.g. self-nihilistic and bodily delusions) which Cotard viewed as accompanying features. The symptoms displayed by the 17 later case reports produced a rather different picture, whereby around three-quarters of the patients believed they were dead. It is important to note that if the majority of more recent authors have viewed the Cotard *syndrome* in terms of the single belief that one is dead, then many cases that are similar to those reported by Cotard may have been unreported, being treated merely as variants of depression, rather than as specific delusional syndromes.

Young and colleagues suggested that the Cotard delusion is the result of a misinterpretation of anomalous perceptual experiences, such as things appearing strange and unfamiliar (Young et al., 1992; Wright, et al. 1993; Young, 1994). Such experiences might be interpreted in many possible ways and, as Kaney and Bentall (1989) have noted, this will depend on social and personal factors. With regard to this, it is relevant that the Cotard delusion typically arises in the context of depression. Beck (1967, 1989) argued that depressed individuals are characterized by a negative cognitive "set", involving negative views of themselves, the external world, and the future. The relevance of this is that depressed individuals tend to attribute negative events to internal causes "It's my fault" rather than to external causes "It's someone else's fault" (Kaney and Bentall, 1989; Candido and Romney, 1990). Wright et al. (1993), drawing from this theory, suggested that individuals' depressed moods contribute to their seeking an internal cause for their perceptual anomalies, and erroneously concluding that they must be dead. That is to say, they (correctly) perceive their altered perceptual experience as being a change in themselves, but (incorrectly) go on to infer that they are dead. Young and his colleagues (e.g. Young, Reid, Wright and Hellawell, 1993) have used this same reasoning to account for the Capgras delusion, in which people claim that some of their relatives have been replaced by duplicates or impostors (Capgras and Reboul-Lachaux, 1923). The Capgras and Cotard delusions are similar in that, for example, both sets of patients have perceptual anomalies and problems in recognizing familiar faces. However, the Capgras delusion is associated with a suspicious mood, and is often accompanied by persecutory delusions. Studies have shown that people with persecutory delusions tend to attribute negative events to external rather than internal causes (Kaney and Bentall, 1989; Candido and Romney, 1990). Hence, Young et al. (1993) hypothesized that in the Capgras delusion, a suspicious mood and the presence of persecutory delusions causes people to misattribute changes in their own perceptions to changes in other people, which in turn leads them to infer that these people must be impostors.

What is particularly striking is that many of the points made by Young and colleagues had been made by Cotard, either directly or implicitly. For example, Cotard (1884) referred to a loss of visual imagery in some of his patients – a deficit often associated with visual recognition deficits (e.g. Charcot and Bernard, 1883; Young and van de Wal, 1996). He believed this to be significant in the formation of the delusion. Hence, he suggested that the delusion was the result of a misinterpretation of the altered perceptual experience and that the delusions were not without logic. Cotard (1882) also noted that one of his patients (case 4) not only believed she was dead but also believed that her daughter was the devil in disguise. She also failed to recognize her family, although, as Cotard implies, this may have been because she ceased to believe in their existence. Nevertheless, the linking of the two types of delusion (i.e. Cotard and Capgras) is clear, as stated in what might be described as an early version of the attribution hypothesis. At the end of his report, Cotard (1882) tables an impressive list of contrasts and parallels between the delusion of negation and that of persecution. He concluded that in delusions of negation "Le malade s'accuse lui-même" (the patient blames himself), whereas in delusions of persecution "Le malade s'en prend au monde extérieur" (the patient blames the outside world). It is of some interest that, more than a century later, Cotard's insights are finally being incorporated into our understanding of these delusions.

KORSAKOFF SYNDROME

A somewhat similar situation applies in the Korsakoff syndrome (Korsakoff, 1889), which is often characterized in the medical textbooks as "a severe deficit of short-term memory with confabulation". In fact, each aspect of this definition is inaccurate, as the syndrome is in no sense a disorder of short-term memory – current, immediate, or working memory are intact, and there is a severe impairment of old memories extending many years back (e.g. Kopelman, 1989; Parkin et al., 1990). Moreover, confabulation is only usually seen in the acute stages, and is relatively rare in chronic patients. There are numerous modern neuropsychological studies which show that short-term memory is intact (Zangwill, 1946; Baddeley and Warrington, 1970; Kopelman, 1985), but this was noted by Korsakoff himself, who remarked: "At first, during conversation with such a patient . . . [he or she] gives the impression of a person in complete possession of his [or her] faculties; he [she] reasons about everything perfectly well, and draws correct deductions from given premises, makes witty remarks, plays chess or a game of cards, in a word comports himself [herself] as a mentally sound person." In other words, the patient displays all the features of an "intact working memory".

Since Sanders and Warrington's (1971) study, numerous investigations have been done looking at the extent of the retrograde amnesia in this syndrome, finding that it can extend back 20 years or more. However, Korsakoff himself had mentioned that "not only memory of recent events is lost, but also of the long past, in which case the impairment may involve memories of up to 30 years earlier". Korsakoff also anticipated the distinction between episodic and semantic memory (Tulving, 1972), arguing that in severe cases only "the amnesia is much more profound . . . the memory of fact is completely lost". One fashionable theory of amnesia, first advocated in recent times by Huppert and Piercy (1976, 1978), was that there is a particular deficit in recalling the temporal sequence or context of memories (Mayes, Meudell and Pickering, 1985; Leng and Parkin, 1988; Hirst, 1982; Johnson, Hashtroudi and Lindsay, 1993). Interestingly, Korsakoff also noted this deficit, but he pinpointed it as the basis of many so-called confabulations:

> In telling us something about the past, the patient would suddenly confuse events and would introduce the events related to one period into the story about another period . . . Telling of a trip she had made to Finland before her illness and describing her voyage in vivid detail, the patient mixed into her story her recollections of Crimea, and so it turned out in Finland people always eat lamb and the inhabitants are Tartars.

Modern studies confirm that so-called "spontaneous" confabulation is present in only a minority of Korsakoff patients (Berlyne, 1972; Kopelman, 1987) and, in fact, it is much more likely to result from frontal lobe pathology (e.g. Stuss et al., 1978; Kapur and Coughlan, 1980). Nevertheless, a recent theory of confabulation, proposed by Schnider, von Däniken and Gutbrod (1996), produced an account of spontaneous confabulation in terms of temporal context memory deficits, consistent with Korsakoff's own examples (Johnson, O'Connor and Cantor, 1997; Kopelman, Ng and Van den Boucke, 1997).

Finally, there has been recent debate as to whether the Korsakoff syndrome can be caused by factors other than alcohol which result in thiamine depletion. In fact, some of the recent cases have been unconvincing in that there has been evidence that there has been at least some degree of heavy drinking (Kopelman, 1995). However, Korsakoff (1889) listed a whole series of non-alcohol cases, most of which in hindsight can be seen to have resulted from thiamine depletion. These included eight cases of persistent vomiting, as well as patients with sepsis postpartum, chronic infection, and other chronic diseases such as neoplasm or lymphadenoma.

It is also sometimes stated that he was unaware of the important work by Wernicke on encephalopathy. This may be true. However, Korsakoff noted that many of the features of encephalopathy (described in parallel by Wernicke) were present in his patients, including ophthalmoplegia, nystagmus, ataxia, and confusion. More worrying is the fact that these neurological signs, and their clinical significance, are still commonly missed in clinical practice.

CONCLUSION

What we are certainly not saying is that modern scientific investigation has not taken us any further since the 19th century. Far from it. Modern neuropsychology has produced a much better empirical documentation of the features of both these disorders and, in the case of the Korsakoff syndrome, we also have a much better medical understanding of its causation. What was forgotten were the clinical observations and the detailed descriptive richness, given by authors such as Cotard and Korsakoff. What tends to go into medical textbooks, crammed in no doubt by authors trying to encompass an enormous scope of topics, is sometimes inaccurate and misleading. As the textbooks become respectable, revered, quoted, and examined upon, minor errors become magnified into larger errors (Bartlett, 1932), and misquotation evolves into misunderstanding. There are many other examples where this has happened. There are also many examples of more recent writers who have anticipated important developments in critical ways – think, for example, of Hebb's (1949) anticipation of contemporary connectionism. In brief, it is always valuable to know one's own literature – but that has been said many times before too!

Section 6

MEDIA WATCH

Paul Kurtz, head of the Committee for the Scientific Investigation of Claims of the Paranormal (CSICOP), which has recently organized a congress on "Science in the Age of (Mis)information", stated that "people understand science through the media, largely. They should get it in school, but it's not required" (Yam, 1997). If the journalists uncritically accept and present unsubstantiated notions, we are likely to take these for granted (Randi, 1992). Just consider the fact that a daily horoscope column is present in several high-profile newspapers. This view that the mass media plays an important role in fostering our beliefs is not new (e.g. Maller and Lundeen, 1932), and the view that its role is increasing with widespread television watching (Gerbner, 1987; Ogles, 1987) has been recently supported by experimental evidence (e.g. Sparks, Nelson and Campbell, 1997).

"Factual" information provided by the media is comforting, while the sceptical scientific approach is perceived as distant and somewhat dull. People like information to be encapsulated; they are impatient with long, discursive explanations (Paulos, 1996, p. 191). Every day we read in the newspaper or hear on the television that somebody has just found a new gene that will make us all ultra-centenarians, that cholesterol is not so bad after all, especially if we assimilate it from chips, that vitamin C or other improbable concoctions can prevent or treat cancer, that we should learn to make good use of the hidden – generally the right – side of our brain, as some eminent previously unknown would-be scientist duly reckoned, and that harmless, though expensive, pills with unlikely names, could improve our memory, our well-being and our sexual satisfaction. The "scoops" surrounding this Pandora's box of omnipotent products and triumphalistic findings, geared at feeding our illusions and hopes, are ballasted only by a blatant catastrophism, equally unjustified. And the media snowball, the last utopia (Garattini and Chiaberge, 1992), rolls. Very rarely are we exposed to any sort of argumentative refutation of previously overwrought claims.

Sometimes the journalists try to be objective and compromise between two positions (e.g. giving a voice to both those in favour of and those against an alleged new therapy which treats all types of cancer, dementia and multiple sclerosis). However, this conciliatory strategy, used in the hope that the audience will make up its own mind, is hazardous. It is similar to attempting to reconcile the two views that $2 + 2$ make 4 versus $2 + 2 = 6$ by suggesting 5 as a compromise total.

Science is the Cinderella of all the topics covered by the media. Dunbar (1995, p. 147) calculated that in a week (for a total of 560 hours of viewing time) the four national UK channels showed 210 programme minutes (i.e. 0.6%) devoted to science, mainly natural history. He also underlined that the newspapers do not fare any better: *The Times*, one of the UK's main newspapers, has a mean science coverage of about 0.5% of the total printed text. The proportion of this time and space dedicated to the neurosciences, is of course, minuscule.

Typically, television reporters interview ordinary people (*la gente*), asking their opinion about scientific developments; *la gente*'s hasty emotional reactions are then treated as evidence for or against an argument, without giving the public any chance to appreciate the real subtleties of the debate. These opinions are averaged, often with the help of extemporaneous polls, and the "average" answer then becomes a fact. It reminds me of a story told by Feynman (1985, p. 269): since nobody was allowed to see the Emperor of China, the length of his nose was anybody's guess and the average of all the guesses would be taken as the accurate length of the great man's nose.

If lay persons had a better understanding of scientific methods and of what science can and cannot provide, maybe they would be more appreciative of its efforts and achievements, and more sympathetic towards its failures. Instead, they feel, for instance, that the ''scientists refuse to accept the reality of psychic phenomena because they fear the damage such acceptance might do to their own belief-system'' (Couttie, 1988, p. 93).

CHAPTER 17

The Media and the Brain

TOBY HOWARD and STEVE DONNELLY

INTRODUCTION

For more than a decade, we have had a sceptical interest in pseudoscience and the paranormal and, in particular, its representation in the media. As editors of the UK's only dedicated sceptical magazine, *The Skeptic* (www.skeptic.org.uk), we have built up a large collection of newspaper clippings, books and other material on a wide range of topics, many of them touching on reports of supposed extensions to known human powers and abilities.

Although respectable academic research in parapsychology is underway in a small number of institutions around the world, it is no exaggeration to say that the reportage in UK newspapers on putative phenomena such as telepathy, clairvoyance and psychokinesis bear almost no relation to the findings of the academic researchers in these areas. Particularly in the tabloid newspapers, but also from time to time in the broadsheets, reports appear that are so far removed from established knowledge that they can only be described as science fiction.

As many of the topics that come under the broad heading of the paranormal are concerned with abilities attributed to the human brain, we were particularly interested to see to what extent knowledge of research into brain mechanisms in general has been misrepresented in parts of the popular media. Our expectations were that all reporting on brain research would be wildly exaggerated in a similar way to reports of paranormal powers; however, as we will show below, this turns out not to be the case.

For logistical reasons we decided to restrict ourselves to three specific areas: articles in newspapers; advertisements in newspapers and general interest magazines (including follow-up literature sent to respondents to advertisements); and, finally, the rapidly burgeoning information available on the World Wide Web.

ARTICLES IN THE PRINT MEDIA

Although we have not attempted to conduct a detailed and formal statistical survey, we feel that our findings are reasonably representative. (In particular, we illustrate our findings with specific clippings that we believe are typical examples.) Our collection of clippings covers the last 10 years and includes articles from tabloid and broadsheet newspapers, as well as some general interest periodicals such as women's magazines. The clippings have been collected by readers of *The Skeptic*, who provide us with articles on a wide range of topics which are not by any means exclusively paranormal. In addition to the search through our clippings, we have conducted a search of the publicly available archives of the *Electronic Telegraph*, an Internet version of the UK broadsheet newspapers *The Daily Telegraph* and *The Sunday Telegraph*. This enabled us to obtain comprehensive information about all major articles published in at least one UK broadsheet newspaper since November 1994.

A wide range of brain-related topics feature in our collection. These include a large number of articles on supposed extrasensory perception and smaller numbers of articles on: dreams and hallucinations, hypnosis, false memory syndrome, right–left brain functions, meditation, behaviour/personality/psychology, drugs and brain chemistry, monitoring of brain activity, intelligence and artificial intelligence, and consciousness studies.

Clearly, it is not realistic in a single chapter of this book to deal in detail with all these subjects. Instead, we will illustrate general points concerning the reporting of supposed incidences of extrasensory perception and of more mainstream brain research using a small number of specific examples from different types of newspaper. Finally, we will draw some general conclusions.

Articles on Paranormal Topics

Although the major thrust of this chapter is not extrasensory perception and other supposedly paranormal phenomena, it is instructive to take a brief look at the coverage of articles on such topics in the print media to provide a contrast with the coverage of less popular aspects of brain function.

According to a recent survey of 8000 adults carried out at Leeds University (Uhlig, 1997), more people believe in telepathy, UFOs and ghosts than in the ability of prayer to change events. Michael Svennevig, research director of the Centre for the Future of Communications at Leeds University, stated: "People are displaying greater irrationality in an increasingly rational world." Although one could query his intended meaning of the phrase "an increasingly rational world" the trend towards irrationality, or at least a shift from irrational beliefs of a traditional religious nature towards irrational beliefs of other types, has been a significant one over the last decade or more – and fuelling this trend is undoubtedly the type of article that appears on paranormal topics in a large range of newspapers and periodicals.

As an example of such articles (but restricted to purported extrasensory phenomena – we ignore subjects such as UFOs, fairies, the Bermuda Triangle and ghosts) we shall discuss three articles, chosen as representative examples, that have appeared in a national broadsheet newspaper, a national tabloid newspaper and a large-circulation local newspaper respectively.

A piece in the *Weekend Guardian* in February 1989 is fairly typical of articles aimed, one assumes, at educated, middle-class readers. The article, entitled "Psychic powers or child's play?", by a freelance journalist, begins with an anecdotal report of the writer's child, named Jack, being supposedly aware by some extrasensory means of a minor accident involving his father (Eason, 1989). The writer poses the question: "But could my son really be psychic or is there a more down-to-earth explanation?"

Among a number of anecdotal tales of telepathic communication, the article contains the assertion that "The Rhine experiments at Duke University have put up a strong case for telepathy." This sentence has the effect of adding apparent academic authority to the otherwise anecdotal musings, and as such is extremely (and probably unwittingly) misleading. The work of J. B. Rhine at Duke University has been roundly criticized by sceptics (e.g. Gardner, 1981, p. 217) and, in particular, in later years was tainted by fraud (Gardner, 1983, p. 16) – although, to be fair, the fraud did not involve Rhine himself. The *Weekend Guardian* article finishes with the assertion: "Whatever the truth of Jack's psychic powers . . . if he does give me a warning . . . I shall drive more carefully." The overall effect of the article is to give the impression that it is probable, with some significant academic supporting evidence, that psychic powers are real and that we should certainly give them "the benefit of the doubt".

The tabloid article chosen is one published in the *Daily Mail* in January 1995 which reports on the telepathic abilities of a dog to predict when its owner is about to return home (Oldfield, 1995). Many articles on this theme have appeared in a range of newspapers in recent years as a consequence of the research project suggested by Dr Rupert Sheldrake in his book *Seven Experiments That Could Change the World* (Sheldrake, 1995).

Once again, although the article is anecdotal in nature, the link with Sheldrake's re-search adds academic support to the thesis of the article – which in this case is that "telepathic behaviour is not uncommon in dogs who wait for their owners to return from work every night". However, the case for telepathy in animals has been even less well established than that for telepathy in humans, the major proponent being Sheldrake himself. None the less, the article leads firmly to the conclusion that the psychic rapport between animals and their caretakers is well established.

The technique of including an indication of academic respectability in an otherwise anecdotal article is a common one that occurs in both broadsheet and tabloid news-papers, although it should be pointed out that the *Daily Mail* pitches itself at the more intellectually worthy end of the tabloid spectrum.

Local newspapers, on the other hand, have no such pretensions. The article we have chosen from a local newspaper comes from the *Manchester Evening News* (Barratt, 1994) and is appropriately concerned with local events: in this case, the British and European Festival for the Spiritual Mind and Body which was being held in the Manchester area in the week that the article appeared. In a matter-of-fact manner that takes for granted the existence of a variety of paranormal diagnostic and healing abilities, the article presents a series of inter-views with an aura reader, a kinesiologist and finally with psychic healer Coby Zvikler.

This last individual is of particular interest because he was informally tested in one of our laboratories (S.E.D.) a number of years ago. His claim to be able to unequivocally demonstrate psychic powers by, for instance, administering a "psychic push" capable of knocking people off balance without any physical contact were totally unsupported by tests – as were his claimed abilities to diagnose medical problems psychically, and so psychokinetically interfere with electrical equipment. Zvikler's puzzlement with the nega-tive results in our tests did nothing to diminish his conviction concerning the reality of his powers, and the *Manchester Evening News* article concludes with the statement from Zvikler that: "My abilities are developing every day and I want them to help more and more people."

Although a faint note of scepticism is injected towards the end of the article, this is immediately negated by the direct reporting of unsubstantiated claims by Zvikler:

> The more sceptical amongst us may dismiss [the intense feeling of penetrating warmth from Zvikler's gaze] as psychosomatic but Coby claims to have corrected severe curvature of the spine and unlocked dislocated shoulders which a physiotherapist was unable to treat successfully.

This is a common technique often found in tabloid articles – inject a note of caution or scepticism, only immediately to negate it with unsubstantiated claims. As with the articles in the national newspapers, the impression picked up from the *Manchester Evening News* article is that a range of psychic abilities is well established and even the sceptical reader should take these abilities seriously.

Newspaper articles concerned with extrasensory abilities attributed to human (and even animal) brains are frequently extremely misleading and have a tendency to bolster wild, scientifically unsubstantiated claims by including a reference to academic research that appar-ently supports the claim, or to negate apparent scepticism by additional dubious claims. Even a literate and intelligent reader whose information on such matters came exclusively from reading a range of UK newspapers would thus conclude that the reality of extrasensory abilities was well established – a conclusion that could hardly be further from the truth.

Articles on Brain Mechanisms

Turning now to articles concerned with brain mechanisms and brain function in areas other than paranormal abilities, the situation appears to be radically different. First, articles on these topics seldom appear in the tabloid newspapers (the majority of our clippings are from the broadsheets). Second, on those rare occasions when articles do appear in tabloid newspapers on these subjects, inasmuch as we are competent to judge, they appear to present a reasonably accurate and responsible picture.

As a first example, which is fairly typical of those found in our clippings from the broadsheets as well as in our perusal of relevant articles in the *Electronic Telegraph* archives (www.telegraph.co.uk), we present an article from *The Daily Telegraph* in April 1997 concerned with the use of brain imaging techniques to examine the effects of sleep on the brain (Highfield, 1987). The article reports on research by Dr Pierre Maquet, of the University of Liege in Belgium, demonstrating that sleep does not provide its resting powers across the brain but has particular effects on certain areas, including those that influence social behaviour and social interactions.

The research used a brain imaging technique to examine eight young men during deep stages of restful slow wave sleep which accounts for 75% of our total sleeping time and is accompanied by a particular pattern of nerve cell activity. To quote from the *Daily Telegraph* article: " 'Our study shows there is a maximal decrease of activity in specific cortical brain areas during slow wave sleep,' said Dr Maquet who reports his work in *The Journal of Neuroscience*." In a manner almost befitting an academic journal, the article makes reference to other research and concludes:

> The find is of particular interest because it dovetails with research on the effects of sleep deprivation by Prof Jim Horne and Dr Yvonne Harrison, of Loughborough University. The "rested" parts of the brain included regions involved in social behaviour and social interactions. "Any benefits of this effect may rapidly deteriorate with sleep deprivation," said Dr Maquet. He said that patients with damage in these areas exhibit impulsive behaviour and loss of social constraint.

Comparison of the research as reported in *The Daily Telegraph* with the abstract of the original research paper in the *Journal of Neuroscience* (Maquet et al., 1997) indicates that the reportage clearly left out most of the detailed technical information contained in the original work but, in the style of popular science journals such as *New Scientist*, extracted some of the main points of the original article to build a story likely to be of interest to non-specialist readers.

It should be pointed out that of all the broadsheet newspapers, *The Daily Telegraph* appears to have the best coverage of science in general and brain research in particular, with apparently well-researched articles appearing fairly regularly.

As a stylistic contrast, the second article comes from *The Guardian* in December 1996 (Mihill, 1996) and has the eye-catching title "Hairy men 'are more intelligent' " together with a photograph of Gary Glitter's luxuriant chest hair. The first paragraph reads:

> It's very good news for men like Gary Glitter and Tom Jones, and it could provoke a boom in chest wigs. Hairy men, according to a psychiatrist speaking at a conference yesterday are definitely brighter.

Despite the rather tabloid-like headline and opening paragraph, somewhat redolent of the kind of hyperbole usual in articles on the paranormal, the article is, in fact, written by a medical correspondent and is based primarily on an interview with the academic responsible for the research leading to the hirsute conclusion, Dr Aikarakudy Alias, of the Chester Mental Health Center, Illinois. Dr Alias's research was presented at a conference of the Association of European Psychiatrists and the Royal College of Psychiatrists in London. The article included some scientific detail when it reported Dr Alias's contention that the link between intelligence and hairiness might be due to a chemical called DHT, a variant of the male hormone testosterone, which not only controls sexual characteristics such as body hair but is also believed to play a role in mental faculties. Slightly more restrained articles on the same topic were also published in *The Independent* and *The Daily Telegraph* on the same day.

The key point here is that, in keeping with many other articles on (non-paranormal) scientific topics, the only "sin" committed by the journalist is to seek human interest in a scientific story. Although the emphasis of the article in being translated into a newspaper article is moved away from the technical detail, the essential facts of the original scientific story are preserved – and this is to be expected in articles in a publication that has a general (and mainly non-scientific) readership. This is, once again, in stark contrast to reports of extrasensory perception and similar topics.

As mentioned above, articles on complex scientific topics such as research into brain mechanisms are relatively scarce in the tabloid newspapers except where the research in question moves from the laboratory into more easily popularizable arenas such as the courtroom. A typical tabloid article is thus one from the *Mail on Sunday* from May 1994, with the headline: "Families who have been torn apart by memory therapy" (Fraser, 1994).

The article is typical in that it concentrates on the courtroom aspects of the phenomenon known as either "recovered memory syndrome" or "false memory syndrome", with particular reference to supposed child abuse cases, including that involving American actress Roseanne Arnold. Unsurprisingly for sceptics familiar with cases of recovered memory of alien visitations and past lives, as more and more repressed memory sexual abuse cases went to trial, it became increasingly clear that the "false memory" designation was the more apt. The article is primarily concerned with a case in which a falsely accused father whose life had been ruined by recovered memory accusations of sexual abuse was awarded half a million dollars in damages against the therapists who had practised repressed memory therapy on his daughter. In a sense, the *Mail on Sunday* article was thus "ahead of the game" when in 1994 it suggested that the father's court success represented "a victory for common sense over medical mumbo-jumbo". Typically for tabloid journalism, however, the article is an emotive one and in no way can be said to report on the scientific facts behind false memory syndrome. If anything, the article could be regarded as anti-scientific in tone (if repressed memory therapy were regarded as having any connection with science). Clearly, the journalist responsible for the article is not a science correspondent and is concerned with the "human interest" aspects of the case, an attitude that is prevalent in those rare articles involving brain function and related topics that make it into the pages of the tabloid newspapers.

The final example in this section, to complete the comparison with coverage of extrasensory perception, is from a large-circulation local newspaper; in this case the (London) *Evening Standard*. The subject of the story, which appeared in March 1990 (and also featured in national newspapers), is a so-called "brain gymnasium" set up in Wimbledon by a management consultant who had encountered the idea in California (Gruner, 1990). Interestingly, the devices used for the mental "work-out" are very similar to those covered later in this chapter when we discuss advertisements for "brain machines".

Essentially, customers pay £30 to "sit in a darkened room for half-an-hour listening to the sounds of the sea and high-tech music through headphones and wearing goggles that flash coloured lights". Interestingly, the journalistic technique previously remarked upon in the context of articles on the paranormal is also used here: the article reports that a senior lecturer in psychology at Hull University is to discuss setting up a research project to determine the efficacy of the mental work-out. Once again, the effect is to lend some academic credibility to what would appear to be a therapy of dubious value.

Discussion

An interesting pattern appears when newspaper articles on brain mechanisms and similar topics are compared with those on the paranormal. When a topic is considered by newspaper editors to be scientific in nature, it is relatively unlikely to be covered by the tabloids or by local newspapers, presumably as a consequence of the fact that they do not employ science correspondents or science editors. On the other hand, where a subject is clearly perceived as having significant human interest, the story is likely to be covered in broadsheet, tabloid and local newspapers alike by non-specialist correspondents who will not sacrifice a good story to scientific accuracy.

In some senses, it is thus fortunate that brain research appears to be regarded as "difficult scientific material" rather than "human interest" and, as a consequence, is not often covered by the tabloids and local newspapers. On the other hand, reportage in the broadsheet newspapers is normally by scientifically knowledgeable correspondents who, although simplifying the scientific complexities, do a reasonably fair job of reporting the stories.

For researchers wishing to see their research covered, without hyperbole, in the broadsheet newspapers, the key would thus appear to be to ensure that the story contained moderately complex scientific information and some human interest angle – but not too much.

Finally, lest we leave readers with the impression that all is entirely well in the world of media reports of brain matters, we would like to present a clipping from an American tabloid, *The Weekly World News* (WWN), now also available in the UK, whose slogan would appear to be: "You always have exclusive stories when you make them up". The opening paragraph of an article in the WWN entitled "Exploding Brain" reads:

> MOSCOW – Doctors are blaming a rare electrical imbalance in the brain for the bizarre death of a chess player whose head literally exploded in the middle of a championship game! No one else was hurt in the fatal explosion but four players and three officials at the Moscow Candidate Masters' Chess Championships were sprayed with blood and brain matter when Nikolai Titov's head suddenly blew apart. Experts say he suffered from a condition called Hyper-Cerebral Electrosis or HCE.
>
> (WWN, 1994)

The article goes on to warn of the dangers of excessive use of one's brain (to which regular readers of the WWN should be fairly immune) and quotes Dr Anatoly Martinenko, "famed neurologist and expert on the human brain who did the autopsy on the brilliant chess expert":

> [HCE] is a condition in which the circuits of the brain become overloaded by the body's own electricity. The explosions happen during periods of intense mental activity when lots of current is surging through the brain. Victims are highly intelligent people with great powers of concentration.

We would therefore advise any readers of the present book who:

(a) spend more than five hours a day reading, balancing a cheque-book, or other thoughtful activity,
(b) sometimes hear a faint ringing or humming sound in their ears,
(c) have a tendency to analyze themselves too much, or
(d) find themselves unable to get a thought out of their heads,

to immediately stop what they are doing and watch a game show on television – to reduce the danger of their heads exploding.

BRAIN FUNCTION IN ADVERTISING

Although we found that broadsheet reportage of brain functioning was by and large reasonable, the same cannot be said for the many advertisements for "miracle" products which claim to directly affect the way in which our brains work.

Many companies are now marketing devices popularly known as "mind machines", or "electronic brain-boosters". The claim is made that these devices can influence the state of the mind of the user by displaying patterns of flashing lights, sometimes accompanied by music, to the user. The publicity for such gadgets ranges from the reasonably sober to the outrageous, but the following excerpt, from an advertisement for the "SuperMind Brainwave Entrainment Computer", is a typical example:

> Amazing new computer synchronises brainwave patterns to zap stress, boost mental powers and electronically 'Zen out' your mind!

This kind of hyperbolic announcement is the hallmark of mind machine publicity. What is it actually saying? "Synchronises brainwave patterns" – with what? "Boost mental powers" – what are mental powers? " 'Zen out' your mind" – Zen out?

The SuperMind machine is still available (www.mindmax.com/supermind), and if you wish to evaluate the claims mentioned above, $199.95 + shipping will reserve your own personal unit. Mind machines, as we shall see, to do not come cheap.

The SuperMind machine is but one of dozens of similar machines on the market. They have names like RelaxMate, MindLab, NovaDreamer, The Dream Light, Galaxy, Deltabeta, and so on. Most of these modern "mind machines" can trace their origins to a wobbly mechanical device called the DreamMachine, invented by the avant-garde poet Brion Gysin (1916–1986). Inspired by a mystical experience he underwent when seeing the sun flickering through trees, Gysin designed a device to simulate the lighting conditions on demand. His machine comprised a vertical cylinder with holes cut into the sides, sitting on a record-player turntable. An electric lightbulb hung in the cylinder, suspended from above. When the turntable was rotated at 78 rev/min, the light flashing through the cylinder openings re-sembled the intermittent sunlight he remembered. For Gysin and his crowd, which included William Burroughs, the DreamMachine was the consciousness-expanding machine of choice.

Although from today's perspective the DreamMachine is "old" technology, it still at-tracts a surprisingly large underground following. As well as being the subject of a recent book (Cecil, 1997), the machine also made headlines when it was alleged that excessive use of it led to the suicide of rock musician Kurt Cobain. You can even find detailed instructions on the World Wide Web for building your own DreamMachine (McIntyre, 1997).

In order to gauge the contrast between the journalist coverage of brain function and the proliferation of "mind control" hardware on sale to the public, we chose a number of advertisements which we regarded as typical of the genre. We responded to each, requesting further information, and in some cases conducted further research if the companies also had a World Wide Web presence. In the following, we present a small sample of our findings, with some analysis of the neuromythology being presented.

The Max Stress Controller

"Do they mean me?" asks "radio broadcaster and TV personality" Derek Jameson, with his trademark toothy grin. He's holding up a small device the size of a bar of soap. It's his Max Stress Controller. The following statement from the publicity material is typical of the angle taken by such products:

> Recent studies have shown that the brain emits electromagnetic "waves" of differing frequencies and that these waves represent ideal states of the mind. (EduCom, 1997a)

The picture painted is of a "hot brain", radiating energy rather like a radio beacon. (It can only be a short step from here to telepathy: surely the electromagnetic energy radiated by one brain can travel across space to meet and influence another brain?)

Max offers surprisingly fine-grained control over exactly how it influences your state of mind, emitting "five frequencies to attune your brain to its five most natural modes of operation". These are: sleep mode, communications mode, memory mode, stress release mode, and optimism mode. But how does the device work? According to the publicity:

> Max emits ultra-low frequency waves similar to those of the brain. If you are within 1 metre of Max, your brain gradually begins to emulate those waves.

No further technical explanation is offered. As for scientific "proof" of the effectiveness of the Max device, the company's Web page states:

> Scientists around the world have conducted numerous studies on the effectiveness of low energy emissions; researchers have exposed people with sleeping difficulties to extremely low-power electromagnetic fields and found that sleep cycles improve considerably, is safe [sic], well-tolerated and induces relaxation. (EduCom, 1997b)

In the above extract, the word "researchers" is a hyperlink to the Web site of the pre-reviewed journal *Sleep* (*Sleep*, 1995). There's no obvious material of any relevance to be found on the target page, but taking as a clue the mention in the paper publicity of the Scripps Clinic and Research Foundation, a search of the *Sleep* Web site reveals a possibly relevant paper, with the title "Effects of Low Energy Emission Therapy in Chronic Psychophysiological Insomnia" (Pasche et al., 1997).

Since they hyperlinked to the Sleep Web site, it's presumably reasonable to make the assumption that the manufacturers of the Max device intend this paper to bolster the claims they make for their machine. However, while Pasche et al. do indeed describe the successful use of low-energy emission therapy to relieve chronic insomnia, there is a significant difference between their technique and that employed in the Max. Pasche et al. used an electrically conducting mouthpiece inserted directly into the subject's mouth. The claimed effectiveness of the Max device, as we have seen, does not depend on any physical contact with the user – merely being within 1 m of the device is sufficient.

The Max publicity on the paper also features the endorsement of Roger Coghill, "professional researcher into EM waves". Interestingly, Mr Coghill is co-author of *The Dark Side of The Brain – Major Discoveries in the Use of Kirlian Photography and Electro-Crystal Therapy* (Oldfield and Coghill, 1994).

"Is Max suitable for everybody?" asks the blurb. "Yes, Max is as natural as talking to a friend" it quickly replies. Prospective purchasers of this device might be advised to do the latter, and save themselves £79.95.

LifeTools

Established in 1993, LifeTools advertises widely in magazines such as *Fortean Times* and *New Scientist*, and markets the "incredible" MindLab Orion, which offers "profound relaxation after 15 minutes use", and which can "help you sleep deeper or learn faster too!" (LifeTools, 1997).

The Orion looks rather like a Sony Walkman cassette player, and comes with stereo headphones and a pair of "liteframe" glasses, in which patterns of light are displayed. The Orion can generate a light show based on arbitrary sounds fed into it from an external audio source such as a CD, or from its own built-in microphone. It also features 23 built-in "sessions" ranging in length from 10 min ("use every 40 to 60 minutes to better integrate material during your studies") to 60 min ("excellent as a training session for learning how to meditate for extended periods"). Other sessions include "Increase your focus, clarity and decision making" (15 min), "stimulate your thought processes for help with problem solving" (20 min) and "energise and increase your vitality with this 'power nap' ".

Although they state in small print on their publicity material "We make no medical claims for the Orion, expressed or implied", LifeTools nevertheless publishes a double-sided A4 leaflet boldly entitled "Here's scientific proof that mind machines really work!" On side one of the sheet we find a curious conglomerate of endorsements – none with complete references – ranging from a report of a study published in the peer-reviewed journal *Headache* to the findings of "Norman Shealy MD, PhD, author of *The Creation of Health*".

The latter is interesting. Norman Shealy is founder-president of American Holistic Medical Association (www.shealyinstitute.com), and his book *The Creation of Health* (Shealy, 1993) was co-authored with a "psychic diagnostician" named Carolyn Myss. According to her Web page, "Since 1982 she has worked as a medical intuitive: one who 'sees' illnesses in a patient's body by intuitive means" (Myss, 1997). Dr Shealy also markets his own mind machine, the RelaxMate.

On the other side of the sheet are testimonials from satisfied customers: "Meditation on micro-chip!", enthuses a Mr Harris; "Within two minutes of putting the liteframes on I'm almost in a coma, I'm that relaxed" says Mr Pudney from Braintree.

The MindLab Orion doesn't come cheap. The basic model costs £249, while the more advanced "PolySync Pro" model, which offers a further 27 kinds of session, is £100 more expensive.

New Age Electronics

New Age Electronics of Berwick-upon-Tweed markets a number of gadgets that almost defy sensible analysis. A Subliminal Tape Unit, a Mind Relaxer and a Dream Machine (not the Gysin variety) rub shoulders with hardwood pyramids, an "EVP Detector" which enables you to "hear voices from the dead", a Crystal Power Rod ("acts as a focus to allow the mind to influence sub-atomic particles") and a Radionic Box ("a psionic device for focusing energies at a subconscious level"). Also on the product list are books entitled *Astral Travel Made Easy: The Astral Realms and How to Get There*, and *Reality Structuring – Create All That You Desire*, and a title which perhaps betrays an underlying theme to all the products under review here: *Change Your Life Without Effort* (New Age Electronics, 1997).

What is interesting about this catalogue of strangeness is that it reveals the increasing overlap of the brain improvement world with the New Age scene.

The Realization System

Another "self-development" regimen that offers spectacular results, such as "how to solve emotional problems of personality", is the Realization System, operated by mail order from Stockport, Cheshire (Heap, R. and W., Publishing Company Limited, 1997). Details of the Realization System arrive through the mail in a package containing a quite cleverly personalized form-letter, pages of testimonials, and "save money now" discount offers. What you get for the basic price of £197.95 is a set of 12 Realization System "lessons", including self-grading test papers with model answers. Naturally, this all comes in a "handsome library sleeve".

If the publicity for the Realization System is correct, then £197.95 is actually a vary fair price to pay for such marvels as "a simple method of banishing pain", "problems of marriage and how to solve them", and "a practical method of memory training". But when one considers, for example, the immense effort into pain research worldwide, and the daily despair of people who suffer chronic pain, the fatuous claims of systems like the Realization System invoke only anger in the sensible reader. Nevertheless, the testimonials, if they are genuine, clearly indicate that, for some people at least, the Realization System has improved their mental abilities and enhanced their spiritual well-being.

The retailers of the Realization System are certainly persistent. After sending off the coupon from the advertisement in a magazine, we received full details by return of post. Within the next month, we received four more unsolicited mailings, each with a different personalized form-letter, offering various money-saving schemes.

Discussion

Despite their inflated claims, regimens like the Realization System are effectively beyond analysis, since they are about introspection and self-motivated change. What about mind machines? Do they work? Much emphasis is placed on the attainment of alpha rhythms, with the claimed consequence that relaxation, serenity, mind development and spiritual liberation will follow. But, as Barry Beyerstein, of the Brain and Behaviour Laboratory at Simon Fraser University, has pointed out, while alpha rhythms are directly related to activity in the visual system, they have no proven links whatsoever to curative powers (Beyerstein, 1985).

A common feature of all the advertisements we researched was that the literature received always hedges its bets with phrases like ''you could benefit from'', ''our product can help you'' and so on. The meaning is all in the ''cans'' and ''coulds''. The advertisers might argue that such imprecise language is necessary because of the impossibility of guaranteeing a 100% success rate, and they might have a point. But the same argument applies to guaranteeing a success rate of 0%, or anything in between.

Given that most mind machines require you to close your eyes, and given that most people begin to produce alpha waves when their eyes are closed, what role does a Mind Machine actually play? Until peer-reviewed research says otherwise, the sceptical answer must be ''not much''.

THE BRAIN ON THE WEB

Although the volatile nature of the Web means that it is somewhat meaningless to quote statistics relating to searches for information, in November 1997 we conducted a number of searches to try and determine what information – if any – about the brain was available on-line. The results surprised us.

Using the AltaVista search engine and the keyword ''brain'', we found just over 200 Web sites. All but six of these sites were academic, and presented either the results of recent research, or were repositories for standard data about brain structure and brain function. At these sites, the quality of information was high. The remaining sites mirrored almost directly the advertisements we had encountered in print media: the marketing of mind machines. We also consulted Yahoo, where indexing and classification of Web sites is undertaken by hand. There, we found nine organizations listed under the ''Mind Machines'' classification (Yahoo, 1997).

We see the same types of machine being marketed, the same claims for instant manipulation of mood, and promises of well-being and an improved lifestyle. The names of the same ''experts'' appear again and again, and as you follow the hyperlinks it becomes clear that the on-line mind machine world is largely self-referential. Everyone endorses each other's products.

Discussion

We believe that the Web follows the trend of the print media: sites which attempt to be informational, are so. The remaining sites are commercial, and make the same dubious claims that we find in the print media. The crucial difference, of course, is that the Web is completely unregulated. Individuals and companies can self-publish whatever they like (subject to the obvious legal constraints). What this means for the mind machine advertisers, for example, is that their advertisements are not subject to any editorial control – their copy is not scrutinized by any manager of advertising space, as would be the case in the print media. Correspondingly, the claims made for the machines become increasingly wilder.

As we write (late 1997), this probably doesn't matter much, because, as we have seen, the number of potentially misleading brain-related Web sites is dwarfed by the presence of the informational sites. However, as the Web becomes more mainstream, we expect this to change in the future. In particular, when the inevitable integration of the Web and television finally occurs, access to unregulated and unlabelled sources of information will become a new problem for society to deal with.

CONCLUSIONS

As a topic, brain function is largely ignored by the popular print media, but where it is covered, reporting appears to be reasonable (within normal journalistic bounds). This contrasts greatly with other (higher-interest) topics such as the paranormal: articles on brain research do not sell newspapers in the way that articles on ghosts, telepathy, or astrology do.

Advertising is another matter. Here we see wild and mostly unsubstantiated claims for controlling mental state and increasing mental abilities. We are not saying that mind machines are entirely valueless, or that ''self-realization'' systems can have no beneficial effects. What does concern us are the misleading impressions left about how our brains work, and the general ''changing your life without effort'' approach to self-development and health.

As we move into the next millennium, and the Web/television synthesis approaches, the quantity of readily available information on brain research is liable to increase. But if unregulated publishing comes to dominate, the quality is in danger of decrease.

References

Aarons, L. (1977) Sleep assisted instruction. *Psychological Bulletin*, **83**, 1–40.

Abel, A. (1997) You looking at me? *Fortean Times*, **101**, 36–39.

Adey, W.R. (1981) Tissue interactions with nonionizing electromagnetic fields. *Physiological Reviews*, **61**, 435–514.

Albert, R.S. (1975) Toward a behavioral definition of genius. *American Psychologist*, **30**, 140–151.

Alcock, J. (1981) *Parapsychology: Science or Magic?* New York: Pergamon.

Alder, H. (1993) *Right Brain Manager: How to Harness the Power of Your Mind to Achieve Personal and Business Success*. London: Piatkus.

Altman, J. (1967) Postnatal growth and differentiation of the mammalian brain, with implications for a morphological theory of memory. In: G. Quarton, T. Melnichuk and F. Schmitt (eds) *The Neurosciences: A Study Program*. New York: Rockefeller University Press, pp. 723–743.

American Psychological Association (1994) Definition and description of hypnosis. *Contemporary Hypnosis*, **11**, 143.

Amiel, S.A. (1995) Organ fuel selection: brain. *Proceedings of the Nutrition Society*, **54**, 151–155.

Anderson, A. (1997) No divine right. *New Scientist*, 13 September, 3.

Anderson, M. (1995) Evidence for a single global factor of developmental change – too good to be true? *Australian Journal of Psychology*, **47**, 18–24.

Anderton, C.H. (1986) The forensic use of hypnosis. In: F.A. De Piano and H.C. Salzberg (eds) *Clinical Applications of Hypnosis*. Norwood, NJ: Ablex, pp. 197–223.

Andrade, J. (1995) Learning during anaesthesia: a review. *British Journal of Psychology*, **86**, 479–506.

Andreasen, N.C. (1987) Creativity and mental illness: prevalence rates in writers and their first degree relatives. *American Journal of Psychiatry*, **144**, 1288–1292.

Angela, P. (1978) *Viaggio nel Mondo del Paranormale*. Milano: Garzanti editore.

Annett, M. (1985) *Left, Right, Hand and Brain: The Right Shift Theory*. London: Erlbaum.

Annett, M. (1995) The right shift theory of a genetic balanced polymorphism for cerebral dominance and cognitive processing. *Current Psychology of Cognition*, **14**, 427–480.

Apkarian, A.V. (1995) Functional imaging of pain: new insights regarding the role of the cerebral cortex in human pain perception. *Seminars in the Neurosciences*, **7**, 279–293.

Armstrong, E., Schleicher, A., Omran, H., Curtis, M. and Zilles, K. (1995) The ontogeny of human gyrification. *Cerebral Cortex*, **5**, 56–63.

Arnheim, R. (1962) *Picasso's Guernica: The Genesis of a Painting*. Berkeley: University of California Press.

Astrup, J. (1982) Energy-requiring cell functions. Their critical supply and possible inhibition in protective therapy. *Journal of Neurosurgery*, **56**, 482–497.

Baddeley, A.D. (1993) *Your Memory. A User's Guide*. London: Prion.

Baddeley, A.D. and Warrington, E.K. (1970) Amnesia and the distinction between long- and short-term memory. *Journal of Verbal Learning and Verbal Behavior*, **9**, 176–189.

Bagchi, B. and Wenger, M. (1957) Electrophysiological correlates of some Yogi exercises. *EEG and Clinical Neurophysiology*, Suppl. 7, 132–149.

Baker, R.A. (1992) *Hidden Memories*. Buffalo: Prometheus Books.

Baker, S.L. and Kirsch, I. (1993) Hypnotic and placebo analgesia: order effects and the placebo label. *Contemporary Hypnosis*, **10**, 117–126.

Bakker, D. and Pauwels, E.K.J. (1997) Stroke: the role of functional imaging. *European Journal of Nuclear Medicine*, **24**, 2–5.

Baltes, P.B. and Lindenberger, U. (1997) Emergence of a powerful connection between sensory and cognitive functions across the lifespan: a new window to the study of cognitive aging? *Psychology and Aging*, **12**, 12–21.

Bancaud, J., Brunet-Bourgin, F., Chauvel, P. and Halgren, E. (1994) Anatomical origin of deja vu and vivid ''memories'' in human temporal lobe epilepsy. *Brain*, **117**, 71–90.

Bandler, R. and Grinder, J. (1979) *Frogs into Princes: Neuro-linguistic Programming*. Moab, UT: Real People Press.

Banyai, E.I. and Hilgard, E.R. (1976) A comparison of active alert hypnotic induction and traditional relaxation induction. *Journal of Abnormal Psychology*, **85**, 218–224.

Baranaga, M. (1997) New imaging methods provide a better view into the brain. *Science*, **276**, 1974–1976.

Barber, J. (1991) The locksmith model: accessing hypnotic responsiveness. In: S.J. Lynn and J.W. Rhue (eds) *Theories of Hypnosis: Current Models and Perspectives*. New York: Guilford, pp. 241–274.

Barber, T.X. (1969) *Hypnosis: A Scientific Approach*. New York: Van Nostrand.

Barber, T.X., Spanos, N.P. and Chaves, J.F. (1974) *Hypnotism, Imagination and Human Potentialities*. New York: Pergamon.

Barker, A.T. (1994) Electricity, magnetism and the body: some uses and abuses. *Journal of the Royal Society of Health*, **114**, 91–97.

Barlow, H.B. (1972) Single units and sensation: a neuron doctrine for perceptual psychology? *Perception*, **1**, 371–395.

Barratt, R. (1994) Getting a kick from the psychic. *Manchester Evening News*, 30 April.

Barrett, S. (1995) The dark side of Linus Pauling's legacy. *The Skeptical Inquirer*, **19**(1), 18–20.

Barron, F. (1955) The disposition toward originality. *Journal of Abnormal and Social Psychology*, **51**, 478–485.

Barron, F. and Harrington, D.M. (1981) Creativity, intelligence and personality. *Annual Review of Psychology*, **32**, 439–476.

Barsley, M. (1970) *Left-handed Man in a Right-handed World*. London: Pitman.

Bartlett, F.C. (1982) *Remembering: A Study in Experimental and Social Psychology*. Cambridge: Cambridge University Press.

Bartley, A.J., Jones, D.W. and Weinberger, D.R. (1997) Genetic variability of human brain size and cortical gyral patterns. *Brain*, **120**, 257–269.

Basil, R. (1988) *Not Necessarily the New Age: Critical Essays*. Amherst, NY: Prometheus Books.

Basser, L.S. (1962) Hemiplegia of early onset and the faculty of speech with special reference to the effect of hemispherectomy. *Brain*, **85**, 427–460.

Baylor, D.A., Lamb, T.D. and Yau, K.-W. (1979) Responses of retinal rods to single photons. *Journal of Physiology*, **288**, 613–634.

Bear, D. (1979) Temporal lobe epilepsy: a syndrome of sensory–limbic hyperconnectionism. *Cortex*, **15**, 357–384.

Beck, A.T. (1967) *Depression: Clinical, Experimental, and Theoretical Aspects*. New York: Harper and Row.

Beck, A.T. (1989) *Cognitive Therapy and the Emotional Disorders*. New York: International Universities Press.

Beecher, H.K. (1955) The powerful placebo. *JAMA*, **159**, 1602–1606.

Bekerian, D.A. and Baddeley, A.D. (1980) Saturation advertising and the repetition effect. *Journal of Verbal Learning and Verbal Behavior*, **19**, 17–25.

Bem, D.J. and Honorton, C. (1994) Does psi exist? Replicable evidence for an anomalous process of information transfer. *Psychological Bulletin*, **115**, 4–18.

Benaron, D.A. and Stevenson, D.K. (1994) Resolution of near infrared time-of-flight brain oxygenation imagining. In: P. Vaupel, R. Zander and D.F. Bruley (eds) *Oxygen Transport to Tissue* XV. New York: Plenum Press, pp. 609–617.

Bennett, W. (1980) Providing for posterity. *Harvard Magazine*, **82**(3), 13–16.

Benson, H. (1975) *The Relaxation Response*. New York: Avon Books.

Benson, H. (1996) *Timeless Healing: The Power and Biology of Belief*. New York: Simon and Schuster.

Benton, A.L. (1984) Hemispheric dominance before Broca. *Neuropsychologia*, **22**, 807–811.

Berger, H. (1929) Uber das elektrencephalogramm des menschen. *Archiv für Psychiatrie Nervenkr*, **87**, 527–570.

Berlyne, N. (1972) Confabulation. *British Journal of Psychiatry*, **120**, 31–39.

Bernheim, H. (1885) Notes et discussions. L'hypnotisme chez les hystériques. *Revue Philosophique*, **19**, 311–316.

Bertrand, L.D. (1989) The assessment annd modification of hypnotic susceptibility. In: N.P. Spanos and J.F. Chaves (eds) *Hypnosis: The Cognitive Behavioral Perspective*. Buffalo, NY: Prometheus, pp. 18–31.

Beyerstein, B.L. (1985) The myth of alpha consciousness. *The Skeptical Inquirer*, **10**(1), 42–59.

Beyerstein, B.L. (1987) The brain and consciousness: implications for Psi phenomena. *The Skeptical Inquirer*, **12**(2), 163–174.

Beyerstein, B.L. (1988) Neuropathology and the legacy of spiritual possession. *The Skeptical Inquirer*, **12**(3), 248–263.

Beyerstein, B.L. (1990) Brainscams: Neuromythologies of the New Age. *International Journal of Mental Health*, **19**(3), 27–36.

Beyerstein, D.F. (1992a) Graphology and the philosophy of science. In: B.L. Beyerstein and D.F. Beyerstein (eds) *The Write Stuff*. Amherst, NY: Prometheus Books, pp. 121–162.

Beyerstein, B.L. (1992b) The origins of graphology in sympathetic magic. In: B.L. Beyerstein and D.F. Beyerstein (eds) *The Write Stuff*. Amherst, NY: Prometheus Books, pp. 163–200.

Beyerstein, B.L. (1992c) Handwriting is brainwriting. So what? In: B.L. Beyerstein and D.F. Beyerstein (eds) *The Write Stuff*. Amherst, NY: Prometheus Books, pp. 397–419.

Beyerstein, B.L. (1996a) Believing is seeing: organic and psychological reasons for anomalous psychiatric symptoms. *Medscape* (on-line medical journal): *http://www.medscape.com/Clinical/Medscape*/MentalHealth/1996/v01.n01/mh65.be

Beyerstein, B.L. (1996b) Graphology. In: G. Stein (ed.) *Encyclopedia of the Paranormal*. Amherst, NY: Prometheus Books, pp. 309–324.

Beyerstein, B.L. (1997) Why bogus therapies seem to work. *The Skeptical Inquirer*, **21**(5), 29–34.

Beyerstein, B.L. and Beyerstein, D.F. (eds) (1992) *The Write Stuff*. Amherst, NY: Prometheus Books.

Beyerstein, B.L. and Freeman, R.D. (1976) Increment sensitivity in humans with abnormal visual experience. *Journal of Physiology* (London), **260**, 497–514.

Bickler, P.E. (1992) Aspectos energéticos del metabolismo cerebral y el transporte de iones. *Clínicas de Anestesiología de Norteamérica*, **3**, 599–611.

Binet, A. and Feret, C. (1885) L'hypnotisme chez les hystériques: 1. Le transfert psychique. *Revue Philosophique de la France et de l'Etranger*, **19**, 1–25.

Birren, J.E. (1956) The significance of age changes in speed of perception and psychomotor skills. In: J.E. Anderson (ed.) *Psychological Aspects of Aging*. Washington DC: American Psychological Association.

Birren, J.E. (1974) Psychophysiology and speed of response. *American Psychologist*, **29**, 808–815.

Birren, J.E. and Williams, M.V. (1980) Cognitive issues: speed of behaviour. In: L.W. Poon (ed.) *Aging in the 1980's: Psychological Issues*. Washington DC: American Psychological Association.

Bishop, D.V.M. (1987) Is there a link between handedness and hypersensitivity? *Cortex*, **22**, 289–296.

Bishop, D.V.M. (1988) Can the right hemisphere mediate language as well as the left? A critical review of recent research. *Cognitive Neuropsychology*, **5**, 353–367.

Blackburn, D. (1911) Confessions of a telepathist: thirty-year hoax exposed. *London Daily News*, 1 September.

Blackmore, S. (1991) Is meditation good for you? *New Scientist*, 6 July, 28–33.

Blackmore, S. (1993) *Dying to Live. Science and the Near-death Experience*. London: Grafton.

Blackmore, S. (1994) Alien abduction: the inside story. *New Scientist*, 19 November, 29–31.

Blakemore, C. (1994) *The Mind Machine*. London: Penguin Books.

Blank, M. and Goodman, R. (1997) Do electromagnetic fields interact directly with DNA? *Bioelectromagnetics*, **18**, 111–115.

Blau, A. (1946) *The Master Hand*. New York: American Orthopsychiatric Association.

Bliznitchenko, L. (1968) Hypnopaedia and its practice in the USSR. In F. Rubin (ed.) *Current Research in Hypnopaedia*. London: Macdonald, pp. 202–207.

Boden, M.A. (1990) *The Creative Mind*. London: Weidenfeld and Nicolson.

Boden, M.A. (1994) Précis of "The creative mind": myths and mechanisms. *Behavioral and Brain Sciences*, **17**, 519–570.

Bogen, J.E. (1969) The other side of the brain. II: An appositional mind. *Bulletin of the Los Angeles Neurological Society*, **34**, 135–162.

Bogen, J.E. (1993) The callosal syndromes. In: K.M. Heilman and E. Valenstein (eds) *Clinical Neuropsychology*, 3rd edn, New York: Oxford University Press, pp. 337–407.

Bogen, J.E. (1997) Does cognition in the disconnected right hemisphere require right hemispheric possession of language? *Brain and Cognition*, **57**, 12–21.

Bogen, J.E., DeZare, R., TenHouten, W.D. and Marsh, J.F. (1972) The other side of the brain: IV. The A/P ratio. *Bulletin of the Los Angeles Neurological Society*, **37**, 49–61.

Bogousslavsky, L. and Caplan, L.R. (1993) Vertebrobasilar occlusive disease: review of selected aspects. *Cerebrovascular Disease*, **3**, 193–205.

Borgens, R.B. (1986) The role of natural and applied electric fields in neural regeneration and development. In: *Ionic Currents and Development*. New York: Ian R. Liss, pp. 239–250.

Bouchard, T.J., Jr (1972) A comparison of two group brainstorming procedures. *Journal of Applied Psychology*, **56**, 418–421.

Bouchard, T.J., Jr (1983) Do environmental similarities explain the similarity of intelligence of identical twins reared apart? *Intelligence*, **7**, 175–184.

Bouchard, T.J., Jr (1992) Genetic and environmental influences on adult personality: evaluating the evidence. In: J. Hettema and I.J. Deary (eds) *Foundations of Personality*. Dordrecht, NL: Kluwer Academic.

Bouchard T.J., Jr (1997) Whenever the twain shall meet. *The Sciences*, **37**(5), 52–57.

Bouchard, T.J., Jr and Hare, M. (1970) Size, performance, and potential in brainstorming groups. *Journal of Applied Psychology*, **54**, 51–55.

Bourru, H. and Burot, F. (1888) *Variations de la Personnalité*. Paris: J.B. Baillière.

Bowers, K.S. (1983) *Hypnosis for the Seriously Curious*. New York: Norton.

Bowers, K.S. and Davidson, T.M. (1991) A neodissociative critique of Spanos's social psychological model of hypnosis. In: S.J. Lynn and J.W. Rhue (eds) *Theories of Hypnosis: Current Models and Perspectives*. New York: Guilford, pp. 105–143.

Bradford, H.F. (1986) *Chemical Neurobiology*. New York: W.H. Freeman and Co.

Bradshaw, J.L. and Rogers, L.J. (1993) *The Evolution of Lateral Asymmetries, Language, Tool Use, and Intellect*. Sydney: Academic Press.

Brandon, R. (1984) *The Spiritualists. The Passion for the Occult in the Nineteenth and Twentieth Centuries*. Amherst, NY: Prometheus Books.

Brandwein, P. (1977) The duality of the brain: a symposium in print with Paul Brandwein and Robert Ornstein. *Instructor*, **58**, 56–58.

Brazier, M.A.B. (1959) The historical development of neurophysiology. In: H.W. Magoun (ed.) *Handbook of Physiology*, Section 1: *Neurophysiology*, Vol. 1. Washington: American Physiological Society, pp. 1–58.

Brazier, M.A.B. (1977) *Electrical Activity of the Nervous System*, 4th edn. Tunbridge Wells: Pitman Medical Publishing Company.

Briere, J. (1992) *Child Abuse Trauma: Theory and Treatment of the Lasting Effects*. Newbury Park, CA: Sage Publications.

Briere, J. (1998). Address to the 12th International Congress on Child Abuse and Neglect (ISPCAN), September 6–9, Auckland, New Zealand.

Brilhart, J.K. and Jochen, E.M. (1964) Effects of different patterns on outcomes of problem solving discussions. *Journal of Applied Psychology*, **48**, 175–179.

British Psychological Society (1992) *The Psychologist*, **5(3)** March, p. 99.

Broca, P. (1865) Sur la siège de la faculté du langage articulé. *Bulletins de la Société d' Anthropologie de Paris*, **6**, 377–393.

Broch, H. (1987) *Los Fenómenos Paranormales: Una Reflexión Crítica*. Barcelona: Crítica.

Broch, H. (1991) *Au Coeur de l'Extraordinaire*. Bordeaux: L'horizon Chimérique.

Brown, W.A. (1998) The placebo effect. *Scientific American*, January, 68–73.

Brown-Sequard, Ch.-E. (1877) Dual character of the brain (Toner lecture). *Smithsonian Miscellaneous Collections* (Washington, DC), **15**, 1–21.

Brunvand, J.H. (1982) *The Vanishing Hitchhiker: American Urban Legends and Their Meaning*. New York: W.W. Norton.

Brunvand, J.H. (1986) *The Study of American Folklore*. New York: W.W. Norton.

Bryan, R.M. (1990) Cerebral blood flow and energy metabolism during stress. *American Journal of Physiology*, **259** (Heart and Circulatory Physiology, **28**), H269–H280).

Bryden, M.P., McManus, I.C. and Bulman-Fleming, M.B. (1994) Evaluating the empirical support for the Geschwind–Behan–Galaburda model of cerebral lateralization. *Brain and Cognition*, **26**, 103–167.

Buchanan, A. (1862) Mechanical theory of the preponderance of the right hand over the left; or, more generally, of the limbs of the right side over the left side of the body. *Proceedings of the Philosophical Society of Glasgow*, **5**, 142–167.

Buchsbaum, M.S. (1995) Positron emission tomography studies of abnormal glucose metabolism in schizophrenic illness. *Clinical Neuroscience*, **3**, 122–130.

Bunge, M. (1980) *The Mind–Body Problem: A Psychobiological Approach*. Oxford: Pergamon Press.

Bunge, M. (1984) What is pseudoscience? *The Skeptical Inquirer*, **9**(1), 36–46.

Burgess, P. (1997) Theory and methodology in executive function research. In: P. Rabbitt (ed.) *Methodology of Frontal and Executive Function*. Hove: Psychology Press.

Burt, C.L. (1937) *The Backward Child*. London: University of London Press.

Butler, S. (1985) *Erewhon*. Penguin Classics: London.

Buzan, T. (1991) *Use your Perfect Memory*. London: E.P. Dutton.

Cabeza, R. and Nyberg, L. (1997) Imaging cognition: an empirical review of PET studies with normal subjects. *Journal of Cognitive Neuroscience*, **9**, 1–26.

Calvino, I. (1991) *Perche' Leggere i Classici* [Why should we read classic works]. Mondadori: Milano.

Campbell, D. (1960) Blind variation and selective retention in creative thought as in other knowledge processes. *Psychological Review*, **67**, 380–400.

Campbell, S., Volow, M.R. and Cavenar, J.O., Jr (1981) Cotard's syndrome and the psychiatric manifestations of typhoid fever. *American Journal of Psychiatry*, **138**, 1377–1378.

Candido, C.L. and Romney, D.M. (1990) Attributional style in paranoid vs. depressed patients. *British Journal of Medical Psychology*, **63**, 355–363.

Capgras, J. and Reboul-Lachaux, J. (1923) L'illusion des ''sosies'' dans un délire systématisé chronique. *Bulletin de la Société Clinique de Médicine Mentale*, **11**, 6–16.

Carnegie, D. (1936) *How to Win Friends and Influence People*. New York: Simon and Schuster.

Carnegie, D. (1944) *How to Stop Worrying and Start Living*. New York: Simon and Schuster.

Caro, R.A. (1990) *Means of Ascent: the Years of Lyndon Johnson*. New York: Alfred A. Knopf.

Cattell, R.B. (1959) The personality and motivation of the researcher from measurements of contemporaries and from biography. In: C.W. Taylor (ed.) *The 1959 University of Utah Research Conference on the Identification of Creative Scientific Talent*. Utah: University of Utah Press.

Cattell, R.B. and Drevdahl, J.E. (1955) A comparison of the personality profile (16PF) of eminent researchers with that of eminent teachers and administrators, and of the general population. *British Journal of Psychology*, **46**, 248–261.

Cecil, P. (1997) *Flickers of the DreamMachine*. Hove: CodeX.

Cerf, C. and Navasky, V. (1984) *The Expert Speak*. Villard Books.

Chance, B. (1994) Non-invasive approaches to tissue bioenergetics. *Biochemical Society Transactions*, **22**, 983–987.

Changeux, J-P. (1983) *L'homme Neuronal* [The neuronal man]. Librairie Arthème Fayard: Princeton UP.

Chaput de Saintonge, D.M. and Herxheimer, A. (1994) Harnessing placebo effects in health care. *Lancet*, **344**, 995–998.

Charcot, J.-M. and Bernard, D. (1883) Un cas de suppression brusque et isolée de la vision mentale des signes et des objets (formes et couleurs). *Le Progrès Médical*, **11**, 568–571.

Chaves, J.F. (1989) Hypnotic control of clinical pain. In N.P. Spanos and J.F. Chaves (eds) *Hypnosis: The Cognitive Behavioral Perspective*. Buffalo, NY: Prometheus Books, pp. 242–272.

Chi, J.G., Dooling, E.C. and Gilles, F.H. (1977) Left–right asymmetries of the temporal speech areas of the human fetus. *Archives of Neurology*, **34**, 346–348.

Chomsky, N. (1959) Review of *Verbal Behavior* by B.F. Skinner. *Language*, **35**, 26.

Chrisjohn, R.D. and Peters, M. (1986) The pernicious myth of the right-brained Indian. *Canadian Journal of Indian Education*, **13**, 62–71.

Churchland, P.M. (1984) *Matter and Consciousness*. Cambridge, Mass: Bradford/MIT Press.

Clark, J.B., Bates, T.E., Almeida, A., Cullingford, T. and Warwick, J. (1994) Energy metabolism in the developing mammalian brain. *Biochemical Society Transactions*, **22**, 980–983.

Clarke, E. and Jacyna, L.S. (1987) *Nineteenth-Century Origins of Neuroscientific Concepts*. Berkeley: University of California Press.

Coe, W.C. (1989) Posthypnotic amnesia: Theory and Research. In: N.P. Spanos and J.F. Chaves (eds) *Hypnosis: The Cognitive Behavioral Perspective*. Buffalo, NY: Prometheus, pp. 110–148.

Coe, W.C., Kobayashi, K. and Howard, M.L. (1972) An approach toward isolating factors that influence antisocial conduct in hypnosis. *International Journal of Clinical and Experimental Hypnosis*, **20**, 118–131.

Coe, W.C., Kobayashi, K. and Howard, M.L. (1973) Experimental and ethical problems of evaluating the influence of hypnosis in antisocial conduct. *Journal of Abnormal Psychology*, **82**, 476–482.

Coe, W.C. and Sarbin, T.R. (1991) Role theory: hypnosis from a dramaturgical and narrational perspective. In: S.J. Lynn and J.W. Rhue (eds) *Theories of Hypnosis: Current Models and Perspectives*. New York: Guilford, pp. 303–323.

Coghlan, A. (1997) Pride and prejudice. *New Scientist*, 13 September, 24.

Cohen, J. (1994) The earth is round (p<0.05). *American Psychologist*, **49**, 997–1003.

Collins, R.C. (1991) Basic aspects of functional brain metabolism. *Ciba Foundation Symposium*, **163**, 6–22.

Conn, J.H. (1972) Is hypnosis really dangerous? *International Journal of Clinical and Experimental Hypnosis*, **20**, 61–79.

Cook, C.M. and Persinger, M.A. (1997) Experimental induction of the "sensed presence" in normal subjects and an exceptional subject. *Perceptual and Motor Skills*, **85**, 683–693.

Cooper, C.E., Matcher, S.J., Wyatt, J.S., Cope, M., Brown, G.C., Nemoto, E.M. and Delpy, D.T. (1994) Near-infrared spectroscopy of the brain: relevance to cytochrome oxidase bioenergetics. *Biochemical Society Transactions*, **22**, 974–980.

Corballis, M.C. (1980) Laterality and myth. *American Psychologist*, **35**, 284–295.

Corballis, M.C. (1983) *Human Laterality*. New York: Academic Press.

Corballis, M.C. (1991) *The Lopsided Ape*. New York: Oxford University Press.

Corballis, M.C. (1997) The genetics and evolution of handedness. *Psychological Review*, **104**, 714–727.

Corballis, M.C. and Beale, I.L. (1976) *The Psychology of Left and Right*. Hillsdale, NJ: Erlbaum.

Corballis, M.C. and Morgan, M.J. (1978) On the biological basis of laterality: I. Evidence for a maturational left–right gradient. *Behavioral and Brain Sciences*, **1**, 261–269.

Coren, S. and Porac, C. (1977). Fifty centuries of right-handedness. *Science*, **198**, 631–632.

Corliss, W.R. (1993) Remarkable capabilities of badly damaged brains. In *Biological Anomalies: Humans II*. Glen Arm, MD: The Sourcebook Project, pp. 263–266.

Cotard, J. (1882) Du délire des négations. *Archives de Neurologie*, **4**, 152–170; 282–295. Translated in S.R. Hirsch and M. Shepherd (eds.) (1974) *Variations in European Psychiatry: An Anthology*. Bristol: John Wright and Sons, Ltd.

Cotard, J. (1884) Perte de la vision mentale dans la mélancholie anxieuse. *Archives de Neurologie*, **7**, 289–295.

Council, J.R., Kirsch, I. and Grant, D.L. (1996) Imagination, expectancy and hypnotic responding. In: R.G. Kunzendorf, N.P. Spanos and B.J. Wallace (eds) *Hypnosis and Imagination*. New York: Baywood, pp. 41–66.

Cousins, N. (1957) Smudging the subconscious. *Saturday Review*, 5 October, 20.

Couttie, B. (1988) *Forbidden Knowledge. The Paranormal Paradox*. Cambridge: Lutterworth Press.

Coxhead, N. (1980). *Los Poderes de la Mente*. Barcelona: Martínez Roca.

Craen, A.J.M., Ross, P.J., de Vries, A.L. and Kleijnen, J. (1996) Effect of colour of drugs: systematic review of perceived effect of drugs and of their effectiveness. *British Medical Journal*, **313**, 1624–1626.

Crawford, H.J. (1996) Cerebral brain dynamics of mental imagery: evidence and issues for hypnosis. In: R.G. Kunzendorf, N.P. Spanos and B.J. Wallace (eds) *Hypnosis and Imagination*. New York: Baywood, pp. 253–282.

Crews, F. (1995) *The Memory Wars: Freud's Legacy in Dispute*. New York: New York Review Book.

Crick, F. and Koch, C. (1990) Towards a neurobiological theory of consciousness. *Seminars in the Neurosciences*, **2**, 262–275.

Culver, R.B. and Ianna, P.A. (1984) *The Gemini Syndrome: A Scientific Evaluation of Astrology*. Buffalo: Prometheus Books.

Czikszentmihalyi, M. (1975) *Beyond Boredom and Anxiety*. San Francisco: Jossey-Bass.

Damasio, H. and Damasio, A.R. (1989) *Lesion Analysis in Neuropsychology*. New York: Oxford University Press.

Damasio, A.R., Tranel, D. and Damasio, H. (1990) Face agnosia and the neural substrates of memory. *Annual Review of Neuroscience*, **13**, 89–109.

Darton, N. (1991) The pain of the last taboo. *Newsweek*, 7 October, 70–72.

Dash, M. (1997) *Borderlands*. London: Heinemann.

Davies, P. (1988) Some considerations of the physiological effects of hypnosis. In: M. Heap (ed.) *Hypnosis: Current Clinical, Experimental and Forensic Practices*. London: Croom Helm, pp. 61–67.

Davis, L. (1991) Murdered memory. *In Health*, **5**, 79–84.

Dax, M. (1865) Lésions de la moitié gauche de l'encéphale coincident avec l'oubli des signes de la pensée. *Gazette Hebdomadaire de Médicine et de Chirurgie (Paris)*, **2**, 259–260.

Dean, G.A. (1992) The bottom line: effect size. In: B.L. Beyerstein and D.F. Beyerstein (eds) *The Write Stuff*. Amherst, NY: Prometheus Books, pp. 269–341.

Dean, W. and Morganthaler, J. (1990) *Smart Drugs and Nutrients*. Santa Cruz, CA: B&J Publications.

Dean, G.A., Kelly, I.W., Saklofske, D.H. and Furnham, A. (1992) Graphology and human judgment. In: B.L. Beyerstein and D.F. Beyerstein (eds) *The Write Stuff*. Amherst, NY: Prometheus Books, pp. 342–396.

De Bono, E. (1976) *Teaching Thinking*. London: Temple Smith.

De Bono, E. (1983) The Cognitive Research Trust (CoRT) thinking program. In: W. Maxwell (ed.) *Thinking: the Expanding Frontier*. Philadelphia, PA: The Franklin Institute Press, pp. 115–128.

Decker, D.R. (1994) The right brain. *The Skeptical Inquirer*, **18**, 210.

De Fleury, A. (1872) Du dynamisme comparé des hémisphères cérébraux dans l'homme. *Association Française pour l'Avancement des Sciences*, **1**, 834–845.

de Groh, M. (1989) Correlates of hypnotic susceptibility. In N.P. Spanos and J.F. Chaves (eds) *Hypnosis: The Cognitive Behavioral Perspective*. Buffalo, NY: Prometheus Books, pp. 32–63.

de Groot, H.P. and Gwynn, M.I. (1989) Trance logic, duality and hidden observer responding. In N.P. Spanos and J.F. Chaves (eds) *Hypnosis: The Cognitive Behavioral Perspective*. Buffalo, NY: Prometheus, pp. 187–205.

Della Sala, S. (1997a) Notes from a fringe watcher. *Physiotherapy, Theory and Practice*, **13**, 113–115.

Della Sala, S. (1997b) The Pope's Neo-Darwinism. *The Skeptical Inquirer*, **21**, 65.

Della Sala, S. and Berrini, R. (1979) Epilessia: pregiudizi e prevenzione. *Il Dialogo*, **22**(8), 8.

Della Sala, S. and Logie, R.H. (1998) Dualism down the drain: thinking in the brain. In: K.J. Gilhooly and R.H. Logie (eds) *Thinking in Working Memory*. Hove: The Psychology Press, pp. 45–66.

Delmonte, M. and Kenny, V. (1985) An overview of the therapeutic effects of meditation. *Psychologia*, **28**, 189–202.

Démonet, J.-F., Wise, R. and Frackowiak, R.S.J. (1993) Les fonctions linguistiques explorées en tomographie par émission de positons. *Médecine/Sciences*, **9**, 934–942.

Dennis, W. (1955) Variations in productivity among creative workers. *Scientific Monthly*, **80**, 277–278.

Dennis, W. (1956) Age and productivity among scientists. *Science*, **123**, 724–725.

Dennis, W. (1958a) Early graphic evidence of dextrality in man. *Perceptual and Motor Skills*, **8**, 147–149.

Dennis, W. (1958b) The age decrement in outstanding scientific contributions. *American Psychologist*, **13**, 457–460.

Dennis, W. (1966) Creative productivity between the ages of 20 and 80 years. *Journal of Gerontology*, **21**, 1–8.

Dennis, M. and Kohn, B. (1975) Comprehension of syntax in infantile hemiplegics after cerebral hemidecortication. *Brain and Language*, **2**, 472–482.

Dennis, M. and Whitaker, H.A. (1976) Language acquisition following hemidecortication: linguistic superiority of the left over the right hemisphere. *Brain and Language*, **3**, 404–433.

De Sanchez, M.A. and Astorga, M. (1983) *Projecto Aprendar a Pensor*. Caracas: Ministerio de Educacion.

Descartes, R. (1985) *The Philosophical Writings of Descartes*. (J. Cottingham, R. Stoothoff and D. Murdock, editors and translators). Cambridge: Cambridge University Press.

De Vernejoul, P., Darras, J.C. and Beguin, C. (1984) Approche isotopique de la visualisation des méridiens d'acupuncture. *Agressologie*, **25**, 1107–1111.

Devinsky, O. (1993) Electrical and magnetic stimulation of the central nervous system. Historical overview. In: O. Devinsky, A. Beric and M. Dogali (eds) *Electrical and Magnetic Stimulation of the Brain and Spinal Cord*. New York: Raven Press, pp. 1–16.

Dhume, V.G., Agshikar, N.V. and Diniz, R.S. (1975) Placebo-induced side-effects in healthy volunteers. *Clinician*, **39**, 289–290.

Diaconis, P. (1985) Statistical problems in ESP research. In: P. Kurtz (ed.) *The Skeptic's Handbook of Parapsychology*. Buffalo: Prometheus Books, pp. 569–584.

Diamond, B.L. (1980) Inherent problems in the use of pre-trial hypnosis on a prospective witness. *California Law Review*, **68**, 313–349.

Dillon, P.C., Graham, W.K. and Aidells, A.L. (1972) Brainstorming on a "hot" problem: effects of training and practice on individual and group performance. *Journal of Applied Psychology*, **56**, 487–490.

Dimond, E.G., Kittle, C.F. and Crockett, J.E. (1960) Comparison of internal mammary ligation and sham operation for angina pectoris. *American Journal of Cardiology*, **5**, 483–486.

Dobelle, W.H. and Mladejovsky, M.G. (1974) Phosphines produced by electrical stimulation of the human occipital cortex and their application to the development of a prosthesis for the blind. *Journal of Physiology* (London), **243**, 553–576.

Dominowski, R.L. and Jenrick, R. (1972) Effects of hints and interpolated activity on solution of an insight problem. *Psychonomic Science*, **26**, 335–338.

Drake, M.E.J. (1988) Cotard's syndrome and temporal lobe epilepsy. *Psychiatric Journal of the University of Ottawa*, **13**, 36–39.

Drake, R.A. (1995) A neuropsychology of deception and self-deception. *Behavioural and Brain Sciences*, **18**, 552–553.

Drevdahl, J.E. and Cattell, R.N. (1958) Personality and creativity in artists and writers. *Journal of Clinical Psychology*, **14**, 107–111.

Druckman, D. and Bjork, R.A. (eds) (1991) *In the Mind's Eye: Enhancing Human Performance*. Washington, DC: National Academy Press.

Druckman, D. and Bjork, R.A. (eds) (1994) *Learning, Remembering, Believing: Enhancing Human Performance*. Washington, DC: National Academy Press.

Druckman, D. and Swets, J. (eds) (1988) *Enhancing Human Performance: Issues, Theories, and Techniques*. Washington, DC: National Academy Press.

Duffy, C.J. and Wurtz, R.H. (1997) Medial superior temporal area neurons respond to speed patterns in optic flow. *Journal of Neuroscience*, **17**, 2839–2851.

Dumontpallier, A. and Magnan, V. (1883) Des hallucinations bilaterales à caractère différent suivant le côté effecté, dans le délire chronique; léçon clinique de M. Magnan, et demonstration expérimentale du siège hémilateral ou bilateral cérébral des hallucinations. *Union Médicale*, 3ème série, **35**, 845–848, 869–875.

Dunbar, R. (1995) *The Trouble with Science*. London: Faber and Faber.

Duncan, J. (1995) Attention, intelligence and the frontal lobes. In: M.S. Gazzaniga (ed.) *The Cognitive Neurosciences*. Cambridge: MIT Press, pp. 721–731.

Duncan, J., Burgess, P. and Emslie, H. (1995) Fluid intelligence after frontal lobe lesions. *Neuropsychologia*, **33**, 261–268.

Dunnette, M.D., Campbell, J. and Jaastad, K. (1963) The effects of group participation on brainstorming effectiveness for two industrial samples. *Journal of Applied Psychology*, **47**, 10–37.

Eadie, B.J. (1992) *Embraced by the Light*. New York: Bantom.

Eason, J. (1989) Psychic powers or child's play? *The Weekend Guardian*, 18 February.

Ebbern, H., Mulligan, S. and Beyerstein, B.L. (1996) Maria's near-death experience: waiting for the other shoe to drop. *The Skeptical Inquirer*, **20**, 27–33.

Eccles, J.C. (1965) *The Brain and the Unity of Conscious Experience*. Cambridge: Cambridge University Press.

Eccles, J.C. (1981) Mental dualism and commissurotomy. *Behavioral and Brain Sciences*, **4**, 105.

Eccles, J.C. (1992) Evolution of consciousness. *Proceedings of the National Academy of Sciences of the USA*, **89**, 7320–7324.

Eco, U. (1997) *Kant e l'ornitorinco*. Bompiani: Milano.

Edelman, G.M. (1989) *The Remembered Present: a Biological Theory of Consciousness*. New York: Basic Books.

Edmonston, W.E. (1991) Anesis. In: S.J. Lynn and J.W. Rhue (eds) *Theories of Hypnosis: Current Models and Perspectives*. New York: Guilford Press, pp. 197–240.

EduCom (1997a) EduCom Limited, Bournehall Hall, Bournehall Road, Bushey, Hertfordshire, WD2 3YG

EduCom (1997b) www.maxproducts.com

Edwards (1979) Drawing on the Right Side of the Brain. Los Angeles: Tarcher.

Edwards, J. and Baldauf, R.B. (1983) Teaching thinking in secondary science. In: W. Maxwell (ed.) *Thinking: the Expanding Frontier*. Philadelphia, PA: The Franklin Institute Press, pp. 129–138.

Eich, E. (1990) Learning during sleep. In: R.R. Bootzin, J.F. Kihlstrom and D.L. Schacter (eds) *Sleep and Cognition*. Washington, DC: American Psychological Association, pp. 88–108.

Eisenberg, L. (1976) The outcome as a cause: predestination and human cloning. *Journal of Medicine and Philosophy*, **1**, 318–331.

Eisenberg, L. (1995) The social construction of the human brain. *American Journal of Psychiatry*, **152**, 1563–1575.

Eisenberg, D.M., Kessler, R.C., Foster, C., Norlock, F.E., Calkins, D.R. and Delbanco, T.L. (1993) Unconventional medicine in the United States. Prevalence, costs, and pattern of use. *New England Journal of Medicine*, **328**, 246–252.

Ellis, A.X., Della Sala, S. and Logie, R.H. (1996) The bailiwick of visuo-spatial working memory: evidence from unilateral spatial neglect. *Cognitive Brain Research*, **3**, 71–78.

Elo, A.E. (1965) Age changes in master chess performance. *Journal of Gerontology*, **20**, 289–299.

Erdelyi, M.J. (1990) Repression, reconstruction, and defense: history and integration of the psychoanalytic and experimental frameworks. In: J.L. Singer (ed.) *Repression and Dissociation*. Chicago: University of Chicago Press, pp. 1–31.

Erdelyi, M.W. (1994) The empty set of hypermnesia. *International Journal of Clinical and Experimental Hypnosis*, **42**, 379–390.

Erecinska, M. and Silver, I.A. (1989) ATP and brain function. *Journal of Cerebral Blood Flow and Metabolism*, **9**, 2–19.

Ericsson, K.A. (1990) Peak performance and age: an examination of peak performance in sports. In: P.B. Baltes and M.M. Baltes (eds) *Successful Aging: Perfpectives from the Behavioural Sciences*. Cambridge: Cambridge University Press.

Ericsson, K.A. and Charness, N. (1994) Expert performance: its structure and acquisition. *American Psychologist*, **49**, 725–747.

Ericsson, K.A., Krampe, R.T. and Tesch-Rohmer, C. (1993) The role of deliberate practice. *Psychological Review*, **100**(3), 363–406.

Ericsson, K.A. and Pennington, N. (1993) The structure of memory performance in experts: implications for memory in everyday life. In: G.M. Davies and R.H. Logie (eds) *Memory in Everyday Life*. Amsterdam: Elsevier, pp. 241–272.

Ericsson, K.A. and Simon, H.A. (1993) *Protocol Analysis: Verbal Reports as Data*, revised edition. Cambridge, Mass: MIT Press.

Ericsson, K.A. and Smith, J. (1991) Prospects and limits of the empirical study of expertise: an introduction. In: K.A. Ericsson and J. Smith (eds) *Towards a General Theory of Expertise*. Cambridge: Cambridge University Press.

Erlich, J. (1992) Brain gain: drugs the boost intelligence. *Omni*, 14 September, 42–47.

Ernst, E. (1992) Placebo forte. *Wiener Medizinische Woohenschrift*, **142**, 217–219.

Evans, F.J. (1979) Contextual forgetting: post-hypnotic source amnesia. *Journal of Abnormal Psychology*, **88**, 556–563.

Evans, F.J. (1991) Hypnotizability: individual differences in dissociation and the flexible control of psychological processes. In: S.J. Lynn and J.W. Rhue (eds) *Theories of Hypnosis: Current Models and Perspectives*. New York: Guilford Press, pp. 144–168.

Evans, F.J. and Kihlstrom, J.F. (1973) Post-hypnotic amnesia as disrupted retrieval. *Journal of Abnormal Psychology*, **82**, 319–323.

Exner, S. (1881) *Untersuchungen uber die localisation der Functionen in der Grosshirnrinde des Menschen*. Vienna: Wilhelme Braumuller.

Eysenck, H.J. (1986) The theory of intelligence and the psychophysiology of cognition. In: R.J. Sternberg (ed.) *Advances in the Psychology of Human Intelligence*, Vol. 3. Hillsdale, NJ: Erlbaums.

Eysenck, H.J. (1994) The measurement of creativity. In: M. Boden (ed.) *Dimensions of Creativity*. Cambridge, MA: MIT Press, pp. 199–242.

Faber, D.S. and Korn, H. (1989) Electrical field effects: their relevance in central nervous system networks. *Physiological Reviews*, **69**, 822–863.

Faith, M. and Ray, W.J. (1994) Hypnotizability and dissociation in a college population: orthogonal individual differences. *Personality and Individual Differences*, **17**, 211–216.

Fedotchev, A.I., Bondar, A.T., Maevskii, A.A. and Zuimach, E.A. (1996) Physiological effects of photostimulation and their relationship with the subjective state parameters. *Human Physiology*, **21(3)**, 203–207.

Fellman, A. and Fellman, M. (1981) *Making Sense of Self: Medical Advice Literature in Late Nineteenth-Century America*. Philadelphia: University of Pennsylvania Press.

Fellows, B.J. (1986) The concept of trance. In: P.L.N. Naish (ed.) *What is Hypnosis?* Philadelphia: Open University Press, pp. 37–58.

Fellows, B.J. (1994) Defining hypnosis: a survey of British opinions on the APA definition. *Contemporary Hypnosis*, **11**, 155–159.

Fenwick, P. (1987) Meditation and the EEG. In: M.A. West (ed.) *The Psychology of Meditation*. Oxford: Clarendon Press, pp. 104–117.

Feynman, R.P. (1985) *Surely You are Joking, Mr. Feynman. Adventures of a Curious Character*. New York: Bantam Books.

Fink, G.R., Markowitsch, H.J., Reinkemeier, M., Bruckbauer, T., Kessler, J. and Heiss, W-D. (1996) Cerebral representation of one's own past: neural networks involved with autobiographical memory. *Journal of Neuroscience*, **16**, 4275–4282.

Fisher, R.P. and Geiselman, R.E. (1992) *Memory Enhancing Techniques for Investigative Interviewing: The Cognitive Interviewer*. Springfield, Ill.: Charles C. Thomas.

Fitzkee, D. (1945) *Magic by Misdirection*. Oakland, California: Magic Ltd.

Fliess, W. (1923) *Der Ablauf der Lebens*. Vienna: Deuticke.

Forem, J. (1973) *Transcendental Meditation: Maharishi Mahesh Yogi and the Science of Creative Intelligence*. New York: Bantam Books.

Forshaw, M. (1994) Expertise and ageing: *the crossword puzzle paradigm*. Unpublished PhD thesis, University of Manchester.

Förstl, H. and Beats, B. (1992) Charles' Bonnett's description of Cotard's delusion and reduplicative paramnesia in an elderly patient (1788). *British Journal of Psychiatry*, **160**, 416–418.

Fox, B.H. and Robbins, J.S. (1952) The retention of material presented during sleep. *Journal of Experimental Psychology*, **43**, 75–79.

Frank, J.D. and Frank, J.B. (1991) *Persuasion and Healing*. Baltimore: J. Hopkins University Press.

Frankel, C. (1973) The nature and sources of irrationalism. *Science*, **180**, 927–931.

Fraser, L. (1994) Families who have been torn apart by memory therapy. *The Mail on Sunday*, 15 May.

Fredrickson, R. (1992) *Repressed Memories: A Journey to Recovery from Sexual Abuse*. New York: Simon & Schuster.

Fried, I., Nenov, V.I., Ojemann, S.G. and Woods, R.P. (1995) Functional MR and PET imaging of rolandic and visual cortices for Neurosurgical planning. *Journal of Neurosurgery*, **83**, 854–861.

Friedman, H. and Davis, M. (1938) ''Left-handedness' in parrots. *Auk*, **55**, 478–480.

Friston, K.J., Frith, C.D., Liddle, P.F. and Frackowiak, R.S.J. (1991) Comparing functional (PET) images: the assessment of significant change. *Journal of Cerebral Blood Flow and Metabolism*, **11**, 690–699.

Friston, K.J., Holmes, A., Poline, J.-B. Price, C.J. and Frith, C.D. (1996) Detecting activations in PET and fMRI: levels of inference and power. *Neuroimage*, **40**, 223–235.

Fritsch, V. (1968) *Left and Right in Science and Life*. London: Barrie & Rockliff.

Fulgosi, A. and Guilford, J.P. (1968) Short term incubation in divergent production. *American Journal of Psychology*, **81**, 241–246.

Fuller, U. (1975) *Confessions of a Psychic*. Teaneck, New Jersey: Karl Fulves.

Fuller, U. (1980) *Further Confessions of a Psychic*. Teaneck, New Jersey: Karl Fulves.

Gambril, E. (1992) Self-help books: pseudoscience in the guise of science? *The Skeptical Inquirer*, **16**(4), 389–399.

Garattini, S. and Chiaberge, R. (1992) *Scoppiare di Salute*. Milano: Rizzoli.

Garattini, S. and Garattini, L. (1993) Pharmaceutical prescriptions in four European countries. *Lancet*, **342**, 1191–1192.

García Márquez, G. (1994) *Strange Pilgrims*. London: Penguin Books.

Gardner, M. (1957) *Fads and Fallacies in the Name of Science*. New York: Dover Publications.

Gardner, M. (1981) *Science: Good, Bad and Bogus*. Buffalo, NY: Prometheus Books.

Gardner, M. (1983) Notes of a psi watcher. *The Skeptical Inquirer*, **7**(4).

Gardner, M. (1985) Parapsychology and quantum mechanics. In: P. Kurtz (ed.) *A Skeptic's Handbook of Parapsychology*. Buffalo: Prometheus Books, pp. 585–598.

Gardner, M. (1989) Water with memory? The dilution affair. *The Skeptical Inquirer*, **13**(2), 132–141.

Gardner, H. (1994) *Creating Minds*. New York: Basic Books.

Garrett, S.V. (1976) Putting our whole brain to use: a fresh look at the creative process. *Journal of Creative Behavior*, **10**, 239–249.

Garry, M., Manning, C.G. and Loftus, E.F. (1997, July) A cognitive whodunnit: thinking about an event can make you think it happened to you. Presented at the second meeting of the Society for Applied Research in Memory & Cognition (SARMAC), Toronto.

Garry, M., Manning, C., Loftus, E. and Sherman, S. (1996) Imagination inflation: imagining a childhood event inflates the confidence that it occurred. *Psychonomic Bulletin and Review*, **3**, 208–214.

Gazzaniga, M.S. (1983) Right hemisphere language following brain bisection: a 20-year perspective. *American Psychologist*, **38**, 525–537.

Gazzaniga, M.S. (1987) Perceptual and attentional processes following callosal section in humans. *Neuropsychologia*, **25**, 119–133.

Gazzaniga, M. (1989) Organization of the human brain. *Science*, **245**, 947–952.

Gazzaniga, M.S. (1992) *Nature's Mind*. Basic Books, New York.

Gazzaniga, M.S., Bogen, J.E. and Sperry, R.W. (1967) Dyspraxia following division of the cerebral commissures. *Archives of Neurology*, **16**, 606–612.

Gerbner, G. (1987) Science on television: how it affects public conceptions. *Issues in Science and Technology*, **3**, 109–115.

Geschwind, N. and Behan, P. (1982) Left-handedness: association with immune disease, migraine, and developmental learning disorder. *Proceedings of the National Academy of Sciences of the USA*, **79**, 5097–5100.

Geschwind, N. and Galaburda, A.M. (1987) *Cerebral Lateralization: Biological Mechanisms, Associations, and Pathology*. Cambridge, MA: Bradford Books/MIT Press.

Geschwind, N. and Levitsky, W. (1968) Human brain: right–left asymmetries in temporal speech region. *Science*, **161**, 186–187.

Ghez, C. (1991) Muscles: effectors of the motor systems. In: E.R. Kandel, J.H. Schwartz and T.M. Jessell (eds) *Principles of Neural Science*, 3rd edn. Norwalk: Appleton & Lange, pp. 548–563.

Ghiselin, B. (1952) *The Creative Process*. New York: Mentor.

Gibson, H.B. (1992) A recent case of a man charged for rape and other sexual offences. *Contemporary Hypnosis*, **9**, 139–148.

Gloor, P., Olivier, A., Quesney, L., Andermann, F. and Horowitz, S. (1982) The role of the limbic system in experiential phenomena of temporal lobe epilepsy. *Annals of Neurology*, **12**, 129–144.

Gloor, P., Salanova, V., Olivier, A. and Quesney, L. (1993) The human dorsal hippocampal commissure. *Brain*, **116**, 1249–1273.

Gold, P.E. (1995) Role of glucose in regulating the brain and cognition. *American Journal of Clinical Nutrition*, **61**(suppl), 987S–995S.

Golding, W. (1955) *The Inheritors*. London: Faber and Faber.

Goleman, D. (1997) Split-brain psychology: fad of the year. *Psychology Today*, **11**, 88–90, 149–150.

Golla, F.L., Hutton, E.L. and Walter, W.G. (1943) The objective study of mental imagery. *Journal of Mental Science*, **89**, 375.

Goodman, E.M., Greenebaum, B. and Marron, M.T. (1995) Effects of electromagnetic fields on molecules and cells. *International Review of Cytology*, **158**, 279–338.

Gorassini, D.R. (1996) Conviction management: lessons from hypnosis research about how self-images of dubious validity can be willfully sustained. In: R.G. Kunzendorf, N.P. Spanos and B.J. Wallace (eds) *Hypnosis and Imagination*. New York: Baywood, pp. 177–198.

Gorassini, D.R. (1997) Strategy selection and hypnotic performance. *Contemporary Hypnosis*, **14**, 37–47.

Gordon, S. (1996) *The Book of Miracles*. London: Headline.

Gorn, G.J. (1982) The effects of music in advertising on choice behavior: a classical conditioning approach. *Journal of Marketing*, **46**, 94–101.

Gould, S.J. (1980) *Ever Since Darwin*. London: Penguin Books.

Gould, S.J. (1981) *The Mismeasure of Man*. New York: W.W. Norton.

Gould, S.J. (1997) Individuality. *The Sciences*, **37**(5), 14–16.

Graceley, R.H., Dubner, R., Deeter, W.R. and Wolskee, P.J. (1985) Clinicians expectations' influence placebo analgesia. *Lancet*, **i**, 43.

Grady, M.P. and Luecke, E.A. (1978) *Education and the Brain* (Fastback 108). Bloomington, IN: Phi Delta Kappa Education Foundation.

Grafton, S.T. (1995) Mapping memory systems in the human brain. *Seminars in the Neurosciences*, **7**, 157–163.

Gray, G. and Flynn, P. (1981) A survey on placebo use in a general hospital. *General Hospital Psychiatry*, **3**, 199–203.

Greenfield, S. (1997) *The Human Brain*. A *Guided Tour*. London: Weidenfeld & Nicolson.

Green, J. (1975) *Thinking and Language*. London: Methuen.

Greenwald, A.G., Spanaberg, E.R., Pratkanis, A.R. and Eskenazi, J. (1991) Double-blind tests of subliminal self-help autotapes. *Psychological Science*, **2**(2), 119–122.

Grossman, S.P. (1967) A *Textbook of Physiological Psychology*. New York: John Wiley, pp. 564–595.

Gruber, H.E. (1980) *Darwin on Man*: A *Psychological Study of Scientific Creativity*, 2nd edn. Chicago: University of Chicago Press.

Gruber, H.E. and Davis, S. (1988) Inching our way up Mount Olympus: the evolving systems approach to creative thinking. In: R.J. Sternberg (ed.) *The Nature of Creativity*: *Contemporary Psychological Perspectives*. Cambridge: Cambridge University Press, pp. 243–270.

Gruner, P. (1990) Scientists to exercise minds at "brain gym". *Evening Standard*, 30 March.

Grünewald-Zuberbier, E., Grünewald, G. and Rasche, A. (1975) Hyperactive behavior and EEG arousal reactions in children. *EEG and Clinical Neurophysiology*, **38**(2), 149–159.

Gruzelier, J. (1988) The neuropsychology of hypnosis. In: M. Heap (ed.) *Hypnosis*: *Current Clinical, Experimental and Forensic Practices*, London: Croom Helm, pp. 68–76.

Guiraud, G.G. and Lile, P.C. (1993) Acupuncture: procédés abusifs de valorisation scientifique. *La Presse Médicale*, **22**, 1249–1250.

Gustin, W.C. (1995) The development of exceptional research mathematicians. In: B.S. Bloom (ed.) *Developing Talent in Young People*. New York: Ballantine Books, pp. 270–331.

Hahnemann, S. (1991) *Organon de la Medicina*. Buenos Aires: Editorial Albatros.

Haier, R.J., Siegel, B.V., Nuechterlein, K.H., Hazlett, E., Wu, J.C., Paek, J., Browning, H.L. and Buchsbaum, M.S. (1988) Cortical glucose metabolic rate correlates of abstract reasoning and attention studied with positron emission tomography. *Intelligence*, **12**, 199–217.

Haier, R.J., Siegel, B.V., MacLachlan, A., Solderling, E., Lottenberg, S. and Buchsbaum, M.S. (1992a) Regional glucose metabolic changes after learning a complex visuospatial/motor task: a positron emission tomographic study. *Brain Research*, **570**, 134–143.

Haier, R.J., Siegel, B.V., Tang, C., Abel, L. and Buchsbaum, M.S. (1992b) Intelligence and changes in regional glucose metabolic rate following learning. *Intelligence*, **16**, 415–426.

Hall, T. (1962) *The Spiritualists*: *The Story of Florence Cook and William Crookes*. Londra (reprinted as: *The Medium and the Scientist*, 1984, Buffalo: Prometheus Books).

Hall, T. (1984) *The Medium and the Scientist*. Buffalo: Prometheus Books.

Hall, T. (1984a) *The Enigma of Daniel Home*. Buffalo: Prometheus Books.

Hamilton, I. (1994) A *Touch more Treason*. Glasgow: Neil Wilson Publishing.

Hammer, J. (1989) Brain boosters: road-testing the new mind machines. In: T. Schultz (ed.) *The Fringes of Reason*. New York: Harmony Books, pp. 130–136.

Hammond, C. (1997) Investigating False Memory for the Unmemorable: a Critique of Experimental Hypnosis and Memory Research. American Society of Clinical Hypnosis International, San Diego, 22–27 June.

Hansson, E. and Rönnbäck, L. (1995) Astrocytes in glutamate neurotransmission. *FASEB Journal*, **9**, 343–350.

Hari, R. and Lounasmaa, O.V. (1989) Recording and interpretation of cerebral magnetic fields. *Science*, **244**, 432–436.

Hari, R. and Salmelin, R. (1997) Human cortical oscillations: a neuromagnetic view through the skull. *Trends in Neurosciences*, **20**, 44–49.

Harmony, T. (1990) Origen del electroencefalograma. *Salud Mental*, **13**(3), 27–34.

Harrington, A. (1985) Nineteenth-century ideas on hemispheric differences and "duality of mind". *Behavioral and Brain Sciences*, **8**, 617–660.

Harrington, A. (1987) *Medicine, Mind, and the Double Brain*. Princeton, NJ: Princeton University Press.

Harrington, A. (ed.) (1997) *The Placebo Effect: An Interdisciplinary Exploration*. Cambridge, Mass: Harvard University Press.

Harris, B. (1985) *Gellerism Revealed*. Calgary: Micky Hades International.

Harris, L.J. (1988) Right-brain training: some reflections on the applications of research on cerebral hemispheric specialization to education. In: D.L. Molfese and S.J. Segalowitz (eds) *Brain Lateralization in Children*. New York: Guilford, pp. 207–235.

Harten, H.-U. (1977) *Física básica para estudiantes de medicina*. Barcelona: Editorial Científico-Médica.

Hartwick, J.J. (1996) *Placebo Effects in Health and Disease: Index of New Information with Authors, Subjects, and References*. Washington: ABBE Publications Associations.

Haug, H., Barmwater, U.J., Eggers, R., Fischer, D., Kuhl, S. and Sasi, N.L. (1983) Anatomical change is aging brain: morphometric analysis of human prosecephalon. *Neuropharmacology*, **21**, 1–12.

Healey, F., Persinger, M.A. and Koren, S.A. (1996) Enhanced hypnotic suggestibility following applications of burst-firing magnetic fields over the right temporoparietal lobes: a replication. *International Journal of Neuroscience*, **87**, 201–207.

Heap, M. and Dryden, W. (1991) *Hypnotherapy: A Handbook*. Milton Keynes: Open University Press.

Heap, R. and W., Publishing Company Limited (1997) Bowden Hall, Marple, Stockport, Cheshire SK6 6NE, UK.

Hebb, D.O. (1949) *Organization of Behavior*. New York: John Wiley.

Hebb, D.O. (1966) A *Textbook of Psychology*. Saunders, Philadelphia.

Heim, A.W. (1970) *The AH 4 Group Test of General Intelligence*. Windsor: NFER-Nelson.

Hembrooke, H.A. and Ceci, S.J. (1997) True and false memories of traumatic childhood events. SARMAC, Toronto.

Henriksen, O. (1994) MR spectroscopy in clinical research. *Acta Radiologica*, **35**, 96–116.

Herman, J.L. and Harvey, M.R. (1993) The false memory debate: social science or social backlash. *Harvard Mental Health Letter*, **9**, April.

Herman, J.L. and Schatzow, E. (1987) Recovery and verification of memories of childhood sexual trauma. *Psychoanalytic Psychology*, **4**, 1–14.

Hermann, N. (1981) The creative brain. *Training and Development Journal*, **35**, 11–16.

Herrnstein, R.J., Nickerson, R.S., de Sanchez, M. and Swets, J.A. (1986) Teaching thinking skills. *American Psychologist*, **41**, 1279–1289.

Hertz, R. (1909) La préeminence de la main droite: etude sur la polarité religieuse. *Revue Philosophique*, **68**, 553–580 (translated in Hertz, 1960).

Hertz, R. (1960) *Death and the Right Hand*. Aberdeen: Cohen & West.

Hewes, G. (1949) Lateral dominance, culture, and writing systems. *Human Biology*, **21**, 233–245.

Highfield, R. (1997) Scientists tap into the secret of sleep. *The Daily Telegraph*, 26 April.

Hilgard, E.R. (1978) States of consciousness in hypnosis: divisions or levels? In: F.H. Frankel and H.S. Zamansky (eds) *Hypnosis at its Bicentennial: Selected Papers*. New York: Plenum, pp. 15–36.

Hilgard, E.R. (1985) Conscious and unconscious processes in hypnosis. In D. Waxman, P.C. Misra, M. Gibson and M.A. Basker (eds) *Modern Trends in Hypnosis*. New York: Plenum, pp. 29–40.

Hilgard, E.R. (1986) *Divided Consciousness: Multiple Controls in Human Thought and Action*. New York: Wiley.

Hilgard, E.R. (1991) A neodissociation interpretation of hypnosis. In: S.J. Lynn and J.W. Rhue (eds) *Theories of Hypnosis: Current Models and Perspectives*. New York: Guilford, pp. 83–104.

Hilgard, E.R. and Hilgard, J.R. (1983) *Hypnosis in the Relief of Pain*. Los Altos, CA: William Kaufmann.

Hilgard, J.R. (1970) *Personality and Hypnosis: A Study of Imaginative Involvement*. Chicago: University of Chicago Press.

Hinke, R.M., Hu, X., Stillman, A.E., Kim, S.-G., Merkle, H., Salmi, R. and Ugurbil, K. (1993) Functional magnetic resonance imaging of Broca's area during internal speech. *Neuroreport*, **4**, 675–678.

Hirsch, H. and Jacobson, M. (1975) The perfectible brain: principles of neural development. In: M. Gazzaniga and C. Blakemore (eds) *Handbook of Psychobiology*. New York: Academic Press, pp. 107–137.

Hirsch, S.R. and Shepherd, S. (1974) *Themes and Variations in European Psychiatry*. Bristol: Wright. Translation of Cotard (1882).

Hirst, W. (1982) The amnesic syndrome: descriptions and explanations. *Psychological Bulletin*, **91**, 435–460.

Holloway, T. (1956) Left-handedness is no handicap. *Psychology*, **20**, 27.

Holmes, D.S. (1984) Meditation and somatic arousal reduction. *American Psychologist*, **39**(1), 1–10.

Holmes, D.S. (1987) The influence of meditation versus rest on physiological arousal: a second examination. In: M.A. West (ed.) *The Psychology of Meditation*. Oxford: Clarendon Press, pp. 81–103.

Holms, A.C. (1969) *The Facts of Psychic Science*. New York.

Hopkins, W.D. (1996) Chimpanzee handedness revisited: 55 years since Finch (1941). *Psychonomic Bulletin and Review*, **3**, 449–457.

Horn, J.L. (1982) The theory of fluid and crystallised intelligence in relation to concepts of cognitive psychology and aging in adulthood. In: F.I.M. Craik and S. Trehub (eds) *Aging and Cognitive Processes*. Boston: Plenum.

Horn, J.L. and Cattell, R.B. (1967) Age differences in fluid and crystallised intelligence. *Acta Psychologica*, **26**, 107–129.

Horwitz, B., McIntosh, A.R., Haxby, J.V. and Grady, C.L. (1995) Network analysis of brain cognitive function using metabolic and blood flow data. *Behavioural Brain Research*, **66**, 187–193.

Houdini, H. (1926) *A Magician Among the Spirits*. Reprint 1972. New York: Arno Press.

Houser, C.R. (1992) Morphological changes in the dentate gyrus in human temporal lobe epilepsy. In: C.E. Ribak, C.M. Gall and L. Moody (eds) *The Dentate Gyrus and its Role in Seizures*. New York: Elsevier, pp. 223–234.

Howe, M.J.A. (1996) *Intelligence*. London: Sage.

Howe, M.J.A. (1997) *IQ in Question: The Truth about Intelligence*. London: Sage.

Howe, M.J.A., Davidson, J.W. and Sloboda, J.A. (1998) Innate talents: reality or myth? *Behavioral and Brain Sciences*, in press.

Hudson, L. (1966) *Countrary Imaginations*. London: Methuen.

Hughes, T. (1992) *Shakespeare and the Goddess of Complete Being*. London: Faber & Faber.

Huppert, F.A. and Piercy, M. (1976) Recognition memory in amnesic patients: effect of temporal context and familiarity of material. *Cortex*, **12**, 3–20.

Huppert, F.A. and Piercy, M. (1978) The role of trace strength in recency and frequency judgements by amnesic and control subjects. *Quarterly Journal of Experimental Psychology*, **30**, 347–354.

Hussein, J.N., Fatoohi, L.J., Al-Dargazelli, S. and Almuchtar, N. (1994) The deliberately caused bodily damage phenomena: mind, body, energy or what? Final part (iii) of a three-part article. *Journal of Alternative and Complementary Medicine*, **12**(11), 25–29.

Huston, P. (1995) China, Chi and chicanery. Examining traditional Chinese medicine and Chi theory. *The Skeptical Inquirer*, **19**, 38–42, 58.

Hutchinson, M. (1994) *Megabrain Power. Transform your Life with Mind Machines and Brain Nutrients*. New York: Hyperion.

Huxley, A. (1972) *Brave New World*. Harmondsworth, Middlesex: Penguin Books Ltd.

Hyman, R. (1977) Cold reading: how to convince strangers that you know all about them. *The Zetetic*, **1**, 18–37.

Hyman, R. (1992) *The Elusive Quarry: A Scientific Appraisal of Psychical Research*. Amherst, NY: Prometheus Books.

Hyman, I., Husband, T. and Billings, F. (1995) False memories of childhood experiences. *Applied Cognitive Psychology*, **9**, 181–197.

Jackson, J.H. (1864) Clinical remarks on cases of defects of expression (by words, writing, signs, etc) in diseases of the nervous system. *Lancet*, **ii**, 604.

Jackson, J. (1905) *Ambidexterity or Two-handedness and Two-brainedness*. London: Kegan Paul, Trench & Trubner.

Jacobs, S. and Gotthelf, C. (1986) Effects of hypnosis on physical and athletic performance. In: F.A. DePiano and H.C. Salzberg (eds) *Clinical Applications of Hypnosis*. Norwood, NJ: Ablex.

James, W. (1890) *The Principles of Psychology*. New York: Henry Holt.

Jamison, K.R. (1995) Manic-depressive illness and creativity. *Scientific American*, **272**, 46–51.

Jarvik, L.F. (1983) Age is in – Is the wit out? In: D. Samuel, S. Algeri, S. Gershon, V.E. Grimm and G. Toffano (eds) *Aging of the Brain*. New York: Raven Press.

Jensen, A.R. (1980) Chronometric analysis of mental ability. *Journal of Social and Biological Structures*, **3**, 181–224.

Jensen, A.R. (1985) The nature of the black–white difference on various psychometric tests: Spearman's hypothesis. *Behavioural and Brain Sciences*, **8**, 193–219.

Jensen, A.R. (1987) Individual differences in the Hick paradigm. In: P.A. Vernon (ed.) *Speed of Information Processing and Intelligence*. Norwood, NJ: Ablex.

Jerison, H. (1982) The evolution of biological intelligence. In: R.J. Sternberg (ed.) *Handbook of Human Intelligence*. Cambridge UK: Cambridge University Press.

Johnson, R.F.Q. (1989) Hypnosis, suggestion and dermatological changes: a consideration of the production and diminution of dermatological entities. In: N.P. Spanos and J.F. Chaves (eds) *Hypnosis: The Cognitive-Behavioral Perspective*. Buffalo, NY: Prometheus, pp. 297–312.

Johnson, M. and Din, (1997) Ethnocultural differences in the analgesic effects of placebo. *Complementary Therapies in Medicine*, **5**, 74–79.

Johnson, M.K., Hashroudi, S. and Lindsay, D.S. (1993) Source monitoring. *Psychological Bulletin*, **114**, 3–28.

Johnson, M.K., O'Connor, M. and Cantor, J. (1997) Confabulation, memory deficits, and frontal dysfunction. *Brain and Cognition*, **34**, 189–206.

Johnson, C. and Persinger, M. (1994) The sensed presence may be facilitated by interhemispheric intercalation: relative efficacy of the mind's eye, Hemi-Sync tape, and bilateral temporal magnetic field stimulation. *Perceptual and Motor Skills*, **79**, 351–354.

Jones, E. (1961) *The Life and Work of Sigmund Freud*. Edited by L. Trilling and S. Marcus. London: Hogarth.

Jones, G.V. (1990) Misremembering a common object: when left is not right. *Memory and Cognition*, **18**, 174–182.

Jones, H.E. and Conrad, H. (1933) The growth and decline of intelligence: a study of a homogenous group between the ages of ten and sixty. *Genetic Psychological Monographs*, **13**, 223–298.

Jones and Flynn (1989) Methodological and theoretical considerations in the study of "hypnotic" effects in perception. In: N.P. Spanos and J.F. Chaves (eds) *Hypnosis: The Cognitive Behavioral Perspective*. Buffalo, NY: Prometheus, pp. 149–174.

Jones, W.H. and Russell, D. (1980) The selective processing of belief disconfirming information. *European Journal of Social Psychology*, **10**, 309–312.

Jones, B. and Spanos, N.P. (1982) Suggestions for altered auditory sensitivity, the negative subject effect and hypnotic susceptibility: a signal detection analysis. *Journal of Personality and Social Psychology*, **43**, 637–647.

Joseph, A.B. (1986) Cotard's syndrome with coexistent Capgras' syndrome, syndrome of subjective doubles, and palinopsia. *Journal of Clinical Psychiatry*, **47**, 605–606.

Joseph, R. (1992) *The Right Brain and the Unconscious: Discovering the Stranger Within*. New York: Plenum.

Jung, C. (1971) *Memories, Dreams and Reflections*. London: Collins.

Kalat, J.W. (1995) *Biological Psychology*, 5th edn. Pacific Grove, CA: Brooks-Cole.

Kamiya, J. (1969) Operant control of the EEG alpha rhythm and some of its reported effects on consciousness. In: C. Tart (ed.) *Altered States of Consciousness*. New York: Anchor Books, pp. 519–529.

Kandel, E.R., Schwartz, J.H. and Jessell, T.M. (eds) (1991) *Principles of Neural Science*, 3rd edn. Norwalk: Appleton & Lange.

Kaney, S. and Bentall, R.P. (1989) Persecutory delusions and attributional style. *British Journal of Medical Psychology*, **62**, 191–198.

Kantor, D. (1980) Critical identity image. In: J.K. Pearce and L.J. Friedman (eds) *Family Therapy: Combining Psychodynamic and Family Systems Approaches*. New York: Grune & Stratton, pp. 137–167.

Kapur, N. and Coughlan, A.K. (1980) Confabulation and frontal lobe dysfunction. *Journal of Neurology, Neurosurgery and Psychiatry*, **43**, 461–643.

Karmiloff-Smith, A. (1993) Is creativity domain-specific or domain-general? Clues from normal and abnormal development. *Artificial Intelligence and Simulation of Behavior Quarterly*, August (**84**), 35–40.

Kasamatsu, J. and Hirai, T. (1966) An electroencephalographic study on the Zen meditation (Zazen). *Folio Psychiatrica et Neurologica Japonica*, **20**, 315–336.

Kienle, G.S. (1995) *Der sogenanute Plazeboeffekt*. Stuttgart: Schattauer.

Kihlstrom, J.F. and Wilson, L. (1984) Temporal organization of recall during posthypnotic amnesia. *Journal of Abnormal Psychology*, **93**, 200–208.

Kihlstrom, J.F., Evans, F.J., Orne, E.C. and Orne, M.T. (1980) Attempting to breach posthypnotic amnesia. *Journal of Abnormal Psychology*, **89**, 603–616.

Kim, S.-G., Ashe, J., Hendrich, K., Ellerman, J.M., Ugurbil, K. and Georgopoulos, A.P. (1993) Functional magnetic resonance imaging of motor cortex: hemispheric asymmetry and handedness. *Science*, **261**, 615–617.

Kinnunen, T., Zamansky, H.S. and Block, M. (1994) Is the hypnotized subject lying? *Journal of Abnormal Psychology*, **2**, 184–191.

Kipling, R. (1901) Kim. London: Macmillan.

Kirsch, I. (1991) The social learning theory of hypnosis. In: S.J. Lynn and J.W. Rhue (eds) Theories of Hypnosis: Current Models and Perspectives. New York: Guilford, pp. 439–466.

Kirsch, I., Montgomery, G. and Sapirstein, G. (1995) Hypnosis as an adjunct to cognitive-behavioural therapy: a meta-analysis. Journal of Consulting and Clinical Psychology, 63, 214–220.

Kirsch, I., Mobayed, C.P., Council, J.R. and Kenny, D.A. (1992) Expert judgments of hypnosis from subjective state reports. Journal of Abnormal Psychology, 101, 657–662.

Kleeimeier, R.W. (1962) Intellectual changes in the senium. Proceedings of the Social Statistics Section of the American Statistical Association, 290–295.

Klippel, M. (1898) La non-equivalence des deux hémisphères cérébraux. Revue de la Psychiatrie, 52–57.

Knox, J.V., Morgan, A.H. and Hilgard, E.R. (1974) Pain and suffering in ischemia: the paradox of hypnotically suggested anesthesia as contradicted by reports from the "hidden-observer". Archives of General Psychiatry, 30, 840–847.

Koestler, A. (1964) The Act of Creation. London: Hutchinson.

Kohn, A. (1986) False Prophets. Oxford: Basil Blackwell Ltd.

Kolata, G. (1997) Clone. The Road to Dolly and the Path Ahead. London: Allen Lane, The Penguin Press.

Kolb, B. and Whishaw, I.Q. (1996) Fundamentals of Human Neuropsychology, 4th edn. New York: W.H. Freeman.

Kopelman, M.D. (1985) Rates of forgetting in Alzheimer-type dementia and Korsakoff's syndrome. Neuropsychologia, 23, 623–638.

Kopelman, M.D. (1987) Two types of confabulation. Journal of Neurology, Neurosurgery and Psychiatry, 50, 1482–1487.

Kopelman, M.D. (1995) The Korsakoff syndrome. British Journal of Psychiatry, 166, 154–173.

Kopelman, M.D., Ng, N. and Van den Boucke, O. (1997) Confabulation extending across episodic memory, personal and general semantic memory. Cognitive Neuropsychology, 14, 683–712.

Korsakoff, S.S. (1889) Psychic disorder in conjunction with peripheral neuritis (translated by M. Victor and P.I. Yakovlev, 1955). Neurology, 5, 394–406.

Krauss, L. (1997) The Physics of Star Trek. New York: Harper Collins.

Krech, D. (1962) Cortical localization of function. In: L. Postman (ed.) Psychology in the Making: Histories of Selected Research Problems. New York: Alfred A. Knopf, pp. 31–72.

Krivacska, J. (1993) Antisexualism in child sexual abuse prevention programs – Good touch, bad touch . . . don't touch? Issues in Child Abuse Accusations, 5, 78–82.

Kuhn, T.S. (1970) The Structure of Scientific Revolutions. Chicago: University of Chicago Press.

Kulikov, V.N. (1964) The question of hypnopaedia. Problems in Psychology, 2, 87–97.

Kunzendorf, R.G. (1990) Post-hypnotic amnesia: dissociation of self concept or self-consciousness? Imagination, Cognition and Personality, 9, 321–334.

Kuschinsky, W. (1987) Coupling of function, metabolism and blood flow in the brain. News in Physiological Sciences, 2, 217–220.

Lachman, R., Lachman, J.L. and Taylor, D.W. (1982) Re-allocation of mental resources over the productive lifespan: assumptions and techniques. In: F.I.M. Craik and S. Trehub (eds) Aging and Cognitive Processes. New York: Plenum Press.

Landau, W.M. (1988) Clinical neuromythology. Neurology, 38, 1496–1499, 1799–1801.

Landau, W.M. (1989) Clinical neuromythology. Neurology, 39, 725–730.

Landau, W.M. (1990) Clinical neuromythology. Neurology, 40, 733–740, 884–886, 1337–1339.

Landau, W.M. and Nelson, D.A. (1996) Clinical neuromythology XV. Feinting science. Neurology, 46, 609–618.

Lasagna, L., Mosteller, F., von Felsinger, J.M. and Beecher, H.K. (1954) A study of the placebo response. American Journal of Medicine, 16, 770–779.

Latour, B. (1998) From the world of science to the world of research. Science, 280, 208–209.

Laurence, J.R. and Perry, C.W. (1988) Hypnosis, Will and Memory: A Psycho-legal History. New York: Guilford.

LeBars, P., Katz, M., Berman, N., Itil, T., Freedman, A. and Schatzberg, A. (1997) A placebo-controlled, double blind, randomized trial of and extract of Ginko Biloba for dementia. Journal of the American Medical Association, 278(16), 1327–1332.

Le Doux, J.E., Wilson, D.J. and Gazzaniga, M.S. (1977) Manipulo-spatial aspects of cerebral lateralization: clues to the origin of lateralization. Neuropsychologia, 15, 743–750.

LeMay, M. (1976) Morphological cerebral asymmetries of modern man, fossil man, and nonhuman primates. *Annals of the New York Academy of Sciences*, **280**, 349–366.

Lehmann, H.C. (1953) *Age and Achievement*. Princeton, NJ: Princeton University Press.

Lehmann, H.C. (1954) Men's creative production rate at different ages and in different countries. *Scientific Monthly*, **78**, 321–326.

Lehmann, H.C. (1957) The chemist's most creative years. *Science*, **127**, 1213–1222.

Leng, N.R.C. and Parkin, A.J. (1988) Double dissociation of frontal dysfunction in organic amnesia. *British Journal of Clinical Psychology*, **27**, 359–362.

LeShan, L. (1942) The breaking of habit by suggestion during sleep. *Journal of Abnormal and Social Psychology*, **37**, 406–408.

Letzelter, M., Jungermann, C. and Frietag, W. (1986) Schwimmleistungen im Alter. *Zeitschrift fur Gerontologie*, **19**, 389–395.

Leuba, C. and Bateman, D. (1952) Learning during sleep. *American Journal of Psychology*, **65**, 301–302.

Levinson, B.W. (1965) States of awareness during general anaesthesia. *British Journal of Anaesthesia*, **37**, 544–550.

Levinthal, F., Macagno, E. and Levinthal, C. (1976) Anatomy and development of identified cells in isogenic organisms. *Cold Spring Harbor Symposia of Quantitative Biology*, **40**, 321–331.

Lévi-Strauss, C. (1970) *The Raw and The Cooked*. London: Cape.

Levitan, I.B. and Kaczmarek, L.K. (1997) *The Neuron. Cell and Molecular Biology*. New York: Oxford University Press.

Levitt, R.E., Aronoff, G., Morgan, C.D., Overley, T.M. and Parrish, M.J. (1975) Testing the coercive power of hypnosis: committing objectionable acts. *International Journal of Clinical and Experimental Hypnosis*, **23**, 59–67.

Lewin, R. (1980) Is your brain really necessary? *Science*, **210**, 1232–1234.

Lewontin, R.C. (1997) The confusion over cloning. *New York Review of Books*, **XLIV**(16), 18–23.

Liddle, P.F. (1996) Functional imaging – schizophrenia. *British Medical Bulletin*, **52**, 486–494.

LifeTools (1997) LifeTools, Freepost SK1852, Macclesfield SK10 2YE, also on the Web at www.lifetools.com.

Lindenberger, U. and Baltes, P.B. (1994) Sensory functioning and intelligence in old age: a strong connection. *Psychology and Aging*, **9**, 339–355.

Llinas, R. and Ribary, U. (1993) Coherent 40–Hz oscillation characterizes dream state in humans. *Proceedings of the National Academy of Sciences of the USA*, **90**, 2078–2081.

Loftus, E.F. (1993) Desperately seeking memories of the first few years of childhood: the reality of early memories. *Journal of Experimental Psychology: General*, **122**, 274–277.

Loftus, E. (1996) *Eyewitness Testimony*. Cambridge, Mass: Harvard University Press.

Loftus, E.F. and Ketcham, K. (1991) *Witness for the Defense*. New York: St Martin's Press.

Loftus, E.F. and Pickrell, J.E. (1995) The formation of false memories. *Psychiatric Annals*, **25**, 720–725.

Lotka, A.J. (1926) The frequency distribution of scientific productivity. *Journal of the Washington Academy of Sciences*, **16**, 317–323.

Ludwig, A.M. (1992) Creative achievement and psychopathology: comparison among professions. *Journal of Psychotherapy*, **46**, 330–356.

Lusted, H.S. and Knapp, R.B. (1996) Controlling computers with neural signals. *Scientific American*, **275**(4), 58–63.

Luys, J.B. (1879) Etudes sur le dédoublement des operations cérébrales et sur le rôle isolé de chaque hémisphère dans les phénomènes de la pathologie mentale. *Bulletins de l'Académie de Médecine*, 2ème série, **8**, 516–534, 547–565.

Luys, J.B. (1881) Recherches nouvelles sur les hémiplégies émotives. *Encéphale*, **1**, 644–646.

Lynn, S.J. (1992) A non-state view of hypnotic involuntariness. *Contemporary Hypnosis*, **9**, 21–27.

Lynn, S.J. and Rhue, J.W. (1991a) An integrative model of hypnosis. In: S.J. Lynn and J.W. Rhue (eds) *Theories of Hypnosis: Current Models and Perspectives*. New York: Guildford, pp. 397–438.

Lynn, S.J. and Rhue, J.W. (eds) (1991b) *Theories of Hypnosis: Current Models and Perspectives*. New York: Guilford.

Lynn, S.J., Rhue, J.W. and Weekes, J.R. (1990) Hypnotic involuntariness: a social cognitive analysis. *Psychological Review*, **97**, 169–184.

Macagno, E.R., Lopresti, V. and Levinthal, C. (1973) Structure and development of neuronal connections in isogenic organisms: variations and similarities in the optic system of *Daphnia magna*. *Proceedings of the National Academy of Sciences*, **70**, 57–61.

MacKinnon, D.Q. (1962) The personality correlates of creativity: a study of American architects. In: *Proceedings of the 14th Congress of Applied Psychology*, Vol. 2. Copenhagen: Munksgaard, pp. 11–39, Excerpts reprinted in P.E. Vernon (ed.) (1970) *Creativity*, Harmondsworth: Penguin Books.

Macklis, R.M. (1993) Magnetic healing, quackery, and the debate about the health effects of electromagnetic fields. *Annals of Internal Medicine*, **118**, 376–383.

Madsen, P.L., Holm, S., Herning, M. and Lassen, N.A. (1993) Average blood flow and oxygen uptake in the human brain during resting wakefulness: a critical appraisal of the Kety–Schmidt technique. *Journal of Cerebral Blood Flow and Metabolism*, **13**, 646–655.

Magistretti, P.J. and Pellerin, L. (1996) Cellular bases of brain energy metabolism and their relevance to functional brain imaging: evidence for a prominent role of astrocytes. *Cerebral Cortex*, **6**, 50–61.

Maller, J.B. and Lundeen, G.E. (1932) Sources of superstitious beliefs. *Journal of Education Research*, **26**, 321–343.

Malone, K. and Malone, J.P. (1992) Remarkable resolution of an uncommon psychosyndrome: epilepsy-induced remission of Cotard's syndrome. *Irish Journal of Psychological Medicine*, **9**, 53–54.

Malott, J.M. (1984) Active-alert hypnosis: replication and extension of previous research. *Journal of Abnormal Psychology*, **93**, 246–249.

Maquet, P. (1997) Positron emission tomography studies of sleep and sleep disorders. *Journal of Neurology*, **244** (suppl. 1), S23–S28.

Maquet, P., Degueldre, C., Delfiore, G., Aerts, J., Peters, J-M., Luxen, A. and Franck, G. (1997) Functional neuroanatomy of human slow wave sleep. *Journal of Neuroscience*, **17**(8), 2807.

Marden, O.S. (1909) *Peace, Power, and Plenty*. New York: Thomas Y. Crowell.

Marden, O.S. (1917) *How to Get What You Want*. New York: Thomas Y. Crowell.

Marg, E., Adams, J.E. and Rutkin, B. (1968) Receptive fields of cells in the human visual cortex. *Experientia*, **24**, 348–350.

Marie, P. (1922) Existe-t-il dans le cerveau humain des centres innés ou préformés de language? *La Press Médicale*, **17**, 117–181.

Marks, D.F. (1986) Investigating the paranormal. *Nature*, **320**, 119–124.

Marks, D. and Kamman, R. (1980) *The Psychology of the Psychic*. Buffalo: Prometheus Books.

Marshall, J. (1997) Everyday tales of ordinary madness. *Nature*, **389**, 29.

Marshall, J.C. and Halligan, P.W. (1988) Blindsight and insight in visuo-spatial neglect. *Nature*, **336**, 766–767.

Martin, J.H. (1991) Coding and processing of sensory information. In: E.R. Kandel, J.H. Schwartz and T.M. Jessell (eds) *Principles of Neural Science*, 3rd edn. Norwalk: Appleton & Lange, pp. 329–340.

Mayes, A.R., Meudell, P.R. and Pickering, A. (1985) Is organic amnesia caused by a selective deficit in remembering contextual information? *Cortex*, **21**, 167–202.

Mazziotta, J.C., Valentino, D., Grafton, S., Bookstein, F., Pelizzari, C., Chen, G. and Toga, A.W. (1991) Relating structure to function *in vivo* with tomographic imaging. *Ciba Foundation Symposium*, **163**, 93–112.

McCann, T.E. and Sheehan, P.W. (1987) The breaching of pseudomemory under hypnotic instruction: implications for original memory retrieval. *British Journal of Experimental and Clinical Hypnosis*, **4**, 101–108.

McCarthy, G., Puce, A., Constable, R.T., Krystal, J.H., Gore, J.C. and Goldman-Rakic, P. (1996) Activation of human prefrontal cortex during spatial and nonspatial working memory tasks measured by functional MRI. *Cerebral Cortex*, **6**, 600–611.

McClearn, G.E., Johansson, B., Berg, S., Pedersen, N.L., Aher, F., Petrill, S.A. and Plomin, R. (1997) Substantial genetic influence on cognitive abilities in twins 80 or more years old. *Science*, **276**, 1560–1563.

McIntyre, T. (1997) ebom.com.au/thom/drmmach.html

McLelland, D.C. (1962) On the dynamics of creative physical scientists. In: H.E. Gruber, G. Teller and M. Wertheimes (eds) *Contemporary Approaches to Creative Thinking*. New York: Atherton, pp. 141–174.

McManus, I.C. (1985) Handedness, language dominance and aphasia: a genetic model. *Psychological Medicine*, **8** (Suppl.) 1–40.

Meadow, A., Parnes, S.J. and Reese, H. (1959) Influence of brainstorming instruction and problem sequence on a creative problem solving test. *Journal of Applied Psychology*, **43**, 413–416.

Melton, J.G. (1988) A history of the New Age. In: R. Basil (ed.) *Not Necessarily the New Age: Critical Essays*. Amherst, NY: Prometheus Books, pp. 35–54.

Melzack, R. (1989) Phantom limbs, the self and the brain: the D.O. Hebb Memorial Lecture. *Canadian Psychology*, **30**(1), 1–16.

Merikle, P.M. and Skanes, H. (1992) Subliminal self-help audio tapes: a search for placebo effects. *Journal of Applied Psychology*, **77**, 772–776.

Merriam-Webster's Collegiate Dictionary (1993) 10th edn. Springfield: Merriam-Webster, Inc.

Meyer, D. (1965) *The Positive Thinkers: A Study of the American Quest for Health, Wealth and Personal Power from Mary Baker Eddy to Norman Vincent Peale*. Garden City, New York: Doubleday Anchor.

Michaels, R.R., Huber, M.J. and McCann, D.S. (1976) Evaluation of transcendental meditation as a method of reducing stress. *Science*, **192**, 1242–1244.

Mihill, C. (1996) Hairy men "are more intelligent". *The Guardian*, 12 December.

Miller, K. (1997) Star struck. LIFE, July, 38–52.

Miller, L. (1995) Freudian Flame Wars. *Salon Magazine*, 2 December. http://www.salon1999.com/02dec1995/reviews/freud.html

Miller, M.E. and Bowers, K.S. (1993) Hypnotic analgesia: dissociated experience or dissociated control? *Journal of Abnormal Psychology*, **102**, 29–38.

Milner, B. (1971) Interhemispheric differences in the localisation of psychological processes in man. *British Medical Bulletin*, **27**, 272–277.

Milner, B. (1975) Psychological aspects of focal epilepsy and its neurosurgical management. *Advances in Neurology*, **8**, 299–321.

Milton, R. (1994) *Forbidden Science*. London: Fourth Estate Limited.

Minsky, M. (1987) *The Society of Mind*. London: Heinemann.

Mintzberg, H. (1976) Planning on the left side and managing on the right. *Harvard Business Review*, **54**, 49–58.

Mitroff, I.I. (1974) *The Subjective Side of Science*. Amsterdam: Elsevier.

Mittenberg, W., Seidenberg, M., O'Leary, D.S. and DiGuilio, D. (1989) Changes in cerebral functioning associated with normal ageing. *Journal of Clinical and Experimental Neuropsychology*, **11**(6), 918–932.

Mittwoch, U. (1977) To be right is to be born male. *New Scientist*, **73**, 74–76.

Mondadori, C. (1994) In search of the mechanisms of action of the nootropics: new insights and potential clinical implications. *Life Sciences*, **55**(25/26), 2171–2178.

Moody, R.A. (1975) *Life after Life*. New York: Bantam.

Moore, T.E. (1982) Subliminal advertising: what you see is what you get. *Journal of Marketing*, **46**, 38–47.

Moore, T.E. (1995) Subliminal self-help auditory tapes: an empirical test to perceptual consequences. *Canadian Journal of Behavioral Science*, **27**, 9–20.

Morse, C.K. (1993) Does variability increase with age? An archival study of cognitive measures. *Psychology and Aging*, **8**, 156–164.

Morton, J. (1967) A singular lack of incidental learning. *Nature*, **215**(5097), 203–204.

Mulholland, J. (1979) *Beware Familiar Spirits*. New York: Charles Scribner's Sons.

Mulholland, T. and Peper, E. (1971) Occipital alpha and accommodative vergence, pursuit tracking, and fast eye movements. *Psychophysiology*, **8**, 556–575.

Murphy, J. (1985) *Las sorprendentes leyes de la fuerza del pensamiento cósmico*. México D.F.: Diana.

Murray, G.J., Cross, H.J. and Whipple, J. (1992) Hypnotically created pseudomemories: further investigation into the "memory distortion or response bias" question. *Journal of Abnormal Psychology*, **101**, 75–77.

Murray, H.G. and Denny, J.P. (1969) Interaction of ability level and interpolated activity in human problem solving. *Psychological Reports*, **24**, 271–276.

Myslobodsky, M.S. (ed.) (1997) *The Mythomanias: The Nature of Perception and Self-deception*. Mahwah, New Jersey: LEA.

Myss, C. (1997) www.powersource.com/myss/caroline.htm.

Nash, M.R. (1991) Hypnosis as a special case of psychological regression. In: S.J. Lynn and J.W. Rhue (eds) *Theories of Hypnosis: Current Models and Perspectives*. New York: Guilford, pp. 171–198.

Needham, R. (1973) *Right and Left: Essays on Dual Symbolic Classification*. Chicago: University of Chicago Press.

Neher, A. (1961) Auditory driving observed with scalp electrodes in normal subjects. EEG *and Clinical Neurophysiology*, **13**, 449–451.

Neher, A. (1962) A physiological explanation of unusual behavior in ceremonies involving drums. *Human Biology*, **34**, 151–160.

Neher, A. (1990) *The Psychology of Transcendence*. New York: Dover Publications.

Nehlig, A. (1993) Imaging and ontogeny of brain metabolism. *Baillière's Clinical Endocrinology and Metabolism*, **7**, 627–642.

Nehlig, A. (1997) Cerebral energy metabolism, glucose transport and blood flow: changes with maturation and adaptation to hypoglycemia. *Diabetes and Metabolism* (Paris), **23**, 18–29.

Neisser, U. (1984) Toward an ecologically oriented cognitive science. In: T.M. Shlechter and M.P. Toglia (eds) *New Directions in Cognitive Science*. Norwood, NJ: Ablee, pp. 17–32.

Neisser, U. (1993) Memory with a grain of salt. Conference on "Memory and Reality", Valley Forge, PA.

Neisser, U. and Harsch, N. (1992) Phantom flashbulbs: false recollections of hearing the news about Challenger. In: E. Winograd, and U. Neisser (eds) *Affect on Accuracy in Recall*. Cambridge: Cambridge University Press, pp. 9–31.

New Age Electronics (1997) 42 Greenwood, Tweedmouth, Berwick-upon-Tweed, TD15 2EB, UK.

Newman, L.S. and Baumeister, R.F. (1996) Toward an explanation of the UFO abduction phenomenon: hypnotic elaboration, extraterrestrial sadomasochism, and spurious memories. *Psychological Inquiry*, **7**, 99–126.

Ney, T. (1988) Expressing your emotions and controlling feelings. In: A. Gale (ed.) *The Polygraph Test: Lies, Truth and Science*. London: Sage.

NHI Conference on Placebo, 1996.

Nicholls, D.G. (1993) The glutamatergic nerve terminal. *European Journal of Biochemistry*, **212**, 613–631.

Nicholson, C.D. (1990) Pharmacology of nootropics and metabolically active compounds in relation to their use in dementia. *Psychopharmacology*, **101**, 147–159.

Nichell, J. (1993) *Looking for a Miracle: Weeping Icons, Relics, Stigmata, Visions and Healing Cures*. Buffalo: Prometheus Books.

Nickerson, R.S. and Adams, M.J. (1979) Long-term memory for a common object. *Cognitive Psychology*, **11**, 287–307.

Nogrady, H., McConkey, K.M., Laurence, J.R. and Perry, C. (1983) Dissociation, duality, and demand characteristics in hypnosis. *Journal of Abnormal Psychology*, **92**, 223–235.

Nordberg, A. (1996) Application of PET in dementia disorders. *Acta Neurologica Scandinavica Suppl*, **168**, 71–76.

Oakley, D.A. and Plotkin, H.C. (eds) (1979) *Brain, Behaviour, and Evolution*. London: Methuen.

O'Brien, R.M. and Rabuck, S.J. (1976) Experimentally produced self-repugnant behavior as a function of hypnosis and waking suggestion: a pilot study. *American Journal of Clinical Hypnosis*, **18**, 272–276.

Office of Population Censuses and Surveys (1980) *Classification of Occupations*. London: HMSO.

Ogawa, S., Menon, R.S., Tank, D.W., Kim, S.-G., Merkle, H., Ellermann, J.M. and Ugurbil, K. (1993) Functional brain mapping by blood oxygenation level-dependent contrast magnetic resonance imaging. A comparison of signal characteristics with a biophysical model. *Biophysical Journal*, **64**, 803–812.

Ogden, J.A. (1988) Language and memory functions after long recovery periods in left-hemispherectomized subjects. *Neuropsychologia*, **26**, 645–659.

Ogden, J.A. (1989) Visuospatial and other "right-hemispheric" functions after long recovery periods in left-hemispherectomized subjects. *Neuropsychologia*, **27**, 765–776.

Ogles, R.M. (1987) Cultivation analysis: theory, methodology, and current research on television-influenced constructions of social reality. *Mass. Comm. Review*, **14**, 43–53.

Oldfield, S. (1995) A smart family pet to set your watch by. *The Daily Mail*, 16 January.

Oldfield, H. and Coghill, R. (1994) *The Dark Side of The Brain – Major Discoveries in the Use of Kirlian Photography and Electro-Crystal Therapy*. Shaftesbury: Element Books.

Olivotto, M., Arcangeli, A., Carlà, M. and Wanke, E. (1996) Electric fields at the plasma membrane level: a neglected element in the mechanisms of cell signalling. *BioEssays*, **18**, 495–504.

Olton, R.M. and Johnson, D.M. (1976) Mechanisms of incubation in creative problem solving. *American Journal of Psychology*, **7**, 617–630.

Oppenheim, J.S., Skerry, J.E., Tramo, M.J. and Gazzaniga, M.S. (1989) Magnetic resonance imaging of the corpus callosum in monozygotic twins. *Annals of Neurology*, **26**, 100–104.

Orne, M.T. (1959) The nature of hypnosis: artifact and essence. *Journal of Abnormal Psychology*, **58**, 277–299.

Orne, M.T. (1962) On the social psychology of the psychological experiment: with particular reference to demand characteristics and their implications. *American Psychologist*, **17**, 776–783.

Orne, M.T. (1970) Hypnosis, motivation and the ecological validity of the psychological experiment. In: W.J. Arnold and M.M. Page (eds) *Nebraska Symposium on Motivation*. Lincoln, Nebraska: Nebraska Press, pp. 187–265.

Orne, M.T. (1971) The simulation of hypnosis: why, how, and what it means. *International Journal of Clinical and Experimental Hypnosis*, **19**, 183–210.

Orne, M.T. (1979) On the simulating subject as quasi-control group in hypnosis research: what, why and how? In: E. Fromm and R.E. Shor (eds) *Hypnosis: Research Developments and Perspectives*. New York: Aldine, pp. 399–443.

Orne, M.T. and Evans, F.J. (1965) Social control in the psychological experiment: antisocial behaviour and hypnosis. *Journal of Personality and Social Psychology*, **1**, 189–200.

Orne, M.T. and Paskewitz, D.A. (1974) Aversive situational effects on alpha feedback training. *Science*, **186**, 458–460.

Orne, M.T., Sheehan, P.W. and Evans, F.J. (1968) Occurrence of posthypnotic behavior outside the experimental setting. *Journal of Personality and Social Psychology*, **9**, 189–196.

Ornstein, R.E. (1972) *The Psychology of Consciousness*. San Francisco: Freeman.

Osborn, A.F. (1953) *Applied Imagination*. New York: Scribners.

Oster, G. (1973) Auditory beats in the brain. *Scientific American*, **229**, 94–102.

Ostrander, S. and Schroeder, L. (1970) *Psychic Discoveries Behind the Iron Curtain*. Englewood Cliffs: Prentice-Hall.

Ostrander, S. and Schroeder, L. (1994) *Superlearning 2000*. New York: Delacorte Press.

Owen, O.E. (1988) Resting metabolic requirements of men and women. *Mayo Clinic Proceedings*, **63**, 503–510.

Pallis, C. and Harley, L.H. (1996) *ABC of Brain Stem Death*. London: BMJ Publishing Group.

Palomar, J. (1991) Viaje al centro del cerebro. *Clarín Revista*, 10 November, 12.

Paredes, J.A. and Hepburn, M.J. (1976) The split brain and the culture-and-cognition paradox. *Current Anthropology*, **17**, 121–127.

Park, R.L. (1997) Alternative medicine and the laws of physics. *The Skeptical Inquirer*, **21**(5), 24–28.

Parkin, A.J., Montaldi, D., Leng, N.R.C., et al (1990) Contextual cueing effects in the remote memory of Korsakoff patients and normal subjects. *Quarterly Journal of Experimental Psychology*, **42A**, 585–596.

Parnes, S.J. and Meadow, A. (1963) Development of individual creative talent. In: C.W. Taylor and F. Barron (eds) *Scientific Creativity: Its Recognition and Development*. New York: John Wiley, pp. 198–212.

Pasche, B., Erman, M., Hayduk, R., Mitler, M., Reite, M., Higgs, L., Kuster, N., Rossel, C., Dafni, U., Amato, D., Barbault, A. and Lebet, J-P. (1997) Effects of low energy emission therapy in chronic psychophysiological insomnia. *Sleep*, **9**(4), 327.

Passingham, R.E. (1982) *The Human Primate*. San Francisco: Freeman.

Patrick, C. (1935) Creative thought in poets. *Archives of Psychology*, **26**, 73.

Patrick, C. (1937) Creative thought in artists. *Journal of Psychology*, **4**, 35–73.

Pattie, F.A. (1935) A report of attempts to produce uniocular blindness by hypnotic suggestion. *British Journal of Medical Psychology*, **15**, 230–241.

Paulos, J.A. (1988) *Innumeracy*. London: Penguin Books.

Paulos, J.A. (1996) *A Mathematician Reads the Newspaper*. London: Penguin Books.

Payne, D.G., Elie, C.J., Blackwell, J. and Neuschatz, J.S. (1996) Memory illusions: recalling, recognizing, and recollecting events that never occurred. *Journal of Memory and Language*, **35**, 261–285.

Pellerin, L. and Magistretti, P.J. (1996) Excitatory amino acids stimulate aerobic glycolysis in astrocytes via an activation of the Na^+/K^+ ATPase. *Developmental Neuroscience*, **18**, 336–342.

Penfield, W. and Perot, P. (1963) The brain's record of auditory and visual experience: a final summary and discussion. *Brain*, **86**(4), 595–696.

Pennisi, E. (1997) The lamb that roared. *Science*, **278**, 2038–2039.

Perlini, A.H. and Spanos, N.P. (1991) EEG alpha methodologies and hypnotizability: a critical review. *Psychophysiology*, **28**(5), 511–530.

Perlini, A.H., Spanos, N.P. and Jones, W. (1996) Hypnotic negative hallucinations: a review of subjective, behavioral and physiological methods. In: R.G. Kunzendorf, N.P. Spanos and B.J. Wallace (eds) *Hypnosis and Imagination*. New York: Baywood, pp. 199–222.

Perry (1992) Countering the stereotypes of hypnosis. *Contemporary Hypnosis*, **9**, 150.

Persinger, M.A. (1974) *The Paranormal: Part I. The Patterns*. New York: MSS Information.

Persinger, M.A. (1985) Death anxiety as a semantic conditioned suppression paradigm. *Perceptual and Motor Skills*, **60**, 827–830.

Persinger, M.A. (1987) *The Neuropsychological Bases of God Experiences*. New York: Praeger Press.

Persinger, M.A. (1993a) Vectorial hemisphericity as differential sources of the sensed presence, mystical experience and religious conversions. *Psychological Reports*, **76**, 915–930.

Persinger, M.A. (1993b) Near-death experiences: determining the neuroanatomical pathways by experimental patterns and simulation in experimental settings. In: L. Bessette (ed.) *Healing: Beyond Suffering or Death*. Quebec: MHH, pp. 227–286.

Persinger, M.A. (1995) Out-of-body-experiences are more probable in people with elevated complex partial epileptic-like signs during periods of enhanced geomagnetic activity: a non-linear effect. *Perceptual and Motor Skills*, **80**, 563–569.

Persinger, M.A. (1996) Feelings of past lives as expected perturbations within the neurocognitive processes that generate the sense of self: contributions from limbic lability and vectorial hemisphericity. *Perceptual and Motor Skills*, **83**, 1107–1121.

Persinger, M.A., Carrey, N.J. and Suess, L. (1980) *TM and Cult Mania*. North Quincy, Massachusetts: Christopher Publishing.

Persinger, M.A. and Makarec, K. (1993) Complex partial epileptic-like signs as a continuum from normals to epileptics. Normative data and clinical populations. *Journal of Clinical Psychology*, **49**, 33–45.

Persinger, M.A. and Richards, P.M. (1995) Vestibular experiences during brief periods of partial sensory deprivation are enhanced when daily geomagnetic activity exceeds 15–20 nT. *Neuroscience Letters*, **194**, 69–72.

Persinger, M.A., Richards, P.M. and Koren, S.A. (1994) Differential ratings of pleasantness following right and left hemispheric application of low energy magnetic fields that simulate long-term potentiation. *International Journal of Neuroscience*, **79**, 191–197.

Petersen, S.E. and Fiez, J.A. (1993) The processing of single words studied with positron emission tomography. *Annual Review of Neuroscience*, **16**, 509–530.

Petersen, S.E., Fox, P.T., Snyder, A.Z. and Raichle, M.E. (1990) Activation of extrastriate and frontal cortical areas by visual words and word-like stimuli. *Science*, **249**, 1041–1044.

Peterson, M.R., Beecher, M.D., Zoloth, S.R., Moody, D.B. and Stebbings, W.C. (1978) Neural lateralization of species-specific vocalizations by Japanese macaques. *Science*, **202**, 324–327.

Petit, T.L. (1982) Neuroanatomical and clinical neuropsychological change in ageing and dementia. In: F.I.M. Craik and S. Trehub (eds) *Ageing and Cognitive Processes*. New York: Plenum Press.

Pezdek, K., Finger, K. and Hodge, D. (1997) Planting false childhood memories: the role of event plausibility. *Psychological Science*, **8**, 437–441.

Phelps, M.E., Mazziotta, J.C. and Huang, S.-C. (1982) Study of cerebral function with positron computed tomography. *Journal of Cerebral Blood Flow and Metabolism*, **2**, 113–162.

Piattelli-Palmarini, M. (1980) *Language and Learning: The Debate between Jean Piaget and Noam Chomsky*. Cambridge, MA: Harvard University Press.

Pinker, S. (1997) *How the Mind Works*. New York: W.W. Norton & Co.

Pistarini, J. (1991) *Biosinergia, maravilla de Acuario*. Buenos Aires: Lumen.

Plato (1995) *The Republic*. London: Everyman.

Plotkin, W.B. (1979) The alpha experience revisited: biofeedback in the transformation of psychological state. *Psychological Bulletin*, **86**, 1132–1148.

Plotkin, W.B. and Rice, K.M. (1981) Biofeedback as a placebo: anxiety reduction facilitated by training in either suppression or enhancement of alpha brainwaves. *Journal of Consulting and Clinical Psychology*, **49**(4), 590–596.

Plum, F. and Posner, J.B. (1980) *The Diagnosis of Stupor and Coma*, 3rd edn. Philadelphia: F.A. Davis Company.

Poincaré, H. (1908) *Science et Methode*. Paris: Flammarion.

Polidoro, M. (1995) *Viaggio tra gli spirit*. Carnago (VA): Sugarco.

Polidoro, M. (1998) L'Illusione del paranormale. Padova: Franco Muzzio Editore.

Polidoro, M. and Rinaldi, G.M. (1997) Eusapia's Sapient Foot: a new consideration of the Fielding Report. *Journal of the Society for Psychical Research*, **62**, 242–256.

Pope, A. (1978) Neuroglia: quantitative aspects. In: E. Schoffeniels, G. Franck, L. Hertz and D.B. Tower (eds) *Dynamic Properties of Glia Cells*. London: Pergamon Press, pp. 13–20.

Popper, K. and Eccles, J.C. (1977) *The Self and its Brain*. Berlin: Springer-Verlag.

Pratkanis, A. (1995) How to sell a pseudoscience. *The Skeptical Inquirer*, **19**(4), 19–25.

Pratkanis, A.R. (1996) Persuasione sublimale. Una pseudoscienza commerciale. *Scienza & Paranormale*, **4**, 30–38.

Pratkanis, A.R., Eskenazi, J. and Greenwald, A.G. (1990) What you expect in what you believe (but not necessarily what you get: a test of the effectiveness of subliminal self-help audio tapes). *Basic and Applied Social Psychology*, **15**, 251–276.

Prodi, G. (1987) *Il Cane di Pavlov*. Milan: Camunia.

Puthoff, H.E. and Targ, R. (1976) A perceptual channel for information transfer over kilometer distance: historical perspective and recent research. *Proceedings of the IEEE*, **64**, 329–354.

Quintero Osso, B. (1992) Equilibrio químico. In: Sanz Pedrero, P. (ed.) *Fisicoquímica para farmacia y biología*. Barcelona: Ediciones Científicas y Técnicas, S.A., pp. 385–408.

Rabbitt, P.M.A. (1993a) Does it all go together when it goes? *Quarterly Journal of Experimental Psychology*, **46A**, 385–434.

Rabbitt, P.M.A. (1993b) Crystal Quest: an examination of the concepts of "fluid" and "crystallised" intelligence as explanations for cognitive changes in old age. In: A.D. Baddeley and L.S. Weiskrantz (eds) *Attention, Selection, Awareness and Control*. Oxford: Oxford University Press.

Rabbitt, P.M.A. (1996a) Do individual differences in speed reflect "global" or "local" differences in mental abilities? *Intelligence*, **22**, 68–88.

Rabbitt, P.M.A. (1996b) Intelligence is not just mental speed. *Journal of Biosocial Science*, **28**, 425–449.

Rabbitt, P.M.A., Bent, N. and McInnes, L. (1997) Health, age and mental ability. *Irish Journal of Psychology*, **18**, 104–131.

Rabbitt, P.M.A. and Yang, Q. (1996) In: C. Hertzog, D. Herman et al. (eds) *Proceedings of 3rd International Conference on Practical Aspects of Memory*. New Jersey: Erlbaums.

Rabbitt, P., Donlan, C., Bent, N., McInnes, L. and Abson, V. (1993) The University of Manchester Age and Cognitive Performance Research Centre and North East Age Research Longitudinal Programmes, 1982 to 1997. *Zeitschrift fur Gerontologie*, **26**, 176–183.

Rabbitt, P.M.A., Watson, P., Donlan, C., Bent, N. and McInnes, L. (1994) Subject attrition in a longitudinal study of cognitive performance in community based elderly people. *Facts and Research in Cognitive Gerontology*, Paris, Sardi.

Rabbitt, P.M.A., Watson, P., Donlan, C., McInnes, L., Bent, N., Horan, M. and Pendleton, N. (1997) Effects of cause and time of death within 11 years on cognitive performance in old age. *Psychology and Aging*, submitted.

Radin, D.I. (1997) *The Conscious Universe*. New York: Harper-Collins.

Radner, D. and Radner, M. (1982) *Science and Unreason*. Belmont, CA: Wadsworth.

Randi, J. (1975) *The Magic of Uri Geller*. New York: Ballantine (reprinted as: *The Truth about Uri Geller* (1982). Buffalo, NY: Prometheus Books).

Randi, J. (1982a) Lourdes revisited. *The Skeptical Inquirer*, **6**, 4.

Randi, J. (1982b) *Flim-Flam!* Buffalo, NY: Prometheus Books.

Randi, J. (1989) The case of the remembering water. *The Skeptical Inquirer*, **13**(2), 142–146.

Randi (1990) The Mark of Nostradamus. New York: Charles Scribner & Sons (paper – Buffalo, NY: Prometheus Books).

Randi, J. (1992) Help stamp out absurd beliefs. *Time*, 13 April, 80.

Reed, G. (1988) *The Psychology of Anomalous Experience*. Buffalo, NY: Prometheus Books.

Regan, D. (1988) *For the Record*. New York: Harcourt Jovanovich.

Reisser, P.C., Reisser, T.K. and Weldon, J. (1987) *New Age Medicine*. Downers Grove: InterVarsity Press.

Reite, M. and Zimmerman, J. (1978) Magnetic phenomena of the central nervous system. *Annual Review of Biophysics and Bioengineering*, **7**, 167–188.

Renault, B. and Garnero, L. (1996) Les perspectives de l'imagerie fonctionnelle cérébrale électrique et magnétique. *Médecine/Sciences*, **12** (Spécial), 119–122.

Richardson, J.T.E. (1992) Remembering the appearance of familiar objects: a study of monarchic memory. *Bulletin of the Psychometric Society*, **30**, 389–392.

Richardson, P.H. (1994) Placebo effects in pain management. *Pain Reviews*, **1**, 15–32.

Richer, P. (1881) *Etudes cliniques sur l'hystéro-épilepsie ou grande hystérie*. Paris: Delahaye et Lacroisnier.

Ricklefs, R.E. and Finch, C.E. (1995) *Aging, A Natural History*. New York: W.H. Freeman.

Rico, G.L. (1983) *Writing the Natural Way: Using Right-brain Techniques to Release Your Expressive Power*. Los Angeles: J.P. Tarcher.

Ridley, M. (1995) Weird science. *The Waterstone's Magazine*, **2**, 4–11.

Ritter, M. (1991) Sudden recall of forgotten crimes in a puzzler for juries, experts say. *Los Angeles Times*, 30 June.

Robbins, T.W., James, M., Owen, A., Sahakian, B.J., McInnes, L. and Rabbitt, P.M. (1994) Cambridge Automated Neuropsychological Test (CANTAB): a factor analytic study of a large sample of normal elderly volunteers. *Dementia*, **5**, 266–281.

Robbins, T.W., James, M., Owen, A.M., Sahakian, B.J. and McInnes, L. (1997) A neural systems approach to the cognitive psychology of ageing. Studies with CANTAB on a large sample of the normal elderly population. In: P.M.A. Rabbitt (ed.) *Methodology of Frontal Executive Function Testing*. Hove, UK: Psychology Press, in press.

Roberts, R.J., Gorman, L.L., Lee, G.P., Hines, M.E., Richardson, E.D., Riggle, T.A. and Varney, N.R. (1992) The phenomenology of multiple partial epileptic-like symptoms without stereotyped spells: an epilepsy spectrum disorder? *Epilepsy Research*, **13**, 167–177.

Roe, A. (1952) A psychologist examines sixty-four eminent scientists. *Scientific American*, **187**, 21–25.

Rogers, S. (1993) How a publicity blitz created the myth of subliminal advertising. *Public Relations Quarterly* (Winter 1992/1993).

Rogo, D.S. (1991) *Miracles. A Scientific Exploration of Wondrous Phenomena*. London: Aquarian Press.

Roland, P.E. (1993) *Brain Activation*. New York: Wiley-Liss.

Rose, S. (1993) No way to treat the mind. *New Scientist*, 17 April, 23–26.

Rose, S. (1996) Minds, brains, and the Rosetta Stones. In: J. Brockman and K. Matson (eds) *How Things Are*. London: Phoenix, pp. 201–212.

Rosen, G.M. (1987) Self-help books and the commercialization of psychotherapy. *American Psychologist*, **42**(1), 46–51.

Rosenberg, N.L. (1996) The neuromythology of silicone breast implants. *Neurology*, **46**, 308–314.

Rosenberg, G.A. and Wolfson, L.I. (1991) Disorders of brain fluids and electrolytes. In: R.N. Rosenberg (ed.) *Comprehensive Neurology*. New York: Raven Press, pp. 201–214.

Rosenzweig, S., Brohier, S. and Zipfel, A. (1995) The placebo effect in healthy volunteers. *British Journal of Clinical Pharmacology*, **39**, 657–664.

Rosenzweig, M.R., Leiman, A.L. and Breedlove, S.M. (1996) *Biological Psychology*. Sunderland, Mass.: Sinauer Associates.

Rosner, B.S. (1974) Recovery of function and localization of function in historical perspective. In: D.G. Stein, J. Rosen and N. Butters (eds) *Plasticity and Recovery of Function in the Central Nervous System*. New York: Academic Press, pp. 2–29.

Rothman, M. (1989) Myths about science . . . and belief in the paranormal. *The Skeptical Inquirer*, **14**, 25–34.

Rothwell, J.C., Thompson, P.D., Day, B.L., Boyd, S. and Marsden, C.D. (1991) Stimulation of the human motor cortex through the scalp. *Experimental Physiology*, **76**, 159–200.

Rowland, L.W. (1939) Will hypnotised persons try to harm themselves or others? *Journal of Abnormal and Social Psychology*, **34**, 114–117.

Rubin, F. (1968) *Current Research in Hypnopaedia*. London: Macdonald.

Rubin, D.C. and Kontis, T.C. (1983) A schema for common sense. *Memory and Cognition*, **11**, 335–341.

Russell, B. (1959) Mysticism and logic. In: *Mysticism and Logic and Other Essays*. London: George Allen and Unwin, pp. 1–32.

Sacks, O. (1985) *The Man Who Mistook His Wife for a Hat and Other Clinical Tales*. New York: Summit Books.

Sacks, O. (1995) Scotoma: forgetting and neglect in science. In: R.B. Silver (ed.) *Hidden Histories of Science*. London: Granta, pp. 141–187.

Sagan, C. (1977) *The Dragons of Eden*. New York: Random House.

Sagan, C. (1996) *The Demon-haunted World. Science as a Candle in the Dark*. London: Headline.

Saletu, B. (1975) Hypno-analgesia and acupuncture analgesia: a neurophysiological reality. *Neuropsychobiology*, **1**, 218–242.

Salthouse, T.A. (1985) *A Theory of Cognitive Aging*. Amsterdam: North Holland.

Salthouse, T.A. (1991) *Theoretical Perspectives on Cognitive Aging*. Mahwah, NJ: Erlbaums.

Salthouse, T.J. (1996) The processing-speed theory of adult age differences in cognition. *Psychological Review*, **103**, 403–428.

Sanders, H. and Warrington, E. (1971) Memory for remote events in amnesic patients. *Brain*, **94**, 661–668.

Sannita, W.G. (1995) Benefits of placebos. *Nature*, **378**, 125.

Sapolsky, R.M. (1998) *Junk Food Monkeys*. London: Headline.

Saradeth, T., Resch, K.L. and Ernst, E. (1994) Placebo for varicose veins – don't eat it, rub it! *Phlebology*, **9**, 63–66.

Saraví, F.D. (1991) Efecto Kirlian y cuerpo astral. *El ojo escéptico*, **4**(1), 14–16.

Saraví, F.D. (1993a) *La trampa de las medicinas alternativas*. Barcelona: CLIE.

Saraví, F.D. (1993b) *Parapsicología œun engaño del siglo XX?* Barcelona: CLIE.

Sarbin, T.R. and Coe, W.C. (1972) *Hypnosis: A Social Psychological Analysis of Influence Communication*. New York: Holt, Rinehart and Winston.

Sarbin, T.R. and Slagle, R.W. (1979) Hypnosis and psychophysiological outcomes. In: E. Fromm and R.E. Shor (eds) *Hypnosis: Developments in Research and New Perspectives*, 2nd edn. Chicago: Aldine, pp. 273–303.

Sargant, W. (1957) *Battle for the Mind: A Physiology of Conversion and Brain-Washing*. London: Pan Books.

Sargant, W. (1973) *The Mind Possessed: From Ecstasy to Exorcism*. London: Pan Books.

Savage-Rumbaugh, S. and Lewin, R. (1994) *Kanzi: The Ape at the Brink of Human Mind*. New York: McGraw-Hill.

Schacter, D.L., Harbluk, J.L. and McLachlan, D.R. (1984) Retrieval without recollection: an experimental analysis of source amnesia. *Journal of Verbal Learning and Verbal Behavior*, **23**, 593–611.

Schacter, D.L., Verfaellie, M. and Anes, M.D. (1997) Illusory memories in amnesic patients: conceptual and perceptual false recognition. *Neuropsychology*, **11**, 1–12.

Schacter, D.L., Verfaellie, M. and Pradere, D. (1996) The neuropsychology of memory illusions: false recall and recognition in amnesic patients. *Journal of Memory and Language*, **35**, 319–334.

Schechter, D.C. (1971) Origins of electrotherapy, Part 1. *New York State Journal of Medicine*, **71**, May, 997–1008.

Schnider, A., von Däniken, C. and Gutbrod, K. (1996) The mechanisms of spontaneous and provoked confabulations. *Brain*, **119**, 1365–1375.

Schousboe, A., Westergaard, N. and Hertz, L. (1993) Neuronal–astrocytic interactions in glutamate metabolism. *Biochemical Society Transactions*, **21**, 49–53.

Schröter, K. (1985) Electroencephalography. In: H. Kresse (ed.) *Handbook of Electromedicine*, 3rd edn. Berlin-Chichester: Siemens AG-John Wiley & Sons, pp. 90–108.

Schultz, T. (ed.) (1989) *The Fringes of Reason*. New York: Harmony Books.

Schultz, R. and Curnow, C. (1988) Peak performance and age among super athletes: track and field, swimming, baseball, tennis and golf. *Journal of Gerontology, Psychological Sciences*, **43**, 113–120.

Schurr, A., Payne, R.S., Miller, J.J. and Rigor, B.M. (1997) Brain lactate, not glucose, fuels the recovery of synaptic function from hypoxia upon reoxygenation: an in vitro study. *Brain Research*, **744**, 105–111.

Schwender, D., Kaiser, A., Klasing, S., Peter, K. and Pöppel, E. (1993) Explicit and implicit memory and mid-latency auditory evoked potential during cardiac surgery. In: P.S. Seber, B. Bonke and E. Winograd (eds) *Memory and Awareness in Anaesthesia*. Englewood Cliffs, New Jersey: Prentice Hall, pp. 85–98.

Seuling, B. (1991) *You Can't Sneeze With Your Eyes Open* . . . Dunton Green: Hodder and Stoughton.

Shaywitz, B.A., Shaywitz, S.E., Pugh, K.R., Constable, R.T., Skudlarski, P., Fulbright, R.K., Bronen, R.A., Fletcher, J.M., Shankweiler, D.P., Katz, L. and Gore, J.C. (1995) Sex differences in the functional organization of the brain for language. *Nature*, **373**, 607–609.

Shealy, N. (1993) *The Creation of Health: The Emotional, Psychological and Spiritual Responses that Promote Health and Healing.* Walpole, NH: Stillpoint Publishing.

Sheldrake, R. (1995) *Seven Experiments That Could Change the World.* New York: Riverhead.

Shermer, M. (1997) *Why People Believe Weird Things: Pseudoscience, Superstition, and Other Confusions of Our Time.* UK: WH Freeman.

Shevelev, I.A., Tsicalov, E.N., Gorbach, A.M., Budko, K.P. and Sharaev, K.P. (1993) Thermoimaging of the brain. *Journal of Neuroscience Methods*, **46**, 49–57.

Silva, C.E. and Kirsch, I. (1987) Breaching hypnotic amnesia by manipulating expectancy. *Journal of Abnormal Psychology*, **96**, 325–329.

Silva, C.E. and Kirsch, I. (1992) Interpretive sets, expectancy, fantasy proneness and dissociation as predictors of hypnotic response. *Journal of Personality and Social Psychology*, **63**, 847–856.

Silva, J. and Miele, P. (1985) *El método Silva de control mental.* México: Diana.

Simkins, L. (1982) Biofeedback: clinically valid or oversold? *Psychological Record*, **32**, 3–17.

Simon, H.A. (1966) Scientific discovery and the psychology of problem solving. In: R.G. Colodny (ed.) *Mind and Cosmos: Essays in Contemporary Science and Philosophy.* Pittsburgh: University of Pittsburgh Press, pp. 22–40.

Simon, C.W. and Emmons, W.H. (1955) Learning during sleep? *Psychological Bulletin*, **52**, 328–342.

Simon, J., Guiraud, G., Esquerre, J.P., Lazorthes, Y. and Guiraud, R. (1988) Les meridiens d'acupuncture démythifiés: apport de la méthodologie des radiotraceurs. *La Presse Médicale*, **17**, 1341–1344.

Simonton, D.K. (1977) Creative productivity, age and stress: a biographical time-series analysis of 10 classical composers. *Journal of Personality and Social Psychology*, **35**, 791–804.

Simonton, D.K. (1984) Creative productivity and age: a mathematical model based on a 2-step cognitive process. *Developmental Review*, **4**, 77–111.

Simonton, D.K. (1988) Creativity, leadership and chance. In: R.J. Sternberg (ed.) *The Nature of Creativity.* Cambridge: Cambridge University Press, pp. 386–428.

Singer, W. (1993) Synchronization of cortical activity and its putative role in information processing and learning. *Annual Review of Physiology*, **55**, 349–374.

Skinner, B.F. (1957) *Verbal Behavior.* New York: Appleton-Century-Crofts.

Skolnick, A. (1991) The Maharishi caper; or how to hoodwink top medical journals. *Newsletter of the National Association of Science Writers*, **39**(3), 5–7.

Skolnick, A. (1992) Special Report: The Maharishi caper: JAMA hoodwinked (but just for a while). *The Skeptical Inquirer*, **16**(3), 254–259.

Skrabanek, P. and McCormick, J (1989) *Follies and Fallacies in Medicine.* Glasgow: The Terragon Press, chapter 1, pp. 3–20.

Sleep (1995) www-leland.stanford.edu/dept/sleep/journal.

Smillie, B. and Strauss, S. (1997) Japanese TV yanks mind-bending show. *The Globe and Mail* (Toronto), December 18, 1997, 1, 14.

Smith, M.C. (1983) Hypnotic memory enhancement of witnesses: does it work? *Psychological Bulletin*, **94**, 387–407.

Smith, B.D., Meyers, M.B. and Kline, R. (1989) For better or for worse: left-handedness, pathology, and talent. *Journal of Clinical and Experimental Neuropsychology*, **11**, 944–958.

Sokoloff, L. (1977) Relation between physiological function and energy metabolism in the central nervous system. *Journal of Neurochemistry*, **27**, 13–26.

Sokoloff, L., Takahashi, S., Gotoh, J., Driscoll, B.F. and Law, M.J. (1996) Contribution of astroglia to functionally activated energy metabolism. *Developmental Neuroscience*, **18**, 343–352.

Spanos, N.P. (1982) A social psychological approach to hypnotic behavior. In: G. Weary and H.L. Mirels (eds) *Integrations of Clinical and Social Psychology.* Oxford: Oxford University Press, pp. 231–271.

Spanos, N.P. (1986) Hypnotic behavior: a social psychological interpretation of amnesia, analgesia, and "trance logic". *Behavioral and Brain Sciences*, **9**, 449–502.

Spanos, N.P. (1989) Experimental research on hypnotic analgesia. In: N.P. Spanos and J.F. Chaves (eds) *Hypnosis: The Cognitive-Behavioral Perspective.* Buffalo, NY: Prometheus, pp. 206–240.

Spanos, N.P. (1991) A sociocognitive approach to hypnosis. In: S.J. Lynn and J.W. Rhue (eds) *Theories of Hypnosis: Current Models and Perspectives.* New York: Guilford, pp. 324–363.

Spanos, N.P. (1992) Compliance and reinterpretation in hypnotic responding. *Contemporary Hypnosis*, **9**, 7–14.

Spanos, N.P. and Chaves, J.F. (eds) (1989) *Hypnosis: The Cognitive-Behavioral Perspective*. Buffalo, NY: Prometheus.

Spanos, N.P., Flynn, D.M. and Gwynn, M.I. (1988) Contextual demands, negative hallucinations, and hidden observer responding: three hidden observers observed. *British Journal of Experimental and Clinical Hypnosis*, **5**, 5–10.

Spanos, N.P. and McLean, J. (1986) Hypnotically created pseudomemories: memory distortions or reporting biases? *British Journal of Experimental and Clinical Hypnosis*, **3**, 155–159.

Spanos, N.P., Radtke, H.L. and Bertrand, L.D. (1984) Hypnotic amnesia as a strategic enactment: breaching amnesia in highly susceptible subjects. *Journal of Personality and Social Psychology*, **47**, 1155–1169.

Spanos, N.P., Menary, E., Brett, P.J., Cross, W. and Ahmed, Q. (1987) Failure of posthypnotic responding to occur outside the experimental setting. *Journal of Abnormal Psychology*, **96**, 52–57.

Spanos, N.P., Gwynn, M.I., Comer, S.L., Baltruweit, W.J. and de Groh, M. (1989) Are hypnotically induced pseudomemories resistant to cross-examination? *Law and Human Behavior*, **13**, 271–289.

Spanos, N.P., Perlini, A.H., Patrick, L., Bell, S. and Gwynn, M.I. (1990) The role of compliance in hypnotic and non-hypnotic analgesia. *Journal of Research in Personality*, **24**, 433–453.

Spanos, N.P., Quigley, C.A., Gwynn, M.I., Glatt, R.L. and Perlini, A.H. (1991) Hypnotic interrogation, pretrial preparation, and witness testimony during direct and indirect cross-examination. *Law and Human Behavior*, **15**, 639–653.

Spanos, N.P., Burgess, C.A., DuBreuil, S.C., Liddy, S., Bowman, K. and Perlini, A.H. (1995) The effects of simulation and expectancy instructions on responses to cognitive skill training for enhancing hypnotizability. *Contemporary Hypnosis*, **12**, 1–11.

Sparks, G.G., Nelson, C.L. and Campbell, R.G. (1997) The relationship between exposure to televised messages about paranormal phenomena and paranormal beliefs. *Journal of Broadcasting & Electronic Media*, **41**, 345–359.

Sperry, R.W. (1982) Some effects of disconnecting the cerebral hemispheres. *Science*, **217**, 1223–1226.

Spiegel, D. (1994) A definition without a definition. *Contemporary Hypnosis*, **11**, 151–152.

Spiegel, D., Bierre, P. and Rootenberg, J. (1989) Hypnotic alteration of somatosensory perception. *American Journal of Psychiatry*, **146**, 749–754.

Spiegel, D., Cutcomb, C., Ren, C. and Pribram, K. (1985) Hypnotic hallucination alters evoked potentials. *Journal of Abnormal Psychology*, **94**, 140–143.

Springer, S.P. and Deutsch, G. (1981) *Left Brain Right Brain*. San Francisco: Freeman.

Springer, S.P. and Deutsch, G. (1998) *Left Brain, Right Brain: Perspectives from Cognitive Neuroscience*, 5th edn. New York: W.H. Freeman and Co.

Stam, H.J. (1989) From symptom to cure. Hypnotic interventions in cancer. In: N.P. Spanos and J.F. Chaves (eds) *Hypnosis: The Cognitive-Behavioral Perspective*. Buffalo, NY: Prometheus, pp. 313–339.

Stanimirovic, D.B., Ball, R. and Durkin, J.P. (1997) Stimulation of glutamate uptake and Na,K-ATPase activity in rat astrocytes exposed to ischemia-like insults. *Glia*, **19**, 123–134.

Stannard, R. (1996) *Science and Wonders. Conversations About Science and Belief*. London: Faber and Faber.

Stead, C.K. (1997) The English patient. *Metro*, Issue No. 190, 84–90.

Stein, M. (1974) *Stimulating Creativity*, Vol. 1. New York: Academic Press.

Stein, M. (1975) *Stimulating Creativity*, Vol. 2. New York: Academic Press.

Steinmetz, H., Herzog, A., Schlaug, G., Huang, Y. and Jänke, L. (1995) Brain (a)symmetry in monozygotic twins. *Cerebral Cortex*, **5**, 296–300.

Stern, N. (1978) Age and achievement in mathematics: A case study in the sociology of science. *Social Studies of Science*, **8**, 127–140.

Stevenson, J.H. (1976) The effect of hypnotic dissociation on the performance of interfering tasks. *Journal of Abnormal Psychology*, **85**, 398–407.

Stillings, D. (1983) Mediterranean origins of electrotherapy. *Journal of Bioelectricity*, **2**, 181–186.

Stoerig, P. and Cowey, A. (1997) Blindsight in man and monkey. *Brain*, **120**, 535–559.

Stringer, C. (1997) The myth of race. *The Observer*, 27 April, p. 31.

Stuart, E.W., Shimp, T.A. and Engle, R.W. (1987) Classical conditioning of consumer attitudes: four experiments in an advertising context. *Journal of Consumer Research*, **14**, 334–349.

Stuss, D.T., Alexander, M.P., Liberman, A. and Levine, H. (1978) An extraordinary form of confabulation. *Neurology*, **28**, 1166–1172.

SuperMind (1993) Advertisement in *The Telling Voice*, Beltane issue, p. 27.

Sussmann, D.J. (1978) *Qué es la acupuntura. Qué puede curar. Cómo actúa*, 4th edn. Buenos Aires: Kier.

Svyadoschch, A.M. (1968) The history of hypnopaedia. In: F. Rubin (ed.) *Current Research in Hypnopaedia*. London: Macdonald, pp. 197–201.

Szeto, A.Y.J. (1983) The field is no longer filled with quacks & black magic. IEEE *Engineering in Biology and Medicine Magazine*, **2**, 12–13.

Tagle, N. (1995) *Kirlian. El diagnóstico preventivo de la salud*. Buenos Aires: Kier.

Tallentyre, S.G. (1906) *The Friends of Voltaire*. London: Smith, Elder & Co.

Tangrea, J.A., Adrianza, M.E. and Helsel, W.E. (1994) Risk factors for the development of placebo adverse reactions in a multicenter clinical trial. *Annals of Epidemiology*, **4**, 327–331.

Tardy, M. (1991) Astrocyte et homéostasie. *Médecine/Sciences*, **7**, 799–804.

Tart, C. (ed.) (1969) *Altered States of Consciousness*. New York: Anchor Books.

Taylor, J. (1976) *Superminds*. London: Pan.

Taylor, D.W., Berry, P.C. and Block, C.H. (1958) Does group participating when using brainstorming facilitate or inhibit creative thinking? *Administrative Science Quarterly*, **3**, 23–47.

Taub, H.A., Mitchell, J.N., Stuber, F.E., Eisenberg, L., Beard, M.C. and McCormack, R.K. (1979) Analgesia for operative dentistry: a comparison of acupuncture and placebo. *Oral Surgery*, **48**(3), 205–210.

Terr, L. (1988) What heppens to early memories of trauma? A study of 20 children under age five at the time of documented traumatic events. *Academy of Child and Adolescent Psychiatry*, **27**, 96–104.

Terr, L. (1994) *Unchained Memories: True Stories of Traumatic Memories, Lost and Found*. New York: Basic Books Inc.

Tessman, I. and Tessman, J. (1997a) Mind and body. *Science*, **276**, 369–370.

Tessman, I. and Tessman, J. (1997b) Troubling matters. *Science*, **278**, 561.

Thatcher, R.W., Walker, R.A. and Guidice, S. (1987) Human cerebral hemispheres develop at different rates and ages. *Science*, **236**, 1110–1113.

The Sceptic (1997) Editorial. Prize Quiz. *The Sceptic*, **10**, 26–27.

The Vancouver Sun (1997) Cartoon sparks convulsions in kids. Reuters/Associated Press story. 18 December, pp. 1 and 2.

Tiller, S.G. and Persinger, M.A. (1994) Enhanced hypnotizability by cerebrally applied magnetic fields depends upon the order of hemispheric presentation: an anisotropic effect. *International Journal of Neuroscience*, **79**, 157–163.

Trubo, R. (1982) How to tap your brain's success circuits. *Success, The Magazine for Achievers*, March issue, unpaginated (cited by Harris, 1988).

Trudeau, G. (1992a) My Story: The Draft. *New York Times*, 30 September, A17.

Trudeau, G. (1992b) My Story: The Holes. *New York Times*, 30 September, A17.

Tulving, E. (1972) Episodic and semantic memory. In: E. Tulving and W. Donaldson (eds.) *Organisation of Memory*. New York: Academic Press, pp. 381–403.

Turner, J.A., Deyo, R.A., Loeser, J.D., Von Korff, M. and Fordyce, W.E. (1994) The importance of placebo effects in pain treatment and research. *Journal of the American Medical Association*, **271**, 1609–1614.

Tversky, A. and Kahneman, D. (1973) Availability: a heuristic for judging frequency and probability. *Cognitive Psychology*, **5**, 207–232.

Tweney, R.D. (1985) Faraday's discovery of induction: a cognitive approach. In: D. Gooding and F. James (eds) *Faraday Rediscovered: Essays on the Life and Work of Michael Faraday, 1771–1867*. New York: Stockton Press, pp. 189–210.

Udolf, R. (1983) *Forensic Hypnosis: Psychological and Legal Aspects*. Lexington, Mass: Lexington Books.

Uglig, R. (1997) X-File Britain puts faith in the irrational. *The Daily Telegraph*, 5 September.

Ullman, M., Krippner, S. and Vaughn, A. (1989) *Dream Telepathy: Experiments in Nocturnal ESP*, 2nd edn. London: McFarland.

Ungerleider, L.G. (1995) Functional brain imaging studies of cortical mechanisms for memory. *Science*, **270**, 769–775.

Usher, J.A. and Neisser, U. (1993) Childhood amnesia and the beginnings of memory for four early life events. *Journal of Experimental Psychology: General*, **122**, 155–165.

Uttal, W. (1978) *The Psychobiology of Mind*. Hillsdale, NJ: Lawrence Erlbaum Assoc.

Van der Thillart, G. and Van Waarde, A. (1996) Nuclear magnetic resonance spectroscopy of living systems: applications in comparative physiology. *Physiological Reviews*, **76**, 799–837.

Van Essen, D.C. (1997) A tension-based theory of morphogenesis and compact wiring in the central nervous system. *Nature*, **385**, 313–331.

Vargha-Khadem, F., Carr, L.J., Isaacs, E., Adams, C. and Mishkin, M. (1997) Onset of speech after left hemispherectomy in a nine-year-old boy. *Brain*, **120**, 159–182.

Vernon, P.E. (1970) *Creativity*. Harmondsworth: Penguin Books.

Veroff, A.E. (1980) The neuropsychology of aging. *Psychological Research*, **41**, 259–268.

Voudouris, N.J., Peck, C.L. and Coleman, G. (1990) The role of conditioning and verbal expectancy in the placebo response. *Pain*, **43**, 121–128.

Wackermann, J., Lehmann, D., Dvorak, I. and Michel, C. (1993) Global dimensional complexity of multi-channel EEG indicates change of human brain functional state after a single dose of a nootropic drug. *EEG and Clinical Neurophysiology*, **86**, 193–198.

Wadden, T. and Anderton, C.H. (1982) The clinical use of hypnosis. *Psychological Bulletin*, **91**, 215–243.

Wagstaff, G.F. (1977a) An experimental study of compliance and post-hypnotic amnesia. *British Journal of Social and Clinical Psychology*, **16**, 225–228.

Wagstaff, G.F. (1977b) Post-hypnotic amnesia as disrupted retrieval: a role-playing paradigm. *Quarterly Journal of Experimental Psychology*, **29**, 499–504.

Wagstaff, G.F. (1981) *Hypnosis, Compliance, and Belief*. Brighton: Harvester.

Wagstaff, G.F. (1982a) Disorganized recall, suggested amnesia and compliance. *Psychological Reports*, **51**, 1255–1258.

Wagstaff, G.F. (1982b) Helping a witness remember – a project in forensic psychology. *Police Research Bulletin*, **38**, 56–58.

Wagstaff, G.F. (1984) The enhancement of witness memory by hypnosis: a review and methodological critique of the experimental literature. *British Journal of Experimental and Clinical Hypnosis*, **2**, 3–12.

Wagstaff, G.F. (1986) Hypnosis as compliance and belief: a sociocognitive view. In: P.L.N. Naish (ed.) *What is Hypnosis?* Philadelphia: Open University Press, pp. 59–84.

Wagstaff, G.F. (1987) Hypnotic induction, hypnotherapy and the placebo effect. *British Journal of Experimental and Clinical Hypnosis*, **4**, 168–170.

Wagstaff, G.F. (1989) Forensic aspects of hypnosis. In N.P. Spanos and J.F. Chaves (eds) *Hypnosis: The Cognitive Behavioral Perspective*. Buffalo, NY: Prometheus, pp. 340–359.

Wagstaff, G.F. (1991a) Compliance, belief and semantics in hypnosis: a nonstate, sociocognitive perspective. In: S.J. Lynn and J.W. Rhue (eds) *Theories of Hypnosis: Current Models and Perspectives*. New York: Guilford, pp. 362–396.

Wagstaff (1991b) Hypnosis and harmful and antisocial acts: some theoretical and empirical issues. *Contemporary Hypnosis*, **8**, 141–146.

Wagstaff, G.F. (1993) What expert witnesses can tell courts about hypnosis: a review of the association between hypnosis and the law. *Expert Evidence: The International Digest of Human Behaviour Science and Law*, **2**, 60–70.

Wagstaff, G.F. (1996) Compliance and imagination in hypnosis. In: R.G. Kunzendorf, N.P. Spanos and B.J. Wallace (eds) *Hypnosis and Imagination*. New York: Baywood, pp. 19–40.

Wagstaff, G.F. and Benson, D. (1987) Exploring hypnotic processes with the cognitive simulator comparison group. *British Journal of Experimental and Clinical Hypnosis*, **4**, 83–91.

Wagstaff, G.F. and Carroll, R. (1987) The cognitive simulation of hypnotic amnesia and disorganized retrieval. *Medical Science Research*, **15**, 85–86.

Wagstaff, G.F. and Frost R. (1996) Reversing and breaching posthypnotic amnesia and hypnotically created pseudomemories. *Contemporary Hypnosis*, **13**, 191–197.

Wagstaff, G.F., Green, K. and Somers, E. (1997) The effects of the experience of hypnosis, and hypnotic depth, on juror's decisions regarding the defence of hypnotic automatism. *Legal and Criminological Psychology*, **2**, 65–74.

Wagstaff, G.F. and Royce, C. (1994) Hypnosis and the treatment of nailbiting: a preliminary trial. *Contemporary Hypnosis*, **11**, 9–13.

Wall, P.D. (1993) Pain and the placebo response. In: P.D. Wall (ed) *Experimental and Theoretical Studies of Consciousness*. Ciba Foundation Symposium 174. Chichester: Wiley, pp. 187–216.

Wallace, R.K. and Benson, H. (1972) The physiology of meditation. *Scientific American*, **226**(2), 84–90.

Wallas, G. (1926) *The Art of Thought*. London: Jonathan Cape.

Walter, W.G. (1963) *The Living Brain*. New York: W.W. Norton.

Warren, T.F. and Davis, G.A. (1969) Techniques for creative thinking: an empirical comparison of three methods. *Psychological Reports*, **25**, 207–214.

Watkins, A. and Bickel, W.S. (1986) A study of the Kirlian effect. *The Skeptical Inquirer*, **10**, 244–257.

Watkins, A. and Bickel, W.S. (1989) The Kirlian Technique: controlling the wild cards. *The Skeptical Inquirer*, **13**, 172–184.

Watson, J.D.G. (1996) Functional imaging studies of human visual cortex. *Clinical and Experimental Pharmacology and Physiology*, **23**, 926–930.

Watts, F.N. and Sharrock, R. (1985) Relationships between spider constructs in phobics. *British Journal of Medical Psychology*, **58**, 149–153.

Webb, J. (1971) *The Flight from Reason*. London: Macdonald.

Weil, A. (1974) Andrew Weil's search for the true Geller. *Psychology Today*, June, 45–50; July, 74–82.

Weisberg, R.W. (1986) *Creativity: Genius and Other Myths*. San Francisco, CA: W.H. Freeman.

Weisberg, R.W. (1988) Problem solving and creativity. In: R.J. Sternberg (ed.) *The Nature of Creativity: Contemporary Psychological Perspectives*. Cambridge: Cambridge University Press, pp. 148–176.

Weiskrantz, L. (1996) Blindsight revisited. *Current Opinion in Neurobiology*, **6**, 215–220.

Weiss, H.R. and Sinha, A.K. (1993) Imbalance of regional cerebral blood flow and oxygen consumption: effect of vascular alpha adrenoceptor blockade. *Neuropharmacology*, **32**, 297–302.

Wernicke, C. (1874) *Der Aphasische Symptomenkomplen*. Brelau: Cohn & Weigart.

West, D.J. (1957) *Eleven Lourdes Miracles*. New York: Helix Press.

West, R.L. (1986) An application of prefrontal cortex function theory to cognitive aging. *Psychological Bulletin*, **120**, 272–292.

West, M.A. (1987) *The Psychology of Meditation*. Oxford: Clarendon Press.

Wheeler, M.A., Stuss, D.T. and Tulving, E. (1997) Toward a theory of episodic memory: the frontal lobes and autonoetic consciousness. *Psychological Bulletin*, **121**, 331–354.

Whelihan, W. and Lesher, E. (1985) Neuropsychological changes in frontal functions with ageing. *Developmental Neuropsychology*, **1**, 371–380.

White, L. Tursky, B. and Schwartz, G. (eds.) (1985) *Placebo: Theory, Research, and Mechanisms*. Guilford Press: New York.

Williams, L.M. (1994) Recall of childhood trauma: a prospective study. *Journal of Consulting and Clinical Psychology*, **62**, 1167–1176 (plus commentary).

Wilmut, I., Schnieke, A.E., McWhir, J., Kind, A.J. and Campbell, K.H.S. (1997) Viable offspring derived from fetal and adult mammalian cells. *Nature*, **385**, 810–813.

Wilson, D. (1872) Righthandedness. *The Canadian Journal*, No. 75, 193–203.

Wilson, S.C. and Barber, T.X. (1982) The fantasy prone personality: implications for understanding imagery, hypnosis and parapsychological phenomena. In: A.A. Sheikh (ed) *Imagery: Current Theory, Research and Application*. New York: Wiley, pp. 340–387.

Winder, B. (1993) Intelligence and expertise in the elderly. Unpublished MSc. Thesis, University of Manchester.

Winick, M. (1976) *Malnutrition and Brain Development*. New York: Oxford University Press.

Wiseman, R. (1994) Modeling the strategems of psychic fraud. *European Journal of Parapsychology*, **10**, 31–44.

Wiseman, R. (1996) Witnesses to the paranormal (how reliable?). In: G. Stein (ed.) *The Encyclopedia of the Paranormal*. Buffalo: Prometheus Books, pp. 829–834.

Wiseman, R. and Morris, R.L. (1995) Recalling pseudo-psychic demonstrations. *British Journal of Psychology*, **86**, 113–125.

Witelson, S.F. and Pallie, W. (1973) Left-hemisphere specialization for language in the newborn: neuroanatomical evidence of asymmetry. *Brain*, **96**, 641–646.

Wolberg, L.R. (1972) *Hypnosis: Is It For You?* New York: Harcourt Brace Jovanovich.

Wolpert, L. (1993) *The Unnatural Nature of Science*. London: Faber and Faber.

Wood, J.M. Bootzin, R.R., Kihlstrom, J.F. and Schacter, D.L. (1992) Implicit and explicit memory for verbal information presented during sleep. *Psychological Science*, **3**, 236–239.

Woodrum, E. (1978) Religious organizational change: an analysis based on the TM movement. *Review of Religious Research*, **24**(2), 89–103.

Woodworth, R.S. (1934) *Psychology*, 3rd edn. New York: Henry Holt.

Woodworth, R.S. and Schlosberg, H. (1954) *Experimental Psychology* 3rd Edn. London: Methuen.

Wright, S., Young, A.W. and Hellawell, D.J. (1993) Sequential Cotard and Capgras delusion. *British Journal of Clinical Psychology*, **32**, 345–349.

Wurtman, J.J. (1988) *Managing Your Mind and Mood Through Food*. New York: Harper Collins.

Wyatt, J.S. (1994) Noninvasive assessment of cerebral oxidative metabolism in the human newborn. *Journal of the Royal College of Physicians of London*, **28**, 126–132.

Wylie, M. (1993) Trauma and memory. *Family Therapy Networker*, **17**, 42–43.

Yahoo (1997) msn.yahoo.com/Business-and-Economy/Companies/Health/Alternative/Meditation/Mind-Machines/. Interested readers might like to browse the following sites: tile.net/theta, www.mindmachine.com, www.mintech.net, www. mindmax.com, www.breakthroughproducts.com/mindmach.htm, www.brain.com, www.geocities.com/HotSprings/7820/benefit.htm, www.mindspring,com/~jasko/brain/index.html, www.lifetools.com/default.htm, www.lucidity.com, www.photoreading.com, www.brainsync.com, www.hscti.com.

Yam, P. (1997) The media's eerie fascination. *Scientific American*. January, pp. 84–85.

Yaniv, I. and Meyer, D.E. (1987) Activation and metacognition of inaccessible stored information: potential bases for incubation effects in problem solving. *Journal of Experimental Psychology: Learning, Motivation and Cognition*, **13**, 187–205.

Yesudian, S. and Haich, E. (1986) *Yoga y salud*. Buenos Aires: Editorial Central.

Young, P.C. (1952) Antisocial uses of hypnosis. In: L.M. Le Cron (ed.) *Experimental Hypnosis*, 2nd edn. New York: Macmillan, pp. 376–409.

Young, R.M. (1970) *Mind, Brain and Adaptation in the Nineteenth Century: Cerebral Localization and its Biological Context from Gall to Ferrier*. Oxford: Clarendon Press.

Young, A.W. (1994) Recognition and reality. In: E.M.R. Critchley (ed.) *The Neurological Boundaries of Reality*. London: Farrand Press, pp. 83–100.

Young, A.W. and Leafhead, K.M. (1996) Betwixt life and death: case studies of the Cotard delusion. In: P.W. Halligan and J.C. Marshall (eds) *Methods in Madness: Case Studies in Cognitive Neuropsychiatry*. Hove, UK: Erlbaum (UK) Taylor & Francis, pp.146–171.

Young, A.W., Leafhead, K.M. and Szulecka, T.K. (1994) The Capgras and Cotard delusions. *Psychopathology*, **27**, 266–231.

Young, A.W. and van de Wal, C. (1996) Charcot's case of impaired imagery. In: C. Code, C.-W. Wallesch, A.R. Lecours and Y. Joanette (eds) *Classic Cases in Neuropsychology*. Hove, UK: Psychology Press.

Young, A.W., Reid, I., Wright, S. and Hellawell, D.J. (1993) Face-processing impairments and the Capgras delusion. *British Journal of Psychiatry*, **162**, 695–698.

Young, A.W., Robertson, I.H., Hellawell, D.J., de Pauw, K.W. and Pentland, B. (1992) Cotard delusion after brain injury. *Psychological Medicine*, **22**, 799–804.

Younkin, D.P. (1993) Magnetic resonance spectroscopy in hypoxic-ischemic encephalopathy. *Clinical and Investigative Medicine*, **16**, 115–121.

Zabalova, N.D., Zukhar', V.P. and Petrov, I.A. (1964) The problem of hypnopaedia. *Problems in Psychology*, **2**, 98–103.

Zaidel, E. (1983) A response to Gazzaniga: language in the right hemisphere, convergent perspectives. *American Psychologist*, **38**, 542–546.

Zamansky, H.S. and Bartis, S.P. (1985) The dissociation of experience: the hidden observer observed. *Journal of Abnormal Psychology*, **94**, 243–248.

Zangwill, O.L. (1946) Some qualitative observations on verbal memory in cases of cerebral lesion. *British Journal of Psychology*, **37**, 8–19.

Zangwill, O.L. (1976) Thought and the brain. *British Journal of Psychology*, **67**, 301–314.

Zdenek, M. (1985) *The Right Brain Experience: An Intimate Programme to Free the Powers of Your Imagination*. London: Corgi.

Zeman, A. (1997) Persistent vegetative state. *The Lancet*, **350**, 795–799.

Zimmermann, M. (1978) Neurophysiology of sensory systems. In: R.F. Schmidt (ed.) *Fundamentals of Sensory Physiology*. New York: Springer-Verlag, pp. 31–80.

Zinberg, N.E. (1984) *Drug, Set, and Setting*. New Haven: Yale University Press.

Zusne, L. (1985) Magical thinking and parapsychology. In: P. Kurtz (ed.) *A Skeptic's Handbook of Parapsychology*. Buffalo: Prometheus Books, pp. 685–700.

Zwicky, F. (1969) *Discovery, Invention, Research*. New York: Macmillan.

Zwicky, J.F., Hafner, A.W., Barrett, S. and Jarvis, W.T. (1993) *Reader's Guide to Alternative Health Methods*. Milwaukee: American Medical Association.

Index

Index compiled by Annette Musker